Bridging the Gap

Bridging the Gap
Examining Polarity in America

Nancy L. Herron
Diane Zabel
Editors

1995

Libraries Unlimited, Inc.
Englewood, Colorado

LIBRARIES UNLIMITED, INC.
P.O. Box 6633
Englewood, CO 80155-6633
1-800-237-6124

Project Editor: Stephen Haenel
Copy Editor: Susan Brown
Proofreader: Lori Kranz
Indexer: Joan Griffitts
Interior Design and Type Selection: Pam Getchell and
Alan Livingston
Layout: Alan Livingston

Library of Congress Cataloging-in-Publication Data

Bridging the gap : examining polarity in America / Nancy L. Herron and
Diane Zabel, editors.
  xv, 380 p. 17x25 cm.
  Includes bibliographical references and index.
  ISBN 1-56308-114-8
  1. United States--Social conditions--Bibliography. 2. United
States--Social policy--Bibliography. 3. Social classes--United
States--Bibliography. I. Herron, Nancy L., 1942- . II. Zabel,
Diane.
Z7164.S66B83 1994
[HN57]
016.306'0973--dc20   94-9792
                                                           CIP

This book is dedicated to all groups of Americans adversely affected by the polarity issues it defines.

Contents

11 The Health Care System—*continued*

12 Changing Family Structures 337

Contributing Authors

Christine Avery
Business Reference Librarian
The Pennsylvania State University

Adele Bane
Librarian
The Pennsylvania State University,
Great Valley campus

Debora Cheney
Head of the Documents/Maps
The Pennsylvania State University
Libraries

Kevin R. Harwell
Government Documents Librarian
The Pennsylvania State University

Nancy Henry
Health Sciences Reference Librarian
The Pennsylvania State University

Steven Herb
Education Librarian
The Pennsylvania State University

Nancy L. Herron
Director of Academic Affairs/
Librarian
The Pennsylvania State University

Helen M. Sheehy
Government Documents Librarian
The Pennsylvania State University

Diane H. Smith
Chief of Reference and
Instructional Services
The Pennsylvania State University

Carol Wright
Reference Librarian
The Pennsylvania State University

Diane Zabel
Social Science Reference Librarian
The Pennsylvania State University

Acknowledgments

We would like to extend our gratitude and thanks to Nancy Struble and her assistant Peggy Myers for the meticulous preparation of the manuscript; to the Interlibrary Loan Department Head Nolene Martin and her staff of the University Libraries, The Pennsylvania State University, for identification and location of numerous works; to Carole M. Peterson, Acting Head Librarian and her assistant Brenda M. Hoffman, of the J. Clarence Kelly Library, McKeesport Campus, for reference work and suggestions; and to Dr. Eugene W. Herron for interjection of scientific logic and theory into the definition of polarity as a concept and keystone for the building of this book.

Introduction

This book is about social issues in American society. It is best described by defining what it is not: It is not a treatise on change, it is not a book of solutions or recommendations, it is not a telescope to the future. In a word, it is descriptive rather than prescriptive, a work whose sole purpose is to focus on social issues through creative works produced by thoughtful Americans in an attempt to clarify and magnify for closer scrutiny the ever-widening gulfs that divide and separate a diverse people.

It is a book that strives to define several of the most pressing issues in twelve bibliographic essays that look to the realities of tough social problems facing American culture, issues that are increasingly vigorous in driving a wedge between generations, sexes, races, and ethnic groups. Each of the chapters can be used independently. Although each chapter is unique, all synthesize the literature on a critical social issue. These include popular culture; public policy and government; law and the administration of justice; poverty, welfare, and unemployment; child care and elder care; hunger and nutrition; homelessness; children and learning; adults and literacy; substance abuse; the health care system; and the changing American family. Chapters begin with a bibliographic essay summarizing diverse opinions on the topic. Also included are strategies for locating additional information, such as useful Library of Congress Subject Headings; listings of indexes and databases; and in some cases, specific periodicals, monographs, and nonprint materials. Listings of selected federal legislation and court cases are included when relevant.

Because this book was prepared before the 1994 elections, it does not reflect the uncertainty over the status of health care reform or the future of assistance programs such as WIC, AFDC, and food stamps. Regardless of any changes that may occur, the issues discussed here have been part of American society for decades and will remain crucial issues for the foreseeable future.

This book is about contrasts, comparisons, divisions, and expectations. It is about hope for the future grounded in the free flow of ideas and the information they provide. To that free flow of information, the life blood of a prosperous society, we dedicate this book.

Reprinted with permission of Tribune Media Services.

When a thing ceases to be a subject of controversy, it ceases to be a subject of interest.
William Hazlett, 1778-1830

1

Polarity

Nancy L. Herron

Every schoolchild learns early that the extremes of longitude on the planet Earth are at the North and South poles. All other places fall somewhere in between and gather from their positioning in relation to the poles their climate, their weather, and their population densities. To be "poles apart" (polarized) is to be positioned the greatest distance of one extreme from the other; to be in a state of diametrical opposition (*Webster's Third New International Dictionary*); or, to be in a state that divides a whole into sharply opposing factions or political groups (*Random House Dictionary of the English Language*).

What was once solely a scientific term has gained widespread usage in the fields of sociology and politics. Formerly "polarity" meant "the state of polar alignment of a physical property," but it now also means "the concentration of groups or forces in two opposing positions." The sociopolitical meanings can be and often are conveyed through the use of both the noun form "polarity" and the verb form "to polarize." Developments in a political situation can polarize public opinion and, to a degree, the members of Congress (*Harper Dictionary of Contemporary Usage*). Controversies over the question of busing schoolchildren, for example, have "polarized" many a community in recent years, with each side vehemently—and sometimes violently—defending its stand.

Nancy L. Herron, Director of Academic Affairs at The Pennsylvania State University, McKeesport Campus, holds the rank of Librarian. She is editor of two books, *The Social Sciences: A Cross-Disciplinary Guide to Selected Sources* (1989) and *The Leisure Literature: A Guide to Sources in Leisure Studies, Fitness, Sports, and Travel* (1992), published by Libraries Unlimited, Inc. Dr. Herron holds Doctor of Philosophy and Master of Library Sciences degrees from the School of Library and Information Science, University of Pittsburgh. At Penn State, she was the 1990-1991 Administrative Fellow in the Office of the President.

Polarity in the societal sense is spatial too. Humankind has always been keenly aware of social extremes: of rich and poor, of strong and weak, of have versus have not. During the first two hundred years of the Republic Americans relished incorporating movement between social extremes into the equation of life, that no matter how low an individual's birth place on the social continuum, where one ended up was directly proportional to the amount of hard work expended, the number of good deeds done, the measure of good luck encountered, and the height of expectations set.

Polarity represents continual struggle in the social, ideological, and political contexts. The social science literature gives substance and structure to the political dynamics of social interaction. In that regard, sociologist Irving H. Horowitz (1984, p. xiv) explained it well when he stated that the best social science is done by those who recognize the existence of polarities (chance and necessity, systems and individuals, past and future, good and evil, and yes, winning and losing) without deciding on behalf of one or the other; indeed they recognize that these ontological categories often blend into each other, or even convert into each other. The end result is often the tension, the drama, and the stuff of life.

ROOTS OF POLARITY

Since the mid-1870s the role of government in social welfare has evolved in several directions. By virtually any standard the old system of laissez-faire has ceased to exist and in its place have arisen numerous ideologies ranging from pure Marxism to Euro-Socialism. The American system, as epitomized in "The New Deal," "The Fair Deal," and "The Great Society," falls into this evolutionary process. At the far extreme stand the revolutionary totalitarian regimes of Soviet Russia and the largest surviving heir of that tradition, the People's Republic of China. In short, government's role is perceived as one guaranteeing a level playing field for various economic players and the redistribution of wealth where widening inequities are perceived as dangerous to the common good. The extent of government involvement, then, depends on the political philosophy of the ruling group.

By the 1960s widening inequities of all types existed in America and resulted in the adoption of a new perception of political and social extremes. The Vietnam War brought antiwar sentiment to college campuses; assassinations brought a new kind of polarity to the political arena; and social decay of the ghetto began spawning revolutionary polarity in the large cities of America as fear followed the looting, burning, and riots that marked that decade's civil rights confrontations.

In the 1970s Richard Nixon, Gerald Ford, and Jimmy Carter entered the presidential arena. The period of years spanning their administrations nurtured a growing sense that economic (and therefore social) expansion was no longer infinite, and this realization overshadowed the entrepreneurial spirit of earlier times. The dominant factor driving this change in perception was that the electorate no longer functioned as collections of voters recognizable as political parties. Their true identities now existed as members of special interest groups, and it was as special interest groups that their collective voices were heard loud and clear by government. "Special interests" are usually thought of as being something out of a Thomas Nast cartoon—big men with cigars conspiring over a biscuit trust, said political humorist P. J. O'Rourke (1991, p. 186). But in fact, a special interest is any person or group that wants to be treated differently from the rest by the government. O'Rourke stated further that politics would not exist if it were not for special interests. If the effect of government were always the same on everyone and if no one stood to lose or gain anything from government except what his fellows did, there would be little need for debate and no need for coalitions, parties, or intrigue. Indeed, during the late 1970s, loss of faith in government, helped along by such events as the Watergate scandal, coincided with the decline of the political party system.

During the 1980s the Iran hostage crisis and the historic turn to the right by the electorate set the tone for the decade. Cognitive dissonance emerged as a political reality underscoring the polarity of social issues fighting for life in the political arenas of state and federal governments: ecological thrusts conflicted with industrial initiatives; special funding for social programs competed for dollars with defense industry programs and contracts; and human rights concerns clashed bitterly with law and order mandates demanded by taxpaying inner city residents.

Enter the 1990s. Juan Williams, a journalist for the *Washington Post*, described the two new images that currently compete for the nation's attention. The first is the picture of a black man being brutally beaten by officers of the law; the second is the scene of rioters looting and destroying homes and neighborhoods. Williams told his readers that "the nation must choose which of these images will shape its sensibilities and guide its policies over the years to come" (1992, p. B1).

CHANGING DEMOGRAPHICS

Defining the gulfs that separate so diverse a people is a difficult and arduous task surpassed in magnitude only by the act of trying to prescribe successful solutions. But insight into the dilemma comes from many quarters and from many schools of social thought. Kevin Phillips, a conservative political analyst, in trying to define the problems of polarity, looked backward for help: "In the '60s there were riots because of rising expectations. Blacks wanted more things more quickly as opportunity dawned. Now we have outbreaks in a decade of diminishing expectations. This time they are frustrated that prospects for a better life are disappearing, for blacks in particular" (Williams, 1992, pp. B1, B5).

One of the major causes of social polarity has been identified in the literature as rapidly changing demographics. In addition to minority/majority population shifts, people are looking for cleaner air, cheaper groceries, and better jobs. An example is the state of California, long the symbol of unlimited American promise; that state is an example of diminished expectations. In 1992, more people left California than moved in to the state, 350,000 compared with 342,000. The last year in which more people left than arrived was 1970 (*Moneyline*, 1992).

One in every six Americans moved their place of residence between March 1990 and March 1991 according to a Census Bureau report, "Geographical Mobility," covering that period (*Cost of living index*, 1992). Increasingly, states like California, Washington, and Florida are being populated by sharply contrasting groups of people: wealthy suburban communities growing richer and older as high real estate costs drive out young people; crowded cities full of poor old people straining local budgets and services; middle-income communities, shaken by the job losses produced by upheavals in aerospace, manufacturing, real estate, banking, and other once-steadily growing industries, fearing the future.

For now, when the widely unpopular Rodney King verdict might shame ruling-class America into facing the nation's widening economic and racial divisions, public attention is being diverted. Flames and violence are, in the mind of affluent America, reinforcing threatening stereotypes of poor black people in the inner city, obliterating what seemed an opportunity for a national awakening to the brutal reality of life on the margins of American society (Williams, 1992, pp. B1, B5).

POPULATION DIVERSITY

Steve Freeman, of the Anti-Defamation League of B'nai B'rith, has written and spoken for years of teaching people about diversity and how to live in a pluralistic society. "We talk and dream about a melting pot, but there are reasons to wonder whether it's working" (Lovely, 1993, p. 4). Traditionally, the assimilation model has not worked. When newcomers are expected to fit in, the burden of making changes falls to them. The business world follows the same principle. Roosevelt R. Thomas, in examining assimilation in the workplace, found that there have been insensitivity and disregard for differences. He found that business has traditionally said: "We have determined in this company that there is a specific culture, and that people who fit a given mold do better than those who do not. As you join us, we're going to hold up a mirror in front of you. In this mirror, you will note that we have sketched the outline of the mold that works here. If you fit, fine, come on in. If you don't, we invite you to allow us to shape you to the appropriate mold. This is for our mutual benefit, as it will help to ensure that you have a productive relationship with the company" (1991, p. 24).

Arthur M. Schlesinger, Jr. (1992) examined the assimilation model, often called the melting pot concept, in detail; his research questions included 1) why differences of race, wealth, religion, and nationality are submerged in the pursuit and exercise of democracy; and 2) why the idea of assimilation into the mainstream is giving ground to the celebration of ethnicity, where the achievements of women, African Americans, Indians, Hispanics, and Asians, among others, are recognized.

He concluded that ethnic awareness has its price, and if it is pressed too far, the nation may be moved to fragmentation, resegregation, and tribalization (1992). But does America have a choice? In the workplace and in the marketplace diversity seems to be here to stay. Consider the following:

- Minorities, immigrants, and women now hold more than half of the jobs in the United States;

- By the year 2000, only about one out of every seven new employees in America will be a white male;

- America's consumers are fast becoming more diverse, demanding a diverse workforce to understand and serve them (Thomas, 1991).

The Hudson Institute report of 1987, *Workforce 2000*, has projected that from 1985 to the year 2000 minorities, women, and immigrants will compose 85 percent of the growth in the workforce. The highest rate of increase will occur among Asian Americans and Hispanics; however, Asian Americans will be less significant numerically than Hispanics because they are growing from a much smaller base (*Workforce 2000*, 1987).

The labor participation growth rate of white women will be relatively smaller, but because they are expanding from a larger base, the increase will be numerically substantial. An equally significant prediction is that overall the workforce will grow at a declining rate. For the decade ending in 1990 the growth rate was 27 percent; for the decade ending in the year 2000, it will be 11 percent. One implication of our changing demographics is the very real potential for a labor shortage. Managers are expected to experience increasing difficulty in meeting staffing needs primarily because individuals composing the bulk of the workforce growth have historically been underrepresented in the occupations where the greatest growth is projected: the health professions, natural sciences, computer science, mathematics, and engineering (Thomas, 1991, p. 6).

Projecting from current trends, managers of all organizations can anticipate a time when the potential labor force will consist of large numbers of minorities and women who will be willing and physically able to work but who will lack the necessary skills to take advantage of occupational opportunities. This scenario has been called the "skills gap." The anticipated surge in baby-boomer retirements will exacerbate this situation. The combined circumstances may create a very real labor problem for America in the next decade.

An informed, sophisticated assessment of the relationship of occupational segregation and low income to level of education is essential to developing concrete proposals for change (Wolfe, 1991, p. ix). For example, it is still true that young women (and minorities for that matter) will adapt to the inferior labor market opportunities that they find open to them, thereby "choosing" what they believe is available. Although the opening of opportunities is critical, helping young women (and their parents and teachers) believe that other opportunities will exist is equally as important (Wolfe, 1991, p. ix).

IMMIGRATION TRENDS

During the decade of the 1980s, the United States admitted 8.6 million immigrants, more than the country admitted in any other decade since 1900-1910. Worldwide, one half of the decade's immigrants have made America their destination. Of them, 11 percent (more than three quarters of a million) chose to settle in Los Angeles, California. By the end of the decade 40 percent of all Angelenos were foreign born; 49 percent spoke a language other than English at home; 35.3 percent spoke Spanish (Miles, 1992).

Other states are also feeling the tensions of rapidly growing immigration numbers. In Coral Springs, Florida, in January 1993 a murder trial focused national attention on the beating death of a Vietnamese-American college student. This, another in a series of shocking "hate crimes," has Americans wondering how well the country really accepts immigrants. The U.S. Commission on Civil Rights warns that across the country violence against Asian Americans has escalated into a serious national problem that occurs with disturbing frequency. Dan Lovely, a freelance writer for the *Fort Lauderdale Sun Sentinel*, writes that during the 1980s, as Asians became the country's fastest-growing minority, violence against them also increased, fueled by economic fears and lingering wartime hate, by ignorance, and by media stereotypes. "As immigration continues to increase—to an estimated total of 1 million people last year—and competition for jobs remains heated, there appears to be more and more incidents against all minorities" (1993, pp. 4-6).

American immigration history, while a stellar example of a nation's commitment to the promise of a better life, has also displayed a dark side. As the number of jobs, dollars, and resources decrease in a downturned economy, societal unrest sparks a strong backlash that works to further polarize American citizens from those who come seeking the American Dream. Past attitudes frequently resembled a two-way street that enabled Americans to care for refugees who sought a better and more democratic way of life. In turn, these immigrants brought with them skills and dedication to their new country. In this decade new arrivals seem to need more help than they can give (*In plain Spanish, No,* 1993, p. 16). This situation is especially true for those who reach this country illegally (Nelson, 1975; Corwin, 1978; Fogel, 1978, Gregory, 1989; Cockcroft, 1986; James, 1991).

Most experts agree that immigration is a major element in U.S. population change (Ethier, 1986; Grant, 1991; McNary, 1992). At current fertility levels, natural increases alone (births minus deaths) would cause the American population to peak around the year 2020 at about 270,000,000 and then slowly take a downturn to 220,000,000 (the 1977 size) by 2090. But immigration is a wild card in efforts to project future U.S. population figures. While legal immigration formulas provide predictable numbers to add to American fertility levels, measuring illegal immigration has become more difficult in recent years due to the nature of the problem and the inability of governmental agencies to substantiate illegal alien numbers. Estimates of persons entering the United States illegally each year vary from 200,000/300,000 (*Trying to count the nation's shadow population,* 1992, p. 366) to around 800,000 persons (Grant, 1991, p. 10). But even if the conservative number is used, a population of approximately 330,000,000 will be a reality by the year 2080. Some experts predict that illegal immigration will be swelling the population beyond the level of sustainability and triggering resource and environmental problems that could prove insurmountable in the years ahead.

Often immigration, legal and illegal, is perceived by U.S. citizens to be a threat to job opportunities. When President George Bush signed the Immigration Act of 1990, he endorsed a reform that aimed to open America's doors to many more people from foreign lands with substantial increases in categories based on skills needed in the U.S. economy (McNary, 1992). But to keep immigration in balance, strong enforcement of employer sanctions and border apprehensions of people who attempt to enter the U.S. illegally were seen by the American people as imperative to good policy maintenance. The Bush administration reiterated that this measure, authorizing additional workers from other nations, in no way reduced America's commitment to strong enforcement of the employer sanction provisions of the Immigration Reform and Control Act (IRCA) of 1986. Rather than a conflict of purposes, they stated, this different treatment of legal and illegal immigration reflected a responsibility to better administer laws fairly and from the broadest possible perspective.

But immigration law had an impact on a series of other national interests as well. IRCA needed to do more than impose sanctions on employers who hire or continue to employ aliens whom they know are not authorized legally to work in the United States. The government moved to provide a generous amnesty policy that enabled nearly 3,000,000 people to legalize their status with the eventual possibility of becoming citizens. IRCA also tried to reflect a national commitment to reduce the flow of illegal aliens through more effective control of America's borders.

Doris Meissner, Clinton administration Immigration and Nationalization Service (INS) head, stated that she also wanted to work to stop illegal immigration so that America could continue opening up the country to legal immigration; her position was that legal and illegal immigration go together and that the Expedited Exclusion and Alien Smuggling Enhanced Penalties Act of 1993, put to Congress on July 27, 1993, was intended to link the two. This proposal was designed to address the growing abuse of America's legal immigration and political asylum systems by illegal aliens holding fraudulent documents and by alien smugglers. It was part of a larger administration initiative announced on June 18, 1993, to combat the illegal entry and smuggling of aliens into the United States (Clinton, 1993).

Much of the current literature indicates that, in addition to fears of job competition from illegal immigrants, Americans also perceive illegal aliens as contributors to insurmountable resource and environmental problems in the years ahead. Uncontrolled population growth is seen as exacerbating problems like urban air pollution; acid precipitation; the greenhouse effect, global warming, and rising sea levels; the need to detoxify nuclear and toxic wastes already generated; the mounting problems of disposing of new toxic and urban wastes; and the proliferation of man-made chemicals in the environment. Current polls indicate that at the mass level, most Americans want stricter enforcement of existing immigration laws to protect themselves and their environment by:

- using technical improvements recommended by INS to help Border Patrols guard the nation's perimeter;

- developing better ways of identifying who is entitled to be in the United States;

- deciding which levels of legal immigration are desirable for humane reasons and which are compatible with the country's economic and environmental sustainability;

- developing a national view as to what fertility levels are necessary to achieve a desirable demographic future.

Since the 1970s all workers, regardless of immigration status, have been entitled to the same labor protections and remedies under the law. But despite these protections, illegal aliens are discriminated against in countless ways. Fears of workplace discrimination have intensified since IRCA was passed in 1986 because the law makes it illegal to hire undocumented workers, and some employers argue that federal labor legislation, including Title VII of the 1964 Civil Rights Act and the Fair Labor Standards Act, no longer covers illegal workers. Thus far, the courts have rejected this argument and have held that undocumented workers can bring lawsuits against employers. But the reality is that undocumented workers are not likely to pursue their legal rights. "Ultimately, most experts agree, the real danger for illegals is that they may become a permanent servant class—latter day indentured servants needed for their labor but living as fearful, second-class citizens on the margins of society" (Griffin, 1992, p. 367).

THE AGE GAP

In 1992 the National Council on the Aging reported that there were over 31 million Americans over age 65. More than one in five working adults provided some care for an elderly relative, usually a parent or parent-in-law, and lost on average one week's work per year, according to social welfare researcher Andrew Scharlach at the University of California, Berkeley. The average age of caregivers was 50 years old (Aburdene & Naisbitt, 1992, p. 238).

For most middle-class Americans, the dilemma of how to prepare for old age has become a threatening experience. If saving has been the retirement strategy, ending up in a nursing home often wipes out savings quickly. The average bed in a nursing facility costs $32,000 a year and some run as high as $80,000. When savings are gone, individuals must use Medicaid, the nation's health insurer to the poor, which, unlike Medicare, will pay for nursing home bills. However, Medicaid coverage begins only after all other resources have been expended. Some argue that if the federal government had a program, like Medicare, that paid for nursing-home care for everyone, then families would not have to spend their savings or compete with the poor for scarce funds. Questions of "who should pay" and "how much" continue to fuel the controversy, polarizing family members, generations, and political parties on an issue that promises to remain in the forefront of national debate into the twenty-first century.

More than 100 different long-term care bills have been introduced in Congress in recent years. The price tags run as high as $42 billion a year and the effort has been lost in the larger debate over reforming the nation's total health care system. In the meantime, a bitter debate rages, the ranks of the nation's elderly keep growing, and so do the costs of caring for them in their last, most expensive years (*Planning to be poor*, 1992).

In part to help bridge the gap with younger generations, older Americans are looking to new strategies to keep fit and contributory. Returning to formal education is one way some choose to keep up with children and grandchildren. Dychtwald and Flower (1989) discussed at length the educating of aging Americans. For example, in 1970 only 22 percent of the college population was over 25; by 1985, the proportion was over 45 percent. By 1990 that number had exceeded 50 percent.

Elderhostel, a self-supporting, nonprofit program based in Boston, has been combining leisure, learning, and travel for older Americans since 1975. In its first year of operation Elderhostel had 220 course enrollments at 5 different sites. By 1988 it counted over 170,000 course enrollments at 1,000 sites in 37 countries, and it was growing at the rate of 20,000-30,000 students per year.

CONCENTRATION OF WEALTH

The apparent concentration of wealth in American society is exacerbating the polarity issue. According to a study by the liberal Economic Policy Institute, in the 1980s the nation's richest households gained most. Over 55 percent of the $2.6 trillion increase in family wealth from 1983 to 1989 was in the top 0.5 percent of households, whereas lower-income families lost $256 billion of wealth (U.S. Department of Labor, Bureau of Labor Statistics, 1986). The study defined wealth as net assets, such as stocks, savings, and real estate, minus debt (*Moneyline*, 1992). This change meant that less than 1 percent of American households were worth more than the other 99 percent (*Poor vs. rich*, 1993).

Another example of financial polarity can be seen in a new study by the state of Pennsylvania based on the U.S. census figures that showed a substantial and growing gap between the household income of rural and inner-city dwellers and those living in the suburbs. The margin of difference threatens to create two separate societies: one rich, the other poor. The study indicated that nearly 30 percent of the state's 4.5 million households have incomes below $17,000. These households are found primarily in rural areas, small towns, and the inner cities. The majority of middle- and upper-income households, meanwhile, are located in suburban communities mostly located around the two largest cities, Pittsburgh in the west and Philadelphia in the east (Robbins, 1993).

ROLE CHANGES WITHIN THE FAMILY

The most malignant effects of the declining fortunes of many young families in America have fallen on those who are both poor and members of minorities. In the 1970s and 1980s marriage rates among black women declined and the number of black female-headed households rose dramatically (Skolnik 1991, p. 216). Many African-American observers agreed that there was indeed a crisis in the black family. In contrast to what many feared, however, changes in black families were not leading indicators of future changes in white family life; rather, the family patterns of the two groups were moving further apart than they had ever been in this century (Laslett, 1989).

In America the traditional nuclear family continues to divide and separate. A recent study conducted by The Pennsylvania State Data Center at The Pennsylvania State University's Harrisburg campus reported that the number of single-father families increased 52.6 percent from 1980 to 1990, to a record 78,997. Single-mother families in the state increased 8.6 percent, to 414,690. Married couples with children decreased 11.3 percent, to 2,065,839. All told, that means, in 1990, 80.7 percent of Pennsylvania families were headed by married couples, 16.2 percent by mothers, and 3.1 percent by fathers (Reeves & Reeves, 1993).

For all intents and purposes no model exists for the American family. Rather, many models are being created, representing many diverse styles and shapes. Fathers work while mothers keep house; mothers work while fathers keep house; fathers and mothers both work outside the home; there are single parents, second marriages bringing together people from unrelated backgrounds, childless couples, unmarried couples with and without children, and gay and lesbian parents. It appears that America is living through a period of historic change in family life.

TECHNONATIONALISM

Polarity can also be a by-product of what Alvin Toffler (1990) called "technonationalism," or a movement toward a more globalized production and marketing that requires capital to flow easily across national boundaries. This, in turn, demands the dismantling of old financial regulations and barriers erected by nations to protect their economies. The result is a larger pool of capital instantly available anywhere. But, if this makes the financial system more flexible and helps it overcome localized cries, it also raises the ante, escalating the risk of massive collapse. The global economy directly affects the national economy and imposes constraints on recessionary spirals and depressed markets.

Perhaps the most important element in the economic picture nationally is job growth and the factors that affect it. Despite some growth in the number of new jobs in the United States over the past decade, union membership has withered. In 1960, 35 percent of all nonagricultural workers in America belonged to a union, but by 1980 that portion had fallen to just under a quarter, and by 1989 to about 17 percent. Excluding government employees union membership was down to 13.4 percent—a smaller proportion even than in the early 1930s before the National Labor Relations Act created a legally protected right to labor representation. Add to that decline a reduction in routine production jobs, which have vanished fastest in traditionally unionized industries (auto, steel, and rubber) where average wages have kept up with inflation. Also vanishing are lower- and middle-level management jobs involving routine production. Between 1981 and 1986, more than 780,000 foremen, supervisors, and section chiefs lost their jobs through plant closings and layoffs (U.S. Department of Labor, 1986).

Overall, Robert B. Reich (1992), Secretary of Labor in the Clinton administration, wrote of the decline in routine jobs and how that factor has hurt men more than women in the workplace. This phenomenon has occurred because the routine production jobs held by men in high-volume, metal-bending manufacturing industries had paid higher wages than the routine production jobs held by women in textiles and data processing. As both sets of jobs have been lost, American women in routine production have gained more equal footing with American men—equally poor footing, that is. This lowering of wages in traditionally male production jobs is a major reason why the gap between male and female wages began to close during the 1980s.

Rapidly changing technology is another important factor affecting jobs. This climate of change, which affects the very fabric of American life, can be seen at every level from supermarket scanners to voice answering systems to electronic transfers of funds across town or across the world. It has, as one cartoonist phrased it, forced people to be "dial tone people in a touch-tone world." America has always employed what Boorstin (1965) called a "technology of haste," or a special attitude to the present and the future and the relation between them. He defined America as follows: "Perhaps America was the land of the future, but Americans seldom thought of themselves as building for the future. More precisely, American technology was a technology of the present, shaped by haste, by scarcity of craftsmanship, of capital, and of raw materials, and by a firm expectation of rapid change in the technology itself" (1965, p. 107).

KNOWLEDGE NEEDS

Since the 1950s an explosion of technology has generated 90 percent of all scientific knowledge and is expected to double that knowledge over the next ten to fifteen years. Once considered simply the dream of science fiction writers, "high tech" is now an exciting and dynamic reality. Scientific and technological advances have changed every aspect of our life, so much so that in 1982 *Time Magazine* selected the computer as its "Man of the Year," and in 1984, President Ronald Reagan signed into law a Congressional Resolution designating September 30 through October 6 as National High Tech Week (Lesko, 1986, p. i). Computers and microprocessors have outnumbered people in the United States since the mid-1980s. Because progress in science and technology depends upon the utilization of existing knowledge, access to technological information is becoming increasingly more important.

New complexities have grown out of individuals' needs for more information and more know-how to function day-to-day at an ever increasing pace. Management guru Peter Drucker (1992) noted that knowledge itself turns out to be not only the source of the most effective power, but also a more important ingredient than force or wealth. Put differently, knowledge has gone from being an adjunct of money power and muscle power to being their ultimate amplifier. This is the key to the power shift that lies ahead, and it explains why the battle for the control of knowledge and the means of communicating that knowledge is heating up all over the world (Drucker, 1992, p. 26).

The sharpest views of polarity are focused where learning gaps appear. The new knowledge-centered society requires its members to have mastered not just reading, writing, and arithmetic, but also basic computer skills, and political, social, and historical systems. Because of the vastly expanding corpus of knowledge, it also requires that its members learn how to learn (Drucker, 1992, p. 27).

This idea is not new. In 1982 for example, Mortimer J. Adler introduced his educational manifesto The Paideia Proposal, in which he called for significant changes in America's approach to basic education. He envisioned schooling of the same high quality for all children, turning each one into a competent citizen by employing a one-track system of public schooling that had the same objectives for all without exception. This system was designed to dissolve the polarity that had been created by a multitrack system that aimed at different goals for different groups of children in public education. He advocated that children be taught to learn!

The pressing need for change and the illusive search for quality in school districts across America have long been chronicled by journalists and writers in the social science literature, and none have done it more vividly than Jonathan Kozol. He examined school districts in East St. Louis, New York, San Antonio, Chicago, Washington, D.C., and Camden, New Jersey, that were literally falling apart. Here, he said, young people are literally being starved in body and mind; where public schools remain both segregated and unequal—and in many cases, more segregated and less equal than in 1954 (Kozol, 1991). In 1954 the Supreme Court ruled, in *Brown* v. *Board of Education*, that educational facilities that were separate but equal were not sufficient to ensure quality under the law and were in violation of the students' constitutional rights.

Another well-known author, Alan Bloom (1987), had examined in much the same way American higher education. Bloom argued that the social and political crisis of the United States in the twentieth century was really an intellectual crisis and that if education's purpose was only to prepare individuals for careers instead of to teach lifelong learning concepts, colleges and universities do not have enough to teach students to justify keeping them enrolled for four years.

Millard examined higher education goals closely during his tenure as President of the Council on Post Secondary Accreditation during the late 1980s. He wrote that American higher education has two primary goals, each with roots going back to the eighteenth century: quality and equity. This history, he maintained, contrasted to that in most other countries. Although one or the other of these goals has tended to dominate in particular historical periods (including recent history), the basic question that must be addressed if Americans are to meet changing demographic, social, economic, and political conditions is whether the two are antithetical or compatible, whether Americans can afford to sacrifice either one in an effort to provide for a more highly educated workforce and citizenry (1991, pp. 206-7).

MULTICULTURALISM MOVEMENT

In 1987 marching Stanford University students chanted, "Hey, hey, ho, ho, Western culture has got to go," and alarmists across the nation predicted the fall of American civilization. Richard M. Huber noted this in his exposé of higher education faculty in *How Professors Play the Cat Guarding the Cream* (1992). At the same time, Stanford faculty, not without heated departmental battles of their own, approved required courses that not only stressed cross-cultural comparisons with Western civilization, but especially emphasized the contributions of minorities and women to American culture.

In response to the Stanford action, many scholarly articles appeared in the periodical literature covering a wide spectrum of opinion on the multiculturalism issue. Many were written in response to the work *Cultural Literacy: What Every American Needs to Know* (Hirsch, 1987). Some of the most vocal scholars included Henry Louis Gates, Jr. (1990, 1992); Donald Kagan (1991); Dinesh D'souza (1992); Forrest McDonald (1982, 1986); and Jacob Neusner (1988, 1991).

Donna Shalala, Secretary of Heath and Human Services for the Clinton administration and former president of the University of Wisconsin at Madison, examined the problem this way: Many campuses are attempting to expand their curricula to reflect overlooked intellectual contributions—from women, minorities, and Third World cultures. "Who should teach? . . . Only White males? We can't provide a first-class education without women and minorities in the classrooms. Traditionalists argue that these changes are coming at the expense of Western culture" (Cleveland, 1991).

The issue of multiculturalism raises a series of key questions about how American history should be perceived: Is the story of America that of a common culture or of many different, perhaps irreconcilable, ones? Given the proliferation over the last 30 years of research in women's history, labor history, black history, and the history of other radical and ethnic groups, is it desirable, or even possible, to impose a single narrative line on the story of America's evolution? If such a grand narrative is possible, what should it be? (Coughlin, 1992, A8).

ENVIRONMENTS AT RISK

As many great polarities have developed over physical and environmental issues as have developed over theoretical ones. Special interest groups who focus their energies on "environments" at risk include Greenpeace, The Sierra Club, and The Wilderness Society, to list only a few. Their focus is on perceived threats to America's natural splendor, and their foes are perceived as agents who work to capitalize on entrepreneurial development and expansion in the name of an increased gross national product and job creation.

Leaders of the Clinton administration came of age during a period when ecological concerns were first emerging; Vice President Gore is an example (1992). Urban air quality, lake water purity, endangered animal species, wild birds, the oceans, and natural forests, to name a few of the most focused issues, all have become battlegrounds for wars between "environmental guardians" and industries that claim to provide jobs and stimulation for a troubled national economy.

In the state of Oregon, the forests of firs vie with logging companies and pulp mills; in Florida, the ecosystem is at odds with a superheated economy and the cutting off of the flow of fresh water for dams, dikes, and ditches; in Alaska, a 19-million-acre preserve above the Arctic Circle, known as America's Serengeti because of its abundant wildlife, is endangered by the potential to open it up to oil drilling; in Arizona, smog from nearby power plants and distant cities besmirches the landscape; in Louisiana, a notorious 250-mile stretch between Baton Rouge and New Orleans is lined with 9 refineries and 85 other industrial facilities, many producing petrochemicals with wastes that threaten the poor, largely black population who live near them and suffer high rates of cancer, miscarriage, and infant mortality; and in Ohio, the city of East Liverpool is home to one of the world's largest toxic-waste incinerators, situated about 1,000 feet from an elementary school (McKibben, 1993, p. 128).

GENDER ISSUES

Gender issues have been identified in the literature as the possible cause celebre for the 1990s and beyond in the crowded field of polarity factors. The quest for women's rights, begun at the dawn of the twentieth century, continues on steadily into the twenty-first. With the quest comes controversy over a wide spectrum of issues that exemplify America's national divisions.

Politically, after two decades of grassroots politicking from the school board to the state house, U.S. women have begun to win offices that will move them into leadership positions. With the backing of female voters, now the majority of the American electorate, as well as men seeking new leadership, a generation of women will take office as governors and congresswomen over the next two decades. By 2008 Aburdene and Naisbitt predict that U.S. women will hold at least 35 percent of governorships and that a woman will be electable, or already elected, as the U.S. president (1992, p. 3).

After the Clarence Thomas Supreme Court confirmation hearings, women, in their anger over sexual harassment, the abortion issue, and the insensitivity of elected officials, seemed to be awakened to political and financial power. Millions of dollars poured into the coffers of women's PACs (political action caucuses) and campaign chests. In March 1992 examples of unprecedented political success occurred, including Carol Mosely Braun's upset of incumbent Senator Alan Dixon of Illinois, one of the 11 Democrats who joined Republicans to vote for Thomas's confirmation. Next came Democrat Lynn Yeakel's nomination and campaign to defeat GOP Senator Arlen Spector from Pennsylvania. Then, Kay Bailey Hutchison from Texas defeated incumbent Robert Krueger for a seat in the Senate in May of 1993.

American perceptions of women as leaders are changing. In a *U.S. News and World Report* poll in April 1992, a stunning 61 percent of those surveyed thought that the country would be governed better if more women held political office. In 1984, the same survey showed that only 28 percent held that view.

But women's groups continue to struggle for recognition in the intellectual establishment. Bloom, for instance, reflecting on the national intellectual and moral climate in *The Closing of the American Mind* (1987), frequently lashed out at the women's movement. A few years after his best-seller on the decline of higher education in America made vibrations throughout academe, he stood by his indictment of feminism in that book. He now says he "underestimated the problem," according to Susan Faludi (1991). "Whether he's deploring the state of scholarship, the emasculating tendencies of music, or the transience of student relationships, the baleful influence he identifies is always the same: the feminist transformation of society that has filled women with demands and desires and depleted men of vim and vigor" (1991, p. 290). She quoted Bloom as follows: "the latest enemy of the vitality of the classic tests is feminism; concerted attacks on the literary canon from '60s student radicals and minorities pale in comparison" (Bloom, 1987, pp. 65-66).

Christopher Lasch also tried to drive a wedge between the sexes in his book *The True and Only Heaven* (1991), a treatise against freedom of choice and feminist challenges to traditional marriage; Roger Kimball in *Tenured Radicals: How Politics Has Corrupted Our Higher Education* (1990) presented an indictment of feminist studies and feminist scholars, alleging that feminists intimidate universities into hiring other feminists and that "their object is nothing less than the destruction of the values, methods, and goals of traditional humanistic study" (Lasch, 1990, p. 31).

The sexual polarity issue has been compounded by what the media have come to call the New Right, politicians who draw attention to ideological differences between women's groups in America. Jerry Falwell has led the way through his discourse on moral conditions (1981), his biography (1987), and his perspective on the abortion issue (1986). He emerged as a right-wing leader during the 1980s, using female spokespersons like Phyllis Schlafly (1977) and Beverly LaHaye (1984), founder of the New Right's Concerned Women for America, to carry the message.

An issue at the forefront of the controversy involves perceptions of traditional patterns of marriage. The feminist revolution of this century has provided the most powerful challenge to traditional patterns of marriage. Paradoxically, it may also have strengthened the institution by giving greater freedom to both partners and by allowing men to accept some of the traditionally female values (Rubenstein, 1990).

The changing views on marriage have had their effect on all sides. But the debate about whether the American family is destroyed or better than ever continues. "Most of us," observed Joseph Featherstone, "debate these matters from our general instinct of where history is tending, from our own lives and those of our friends. . . . One of the difficult things about the family as a topic is that everyone in the discussion feels obliged to defend a particular set of choices" (1979, p. 20).

Although many other issues permeate the controversy between feminist and nonfeminist groups of women, the one most likely to inspire strong stands is the abortion question. "People may not think sexual harassment is a voting issue," said Massachusetts pollster Gerry Chervinsky, "but they will vote on abortion." In 1990, pro-choice forces won in gubernatorial races in Florida and Texas, whereas anti-abortion forces won in Kansas and Pennsylvania. Some observers say abortion has already cost Republicans the governorships in Virginia, New Jersey, and Texas (Aburdene & Naisbitt, 1992, p. 24).

The landmark *Roe* v. *Wade* decision legalized abortion in 1973. Since then, the controversy has raged between anti-abortion and pro-choice supporters. The extremes of passion reached a pinnacle at the killing of a Florida abortion clinic physician by a pro-life extremist in the spring of 1993.

The abortion controversy has forced some women's groups to reexamine alternatives. One option being reintroduced by women fearing physical retaliation from visits to family planning facilities is the procedure called menstrual extraction (ME). ME is a controversial, illegal form of nonmedical abortion, practiced by a women's self-help underground. Advocates for the procedure have formed the self-help underground in cities like New York and Los Angeles, on college campuses, and in inner cities in the South and Midwest. Members of the underground feel it provides an alternative in locations where abortion rights are threatened. Predictably, doctors express concern and serious reservations about the practice, as do other groups. Patricia Ireland, president of the National Organization for Women (NOW), stated that the practice was "interesting as part of the women's health movement, which centers around taking control of our bodies, but our main concern is women's safety. It's critical that people who are performing abortions be adept" (Dogar, 1993).

The works of founding feminists still drive present opinion. Writers like Betty Freidan (1983, 1991) and *Ms.* magazine's founder, Gloria Steinem (1983, 1992), continue to be the focus of the country's views of the feminist movement. But other well-known and often-quoted feminist writers have produced classics in the genre and have, through their writings, provided a chronicle of the women's movement over the last twenty years: Germaine Greer (1971, 1984, 1989), Susan Brownmiller (1975, 1984), Jean Baker Miller (1986), Ellen DuBois and Vicki L. Ruis (1990), Carol Gilligan (1982, 1988), and Marcia Cohen (1988).

The issue of better educating women has also been at the forefront of the women's movement. Donna L. Shavlik, Director of ACE's Office of Women in Higher Education, and Judith G. Touchton, Deputy Director (1991), outlined the central message that educating women means more than admitting and graduating them. Their contention is that "more" means understanding the culture of women. Men have also been deeply affected by the changes women have made in society. They are seeking to respond with their own new questions and formulations of possible new roles. The following are some questions that Shavlik and Touchton put forward to initiate thought and discussion.

- Do women and men use different language in talking about the issue?

- Do men and women have different experience with the issue?

- Do women and men ascribe different meanings to the issue? Why?

- Do the metaphors, images, and myths that shape women's and men's thinking about the issue carry equal power? (1992, p. 54)

GAY AND LESBIAN ISSUES

Gender equity expanded to the gay community is viewed by that group as a human rights issue. Over the last two decades, homosexual-heterosexual polarity has affected local, state, and federal legislation, as well as the politics associated with it. Major topics include domestic partnership ordinances that allow gay and lesbian couples to seek the legal protections that married heterosexuals enjoy; the addition of formal gay and lesbian service programs to those offered for women, veterans, disabled people, and others; funding for AIDS research and the health care costs and services associated with the treatment of the disease.

In November 1992, the state of Colorado led the nation in an anti-gay-rights revolt when voters approved Amendment Two, a measure promoted by right-wing, Christian fundamentalist groups that repealed existing gay-rights laws and banned all such future laws. Opponents of Amendment Two argue that it and similar measures violate the federal constitution by denying gay men and women equal participation in the political process by prohibiting legislative protections for them (*Constitutional limits on anti-gay-rights initiatives*, 1993; Friedman, 1993). Later the amendment was blocked by a Colorado Supreme Court injunction but not before the state lost some $39 million in business due to boycotts by some 63 groups who cancelled conventions in the state (Peterson, 1993). The State of California, conversely, has recently enacted a law barring job discrimination against homosexuals (*Action in the states: Homosexuals*, 1993).

Robert F. Gentry, associate dean of students at the University of California at Irvine and a vocal and outspoken gay activist, is also mayor of Laguna Beach. In interviews and articles he is a strong spokesperson for the movement. He stated that he seeks not only physical safety for homosexuals but psychological safety as well. "My agenda for gay and lesbian rights is very basic—a safe environment and equal treatment" (Biemiller, 1992, p. A5).

Some change in perspective toward gay and lesbian issues has begun in several arenas. One is the business community. Several companies across America, like Levi Strauss, Apple, Digital Equipment Corporation, AT&T, Boeing, Coors, DuPont, Hewlett-Packard, Lockheed, and Sun Microsystems, to name only a few, are becoming more sensitized to employee needs. Gays and lesbians are winning corporate family benefits. As an example, in April 1991, New York's Monefiore Medical Center became the first large private employer to offer health and life insurance to the long-term partners of homosexual employees. Unmarried heterosexual couples are not eligible (Aburdene & Naisbitt, 1992, p. 239).

In the summer of 1993, at the University of Pittsburgh, a controversy raged over an effort to expand employee benefits to same-sex domestic partners (bereavement leave, tuition credit, and courtesy benefits). Much of the university's policy has polarized and angered heterosexual domestic partners who are not married but living together; they claimed that they were denied benefits based on their sexual orientation. The university reasoned that heterosexuals have the opportunity to commit legally through marriage (Casey, 1993).

THE ARBITERS OF POLARITY

After all has been said and written about polarity issues in the United States, one question remains. Who defines the parameters of a polar situation and who defines the poles? Certain "givens" must apply:

1. For those in a given situation it is virtually impossible to define where the poles are. In 1939, to a die-hard National Socialist in Germany and a deeply committed Communist in Russia, the field of political philosophy between the two seemed crystal clear, disparate, and great. What they could not see was that the ground behind, littered with the memories of disappeared comrades and foes alike, was perilously close. Like the two extremes of negative and positive infinity, they had met somewhere on the far reaches of logic carried to illogical extremes, as each carried out their respective visions in terror, night and fog, and death. Only the outsider sighting from a distance could see the true situation, political and economic dominance from east or west.

2. From "Given 1" comes "Given 2." Neither the situation nor the polarities are static. Attempting to assign a vector or vector strength to a pole is frequently an exercise in futility. In the affairs of human beings, alliances and coalitions change the shape of polarities in such a way that

they cannot be viewed as a bar magnet but rather as a force field shaped like an egg in which the wide end and the narrow end frequently exchange dimensions. From this instability can be derived "Given 3."

3. The perceived shapes of the polarities are usually as frozen in time as the view of a new star arriving millions of light years after its birth. In short, like Heisenberg's principle of uncertainty, we can see where it is or what it is but cannot do both simultaneously; nor can we predict its next configuration.

With these givens in mind, examine some of the expostulaters of various polarities. Think of that egg as a metaphor for any polar situation and explore how the following individuals would see it.

The Critic

The critic as a contemporary must be seen as inside the situation, in other words, inside the egg. From Socrates through Petronius Arbiter through Peter Abelard, Martin Luther, Voltaire, and Thomas Jefferson, the naming of one pole as good or one as evil has always implied the critic's bias toward good. Yet, as Lord Russell once said, "there has never been a war between good and evil" (except as defined by the victor). The insider never doubts he or she is on the side of good.

Think about this bias in terms of the media. As critic or information provider to millions (either through newspapers, television cable news channels, or radio) what role does the media play in formulating opinion and defining America's polarities? What role is appropriate?

The Analyst

Think of the analyst examining the egg. He or she stands outside the egg because it is simpler to determine the end with the wider radius by standing outside. The real challenge is to find the right egg to analyze, especially when the analyst starts with a preconceived point of view. This type is comparable to the author of fiction who carefully selects the egg, meticulously describes it, and presents it for the reader to generate feelings and ideas from. In this case, eggs are seldom considered in random array; one starts with a pullet, hen, or ostrich and goes on to describe the egg as in any other situation. The major warning to readers of these writers: The viewer at the one end may see the egg as round when, indeed, it is not.

The Student

Think also of the student examining the egg. The farther in time the student is from the egg, the more accurate the description of the shell and the less accurate the knowledge of its contents. The student may be studying to be an historian, sociologist, anthropologist, paleontologist, or astrophysicist. Regardless of his or her discipline or interest, the description of the poles and polarities may be accurate to a great degree, but the knowledge of the contents or occupants of the poles of the egg grow dimmer with time while the latitude of conjecture grows broader.

The Innocent Outsider (The Disaffected)

This individual stands alone at one end of the egg. He or she is like an invader from another planet. Everyone else is clustered at the other end. Many stories have been told about a Martian who arrives on Earth to find an alien culture. The Martian makes inquiries regarding religious or political customs and then arrives at logically illogical conclusions. This is the stuff of Jonathan Swift and *Gulliver's Travels*. From a spectator's standpoint, these analyses betray a person who has defined his or her own pole with all others at the other pole. All this being said, does it negate the whole concept of polarities and devices for analysis?

Short of chaos theory and anarchy, which in a world of motivated, socialized creatures is truly only a mathematical possibility, it must be presumed that humans, even if carrying out their own personal agenda, do, at times, act together as a group.

It must also be presumed that other motivated, socialized creatures with other agendas individually and socially will act in opposition. Sagan and Druyan (1992) point out that polarities are not confined to human beings but exist in other mammals, especially the primates. Thus, since polarities seem to exist at many levels in the animal kingdom, they become a proper subject of study. This book will attempt to present a few of these polarities that have become flashpoints in American culture.

REFERENCES

Abramson, J. B.; Arterton, F. C.; & Orren, G. R. 1988. *The electronic commonwealth: The impact of new media technologies on democratic politics*. New York: Basic Books.

Aburdene, P., & Naisbitt, J. 1992. *Megatrends for women*. New York: Villard Books.

Action in the states: Homosexuals. 1993. *CQ Researcher* 3, 9 (5 March): 208.

Adler, M. 1982. *The Padiea proposal: An educational manifesto*. New York: Macmillan.

Biemiller, L. 1992. The dean who is a mayor and a gay activist. *The Chronicle of Higher Education*, 17 June, A5.

Birkerts, S. 1992. Mapping the new reality. *Wilson Quarterly* 16, 2 (Winter): 102-10.

Bloom, A. 1987. *The closing of the American mind*. New York: Simon & Schuster.

Boorstin, D. J. 1965. *The Americans: The national experience*. New York: Vintage Books.

Brownmiller, S. 1975. *Against our will: Men, women, and rape.* New York: Simon & Schuster.

———. 1984. *Femininity.* New York: Fawcett Columbine.

Casey, K. 1993. Couples mixed on Pitt change. *Tribune Review*, 1 July, B1.

Cleveland, C. 1991. Campus CEO is taking on racial antagonism, sexual discrimination and the whole football team. *Working Woman* (December): 60-63.

Clinton, William J. 1993. Message to Congress transmitting proposed legislation on illegal immigration. *Weekly Compilation of Presidential Documents* 29, 30 (2 August): 1463-64.

Cockcroft, J. D. 1986. *Outlaws in the promised land.* New York: Grove Press.

Cohen, L. R., & Noll, R. G. 1991. *The technology pork barrel.* Washington, DC: Brookings Institution.

Cohen, M. 1988. *The sisterhood: The inside story of the women's movement and the leaders who made it happen.* New York: Fawcett Columbine.

Constitutional limits on anti-gay rights initiatives. 1993. *Harvard Law Review* 106, 81 (June): 1905-25.

Cornfield, M. 1992. How to read the campaign. *Wilson Quarterly* 16, 2 (Spring): 38-48.

Corwin, A. F., ed. 1978. *Immigrants—and immigrants.* Westport, CN: Greenwood Press.

Cost of living index. 1992. Louisville, KY: American Chamber of Commerce Researchers Association.

Coughlin, E. K. 1992. Scholars confront fundamental question: Which vision of America should prevail? *The Chronicle of Higher Education*, 29 January, A8.

Dogar, R. 1993. Controversy. *Self* (June): 90-91.

Donovan, R., & Scherer, R. 1992. Politics transformed. *Wilson Quarterly* 16, 2 (Spring): 18-58.

Drucker, P. F. 1989. *The new realities, in government and politics, in economics and business, in society and world view.* New York: Harper & Row.

———. 1992. *Managing for the future: The 1990s and beyond.* New York: E. P. Dutton.

D'souza, D. 1992. *Illiberal education: The politics of race and sex on campus.* New York: Vintage Books.

DuBois, E. C., & Ruis, V. L., eds. 1990. *Unequal sisters: A multicultural reader in U.S. women's history.* New York: Routledge.

Dychtwald, K., & Flower, J. 1989. *Age wave: The challenges and opportunities of an aging America.* Los Angeles: Jeremy P. Tarcher.

Ethier, W. J. 1986. Illegal immigration. *American Economic Review* 76, 2 (May): 258-62.

Faludi, S. 1991. *Backlash: The undeclared war against American women.* New York: Crown.

Falwell, J. 1981. *Listen America!* New York: Bantam Books.

———. 1986. *If I should die before I wake.* Nashville, TN: Thomas Nelson.

———. 1987. *Strength for the journey.* New York: Simon & Schuster.

Featherstone, J. 1979. Family matters. *Harvard Educational Review* 49: 20-52.

Fogel, W. 1978. *Mexican illegal alien workers in the United States.* Los Angeles: Institute of Industrial Relations, University of California.

Friedan, B. 1983. *The feminine mystique.* New York: Dell.

———. 1991. *The second stage.* New York: Dell.

Friedman, S. 1993. Colorado's Amendment 2 blocked. *ABA Journal* 79 (October): 48-49.

Gates, H. L., Jr. 1990. *Reading black, reading feminist: A critical anthology.* New York: Meridian Books.

———. 1992. *Loose canons: Notes on the culture wars.* New York: Oxford University Press.

Gilligan, C. 1982. *In a different voice: Psychological theory and women's development.* Cambridge: Harvard University Press.

Gilligan, C., et al., eds. 1988. *Mapping the moral domain: A contribution of women's thinking to psychological theory and education.* Cambridge: Harvard University Press.

Gore, A. 1992. *Earth in the balance: Ecology and the human spirit.* Boston: Houghton Mifflin.

Grant, L. 1991. Facing the consequences of illegal immigration. *USA Today. The Magazine of the American Scene* 119, 2548 (January): 10-12.

Greer, G. 1971. *Female eunuch.* New York: McGraw-Hill.

———. 1984. *Sex and destiny.* London: Secker & Warburg.

———. 1989. *Daddy, we hardly knew you.* New York: Alfred Knopf.

Gregory, P. 1989. *Undocumented migration to the United States: Can the flow be stemmed?* Albuquerque: Latin American Institute, The University of New Mexico. Research Paper Series No. 22.

Griffin, R. D. 1992. Illegal immigration. *CQ Researcher* 2, 16 (24 April): 363-6+.

Hallin, D. C. 1992. Sound bite democracy. *Wilson Quarterly* 16, 2 (Spring): 34-37.

Harper dictionary of contemporary usage. 1985. 2nd ed. New York: Harper & Row.

Hirsch, E. D., Jr. 1987. *Cultural literacy: What every American needs to know.* Boston: Houghton Mifflin.

Horowitz, I. L. 1984. *Winners and losers: Social and political polarities in America.* Durham, NC: Duke University Press.

Huber, R. M. 1992. *How professors play the cat guarding the cream: Why we're paying more and getting less in higher education.* Fairfax, VA: George Mason University Press.

In plain Spanish, No. 1993. *National Review* 45, 14: 16(2).

James, D. 1991. *Illegal immigration: An unfolding crisis.* Lanham, MD: University Press of America.

Kagan, D., et al. 1991. *The western heritage.* New York: Macmillan.

Kimball, R. 1990. *Tenured radicals: How politics has corrupted our higher education.* New York: Harper & Row.

Kozol, J. 1991. *Savage inequalities: Children in America's schools.* New York: Crown.

LaHaye, B. 1984. *The restless woman.* Grand Rapids, MI: Zondervan.

Lasch, C. 1991. *The true and only heaven: Progress and its critics.* New York: W. W. Norton.

Laslett, P. 1989. *A fresh map of life: The emergence of the third age.* London: Weidenfeld & Nicolson.

Lesko, M. 1986. *Lesko's new tech sourcebook: A directory to finding answers in today's technology-oriented world.* New York: Harper & Row.

Lovely, D. 1993. *USA Weekend,* 8-10 January, 4-6.

Luke, T. H. 1989. *Screens of power: Ideology, domination, and resistance in information society.* Urbana: University of Illinois Press.

MacDonald, F. 1982. *Black is the color of the cosmos.* New York: Garland Publications.

———. 1986. *A constitutional history of the United States.* Malabar, FL: R. E. Krieger.

Mansfield, E. 1971. *Technological change: An introduction to a vital area of modern economics.* New York: W. W. Norton.

McKibben, B. 1993. The ten most endangered places. *Self* (June): 128-30.

McNary, G. 1992. Curbing illegal immigration: Employers must help. *USA Today. The Magazine of the American Scene* 12, 2568 (September): 22-23.

Miles, J. 1992. Blacks vs. browns. *The Atlantic* (October): 41-69.

Millard, R. M. 1991. *Today's myths and tomorrow's realities.* San Francisco: Jossey-Bass.

Miller, J. B. 1986. *Toward a new psychology of women.* Boston: Beacon Press.

Moneyline: Rich get richer. 1992. *USA Today,* 30 October, B1.

Morris, W., & Morris, M. 1975. *Harper dictionary of contemporary usage.* New York: Harper & Row.

Nelson, E., comp. 1975. *Pablo Cruz and the American dream.* Salt Lake City, UT: Peregrine Smith.

Neusner, J. 1988. *Paradigms in passage: Patterns of change in the contemporary study of Judaism.* Lanham, MD: University Press of America.

———. 1991. *Introduction to Judaism: A textbook and reader.* Louisville, KY: Westminster/John Knox Press.

The new Encyclopaedia Britannica. 1992. Macropaedia, vol. 16. Chicago: Encyclopaedia Britannica.

O'Rourke, P. J. 1991. *Parliament of whores.* New York: Atlantic Monthly Press.

Oxford English dictionary. 1991. 2nd ed. Vol. 7. Oxford: Clarendon Press.

Pearson, C. S.; Shavlik, D. L.; & Touchton, J. G.; eds. 1991. *Educating the majority: Women challenge tradition in higher education.* New York: Macmillan.

Peterson, J. 1993. Punishing the less guilty? *SKI* 58, 4 (December): 38.

Planning to be poor. 1992. *Newsweek,* 30 November, 66-67.

Poor vs. rich: The widening gap. 1993. *Rural Pennsylvania* 2, 2 (March/April): 1.

Random House dictionary of the English language. 1987. 2nd ed. New York: Random House.

Reeves, F., & Reeves, T. 1993. Political watch. *Pittsburgh Post Gazette,* 20 June, A15.

Reich, R. B. 1992. *The work of nations: Preparing ourselves for 21st century capitalism*. New York: Vintage Books.

Robbins, R. 1993. Rural vs. rich: Income gap grows. *Tribune Review*, 21 March, A1.

Rostow, W. W. 1990. *Theorists of economic growth from David Hume to the present: With a perspective on the next century*. New York: Oxford University Press.

Rubenstein, H. 1990. *The Oxford book of marriage*. New York: Oxford University Press.

Sagan, C., & Druyan, A. 1992. *Shadows of forgotten ancestors: A search for who we are*. New York: Random House.

Schlafly, P. 1977. *The power of the positive woman*. New Rochelle, NY: Arlington House.

Schlesinger, A. M., Jr. 1992. *The disuniting of America*. New York: W. W. Norton.

Shavlik, D., & Touchton, J. G. 1992. *Educational Record* (Fall): 47-55.

Skewes, E. A. 1993. Can our cities survive? *Dickinson Magazine* (Winter): 12-17.

Skolnick, A. 1991. *Embattled paradise: The American family in an age of uncertainty*. New York: Basic Books.

Sowell, T. 1991. A world view of cultural diversity. *Society* 29, 1 (November/December): 37-44.

Steinem, G. 1983. *Outrageous acts and everyday rebellions*. New York: American Library.

———. 1992. *Revolution from within: A book of self-esteem*. New York: Little, Brown.

Thomas, R. R., Jr. 1991. *Beyond race and gender: Unleashing the power of your total work force by managing diversity*. New York: AMACOM (American Management Association).

Toffler, A. 1970. *Future shock*. New York: Random House.

———. 1981. *The third wave*. New York: Bantam Books.

———. 1990. *Powershift: Knowledge, wealth, and violence at the edge of the 21st century*. New York: Bantam Books.

Trying to count the nation's shadow population. 1992. *CQ Researcher* 2, 16 (April 24): 366-67.

U.S. Department of Labor. Bureau of Labor Statistics. 1986. Reemployment increases among displaced workers. *BLS News* USDL 86-414, October 14, Table 6.

Williams, J. 1988. *Eyes on the prize: America's civil rights years, 1954-1965*. New York: Penguin.

———. 1992. Learning the right lesson. *The Pittsburgh Press*, 10 May, B1, B5.

Wolfe, L., ed. 1991. *Women, work, and school: Occupational segregation and the role of education*. Boulder, CO: Westview Press.

Workforce 2000: Work and workers for the 21st century. 1987. Indianapolis: Hudson Institute.

SOURCES OF ADDITIONAL INFORMATION

Indexes/Databases

ABI/Inform
UMI/Data Courier
620 South Third Street
Louisville, KY 40202-2475
800-626-2823
Online and CD-ROM formats

Academic Index
Online Services
Information Access Company
362 Lakeside Drive
Foster City, CA 94404
415-378-5200
Online and CD-ROM formats

Alternative Press Index
Alternative Press Center
P.O. Box 33109
Baltimore, MD 21218
410-243-2471
Print format

Business Periodicals Index
H. W. Wilson Company
950 University Avenue
Bronx, NY 10452
212-588-8400
Print, online, and CD-ROM formats

CENDATA
Bureau of the Census
Federal Center
Suitland, MD 20233
301-763-5820
Online format

CIS Index
Congressional Information Service
4520 East-West Highway
Bethesda, MD 20814-3387
301-654-1550
Print, online, and CD-ROM formats

Editorials on File
Facts on File
460 Park Avenue South
New York, NY 10016
800-322-8755
Print, online, and CD-ROM formats

ERIC
U.S. Department of Education
2440 Research Boulevard, 5th Floor
Rockville, MD 20850
301-656-9723
Print, online, and CD-ROM formats

Facts on File
Facts on File
460 Park Avenue South
New York, NY 10016
800-322-8755
Print, online, and CD-ROM formats

General Periodical Index
Online Services
Information Access
362 Lakeside Drive
Foster City, CA 94404
800-227-8431
Online and CD-ROM formats

National Newspaper Index
Online Services
Information Access
362 Lakeside Drive
Foster City, CA 94404
800-227-8431
Online and microfiche formats

New York Times Index
New York Times
299 West 43d Street
New York, NY 10036
212-556-1234
Print, online, and CD-ROM formats

PAIS INTERNATIONAL
Public Affairs Information Service, Inc.
521 West 43rd Street
New York, NY 10036
212-736-6639
Print, online, and CD-ROM formats

Readers' Guide to Periodical
Literature
H. W. Wilson Company
950 University Avenue
Bronx, NY 10452
215-588-8400
Print, online, and CD-ROM formats

Social Sciences Citation Index
Institute for Scientific Information
3501 Market Street
Philadelphia, PA 19104
1-800-523-4092

Social Sciences Index
H. W. Wilson Company
950 University Avenue
Bronx, NY 10452
215-588-8400
Print, online, and CD-ROM formats

Social Work Abstracts
National Association of Social Workers
7981 Eastern Avenue
Silver Spring, MD 20910
301-565-0333
Print, online, and CD-ROM formats

Sociological Abstracts
Sociological Abstracts, Inc.
P.O. Box 2206
San Diego, CA 92122
619-695-8803
Print, online, and CD-ROM formats

Women Studies Abstracts
Transaction Periodicals Consortium
Rutgers University
New Brunswick, NJ 08903
908-932-2280
Print format

Work Related Abstracts
Harmonie Park Press
23630 Pinewood
Warren, MI 48091
313-715-3080
Print format

Useful Library of Congress
Subject Headings

Abortion
Abortion—Religious Aspects
Abortion—United States
Academic freedom—United States
Afro-American Literature and Culture
Afro-Americans
Afro-Americans—Civil Rights—History
Aging—Social Aspects
Analogy
Anti-abortion
Anti-abortion—United States
Civilization, Modern—20th Century—
    Psychological Aspects
Conduct of Life
Discrimination
Discrimination in Higher Education—
    United States
Economic Conditions
Education
Education—United States
Educational Equalization—United
    States

Environment
Environment—United States
Environmental Issues—United States
Ethnicity
Ethnology—United States
Ethnology—United States—Statistics
Femininity (Psychology)
Feminism
Feminism—United States—History—
    20th Century
Feminism and Literature—United
    States
Feminists—United States
Gay Rights
Gay Rights—United States
Gays
Gays—United States
Higher Education—United States
Higher Education—United States—
    Curricula
Higher Education—United States—
    Political Aspects

Homophobia
Homosexuals
Ideology
Immigration—United States
Immigration—United States—
    Statistics
Intercultural Education—United
    States
Interdisciplinary Approach in
    Education
Interdisciplinary Approach to
    Knowledge
Legal Positivism
Lesbian Rights
Lesbian—United States
Logic
Minorities—Education
Minorities—Education (Higher)
Minorities—United States
Minorities—United States—
    Congresses
Multiculturalism
Multiculturalism—United States
Philosophy
Polarity
Polarity (Philosophy)
Political Sociology
Poor—United States
Pro-choice
Pro-choice—United States

Pro-life
Pro-life—United States
Psychology and Philosophy
Quality of Life—United States
Racism—United States
Refugees—United States
Sex Roles
Sociology
Student Movements—United States
United States—Census, 20th, 1980
United States—Economic Policy
United States—Ethnic Relations
United States—Moral Conditions
United States—Politics and
    Government
United States—Population
United States—Race Relations
United States—Social Conditions
United States—Social Policy
United States—Social Policy—
    Congresses
Wealth—United States
Women
Women—United States
Women—United States—History—
    Cross Cultural Studies
Women—United States—Social
    Conditions
Women's Rights—United States
Women's Studies—United States

Government, as the most conspicuous object in society, is called upon to give signal of what shall be done; and, in many ways, to preside over, further, and command the doing of it. But the government cannot do, by all its signaling and commanding, what the society is radically indisposed to do.

Thomas Carlyle, 1843

2

The Government's Role in "Bridging the Gap"

Diane H. Smith

The goal of this chapter is to discuss the role that federal and state governments have played in developing public policies aimed at bridging and limiting social inequalities in America. In today's society many inequities that we see daily, through our own experiences or through the media, are personally shocking and unjust. Our initial reaction is that the government ought to do "something." Yet, now, as in the past, there is no consensus about what is the correct social welfare policy. Some of the major American political and social battles of the twentieth century were fought over precisely what that "something" should be (Critchlow & Hawley, 1988; Patterson, 1986; Weir, Orloff, & Skocpol 1988). Additionally, because most of us have reached adulthood during a period of extensive government public policy intervention, our perceptions are

Diane H. Smith is currently Chief of Reference and Instructional Services at The Pennsylvania State University. Before that she served as the United States Librarian and Head of Documents/Maps at Penn State. She has held several offices in ALA/GODORT, including Chair in 1985-1986. She also has been a member and chair of the Depository Library Council to the Public Printer. She has written and spoken widely on the issues of technology in documents collection and on U.S. information policy. With Diane Garner, Ms. Smith co-authored *The Complete Guide to Citing Government Documents*.

that government should take action. However, people have not always reacted this way. In fact, it was not until the Great Depression that people even seriously discussed whether the government had a mandate to be involved actively in social issues. The central objective of this chapter is to chart the evolution of society's perceptions of the government's role in public policy issues. This evolving role is played against the backdrop of vying economic philosophies, the question of federalism and states' rights, the power of the two major American political parties, and the constant "checks and balances" of presidential and congressional power (Hofstadter, 1948).

WHAT IS PUBLIC OR SOCIAL POLICY?

Public or social policy is what governments choose to do or not to do for the citizens of a country (DiNitto, 1991; Dye, 1987; Morris, 1985). Government action or inaction can have broad ramifications on society and the economy of a country. Public policy is a decision-making procedure that is entangled in a process of intensive compromise and adjustment. Studying the public policy of an issue can be valuable for three reasons. First, understanding public policy improves one's knowledge of that aspect of society. Second, comprehending why and how a government has reacted to a problem in the past helps to predict how it will react to a similar problem in the future. Third, understanding social policies can help in articulating "correct" policies for the future. This last objective is, however, fraught with the question of what constitutes "right" when the issue is a social one and there are widely varying solutions.

HISTORY OF GOVERNMENT SOCIAL POLICY

Eighteenth-Century America

"The basic tenets and programs of any social welfare system reflect the values of the society in which the system functions" (Trattner, 1984, p. 1). This opening sentence of Trattner's classic treatise on the development of the American welfare state explains why little, if any, government social welfare policy existed in colonial and pre-industrial America. The facts are simple and known by most who have studied this period: America was primarily an agricultural economy, evolving from the feudal traditions and economy of Europe. There was work for all to clear the land and develop the economy; the idea of unemployment was totally foreign. There were extensive lands to be farmed and owned, unlike Europe in which natural resources were controlled by a few privileged individuals. The general belief was that pauperism and poverty could not occur in such a utopia. This myopia blinded the early colonists to the social welfare needs within their society (Axinn, 1982; Katz, 1986; Jansson, 1988). Most settlers and immigrants were northern European, usually English, with a strong tradition of Protestant work ethic and charitable giving through private organizations to those less fortunate. This ethnic and religious background fostered the development of a strong American ethos that emphasized individuals' sole responsibility for themselves and their families' well-being. Reflecting the societal norms of the time, there was also little concern for the disenfranchised of society: Native Americans, black slaves, indentured servants, and women. Concurrently, with the evolution of the thirteen colonial governments into a single federal system, people held a deep distrust of a strong centralized government. As a result, the Constitution was written to limit the powers of a central government and empower the local governments. This division of responsibilities clearly assigned any responsibility for social welfare to the state and local authorities rather than the federal government.

Nineteenth-Century America

As the country grew in population and size, the problems inherent in all societies also grew. Increased immigration, especially into the larger cities, heightened awareness of these problems. However, most Americans at this time viewed these social problems as signs of moral deficiencies, not the results of economics. The response from local governments and charities was to develop institutions to deal with the criminals, drunkards, the mentally ill, and children's welfare. These "reform movements" created several types of institutions that were later pulled into the field of "charity and correction" (Leiby, 1978, p. 48; Lubove, 1972).

During the period of major industrialization that occurred after the Civil War, particularly in the North, these problems began to intensify. The agricultural utopia of America was quickly being replaced by the sweatshops of the big cities. The wounded, widowed, or orphaned of the war were in need. The emancipation of the slaves had led to a new class of neglected workers. Government made little attempt to regulate industries, and unbridled industrial development flourished, making fortunes for a few and developing discontent among a growing working class. "By the end of the nineteenth century, Americans had developed a conservative consensus in which they took moralistic and punitive stances toward destitute persons, possessed a restrictive concept of social obligations, perceived social problems to be temporary rather than endemic to the social fabric, and favored limited government" (Jansson, 1988, p. 83).

The Progressive Era and Its Legacy

As the problems of an industrialized economy continued to develop, the progressive reform era began. This movement, which attacked a variety of political, economic, and social conditions, was based on a combination of traditional nineteenth-century liberalism and the theory of Social Darwinism. This mixture resulted in a subtle but significant change in the American view of the individual: The social and collective good might be more important than that of the individual. Additionally, there were areas of social welfare (health, safety, and morals) in which the state had responsibilities for the collective good and the individual did not need to battle conditions alone. A key philosophy behind this reform movement was the economic notion that there were normal standards of living and a defined poverty line. The object of social reform was to develop policies and programs that would prevent most working people from falling below this line (Leiby, 1987). No longer was the goal of social work to help those in poverty, but rather to prevent people from going into poverty. Robert Hunter's 1904 book *Poverty* contained one of the first calls for legislative action in this area. In this work Hunter challenged the government to institute minimum standards for immigration; to prohibit child labor; to regulate work hours, especially for women and children; to make factories and tenements safe; to eradicate diseases; to regulate dangerous trades; to provide educational and recreational institutions; and to provide for those unemployed, ill, or aged. This list of government actions clearly laid out an agenda for a welfare state, an agenda the government adopted in large part thirty years later. Additional works, such as Jacob Riis's *How the Other Half Lives*, Upton Sinclair's *The Jungle*, and Jane Addams's *Twenty Years at Hull House*, further fueled the desire for regulatory reform and some level of social legislation.

Key among the legislative actions that were undertaken during the Progressive Era were the laws and regulations that affected women, children, and workmen's compensation. Although not significant in number, these legislative actions were indicative of the changing American philosophy of government's responsibility for individuals. Such legislation included laws limiting hours and controlling working conditions for women and children; the Mann Act, prohibiting the interstate transportation of nonconsenting women; various state enactments of mothers' pension and workmen's compensation laws; the establishment of the federal Children's Bureau to deal with child welfare issues; and the passage of the Sheppard-Towner Act to provide federal funds for clinics for children and pregnant women.

The 1920s and the Great Depression

With the end of World War I, America experienced a period of rapid industrial and economic development. The only world power to have emerged from the war both unscathed and a creditor to the rest of the world, America turned inward and funneled its energies into a decade of economic prosperity. Growing consumer demands, tax cuts, and a new age of industrial growth tied to technology and scientific management methods all fueled an economy that turned its back on the needs of the poor and underrepresented. The beliefs of the Progressive Era and many of its policies, programs, laws, and regulations were quickly discarded in the face of such prosperity. The political and social philosophy of this decade of Republican presidents was aptly summed up by Harding's famous quote: "What we want in America is less government in business and more business in government." This philosophy would reappear sixty years later in the Reagan and Bush administrations.

The stock market crash of 1929 brought a harsh new social and economic reality to America. The belief that unemployment and poverty were problems that could not affect most Americans quickly changed. The utopia myth was destroyed by the images of bread lines, apple vendors, and abandoned farms. The unemployed could be anyone, from any social stratum, educational level, occupation, or location. The nation's charitable relief organizations simply could not deal with the numbers of people in need of aid. Nonetheless, Herbert Hoover staunchly stood by his beliefs that it was not appropriate for the government to involve itself in welfare issues. Although he finally did support both the passage of the Reconstruction Finance Corporation, a federal entity that could finance corporation and bank projects at the verge of bankruptcy, and the Emergency Relief and Construction Act of 1932, the economy was in dire condition by the time Roosevelt was elected in November 1932. That this financial crisis was international in scope only heightened American isolationism and reinforced the belief that the government had limited ability to deal with the crisis (Hill, 1988).

The New Deal

Roosevelt's administration was a watershed event in the history of American welfare and American politics (Schlesinger, 1957-1960). The programs introduced had a permanent effect on the American perception of government and its role in the fabric of daily life. The philosophy embodied within these programs continues to affect political and economic actions fifty years after their initial implementation (Fraser & Gerstle, 1989; Sitkoff, 1985). For the first time the idea that government had a role in social welfare was popularized. As noted by a 1933 *New York Times Magazine* article, "There is a country-wide dumping of responsibility on the Federal Government. If Mr. Roosevelt goes on collecting mandates, one after another . . . it is because all other powers . . . virtually abdicate in his favor. America today literally asks for orders. . ." (Friedel, 1964, p. 5).

With this mandate came the power to try new approaches to economic and social problems. In Roosevelt's administration vigorous and bold programs were undertaken to put America back on its feet. Among legislation undertaken were the Federal Emergency Relief Act (FERA), which provided federal monies as grants-in-aid to local agencies; the

Agricultural Adjustment Act (AAA), designed to subsidize farm economies; the National Industrial Recovery Act (NIRA), aimed at reviving manufacturing; and the National Labor Relations Act (NLRA) and the Fair Standards Labor Act, passed to facilitate resolution of labor disputes and guarantee minimum wages and conditions for employees. Through the Civil Works Administration (CWA), the Public Works Administration (PWA), the Civilian Conservation Corps (CCC), and the Works Progress Administration (WPA), the government tried to put men and women back to work. Each of these programs chipped away at the American myth of individual responsibility and fueled the belief that there was a role for the federal government in social and economic welfare. This public opinion was only reinforced when America entered the war and the power of the government reached into all lives through war effort programs, rationing, and selective service.

However, although Roosevelt's legislative activities in 1933-1934 were important in restoring some American confidence, the keystone to the New Deal program was the Social Security Act of 1935. Central to the act were the provisions of Old Age Insurance (OAI), which mandated annuities for workers at age sixty-five. Other provisions included a state-federal system of unemployment insurance and federal aid to women with children (Abbott, 1940; Abbott, 1941; Altmeyer, 1966; Lubove, 1986; Witte, 1962). Developed by the Committee on Economic Security and the product of inevitable political compromise, this act established the first permanent role for the federal government in welfare issues and its passage laid the groundwork for America's current welfare state.

Postwar America and the 1950s

The end of World War II brought a period of relative affluence and complacency to the United States. Over time political opposition to the New Deal and its Democratic reforms dismantled many policies and programs that Roosevelt had established. Yet the belief that the federal government had a role in creating social and economic policies could not be so easily eliminated. Simply too many Americans had suffered from the Depression and had survived due to government intervention.

During this time the federal government maintained a presence in four areas: health, education, child care, and race relations. A major concern during the war years was the health of soldiers and their dependents, as demonstrated by the 1943 passage of the Emergency Maternity and Infant Care Act. Emphasis on health issues continued after the war with the passage of the National Mental Health Act of 1946 and the thwarted attempt in 1948 by Truman to pass a national health insurance act. Educational issues came to the forefront in 1944 with the passage of the Servicemen's Readjustment Act (GI Bill). This piece of legislation developed a trained and educated workforce that would later fuel the economic growth of the 1950s and 1960s. As the returning veterans resumed civilian life, the generation known as the baby-boomers were conceived. Their birth encouraged further steps by the government in child care and education issues, with the passage of the National School Lunch Program (1946) and the special Milk Program in 1954. However, nothing was to be as significant socially, or as traumatic to the American psyche, as the rising pressure of civil rights demands that would erupt in the 1960s. Key to this change was the 1954 Supreme Court decision of *Brown* v. *the Board of Education*, eliminating the concept of "separate but equal" educational facilities and laying the foundation for substantial federal civil rights legislation in the 1960s.

The 1960s and the Great Society

With the election of Kennedy to the presidency, the Democrats again had an opportunity to re-create the types of social welfare programs that Roosevelt had originally introduced and upon which the Democrats had built much of their political clout and reputation. During the next eight years of Democratic rule the most important pieces of welfare legislation since the New Deal were passed and "a generation's backlog of ideas and legislation" were harvested (Kaplan & Cuciti, 1986, p. 1). Aided by the best and the brightest of their generation, the Kennedy and Johnson administrations tried to respond to the social problems of unemployment, civil rights, education, and health (Aaron, 1978; Sundquist, 1968). Under the Johnson administration the government improved income mainte- nance programs and developed a plan to provide direct services to indi- viduals, services that previously had been provided solely by local agencies. Overall these services pushed the country a few inches closer to an American variety of the welfare state. Johnson's "Great Society" was clearly an attempt to continue the work of the New Deal (Bornet, 1983; Moynihan, 1973a).

A whole series of new laws, programs, and abbreviations entered the American vocabulary. Key among them were the Manpower Development Training Act of 1961; the Food Stamp Act of 1964; the Civil Rights Act of 1964; the Aid to Families with Dependent Children Act of 1961 (AFDC); the Economic Opportunity Act of 1964; Medicare and Medicaid programs as amendments to the Social Security Act of 1965; the Elementary and Secondary Education Act of 1965; the Older Americans Act of 1965; the WIC and Headstart programs; and employment programs, such as VISTA, WIN, and the Job Corps. All of this legislation was developed against a backdrop of rising civil disorders and demands for civil rights (U.S. National Advisory Commission on Civil Disorder, 1968); increasing awareness of Americans that their land of plenty contained significant pockets of poverty (Harrington, 1962; U.S. National Advisory Commission on Rural Poverty, 1967; U.S. President's Commission on Income Mainte- nance, 1969-1970); the phenomenon of the "working poor" that under- mined that very basic American belief of hard work paying off; the steadily increasing numbers of individuals receiving welfare support (Piven & Cloward, 1971); and America's escalating military involvement in Vietnam. Whether Johnson's policies would have been effective in the long term is an academic question that is hotly debated in the literature (Bremner, Reichard, & Hopkins, 1986; Haveman, 1977; Levine, 1970; Levitan, 1969; Levitan, 1976; Matusow, 1984; Plotnick, 1975; Schwarz, 1988; Steiner, 1971). What truly destroyed the "Great Society" was not the social agenda, but Vietnam. As opposition to the war increased, Johnson's popularity steadily plummeted and convinced him not to seek reelection in 1968. This election proved to be a turning point that would affect and influence social welfare policy for the next twenty-five years.

Nixon and the 1970s

The election of Richard Nixon brought the Republican party back to power and signaled a major shift of the American mood to the right (Reichley, 1981). However, for the first three years of his presidency, Nixon, contrary to popular belief, continued the reforms of Johnson, Kennedy, and Roosevelt (Levitan, 1976; Levitan & Johnson, 1984; Plotnick, 1975). During his administration federal spending for social programs doubled over expenditures (Jansson, 1988, p. 188). This phenomenal increase in spending was due in large part to the programs that Nixon undertook (Burke & Burke, 1974). Key among these programs was the decision to establish automatic indexing for Social Security payments. Previously, any increases were periodically proposed and evaluated; now the increases could potentially exceed the inflation rate. Other significant Nixon reforms were revisions to the Food Stamp program, the Supplemental Security income program to assist older Americans living on Social Security, the consolidation of federally sponsored social services under Title XX of the Social Security Act, and the passage of the Comprehensive Employment and Training Act (CETA). He also introduced the Family Assistance Program (FAP), a piece of legislation that would have substantially reformed welfare programs and that rivaled many of Roosevelt's plans (Moynihan, 1973b). Unfortunately, due to political infighting, the program was defeated. With Nixon's resignation in 1974 American interest in social policy waned and public interest in welfare lessened considerably. Reflecting the mood of the time and the recession-plagued economy reeling from the development of the global oil economy, few legislative or policy initiatives were undertaken in either the Ford or Carter administration.

The Reagan and Bush Legacy

The elections of Ronald Reagan and George Bush during the 1980s heralded the return to conservatism, and their policies have been frequently touted by the press as the "Reagan Revolution" or as a "counter-revolution" to the policies of the 1960s and 1970s (Dallek, 1984; Leuchtenburg, 1989; Stockman, 1986). The primary goals of the revolution were to decrease government regulation and spending in the areas of social policy and increase spending in the defense and military complex.

The solution to growing unemployment and inflation was to depend on the theory of "supply-side" economics, forsaking the fifty years of Keynesian theory (Niskanen, 1988). The tremendous increases in military expenditures were financed not through increased taxes that would have been politically untenable, but through the ever-growing federal deficit and massive cuts in social programs (Bawden, 1984; Hulten & Sawhill, 1984; Piven, 1982). To support the level of cuts during these years of Republican control there was a systematic disassembling of the social welfare state that had been constructed through years of Democratic agendas (Burt, 1985; Champagne & Harphan, 1984; Palmer & Sawhill, 1984; Schorr, 1986). Key legislation during the Reagan years was the Omnibus Budget Reconciliation Act (OBRA) and the Tax Equity and Fiscal Responsibility Act (TEFRA), both of which substantially cut into federally funded welfare programs; the passage of the Job Training Partnership Act (JTPA) in favor of CETA; and new regulations and cuts into the Medicare and Social Security programs.

With the election of George Bush in 1988 the pattern continued. Immersed in issues of international and military policy, the Bush agenda for social policy was simply a continuation of Reagan's programs, with an emphasis on federal budget cuts and tax reductions in light of a growing recession (Barilleaux & Stuckey, 1992; Campbell & Rockman, 1991; Duffy, 1992; Jansson, 1987). Whether the election of Bill Clinton in 1992 can be interpreted as a clear signal from the American people in favor of the developing welfare state will need to be researched in the future. The election certainly was viewed by those with pro-active social policy agendas as a significant point in American political history and Clinton's first-year emphasis on domestic and health policy in lieu of foreign policy concerns has reaffirmed this belief.

RECURRING THEMES
IN FEDERAL SOCIAL POLICY

In any discussion of federal social policy there are three factors that are central to understanding the past and are crucial in predicting the actions of the American government and the response of the American populace. These issues—federalism, politics, and economics—are so intertwined that it is difficult to separate one totally from another. The remainder of this chapter briefly discusses these issues and their relevance to federal social policy.

Federalism

A key question in the controversy concerning national social policy revolves around the role of the federal government in relation to local governments. Over time the varying governmental roles have proven to be constantly changing because of fiscal constraints, political agendas, and judicial interpretations. An excellent source for information about these relations in the last twenty years can be seen in the many publications of the Advisory Commission on Intergovernmental Relations (1980, 1982, 1984).

As originally conceived in the Constitution, all powers, except those specifically assigned as federal in nature, were delegated to the states. Before 1930 initiatives in the area of welfare services tended to be a loose form of "cooperative federalism," focusing on grants-in-aid and federal standards of performance. However, through Roosevelt's New Deal policies the transition to national responsibility for welfare strongly advanced. The programs and agencies that developed because of the Depression were watershed events in the redefinition of a strong federal, state, and local relationship (Brock, 1988; Carey 1938). With the War on Poverty a new definition of federalism arose: "creative federalism" (Henig, 1985, p. 15). A key characteristic of this style of federalism was that the government used explicit incentives to force local and state compliance in the management of welfare programs. With the Nixon administration "new federalism" became the byword for social policies. New federalism stressed the principles of general revenue sharing and block grants (Elazar, 1974; Reagan, 1972; Sundquist, 1975). Finally, with the Reagan administration yet another form of "new federalism" emerged; a federalism that reversed the fifty-year role of federal government and returned significant authority and fiscal obligations to the state and local governments (Swartz & Peck, 1990), frequently with a negative impact on local budgets.

Politics

Probably more than any other factors in the twentieth century, politics, party loyalty and platforms, and special interest groups have played a significant role in the development of federal social policy (Beck, 1982; Browning 1985; Browning, 1986; Sinclair, 1984; Steiner, 1966). Constant shifts within the political power structure of Washington have occurred with the rising and falling fortunes of the Republicans and Democratic political parties. These changes, reacting with national economic patterns, have resulted over the years in a schizophrenic pattern of federal social policies and programs (Browning, 1986), a pattern reflecting the mood, interests, and opinions of congressional constituents.

However, the relationship between the president and Congress has also played a major role in the development and "stalemate" of social programs (Mezey, 1986; Mezey, 1989, p. 109). The success of any administration has been determined by its ability to use its resources to wend its way through the political legislative process (Light, 1982, p. 13; Light, 1985). History shows that some have been more successful than others in their endeavors to implement social policy (McKay, 1989; Sundquist, 1968).

Economics and Budgeting

Inevitably, in all discussions about the role of the federal government in welfare and public policy, the issue of economics and costs arises as the deciding factor. Whether the program is morally right or whether it will benefit many citizens, the final question always arises: "Can the government and can society (i.e., the taxpayers) afford the costs that will be incurred in developing or continuing such a social program, and, if so, at what cost to other programs?" The extent to which the federal budget can support expensive social programs is, thus, a significant part of this economic question. Within this debate there arise the politics and processes of budget preparation and taxation (Ippolito, 1990; Wildavsky, 1984); the issues surrounding federal deficits versus balanced budgets (Savage, 1988; Stein, 1969) the question of entitlement programs and their automatic indexation (Peterson & Howe, 1988; U.S. Congress. House, 1981; Weaver, 1988); and finally the sheer amounts of the federal budget spent in social services (Bixby, 1991; U.S. Health, Education, and Welfare, 1968).

In the field of political economy there are also vying economic philosophies outlining the proper role for the government in everyday economic and social matters. These theories range from governmental laissez-faire to socialism. Within America one encounters an equally wide spectrum of ideas as to what the proper governmental role in social policy should be. These different opinions, arising from the variety of regional, ethnic, religious, social, educational, and economic backgrounds of Americans, are essential in understanding the development of federally supported welfare policies in this country.

Historically the dream of economic freedom and democracy is built upon the notion that every individual is capable of "pulling one's self up by one's bootstraps" and attaining prosperity through hard work. This was the immigrant dream, the tale of a land of infinite opportunity, and was strongly engrained in the American personality. This belief was built on the idea of a laissez-faire government and an economy in which market forces were allowed to operate freely. However, according to theorists in the field of political economy and history, there was considerable intervention in the economy in the eighteenth and nineteenth centuries (Bourgin, 1989; Fine 1964; Hughes, 1991). Later, the New Deal's dependence on Keynesian economics had a significant impact on Americans' perceptions of the role of the government in welfare policy (Fraser & Gerstle, 1989; Schlesinger, 1957-1960). The successes and failures of the "Great Society" also molded further a developing American form of a welfare state (Anderson, 1978). The most recent addition to the spectrum of American economic theory has been the philosophy of "Reaganomics" or "trickle-down economics" (Niskanen, 1988). America, relying on this economic theory of less government spending in welfare, more dependence on private or charitable giving, and business stimulation in the hopes that the money would "trickle" down to the needy, has experienced the greatest growth of individuals in need of welfare since the Depression.

Future Trends

"The welfare state is, first and foremost, a political artifact. As such, it is the product of historical accretion and political compromise. Different bits have been added, over the years, by different people with different purposes in mind. . . . Basically, it means that the 'welfare state' is not itself a single, unified, unambiguous entity. It is instead a ragbag of programs, only vaguely related and only imperfectly integrated" (Goodin, 1988, p. 3). Given this assessment, the question before us is not if, but how, the American patchwork welfare state will continue to develop in the future. As America enters the last decade of this century, the arguments for and against government involvement in social welfare issues continue to be debated. For some less government is the best government (Crane & Boaz, 1989; Glazer, 1988). For others "the evolution of the American welfare system can be viewed as the product of both increasing public sensitivity to the defects of the free markets and expanding resources for ameliorating social ills" (Levitan & Johnson, 1984, p. 3). According to them, the future American welfare state is desirable and affordable (Aaron, 1990; Vedlitz, 1988) and compatible with the strong American tradition of individualism (Marmor, Mashaw, & Harvey, 1990). Whatever the future holds, it is assured that politics, economics, and public opinion will develop a welfare state uniquely American.

REFERENCES

Aaron, H. J. 1978. *Politics and the professors: The great society in perspective.* Washington, DC: Brookings Institution.

———. 1990. *Setting national priorities: Policy for the nineties.* Washington, DC: Brookings Institution.

Abbott, E. 1940. *Public assistance.* Chicago: University of Chicago Press.

———. 1941. *From relief to social security.* Chicago: University of Chicago Press.

Addams, J. 1910. *Twenty years at Hull House.* New York: Macmillan.

Advisory Commission on Intergovernmental Relations. 1980. *Public assistance: The growth of a federal function.* Washington, DC: Government Printing Office.

———. 1982. *State and local roles in the federal system.* Washington, DC: Government Printing Office.

———. 1984. *Significant features of fiscal federalism.* Washington, DC: Government Printing Office.

Altmeyer, A. J. 1966. *The formative years of social security.* Madison: University of Wisconsin Press.

Anderson, M. 1978. *Welfare: The political economy of welfare reform in the United States.* Stanford, CA: Hoover Institution Press.

Axinn, J. 1982. *Social welfare: A history of the American response to need.* 2nd ed. New York: Harper & Row.

Barilleaux, R. J., & Stuckey, M. E. 1992. *Leadership and the Bush presidency: Prudence or drift in an era of change?* Westport, CT: Praeger.

Bawden, D. L., ed. 1984. *The social contract revisited: Aims and outcomes of President Reagan's social welfare policy.* Washington, DC: Urban Institute Press.

Beck, N. 1982. Parties, administrations, and American macroeconomic outcomes. *American Political Science Review* 76: 83-93.

Bixby, A. K. 1991. Overview of public social welfare expenditures, fiscal year 1989. *Social Security Bulletin* 54: 28-30. (Note: This is an article that appears annually with new data in the *Social Security Bulletin.*)

Bornet, V. D. 1983. *The presidency of Lyndon B. Johnson.* Lawrence: University of Kansas.

Bourgin, F. 1989. *The great challenge: The myth of laissez-faire in the early republic.* New York: G. Braziller.

Bremner, R.; Reichard, G. W.; & Hopkins, R. J.; eds. 1986. *American choices, social dilemmas and public policy since 1960.* Columbus: Ohio State University Press.

Brock, W. R. 1988. *Welfare, democracy, and the new deal.* Cambridge: Cambridge University Press.

Browning, R. X. 1985. Presidents, Congress, and policy outcomes: U.S. social welfare expenditures, 1949-1977. *American Journal of Political Science* 29: 197-216.

―――. 1986. *Politics and social welfare policy in the United States.* Knoxville: University of Tennessee Press.

Burke, V., & Burke, V. 1974. *Nixon's good deed: Welfare reform.* New York: Columbia University Press.

Burt, M. R. 1985. *Testing the social safety net: The impact of changes in support programs during the Reagan administration.* Washington, DC: Urban Institute Press.

Campbell, C., & Rockman, B. A. 1991. *The Bush presidency: First appraisals.* Chatham, NJ: Chatham House.

Carey, J. P. 1938. *The rise of a new federalism: Federal-state cooperation in the United States.* New York: Columbia University Press.

Champagne, A., & Harphan, E. J. 1984. *The attack on the welfare state.* Prospect Heights, IL: Waveland Press.

Crane, E. H., & Boaz, D., eds. 1989. *An American vision: Policies for the 90's.* Washington, DC: Cato Institute.

Critchlow, D. T., & Hawley, E. W., eds. 1988. *Federal social policy: The historical dimension.* University Park: Pennsylvania State University Press.

Dallek, R. 1984. *Ronald Reagan: The politics of symbolism.* Cambridge: Harvard University Press.

DiNitto, D. M. 1991. *Social welfare: Politics and public policy.* 3rd ed. Englewood Cliffs, NJ: Prentice-Hall.

Duffy, M. 1992. *Marching in place: The status quo presidency of George Bush.* New York: Simon & Schuster.

Dye, T. R. 1987. *Understanding public policy.* 6th ed. Englewood Cliffs, NJ: Prentice-Hall.

Elazar, D. J. 1974. The new federalism: Can the states be trusted? *The Public Interest* 35: 89-102.

Fine, S. 1964. *Laissez-faire and the general welfare state: A study of conflict in American thought, 1865-1901.* Ann Arbor: University of Michigan Press.

Fraser, S., & Gerstle, G., eds. 1989. *The rise and fall of the New Deal order, 1930-1980.* Princeton, NJ: Princeton University Press.

Friedel, F., ed. 1964. *The New Deal and the American people.* Englewood Cliffs, NJ: Prentice-Hall.

Glazer, N. 1988. *The limits of social policy.* Cambridge: Harvard University Press.

Goodin, R. E. 1988. *Reasons for welfare: The political theory of the welfare state.* Princeton, NJ: Princeton University Press.

Harrington, M. 1962. *The other America: Poverty in the United States.* New York: Penguin Books.

Haveman, R. H., ed. 1977. *A decade of federal antipoverty programs, achievements, failures, and lessons.* New York: Academic Press.

Henig, J. R. 1985. *Public policy and federalism: Issues in state and local politics.* New York: St. Martin's Press.

Hill, K. Q. 1988. *Democracies in crisis: Public policy responses to the Great Depression.* Boulder, CO: Westview Press.

Hofstadter, R. 1948. *The American political tradition and the men who made it.* New York: Knopf.

Hughes, J. R. T. 1991. *The governmental habit redux: Economic controls from colonial times to the present.* Princeton, NJ: Princeton University Press.

Hulten, C. R., & Sawhill, I. V., eds. 1984. *The legacy of Reaganomics.* Washington, DC: Urban Institute Press.

Hunter, R. 1904. *Poverty.* New York: Macmillan.

Ippolito, D. S. 1990. *Uncertain legacies: Federal budget policy from Roosevelt through Reagan.* Charlottesville: University of Virginia Press.

Jansson, B. S. 1987. Federal social legislation since 1961. In *Encyclopedia of social work,* vol. 1. Silver Spring, MD: National Association of Social Workers, 593-600.

———. 1988. *The reluctant welfare state: A history of American social welfare policies.* Belmont, CA: Wadsworth.

Kaplan, M., & Cuciti, P. L., eds. 1986. *The great society and its legacy: Twenty years of U.S. social policy.* Durham, NC: Duke University Press.

Katz, M. B. 1986. *In the shadow of the poorhouse: A social history of welfare in America.* New York: Basic Books.

Leiby, J. 1978. *A history of social welfare and social work in the United States, 1815-1972.* New York: Columbia University Press.

———. 1987. History of social welfare. In *Encyclopedia of social work,* vol. 1. Silver Spring, MD: National Association of Social Workers, 755-88.

Leuchtenburg, W. E. 1989. *In the shadow of FDR: From Harry Truman to Ronald Reagan.* Ithaca, NY: Cornell University Press.

Levine, R. A. 1970. *The poor ye need not have with you: Lessons from the war on poverty.* Cambridge: MIT Press.

Levitan, S. A. 1969. *The great society's poor law: A new approach to poverty.* Baltimore, MD: Johns Hopkins University Press.

———. 1976. *The promise of greatness.* Cambridge: Harvard University Press.

Levitan, S. A., & Johnson, C. M. 1984. *Beyond the safety net: Reviving the promise of opportunity in America.* Cambridge, MA: Ballinger.

Light, P. C. 1982. *The president's agenda: Domestic policy choice from Kennedy to Carter.* Baltimore, MD: Johns Hopkins University Press.

———. 1985. *Artful work: The politics of social security reform.* New York: Random House.

Lubove, R. 1972. *Poverty and social welfare in the United States.* New York: Holt, Rinehart & Winston.

———. 1986. *The struggle for social security, 1900-1935.* 2nd ed. Pittsburgh, PA: University of Pittsburgh Press.

Marmor, T. R.; Mashaw, J. L.; & Harvey, P. L. 1990. *America's misunderstood welfare state: Persistent myths, enduring realities.* New York: Basic Books.

Matusow, A. J. 1984. *The unraveling of America: A history of liberalism in the 1960s.* New York: Harper & Row.

McKay, D. H. 1989. *Domestic policy and ideology: Presidents and the American state, 1964-1987.* Cambridge: Cambridge University Press.

Mezey, M. L. 1986. The legislature, the executive, and public policy: The futile quest for congressional power. *Congress and the Presidency* 13: 1-20.

———. 1989. *Congress, the president, and public policy.* Boulder, CO: Westview Press.

Morris, R. 1985. *Social policy of the American welfare state: An introduction to policy analysis.* 2nd ed. New York: Longman.

Moynihan, D. P. 1973a. *Maximum feasible misunderstanding.* New York: Random House.

———. 1973b. *The politics of a guaranteed income: The Nixon administration and the family assistance plan.* New York: Vintage Books.

Niskanen, W. A. 1988. *Reaganomics: An insider's account of the policies and the people.* New York: Oxford University Press.

Palmer, J. L., & Sawhill, I. V. 1984. *The Reagan record: An assessment of America's changing domestic priorities.* Washington, DC: Urban Institute Press.

Patterson, J. T. 1986. *America's struggle against poverty, 1900-1985.* Cambridge: Harvard University Press.

Peterson, P. G., & Howe, N. 1988. *On borrowed time: How the growth in entitlement spending threatens America's future.* San Francisco: ICS Press.

Piven, F. F. 1982. *The new class war: Reagan's attack on the welfare state and its consequences.* New York: Pantheon Books.

Piven, F. F., & Cloward, R. A. 1971. *Regulating the poor: The functions of public welfare.* New York: Vintage Books.

Plotnick, R. D. 1975. *Progress against poverty: A review of the 1964-1974 decade.* New York: Academic Press.

Reagan, M. D. 1972. *The new federalism.* New York: Oxford University Press.

Reichley, J. 1981. *Conservatives in an age of change: The Nixon and Ford administrations*. Washington, DC: Brookings Institution.

Riis, J. 1890. *How the other half lives*. New York: Charles Scribner's Sons.

Savage, J. D. 1988. *Balanced budgets & American politics*. Ithaca, NY: Cornell University Press.

Schlesinger, A. M. 1957-1960. *The age of Roosevelt*. Boston: Houghton Mifflin.

Schorr, A. L. 1986. *Common decency: Domestic policies after Reagan*. New Haven, CT: Yale University Press.

Schwarz, J. 1988. *America's hidden success: A reassessment of public policy from Kennedy to Reagan*. New York: W. W. Norton.

Sinclair, B. D. 1984. The policy consequences of party realignments: Social welfare legislation in the House of Representatives, 1933-1954. *American Journal of Political Science* 22: 83-105.

Sinclair, U. 1906. *The Jungle*. New York: The Jungle Publishing Company.

Sitkoff, H., ed. 1985. *Fifty years later: The New Deal evaluated*. New York: Knopf.

Stein, H. 1969. *The fiscal revolution in America*. Chicago: University of Chicago Press.

Steiner, G. Y. 1966. *Social insecurity: The politics of welfare*. Chicago: Rand McNally.

———. 1971. *The state of welfare*. Washington, DC: Brookings Institution.

Stockman, D. 1986. *The triumph of politics*. New York: Harper & Row.

Sundquist, J. L. 1968. *Politics and policy: The Eisenhower, Kennedy, and Johnson years*. Washington, DC: Brookings Institution.

———. 1975. *Making federalism work*. Washington, DC: Brookings Institution.

Swartz, T. R., & Peck, J. E., eds. 1990. *The changing face of fiscal federalism*. Armonk, NY: M. E. Sharpe.

Trattner, W. I. 1984. *From poor law to welfare state: A history of social welfare in America*. New York: Free Press.

U.S. Congress. House. Committee on the Budget. 1981. *Indexing and the federal budget*. Washington, DC: Government Printing Office. (Y4.B85/3:In2/3).

U.S. Department of Health, Education and Welfare. Social Security Administration. Office of Research and Statistics. 1968. *Social welfare expenditures under public programs in the United States, 1929-1966*. Washington, DC: Government Printing Office. (FS 3.49:25).

U.S. National Advisory Commission on Civil Disorders (Kerner Commission). 1968. *Report*. Washington, DC: Government Printing Office. (Pr 36.8:C49/R29).

U.S. National Advisory Commission on Rural Poverty. 1967. *The people left behind*. Washington, DC: Government Printing Office. (Pr 36.8:R88/P39).

U.S. President's Commission on Income Maintenance. 1969-1970. *Poverty amid plenty: The American paradox*. Washington, DC: Government Printing Office. (Pr 36.8:In2/P86).

Vedlitz, A. 1988. *Conservative mythology and public policy in America*. New York: Praeger.

Weaver, R. K. 1988. *Automatic government: The politics of indexation.* Washington, DC: Brookings Institution.

Weir, M.; Orloff, S. O.; & Skocpol, T.; eds. 1988. *The politics of social policy in the United States.* Princeton, NJ: Princeton University Press.

Wildavsky, A. 1984. *The politics of the budgetary process.* 4th ed. Boston: Little, Brown.

Witte, E. E. 1962. *The development of the Social Security Act.* Madison: University of Wisconsin Press.

SOURCES OF
ADDITIONAL INFORMATION

Researching the history and issues central to federal social welfare policy requires concentration in many resources and databases. Particularly valuable are resources in the social sciences and history. Since the topic itself is diffuse, research in this area itself reflects the many facets of the topic.

Selected Federal Legislation and Court Cases Relevant to Social Policy

Included are citations to the original statute and today's code, if applicable and reasonable to list, presented in chronological order. If the code listing would be unwieldy, the reader should consult the index tables of the *United States Code (USC)*. Due to the numerous amendments and complexity of many of these pieces of legislation, to guarantee that one has located all amendments it is essential to consult the current *United States Code*. All court cases are cites to United States Supreme Court decisions. Previous cites to the case on its way to the Supreme Court have not been included; consult the appropriate volume of Shepard's to identify those cases.

Food and Drug Act (July 1, 1902; c. 1357, 32 Stat 632; 21 USC 16, 17, 301 et seq.)

Mann Act (Mar. 26 and June 25, 1910; 36 Stat 263; 36 Stat 825; 18 Stat 2421 et seq.)

Children's Bureau Act (Apr. 9, 1912; c. 73, 37 Stat 79; 42 USC 191-194)

Harrison Narcotic Act (Dec. 17, 1914; c. 1, 38 Stat 785)

Vocational Rehabilitation Act of 1918 (June 27, 1918; 40 Stat 617; 38 USC 1502)

Maternity and Infancy Hygiene Act (Sheppard-Towner Act) (Nov. 23, 1921; c. 135, 42 Stat 224)

Emergency Relief and Construction Act of 1932 (July 21, 1932; c. 520, 47 Stat 709; 12 USC 343, 1148)

Civilian Conservation Corps Act (Mar. 31, 1933; c. 17, 48 Stat 22)

Agricultural Adjustment Act (May 12, 1933; c. 25, 48 Stat 31; 7 USC 601 et seq., 1281 et seq., 1308, 1309, 1421 note, 1441, 1444, 1444c, 1445b)

Federal Emergency Relief Act (May 13, 1933; c. 30, 48 Stat 55)

National Industrial Recovery Act (June 16, 1933; c. 90, 48 Stat 195 and June 14, 1935; c. 246, 49 Stat 375; see *USC Index* for relevant sections)

National Housing Act of 1934 (June 27, 1934; c. 847, 48 Stat 1246; 12 USC 1701 et seq.)

National Labor Relations Act (July 5, 1935; c. 372, 49 Stat 449; 29 USC 151 et seq.)

Social Security Act of 1935 (Aug. 14, 1935; c. 35, 49 Stat 620; 42 USC 301 et seq.)

Marihuana Tax Act (Aug. 2, 1937; c. 553, 50 Stat 551)

Works Progress Administration Act (June 21, 1938; c. 554, 52 Stat 809)

Fair Labor Standards Act of 1938-1939 (June 25, 1938; c. 676, 52 Stat 1060; 2 USC 60k; 29 USC 201 et seq.)

Child Labor Act (Fair Labor Standards) (June 25, 1938; c. 676, 52 Stat 1060; 29 USC 212, 213)

Food, Drug, and Cosmetic Act (June 25, 1938; c. 675, 52 Stat 1040; 21 USC 301 et seq.)

Lanham Act (Community Facilities) (June 28, 1941; c. 260, 55 Stat 361)

Aid to Dependent Children (June 14, 1944; c. 257; 58 Stat 177; check *USC Index* for all relevant sections)

Servicemen's Readjustment Act (June 22, 1944; c. 268, 58 Stat 284)

Public Health Service Act (July 1, 1944; c. 372, 58 Stat 682; see *USC Index* for relevant sections)

Full Employment Act of 1946 (Feb. 20, 1946; c. 33, 60 Stat 23; 15 USC 1021 et seq.)

National School Lunch Act (June 4, 1946; c. 281, 60 Stat 230; 42 USC 1751 et seq.)

National Mental Health Act (July 3, 1946; c. 538, 60 Stat 421; 42 USC 201 et seq.)

Hospital Survey and Construction Act (Hill-Burton Act) (Aug. 13, 1946; c. 958, 60 Stat 1040; see *USC Index* for relevant sections)

Housing Act of 1940 (Oct. 14, 1949; c. 862, 54 Stat 1125; 42 USC 1501 et seq.)

Brown v. *the Board of Education of Topeka, Kansas*, 347 US 483 (May 17, 1954)

Medical Facilities Survey and Construction Act (July 12, 1954; c. 471, 68 Stat 461)

Survey and Construction Act (July 12, 1954; c. 471, 68 Stat 461)

National Health Survey Act (July 3, 1956; c. 510, 70 Stat 489)

National Defense Education Act (Sept. 2, 1958; 72 Stat 72; 20 USC 401 et seq.)

Kerr-Mills Act (Sept. 13, 1960; 74 Stat 924; 26 USC 1401 et seq., 3301 et seq.; 42 USC 301 et seq.)

Area Redevelopment Act of 1961 (May 1, 1961; 75 Stat 47; 15 USC 696; 40 USC 461; 42 USC 1464)

Juvenile Delinquency and Youth Offenses Control Act of 1961 (Sept. 22, 1961; 75 Stat 572)

Manpower Development and Training Act of 1962 (Mar. 15, 1962; 76 Stat 23)

Aid to Families with Dependent Children Act of 1961 (May 8, 1962; 75 Stat 75; see *USC Index* for relevant sections)

Gideon v. *Wainwright*, 372 U S 355 (Mar. 18, 1963)

Health Professions Educational Assistance Act (Sept. 24, 1963; 77 Stat 164; see *USC Index* for relevant sections)

Mental Retardation Facilities and Community Mental Health Centers Construction Act of 1963 (Oct. 21, 1963; 77 Stat 282)

Civil Rights Act of 1964 (July 2, 1964; 78 Stat 241; check *USC Index* for all relevant sections)

Food Stamp Act of 1964 (Aug. 31, 1964; 78 Stat 703; 7 USC 2011 et seq.)

Nurse Training Act (Sept. 4, 1964; 78 Stat 908; see *USC Index* for relevant sections)

Elementary and Secondary Education Act of 1965 (Apr. 11, 1965; 79 Stat 27; 20 USC 236 et seq., 241 et seq., 821 et seq.)

Older Americans Act (July 14, 1965; 79 Stat 218; 42 USC 3001 et seq.)

Medicaid Act (Title XIX of Social Security Act) (July 30, 1965; 79 Stat 286; see *USC Index* for relevant sections)

Medicare Act (Title XVIII of Social Security Act) (July 30, 1965; 79 Stat 286; 42 USC 1395 et seq., 1396 et seq.)

Economic Opportunity Act of 1964 (Aug. 20, 1965; 78 Stat 508; 42 USC 2701 et seq.)

Economic Development Act of 1965 (Aug. 26, 1965; 79 Stat 552; 42 USC 3121 et seq.)

Miranda v. *the State of Arizona*, 384 US 436 (June 13, 1966)

Child Nutrition Act of 1966 (Oct. 11, 1966; 80 Stat 885; 42 USC 1771 et seq.)

Demonstration Cities and Metropolitan Development Act of 1966 (Nov. 3, 1966; 80 Stat 1255; see *USC Index* for relevant sections)

Child Health Act of 1967 (Jan. 2, 1967; 81 Stat 821; 42 USC 701 et seq.)

In re Gault, 387 US 1 (May 15, 1967)

King v. *Smith*, 392 US 309 (June 17, 1968)

Shapiro v. *Thompson*, 394 US 618 (Apr. 21, 1969)

Sniadach v. *Family Finance Corporation*, 395 US 337 (June 9, 1969)

Goldberg v. *Kelly*, 397 US 254 (Mar. 23, 1970)

Dandridge v. *Williams*, 397 US 471 (Apr. 6, 1970)

Emergency Health Personnel Act (Dec. 31, 1970; 84 Stat 1868; 42 USC 233)

Wyman v. *James*, 400 US 309 (Jan. 12, 1971)

Boddie v. *Connecticut*, 401 US 371 (Mar. 2, 1971)

James v. *Valtierra*, 402 US 137 (Apr. 26, 1971)

Jefferson v. *Hackney*, 406 US 535 (May 30, 1972)

Fuentes v. *Shevin*, 407 US 67 (June, 12, 1972)

Supplemental Security Income (Oct. 30, 1972; 86 Stat 1329; see *USC Index* for relevant sections)

United States v. *Kras*, 409 US 434 (Jan. 10, 1973)

Ortwein v. *Schwab*, 410 US 656 (Mar. 6, 1973)

Agriculture and Consumer Protection Act of 1973 (Aug. 10, 1973; 87 Stat 221; 7 USC 1301 et seq.)

Rehabilitation Act of 1973 (Sept. 26, 1973; 87 Stat 355; see *USC Index* for relevant sections)

Emergency Medical Services System Act (Nov. 16, 1973; 87 Stat 594; 42 USC 295g-9, 300d et seq.)

Comprehensive Employment and Training Act (Dec. 28, 1973; 87 Stat 839; 29 USC 801 et seq.)

Health Maintenance Organization (HMO) Act (Dec. 29, 1973; 87 Stat 914; 42 USC 280c, 300e et seq.)

Child Abuse Prevention and Treatment Act (Jan. 21, 1974; 88 Stat 4; 42 USC 5101 et seq.)

Memorial Hospital v. *Maricopa County*, 415 US 250 (Feb. 26, 1974)

Mitchell v. *W. T. Grant Co.*, 416 US 600 (May 13, 1974)

Legal Services Corporation Act (July 25, 1974; 88 Stat 378; 42 USC 2996 et seq.)

Social Service Amendments of 1974 (Jan. 4, 1975; 88 Stat 2337; see *USC Index* for relevant sections)

National Health Planning and Resources Development Act of 1974 (Jan. 4, 1975; 88 Stat 2225; 42 USC 300e-4, 300k et seq.)

Warth v. *Seldin*, 422 US 490 (June 25, 1975)

Education of All Handicapped Children Act (Nov. 29, 1975; 89 Stat 773; 20 USC 1401 et seq.)

Runaway and Homeless Youth Act (Oct. 3, 1977; 91 Stat 1048; see *USC Index* for relevant sections)

Full Employment and Balanced Growth Act of 1978 (Oct. 27, 1978; 92 Stat 1887; 12 USC 225a; 15 USC 1021 et seq., 3101 et seq.; 31 USC 632,636)

Omnibus Budget Reconciliation Act (Aug. 13, 1981; 95 Stat 357; see *USC Index* for relevant sections)

Food Stamp and Commodity Distribution Amendments of 1981 (Dec. 22, 1981; 95 Stat 1213; 7 USC 2021 et seq.)

Tax Equity and Fiscal Responsibility Act (Sept. 8, 1982; 96 Stat 324; see *USC Index* for relevant sections)

Job Training Partnership Act (Oct. 13, 1982; 96 Stat 1322; 29 USC 1501, 1503, 1522, 1516, 1518, 1533, 1534, 1582, 1602, 1603, 1630 et seq., 1651, 1652, 1707, 1733, 1736)

Temporary Emergency Food Assistance Act of 1983 (Mar. 24, 1983; 97 Stat 13; see *USC Index* for relevant sections)

Social Security Amendments of 1983 (Apr. 20, 1983; 97 Stat 65; see *USC Index* for relevant sections)

Balanced Budget and Emergency Deficit Control Act (Dec. 12, 1985; 99 Stat 1037; see *USC Index* for relevant sections)

Food Security Act of 1985 (Dec. 23, 1985; 99 Stat 1354; see *USC Index* for relevant sections)

Consolidated Omnibus Budget Reconciliation Act of 1985 (Apr. 7, 1986; 100 Stat 82; see *USC Index* for relevant sections)

Education of the Handicapped Act (Oct. 8, 1986; 100 Stat 1145; 20 USC 1400 et seq.)

Homeless Eligibility Clarification Act (Oct. 27, 1986; 100 Stat 3207; see *USC Index* for relevant sections)

Health Care Quality Improvement Act (Nov. 14, 1986; 100 Stat 3743: 42 USC 11101 et seq.)

Medical and Medicaid Patient and Program Protection Act (Aug. 18, 1987; 101 Stat 680; see *USC Index* for relevant sections)

Family Support Act of 1988 (Oct. 13, 1988; 102 Stat 2443; see *USC Index* for relevant sections)

Workplace Act of 1988 (Nov. 19, 1988; 102 Stat 4181, sec. 5151 et seq; 41 USC 701 et seq.)

Stewart B. McKinney Homeless Assistance Act (July 22, 1991; 101 Stat 482; see *USC Index* for relevant sections)

Child Nutrition and WIC Reauthorization Act of 1991 (Nov. 10, 1991; 103 Stat 877; 42 USC 1751 et seq.)

Family and Medical Leave Act (Feb. 5, 1993; 107 Stat 6; see *USC Index* for relevant sections)

Government Publications and Legal Resources

Depending upon the focus of research, government publications are a potentially valuable source. Congressional hearings and documents on programs give additional background material and may provide legislative intent for the establishment of particular programs. Because these types of publications are rarely reflected in standard library catalogs, it is necessary to use specific book catalogs and indexes that provide subject access. Excellent resources in this area are:

CIS Index to Congressional Publications and Legislative Histories

CIS Index to Unpublished US Senate Committee Hearings

CIS Index to US Senate Executive Documents and Reports

CIS US Congressional Committee Prints Index

Legal resources also provide the full text of laws and bills proposed to amend federal social policy. As is true with books and government publications, a specific topic should be researched, rather than the broad issue of federal policy. Appropriate resources are:

Code of Federal Regulations (a listing of all current federal regulations)

Legi-Slate (a database that tracks all currently proposed federal legislation)

LEXIS (a database through which one can research court cases and statutes)

Statutes at Large of the United States (a chronological full-text listing of all laws as they were enacted)

United States Code (full text of all current laws by subject organization)

WESTLAW (a database through which one can research court cases and statutes)

Indexes

Research in the area of government social policy takes one into the disciplines of history, economics, politics, and social work. There are many indexes that can be employed to locate specific articles of interest. Several of these are available both in paper and electronic formats. Examples of these indexes are:

America: History and Life

Index to Economic Articles in Journals and Collective Volumes

PAIS International in Print

Social Sciences Index

Social Work Abstracts

Useful Library of Congress Subject Headings

There are few books that deal solely with federal social welfare policy; rather national policy is reflected in books dealing with broader themes. Appropriate general Library of Congress subject headings that describe the politics and economics of potential interest are:

Federal Aid to Public Welfare—United States—History

Government Spending Policy—United States—History

Intergovernmental Fiscal Relations—United States

Political Parties—United States

Public Welfare—United States—History

Social Service—United States—History

United States—Economic Conditions

United States—Politics and Government

United States—Social Policy

Unfortunately, none of these subject headings are very specific and one must look through numerous books to identify items related to this research topic. Another approach is to research titles specific to a chronological period, a presidency, or a topic. This approach culls more relevant titles, but one still must look through the sources to see if they are applicable. Common Library of Congress subject headings that might be of value are:

Child Welfare—United States

Entitlement Spending—United States

New Deal, 1933-1939

Presidents—United States—History

Roosevelt, Franklin Delano, 1882-1945

Social Security—United States—History

A third research approach to the topic is to use known sources as a starting point. Frequently bibliographies and footnotes from relevant texts can be used to locate earlier works. Similarly, using the *Social Sciences Citation Index*, one can locate items that later cited the articles and books in hand. Thus, through citation indexes and bibliographies one can frequently locate sources that might never appear in catalogs and standard indexes.

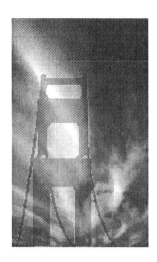

Substantive and procedural law benefits and protects landlords over tenants, creditors over debtors, lenders over borrowers, and the poor are seldom among the favored parties.
John Turner, 1969

3

Law and Criminal Justice

Kevin R. Harwell

The widespread perception that the American judiciary is the ultimate protector of equality is reinforced by many symbols in American law and government. From the Goddess of Justice weighing rights and issues, blind to personal and political interests, to the old saw, "everyone gets their day in court," the expectation of fair treatment by the courts is manifested at all levels of society. In reality, the legal environment, including the courts, is predisposed to favor the powerful and affluent. The actors of government, including the courts, have many resources for defending themselves and asserting their agenda.

In criminal proceedings, the poor are arrested more often and treated more harshly than those who are not poor. The poor are less likely to pursue justice in civil disputes due to lack of resources, lack of information, and lack of faith that their complaints will be heard and acted upon. The administrative bureaucracies that manage programs established to benefit the poor often give field workers inappropriately broad discretion in determining eligibility. The result of too much discretion that is not centrally controlled is that some people receive benefits unjustly and some people are denied benefits unjustly.

Kevin R. Harwell has been a government documents librarian specializing in legal resources and patents at The Pennsylvania State University, University Park, since 1990. Before that he was a documents and patents librarian at Oklahoma State University. His current research interests include a survey of outreach activities among academic, public, and other types of libraries. He holds an M.L.I.S. degree from the University of Texas at Austin.

For those who are not powerful or affluent, lack of income does not diminish their need for legal services. Not unlike others, some poor people are arrested and accused of crimes. They have disagreements with merchants, neighbors, landlords, and employers. They need access to medical care and other benefits. For the poor, as for anyone else, the availability of legal services is an important key to whether they use the law and the courts. Unfortunately, attorney's fees, document preparation fees, court costs, trial preparation costs, and other expenses of legal services are insurmountable obstacles for many people.

According to data collected during the 1990 census, 31,742,864 Americans had incomes within the established poverty range. This figure represents a 13.7 percent increase over 1980 figures, an increase in proportion that is more than twice the increase of the total U.S. population. Poverty status is determined by an arbitrary formula defined in 1964 by the Social Security Administration and prescribed by the Office of Management and Budget in Directive 14 as the standard to be used by federal agencies for statistical purposes (U.S. Bureau of the Census, 1994). The formula establishes a sliding scale based on family size and number of minors. It sets very low thresholds for family income. If a family's income is less than the threshold for its size, that family is below the poverty "line," so that family has been determined to be a poverty-status family. A family's income can be well above the officially recognized poverty line and still not provide enough disposable income to support access to legal services. This situation affects many people not traditionally regarded as poor, people who would otherwise be ineligible for legal services earmarked specifically for low-income individuals.

Even in the last thirty years, when attempts have been made to provide legal services to the poor by means of government-sponsored programs, few scholars have studied the ways that poor people are disfranchised in criminal and civil justice. Christopher E. Smith is an important exception. He has compiled a comprehensive overview of the social science and legal scholarship on the courts in order to examine wealth discrimination, a primary source of advantages and disadvantages for individuals within the judicial process. In particular, he examined the various stages of the judicial process as well as court cases affecting the poor. His book may be regarded as a definitive source for this topic, providing many references to books, cases, and law review articles (Smith, 1991).

There are several possible reasons why wealth discrimination in legal systems has received little attention. Wealth or income bias is often more difficult to identify than other forms of discrimination. Although the U.S. Constitution addresses racial and gender discrimination, it has few explicit prohibitions against wealth discrimination. Too, there is the unstated belief that people who have more money are more deserving of certain services and benefits than people who have fewer resources.

Income discrimination exists in both obvious and subtle ways. The framers of the U.S. Constitution and its amendments had aspirations about balance of powers, impartial justice, and equal protection of the law. However, those who establish, execute, and interpret laws have personal and political interests that come to bear in the processes of government. Critics have charged that many people in government and the courts may have lost touch with the social forces affecting poor people (as well as the middle class), thus magnifying the disadvantages that the poor experience.

CRIMINAL LAW AND THE POOR

The causes of criminal behavior have been theorized and studied by many people. Wilson and Herrnstein (1985) present an extensive review of the literature on the causes of criminal behavior in *Crime and Human Nature*. They note that several linkages between crime and poverty have been observed or hypothesized. Some observers have argued that poverty leaves many youths without opportunities to succeed in mainstream society. Others have noted a pattern where those who succeed in surmounting the obstacles of poverty move away from their communities, thus depriving young people of positive role models. Some social critics contend that the dynamics of the American free enterprise system create a pattern that starts with unemployment, followed by poverty, and ends in social disorder. The political elite responds to social disorder with repressive countermeasures (Smith, 1991). Obviously, the relationship between crime and poverty is difficult to measure precisely. Very many factors influence human, and therefore criminal, behavior.

As an important theorist in the area of society's response to crime, Scott Gordon (1980) has contributed an extended essay on the concepts of welfare, justice, and freedom, designed to clarify the basic issues of political philosophy. Gordon draws much of his discussion from the writings of economists Frank Knight, Milton Friedman, Henry Simons, F. A. Hayek, J. M. Clark, J. A. Schumpeter, and James Buchanan, and philosophers John Rawls and Robert Nozick. Samuel Walker (1989) demonstrated that continual tinkering with the criminal justice system has not significantly produced reductions in serious crime. He provides realistic evaluations of programs that have been tried, commenting on those that have worked and those that have not. Notably, he challenges both conservative and liberal prescriptions for crime reduction. Another useful work is William J. Chambliss's sourcebook on the sociology of criminal law, *Crime and the Legal Process*. Though dated, this work describes empirical studies of the American criminal-law process in the fields of anthropology, law, philosophy, political science, psychology, sociology, and economics (Chambliss, 1969).

In the realm of criminal law, the poor are disfranchised in many ways. Although certain acts are almost universally regarded as criminal, such as rape and murder, for the most part criminal behavior is defined by those in power and by those with the influence to have laws established or interpretations argued in their favor. For example, the consumption of alcoholic beverages is legal, but marijuana is not, even though both substances are subject to abuse and can cause serious medical and social consequences. An important factor in this paradox is that marijuana was used by poor members of racial minority groups when it was outlawed. Some acts, such as loitering and vagrancy, seem to be deemed criminal only to keep poverty out of sight and out of mind. Although prohibitions against loitering and vagrancy are certainly justified at times to protect persons and property, they are often used to remove offensive social problems associated almost exclusively with the poor. In 1981, John Irwin interviewed and followed 200 randomly selected inmates of the San Francisco jails through the jail and court procedures until each case was resolved and found that most of them were detached and disreputable persons who were arrested more because they were offensive than because they had committed crimes (Irwin, 1985). Critics charge that vagrancy and loitering receive too much attention compared to more serious crimes, such as rape, murder, and arson.

To compound the problems, the defining of criminal activity occurs in a constantly changing environment. An example can be found in reviewing literature from the 1960s on ghetto life that described criminal harassment against participants in neighborhood gambling operations. Some of these operations employed large numbers of people and provided venture capital for the community. One classic study is Liebow's *Tally's Corner* (1967), which described people constantly trying to maintain conventional values of success but repeatedly failing. Beginning in the 1970s, though, some state governments began to turn to organized lotteries to assume control of gambling and to raise money. What was once illegal in the hands of people with limited resources is now legal as a source of public revenue.

Defining criminal behavior can also discriminate, but more subtly. White-collar crimes are said to account for a great economic loss to society, yet critics say that because they are committed by people who are affluent these crimes receive relatively little attention from authorities (Kramer, 1984). (The few convictions resulting from the Savings and Loan scandal of the late 1980s would seem to uphold such contentions.) When the action of one person results in the death of another, it is often regarded as murder. However, some related actions are masked behind professional protections, such as malpractice sanctions, or corporate understandings like occupational health and safety penalties. Charles E. Silberman articulated many related issues in *Criminal Violence, Criminal Justice* (1978). His objective was to change the way that Americans think about criminals, crime, and the criminal justice system. Silberman called for a change about the way we think about race, ethnicity, poverty, and social class, as well as about police, courts, prisons, and jails, in order to minimize disadvantages placed upon the poor.

The legal machinery for processing cases of the criminally accused is highly selective, involving a wide range of discretion. Criminal justice agencies must conserve scarce resources of time, money, information, and personnel. Some offenders can afford to create legal and procedural trouble for officials if the laws they have violated are enforced carefully. Although personal and political interests are not always consciously acknowledged by police, prosecutors, judges, and others, it is often easier and less costly to prosecute those who lack sufficient resources to defend themselves. The political environment of the criminal justice arena is significant. A study of how the legal profession's social structure and judicial politics are strongly related was conducted by Jerome R. Corsi (1984). Corsi presented the perspective that law is a socially structured profession and that justice and politics are intermingled. The result of political maneuvering and expeditious processing is that cases are systematically filtered out of the system prior to trial. Statistical studies have shown time and again that poor people are arrested more often, convicted more frequently, sentenced more harshly, and rehabilitated less successfully than the rest of the population (see, for example, Chambliss, 1969). Lois G. Forer (1984), a trial judge, presented a more personal perspective, having confronted drastic differences in the way cases are handled in the courts on a daily basis. Forer reported that people were treated quite differently depending on whether their case was criminal or civil. She also addressed the injustices created by the high cost of legal fees and the inadequacy of legal services for the poor.

In cases of civil justice, individuals must initiate action to seek remedies to disputes, unlike criminal cases where the federal, state, or local government or its representative instigates a charge of criminal behavior. An example of civil justice is found in an incident known as the Buffalo Creek Disaster. In February 1972, a dam made of coal mining refuse, holding back a stream in Middle Fork Hollow in West Virginia, collapsed releasing more than 130 million gallons of water and waste into the Buffalo Creek Valley, killing 125 people and destroying over 1,000 homes. Gerald M. Stern (1976) related his experience as legal counsel representing the survivors in an excellent description of litigation against corporate irresponsibility in his case history of the incident. This case is illustrative of the fact that far more time and money are spent on civil disputes than on criminal cases. The case is unusual in that the survivors continued their pursuit of justice until the issue was resolved. Because money is a limiting factor for the poor, civil justice is often an avenue that may be closed to them. For lack of resources and for other reasons, grievances are often dropped prematurely. Individuals of limited economic means and education may be inadequately informed about possible avenues for remedies. Better-educated people are more likely to be informed about such choices and are more likely to pursue them. People who are accustomed to living in an oppressive environment may be unwilling to advance a dispute for fear of reprisal or that official channels that ought to provide remedies will be unresponsive. Confrontational self-help is sometimes seen as the only avenue to settle disputes. Such confrontations occasionally result in retaliatory property damage or violence (Smith, 1991).

ADMINISTRATIVE JUSTICE

Administrative justice is an area of law that has special relevance for the poor. Government agencies charged with the responsibility of administering various relief programs, including Aid to Families with Dependent Children (AFDC), Supplemental Security Income, food stamps, WIC, and others, make decisions that affect survival for many people who live on the economic margin. Standards for determining whether individuals or families would be eligible for benefits, or continue to be eligible, are set by state agencies that often give broad discretion to field workers. Some of the discretion is intentional, enabling the states to determine the most appropriate means to address local poverty problems. Critics have claimed that too much discretion is given to field workers and not enough direction and authority over eligibility are administered by centralized offices.

Joel F. Handler has written important books describing problems with the administration of relief programs. He co-authored *The "Deserving Poor": A Study of Welfare Administration* (1971) with Ellen Jane Hollingsworth, a study written against the background of political and journalistic discussion with professional comment by social workers and lawyers about the Aid to Families with Dependent Children program as it was administered in Wisconsin. Although the Wisconsin program was characterized as "benign" rather than dehumanizing, the authors called for more concrete legislative and administrative regulation, reducing the discretion of "out of control" field workers. In a later study, written after a decade of research, and subsequent to *Goldberg* v. *Kelly*, a U.S. Supreme Court case that reduced the procedural formality necessary in social welfare hearings, Handler examined the treatment of entitlement recipients and concluded that abuses of official discretion should necessitate consumer protection for social service clients, particularly the poor (Handler, 1979).

Others have also written important works on the problem of administrative justice. Daniel J. Baum (1974) provided an analytical study presented as background material for a June 1973 conference called by the Center for Administrative Justice of the American Bar Association. This in-depth examination looked at the "fair hearing" process in the administration of the categorical welfare program of aid to dependent children (AFDC). It identified the kinds of problems that confront the welfare adjudicative processes. Jerry L. Mashaw (1983) presented a study of hearings and appeals in the Social Security disability program that attempted to determine whether complaints about the program gave an accurate reflection of it, or whether the complaints were a manifestation of conventional displacement of blame. Mashaw concluded that bureaucratic rationality is actually a promising form of administrative justice for the Social Security Administration.

WEALTH DISCRIMINATION VERSUS RACIAL DISCRIMINATION

Wealth discrimination should not be confused with racial discrimination. However, because members of racial minority groups are disproportionately overrepresented among the poor (U.S. Bureau of the Census, 1994), a substantial number of people are subjected to both. It can be expected that if a higher percentage of members of racial minorities are poor, a higher proportion of minorities will experience problems in securing legal services. Strong associations between poverty and crime may also be observed among the disproportionately large group of poor members of racial minorities.

Controversial author William Julius Wilson in *The Declining Significance of Race* (1980) has argued that factors other than race are showing increasing strength in determining socioeconomic status of families. He elaborated on the problems of the ghetto underclass and spelled out policy implications of his findings in a comprehensive analysis written in response to critics of his first study in *The Truly Disadvantaged: The Inner City, the Underclass, and Public Policy* (1987). One prevalent pattern he observed has occurred when black families have moved from rural areas to inner cities, only to find a lack of long-term job opportunities for semi-skilled and unskilled workers. This situation has led to an increase in the number of female-headed households in the inner cities. This increase also corresponds with an increase in the difference between median black family income and median white family income from 1970 to 1980.

Studies of population growth, race, unemployment, and crime have shown that black teenagers did not fair as well as their white cohorts during the period from 1950 through 1979. White teenage unemployment rose only slightly during this time. The size of the white teenage population also remained relatively stable. Black teenage unemployment and black teenage population both grew substantially faster than those of white teenagers, limiting the chances of black teenagers to reap the benefits of a relatively prosperous economy. Lack of employment opportunities is blamed for having created what may be an underclass of permanently poor people (Walker, 1989).

Affirmative action programs have not worked for very poor members of minority groups. These programs have sought to access opportunities in higher education and in white-collar jobs. Poor persons often lack sufficient preliminary education and skills to participate (Smith, 1991).

In criminal justice, overt racism has been dramatically reduced over the years. However, numerous statistical studies show that blacks and members of other minority groups continue to receive harsher treatment than whites. Paul L. Brady (1990), a federal administrative judge, contends that the white majority has willfully blinded itself to the humanity and worth of Americans of African descent. Much of his book, *A Certain*

Blindness: A Black Family's Quest for the Promise of America, is introspective of Brady's personal experiences and those of his parents and grandparents.

PROGRAMS FOR LEGAL SERVICES

Although legal services are too expensive for people with few resources, compassionate attorneys do take up the cases of clients who have no means to pay. The American Bar Association encourages such benevolence in its Model Rules of Professional Conduct, Rule 6.1, *"Pro Bono Publico* Service." Many firms have regular programs for *pro bono* work. Unfortunately, the expectation that all attorneys will provide services to some clients at no fee or a reduced fee clashes with the business goals of most private law firms. The reality is that time devoted to *pro bono* is very limited.

A number of other programs have been undertaken through the years to provide people of limited resources with needed legal services. However, before the 1960s, most efforts were initiated by private organizations on a piecemeal basis. Since 1876, limited assistance has been available for certain groups for certain legal purposes by legal aid societies. The first society in the United States was *Der Deutsche Rechtsschutz Verein*, a society of lawyers who assisted German immigrants in New York with landlord-tenant disputes and family law. Hundreds of legal aid societies were established, mostly in New York and Chicago, surviving on charitable contributions (Smith, 1919).

In 1919, Reginald Herbert Smith, the organizer of the Boston Legal Aid Society, published the first definitive treatment of inequality in the administration of civil justice, *Justice and the Poor* (Smith, 1919). The American Bar Association responded by devoting an entire session of its 1920 Annual Convention to legal aid and by establishing the Special Committee on Legal Aid, which later became the Standing Committee on Legal Aid. Smith's treatise also resulted in the establishment of the National Association of Legal Aid Organizations, later renamed the National Legal Aid and Defender Association (NLADA).

Legal aid societies were hampered by several factors. Distribution of societies was uneven. Legal aid societies were never able to offer generalized legal services to all who needed them because there were relatively few legal aid lawyers compared to millions of poor people. Economics worked against them, usually when they were stressed the most. For example, during the economic depression of the 1930s, charitable contributions were very low, yet more people needed legal aid than ever. Some societies would only take cases that would enable the society to advance the political agenda of its supporters. Organizers often found it difficult to "sell" the idea of legal aid to local bar associations, which viewed such efforts as competitive to the market interests of their members (Kessler, 1987).

An important concept concomitant to the provision of legal assistance in civil matters is the right to counsel, which is guaranteed by the Sixth Amendment of the U.S. Constitution. The original interpretation given to this right was that counsel would not be denied to those who could afford it. That right has been extended over the years to indigents who, although they could not afford counsel, would receive counsel in the form of a public defender or court-appointed counsel if the defendant desired such assistance. One of the first comprehensive treatises on the topic was written by William M. Beaney (1955) and was especially valuable for its treatment of the history of the right to counsel in America, beginning with coverage of English common law.

Although the Equal Opportunity Act and the Economic Opportunity Act, both of 1964, spearheaded President Lyndon B. Johnson's War on Poverty and established the Office of Equal Opportunity (OEO), they offered no legal aid for the poor. The Equal Opportunity Amendments of 1967 established the OEO as oversight agency, in cooperation with the American Bar Association (ABA), for providing such services. Guidelines were established by OEO and ABA for client advisory boards and eligibility of local poor persons' organizations. OEO could not initiate local programs or deliver services directly. Proposals for local programs had to be drawn from local agencies. Services for clients and financial eligibility guidelines were to be developed at the local level (Rowley, 1992).

Local programs were initially slow to develop. Many local bar associations, hostile to perceived competition for clients, sought OEO funding for judicare programs, programs in which services provided by private practices would be reimbursed for handling the cases of poor persons. The OEO refused to fund such plans, expecting them to be expensive and not to be aggressive in behalf of poor clients (Kessler, 1987).

During the 1960s, many studies were conducted to assess American culture, crime, and the status of law and the poor in the United States. The most influential of them was the *Report of the National Advisory Commission on Civil Disorders* (1968). Also known as the "Kerner Commission Report," and the "U.S. Riot Commission Report," this report was written in response to President Johnson's Executive Order 11365, issued on July 29, 1967. During the summer of 1967, more than 150 American cities reported racial disorder ranging from minor disturbances to major outbursts involving sustained and widespread looting and destruction of property. Much attention was given to the social and economic environment in which black Americans lived at the time it was written. Another enormously influential book in its time, Cloward and Ohlin's *Delinquency and Opportunity* (1960) summarized the dominant themes in American theoretical criminology. Ohlin was one of four associate directors of the President's Crime Commission. This book was particularly influential in the War on Poverty.

Another important study was a state-by-state audit, by Lee Silberstein (1965), of efforts to provide adequate defense for indigent defendants in criminal cases. This audit was conducted with the assistance of hundreds of lawyers throughout the United States. Silberstein's report was particularly beneficial in helping the states to develop programs for providing adequate defense after such became a requirement following *Gideon* v. *Wainwright*. A symposium, Conference on the Law of the Poor, was held at the University of California, Berkeley, in 1966, to provide a critical review of the rules and procedures, doctrines, and presuppositions of the law applicable to the poor. The proceedings were edited by Jacobus Ten Broek (1966).

John P. Comer (1966) provided a historical survey of efforts to give indigents free access to the federal courts, including routes that indigent persons have taken to reach an approximation of equality in the protection of their rights and consideration of judicial procedures used in specific cases. Samuel Mencher (1967) also provided background for understanding the multifaceted arena of modern public assistance programs by surveying the economic environment and the ideological perspectives that prevailed at various times during American history. A revealing and detailed field study of the legal problems of the rural poor in an eastern North Carolina county typical of the rural poverty belt was reported by the Staff of the Duke Law Journal in 1969. For a good distillation of what indigent persons could expect, Sylvia Law provided poor persons with information needed to obtain subsistence benefits in the form of a handbook, *The Rights of the Poor* (1973). It explained what people were eligible, what types of assistance were available, what the requirements were, and what administrative procedures, such as hearings, were important facets of getting assistance.

Policies of the OEO Legal Services Program, nationally, shifted away from client service to legal reform in an attempt to capitalize on the conservative ideals of the legal profession and to effect a much wider political reach on behalf of the poor. Law centers were developed at progressive law schools, specializing in specific fields of poverty law and supported by nationwide publications, such as *Clearinghouse Review* (Johnson, 1974).

The OEO Legal Services Program was distinguished from efforts of legal aid societies in several important respects. The Legal Services Program provided services to the poor residents of an area as a whole, not just to members of one group. The poor themselves determined the direction of the services. OEO was committed to redressing inadequacies in the enforcement of legal rights of poor people in the face of a historical lack of access to the courts. Legal needs of the poor were also addressed through community education and outreach programs. A comprehensive range of services and advocacy instrumentation was established to implement policies on behalf of the poor (Kessler, 1987).

The Legal Services Program has been subject to strong opposition throughout its existence. Several attempts were made to limit its power to bring legal actions against federal, state, and local governments, usually in response to initiatives for reform typified by those of one of OEO's best programs. The California Rural Legal Assistance Program (CRLA) was progressive and controversial. Its successful record of legal reform included the restoration of $210 million in cutbacks imposed by then-Governor Ronald Reagan on the state program for medical care, Medi-Cal (*Morris* v. *Williams*, 63 Cal. Rptr. 689, 1967). In 1970, a critical report from the California Office of Equal Opportunity convinced Reagan to veto the CRLA program grant. An OEO commission established in response countered with its own study that found that CRLA was quite effective and responsive to the legal needs of the poor. The director of OEO used this report to convince Reagan to withdraw the veto in return for OEO funding of a demonstration judicare program.

A widespread feeling developed that the strength of local programs was being undermined by the lack of centralized control mechanisms. The OEO Legal Services Program had become geographically diverse. Local programs diverged greatly with respect to eligibility requirements, caseloads, and community participation. Long-term funding was not available, leaving the programs vulnerable to political winds. On the other hand, in the absence of centralized control the individual programs were notably action oriented. Lack of bureaucracy was seen by some as an advantage. On balance, however, the weaknesses of decentralization seemed to outweigh its strengths. This assessment germinated the concept of a national legal services corporation that would provide a centralized program of legal services for the poor while delegating specific powers to appropriate legal agencies (Kessler, 1987).

The redefining of the relationship between the poor and law that was occurring during this dynamic period also found expression in both political theory and in political reality. Piven and Cloward (1971) sought to explain why relief, or welfare, arrangements exist and why the number of people on relief fluctuates from time to time. The authors asserted that relief arrangements are expanded during times of civil disorder and contracted during times of political stability. Although relief is understood in terms of trying to reinforce work norms, it is also responsible for maintaining social and economic inequities. Barlow F. Christensen spearheaded a project to provide the American Bar Association Special Committee on the Availability of Legal Services with research support for making recommendations to the Association's House of Delegates. One result is his *Lawyers for People of Moderate Means: Some Problems of Availability of Legal Services* (Christensen, 1970). This compilation of analytical and polemical papers, incidentally, is a good source for law review references about developments in legal services for the poor during the 1950s and 1960s. Another recommended study is one by Earl Johnson, Jr. (1974), the 1967 director of the OEO Legal Services Program, who described the personalities, forces, decisions, and negotiations that carried the program into collision with reactionary political elements during the formative era of the program.

The fruit of the political posturing and maneuvering that followed was the passage of the Legal Services Corporation Act of 1974, which was signed into law by President Richard M. Nixon just fourteen days before his resignation from office. Under the Legal Services Corporation (LSC), most of the activities that had been pursued under OEO were permitted to continue. Certain areas of law were exempted from the assistance the

LSC was allowed to provide and limitations were placed on the outside activities of staff attorneys (Rowley, 1992).

The most serious threat to the LSC since its inception has been the sentiment that private attorneys should be responsible for assisting the poor, rather than the government. President Ronald Reagan attempted to abolish legal services programs. Failing that, he cut the LSC program budget every year he was in office and appointed directors who were opposed to the program. The program was weakened, but Congress has not allowed the budget cuts to be lethal. The LSC remains an important, if limited, avenue for legal assistance for the poor (Kessler, 1987).

Studies that addressed legal services to the poor continued through the 1970s to the present. Criminal lawyers for the poor were the focus of an empirical study carried out in New York City, Los Angeles, and Washington, D.C., by Robert Hermann (1977), which tried to determine whether there were discernible differences in the quality of legal representation in criminal cases. The study also tried to discover reasons behind the differences that were observed. Handler and Hollingsworth once again examined the delivery of services, this time joined by Howard S. Erlanger (1978). In *Lawyers and the Pursuit of Legal Rights*, the authors interviewed a large number of lawyers in many types of legal practice to study the role of the Legal Services Program in trying to improve the law profession's provision of services to the poor. They found that the legal profession was highly flexible, that socialization was taking place in new ways, and that bar organizations were becoming well rooted in communities. They also found that older organizations were being revived and reconstituted. Rights of the poor were being articulated much more clearly and thoroughly than before and more attorneys were working on their behalf.

Jack Katz sought to address an array of conceptual questions about equal justice in *Poor People's Lawyers in Transition* (1982), which presents a historical case study of professional staffs and organizations of Chicago legal assistance programs that have specialized in providing civil legal service to the poor. Katz tried to determine the elements of organizational structure and personal experience that have come to bear on the motivation for action among legal assistance attorneys. He also tried to determine which philosophies characterizing legal assistance have been associated with social and political movements. Mark Kessler (1987) provided a look at the political role of the legal system directed toward learning whether the legal system could be utilized to effect social reform, whether conditions under which lawyers will bring legal actions against powerful interests could be anticipated, and whether political obstacles that limit the amount of social reform activity pursued by attorneys could be identified.

A conference sponsored by the 1988 Commission on the Cities, the University of New Mexico Institute for Public Policy, and the Johnson Foundation 20 years after the Kerner Commission Report, produced an impressive collection of papers (Harris & Wilkins, 1988). It was found that during the 20-year interval, poverty had become worse, that black, white, and Hispanic societies were becoming more separate, that a largely black and Hispanic underclass was growing, and that although the riots of 20 years before were over, more contemporary social problems such as unemployment, poverty, and segregation were even more destructive to human life. In a similar vein, Norman C. Amaker produced a rigorous analysis (1988) of President Reagan's civil rights record, demonstrating that the Reagan administration's civil rights enforcement record was weaker than the record of all six of his predecessors with federal enforcement responsibility.

The Bush administration did not display the hostility shown by the Reagan administration. In fact, Bush brought some restorative improvements to the Legal Services Corporation budget. However, evaluation of the LSC has continued. In *Legal Services for the Poor: Time for Reform* (1990), Douglas J. Besharov attempted to open dialogue about the orientation, operations, and management of the Legal Services Corporation. He was quite critical of bureaucratic inefficiency and inertia that he observed. He asserted that if the priorities were set by flexible management rather than by the corporation's lawyer-dominant system, LSC would be better focused to address the most pressing needs of the poor. A major independent study was commissioned by John Bayly, President of the Legal Services Corporation, to evaluate the LSC (Rowley, 1992). The research drew significantly on newly developed analytical techniques of public choice. The report based on the study was intended to raise awareness of the participants in legal services to motivate the forces to work together on behalf of the poor.

LEGAL REFORM

For many years, scholars, practitioners, and policymakers have sought to reform the American legal system and the administration of justice in order to simplify them, reduce their inherent delays, and cut costs. Certainly, success in any of these areas would benefit the poor as well. Various terms used to describe such efforts include delegalization, informalism, and mediation. Often referred to as alternative dispute resolution (ADR) programs, they exist all over the country, handling everything from interpersonal disputes among individuals to conflicts between nations. These reforms are very broad based and fragmented to the point that ADR is not a single movement, but a way to refer to the combined efforts of many programs (Harrington, 1985).

One facet of alternative dispute resolution is particularly suited to providing relief to the poor. Neighborhood justice centers provide an arena for resolving minor disputes before they erupt into much larger incidents that disrupt social order, and for handling minor complaints that have originated from inevitable incongruities of society and culture. Minor criminal and civil complaints are referred to the centers by police, prosecutors, and lower court judges (Tomasic & Feeley, 1982).

Neighborhood justice centers vary widely in structure and mission; however, as alternatives to courts they employ techniques of mediation and compromise rather than compulsory formality. They tend to be informal, like Small Claims Courts, Domestic Relations Courts, and Housing Courts, but they are more decentralized and, presumably, more accessible. Proponents say that neighborhood justice centers, as well as other alternative dispute resolution programs, not only reduce burdens of formal justice systems, but also preserve public order, promote harmony among citizens, and advance equal access to justice. Some argue that they are more likely than the courts to discover the root causes of grievances and effect lasting settlements (Tomasic & Feeley, 1982). Critics have charged that Neighborhood Justice Centers shortchange justice by encouraging complainants to resolve conflict prematurely. There is also suspicion that efforts by the federal government and legal and judicial elites to support neighborhood justice centers will advance only the interests of the formal justice system (Smith, 1991).

Roman Tomasic and Malcolm M. Feeley (1982) provide a hard look at Neighborhood Justice Centers. They present key rationales and concerns of the neighborhood justice movement. Case studies are used to evaluate several programs already in operation, including one of the earliest, located in Dorchester, Massachusetts. Criticisms of the movement as a whole, its assumptions, and its problems are offered. An extensive bibliography is included. For a different perspective, Christine B. Harrington (1985) seeks to further the perspective that dispute resolution is a political resource by examining the ideology and institutionalization of order maintenance practices of dispute process in *Shadow Justice: The Ideology and Institutionalization of Alternatives to Court*.

THE SUPREME COURT

Throughout American history, the U.S. Supreme Court has made decisions that have come to bear on the protection of the interests of the poor in noncriminal areas. The history of the court itself has developed in the midst of economic conservatives and economic liberals. Russell W. Galloway (1991) asserts that the justices themselves have brought to the Supreme Court their own perspectives in this light. His analysis shows the movements from conservatism to liberalism and vice versa, which have occurred from time to time, depending upon who was serving on the court.

Legal services programs, specially interpreted protections such as the right to counsel, and other issues of relevance to the poor have not developed as entirely separate entities. A number of scholars have noted the concurrence of certain events that have had important cumulative effects. The Supreme Court under Chief Justice Earl Warren set policy through case decisions that expanded the rights of the poor at about the same time that Congress was becoming interested in and establishing programs on behalf of the poor. This was not entirely coincidental. Susan E. Lawrence (1990) examined why the justices were so responsive to the opportunities for decision when the Legal Services Program brought cases before the court and how these opportunities for decision affected subsequent court cases in *The Poor in Court: The Legal Services Program and Supreme Court Decision Making.* When Warren E. Burger succeeded Earl Warren as chief justice of the United States in 1969, many expected to see the "constitutional revolution" created by the Warren Court rolled back by Burger and Supreme Court appointees of Republican presidents. Vincent Blasi's *The Burger Court* (1983) sheds light on why many policy-setting Warren Court decisions, such as *Brown* v. *Board of Education, Miranda,* and important criminal-law decisions, remained intact or were reinforced by the Burger Court.

Carl T. Rowan's biography, *Dream Makers, Dream Breakers: The World of Justice Thurgood Marshall* (1993), contributes to the social, legal, economic, political, and moral history of most of the twentieth century. U.S. Supreme Court Justice Marshall was controversial, struggling throughout his life and career to liberate Americans who were black or members of other racial minority groups. He was also a champion of the rights of the poor and chastised his fellow justices when Supreme Court decisions were made without sensitivity or understanding of their plight.

Most of the references cited in the bibliography below cover more cases and provide more description than are appropriate to provide here. However, the cases in the following chronologically arranged lists resulted in decisions by the U.S. Supreme Court that were pivotal in terms of interpreting the rights of poor persons.

- Cases in which judicial procedure and right to counsel were at issue:

  Gideon v. *Wainwright* (1963): The U.S. Supreme Court decided that the right to counsel in criminal cases is fundamental to defendants not only in federal courts, but also in state courts.

  Sniadach v. *Family Finance Corporation* (1969): Wage garnishment requires notice and prior hearing.

  Boddie v. *Connecticut* (1971): The U.S. Supreme Court decided that states cannot deny access to their courts to people seeking divorces only because of inability to pay court costs.

  Fuentes v. *Shevin* (1972): Seizure of debtors' property requires prior hearing.

  United States v. *Kras* (1973): The U.S. Supreme Court ruled that a federal statute requiring payment of a $50 fee for an individual to file a bankruptcy petition did not violate equal protection guarantees of the Fifth Amendment when the fee was not waived for an unemployed indigent.

Ortwein v. *Schwab* (1973): Upheld; states refusal to waive filing fee to have court review of administrative reduction of welfare benefits.

Mitchell v. *W. T. Grant Co.* (1974): Upheld; state statute permitting creditors to secure repossession of goods without prior notice to debtor.

Warth v. *Seldin* (1975): Plaintiffs in a suit alleging that Penfield, New York, zoning laws were discriminatory were denied standing. Those who were residents had no cause for the suit because the laws had not kept them out. Those who were not residents could not demonstrate that they were a proper party to the suit because the laws in question did not apply to the jurisdiction in which they lived.

- Cases in which administrative justice and eligibility for benefits were at issue:

King v. *Smith* (1968): The U.S. Supreme Court ruled that Alabama could not deny federal AFDC benefits to children because their mother cohabits with a man who is not their father. Alabama's goal to discourage illicit sexual relationships and illegitimate births could not be used to disqualify aid to needy children.

Shapiro v. *Thompson* (1969): The Supreme Court ruled that one-year residency requirements imposed on welfare recipients by the District of Columbia and other states was unconstitutional in that it purposefully and discriminately interfered with the fundamental right of interstate movement.

Goldberg v. *Kelly* (1970): The Supreme Court ruled that welfare recipients must be given an opportunity for an evidentiary hearing prior to the termination of public assistance payments.

Dandridge v. *Williams* (1970): A Maryland regulation imposing a $250 per month cap on AFDC benefits, regardless of the size of the family, was upheld as rationally based and free from discrimination.

Wyman v. *James* (1971): The Supreme Court ruled that periodic home visits made by caseworkers, as structured by New York statutes and regulations, constituted a reasonable administrative tool for the dispensation of the AFDC program.

James v. *Valtierra* (1971): A California statute required that federally funded, low-rent housing development projects must be approved by the majority of those voting at a community election. The U.S. Supreme Court upheld the statute.

Jefferson v. *Hackney* (1972): A Texas plan for reducing welfare benefits differentially, based on type of assistance, was upheld. Although the plan reduced benefits more for AFDC recipients than for recipients of old-age benefits and blindness and disability benefits, it was found not to be invidious or irrational.

Memorial Hospital v. *Maricopa County* (1974): An Arizona law requiring a one-year residence in a county as a condition for an indigent to receive nonemergency hospitalization or medical care at the county's expense was held to be in violation of the equal protection clause of the U.S. Constitution.

SUMMARY OF TRENDS AND ISSUES

Many of the legal and judicial problems of the poor are systemic. A strong case can be made that legislative processes, social controls, and systems for establishing justice foster polarity between the affluent and those who have fewer resources. The track record for addressing these problems in the United States has not been promising, as of yet.

In order to reverse the oppressiveness of the current systems, participants on all levels will have to begin thinking about justice in different ways, especially with regard to poverty, social class, ethnicity, and race. Use of official discretion will also have to be examined carefully, whether in the criminal justice arena or in administrative bureaucracy. A substantial confounding factor is simply the very large number of individuals involved in making decisions ranging from individual cases to national policies.

Logic dictates that the continuing high costs of legal services will prevent the poor from using them, or using them effectively. Through the Legal Services Corporation, many have received access. Unfortunately, the existence of LSC and its funding seems to be very vulnerable politically.

U.S. Supreme Court rulings have forced state and federal courts to protect the right to counsel. Through public defenders and court-appointed attorneys, more indigent defendants have legal representation than they would have otherwise, yet these service providers are almost hopelessly overextended. Many have such large caseloads and are so poorly supported that they have difficulty providing adequate counsel (Smith, 1991). If American society can successfully reverse the current trend and significantly reduce the number of people living in poverty, providers of legal services for the poor may be able to address their needs more effectively.

REFERENCES

Amaker, N. C. 1988. *Civil rights and the Reagan administration*. Washington, DC: Urban Institute Press.

Baum, D. J. 1974. *The welfare family and mass administrative justice*. Praeger Special Studies in U.S. Economic, Social, and Political Issues. New York: Praeger.

Beaney, W. M. 1955. *The right to counsel in American courts*. Ann Arbor: University of Michigan Press.

Besharov, D. J., ed. 1990. *Legal services for the poor: Time for reform*. Washington, DC: AEI Press.

Blasi, V., ed. 1983. *The Burger court: The counter-revolution that wasn't*. New Haven, CT: Yale University Press.

Blumenthal, R., & Soler, M. I. 1971. The Legal Services Corporation: Curtailing political interference. *Yale Law Journal,* 81: 231-86.

Brady, P. L. 1990. *A certain blindness: A black family's quest for the promise of America*. Atlanta: ALP.

Brown, R. N. 1989. *The rights of older persons*. 2nd ed. American Civil Liberties Union Handbook. Carbondale: Southern Illinois University Press.

Chambliss, W. J. 1969. *Crime and the legal process*. New York: McGraw-Hill.

Christensen, B. F. 1970. *Lawyers for people of moderate means: Some problems of availability of legal services*. Chicago: American Bar Foundation.

Cloward, R. A., & Ohlin, L. E. 1960. *Delinquency and opportunity*. New York: Free Press.

Comer, J. P. 1966. *The forging of the federal indigent code*. San Antonio: Principia Press of Trinity University.

Corsi, J. R. 1984. *Judicial politics: An introduction*. Englewood Cliffs, NJ: Prentice-Hall.

Feld, B. C. 1993. *Justice for children: The right to counsel and the juvenile courts*. Boston: Northeastern University Press.

Forer, L. G. 1984. *Money and justice: Who owns the courts?* New York: W. W. Norton.

Galloway, R. W. 1991. *Justice for all? The rich and poor in Supreme Court history 1790-1990*. Durham, NC: Carolina Academic Press.

Gordon, S. 1980. *Welfare, justice, and freedom*. New York: Columbia University Press.

Handler, J. F. 1979. *Protecting the social service client: Legal and structural controls on official discretion*. Institute for Research on Poverty, Poverty Policy Analysis Series. New York: Academic Press.

Handler, J. F., & Hollingsworth, E. J. 1971. *The "deserving poor": A study of welfare administration*. Institute for Research on Poverty Monograph Series. Chicago: Markham.

Handler, J. F.; Hollingsworth, E. J.; & Erlanger, H. S. 1978. *Lawyers and the pursuit of legal rights*. Institute for Research on Poverty, Poverty Policy Analysis Series. New York: Academic Press.

Harrington, C. B. 1985. *Shadow justice: The ideology and institutionalization of alternatives to court*. Contributions in Political Science, Number 133. Westport, CT: Greenwood Press.

Harris, F. R., & Wilkins, R. W., eds. 1988. *Quiet riots: Race and poverty in the United States*. New York: Pantheon Books.

Hermann, R. 1977. *Counsel for the poor: Criminal defense in urban America*. Lexington, MA: Lexington Books.

Irwin, J. 1985. *The jail: Managing rabble in American society*. Berkeley: University of California Press.

Johnson, E. 1974. *Justice and reform: The formative years of the OEO Legal Services Program*. New York: Russell Sage Foundation.

Kapp, M. B., ed. 1988. *Legal aspects of health care for the elderly: An annotated bibliography*. Bibliographies and Indexes in Gerontology, No 7. New York: Greenwood Press.

Katz, J. 1982. *Poor people's lawyers in transition*. Crime, Law, and Deviance. New Brunswick, NJ: Rutgers University Press.

Kessler, M. 1987. *Legal services for the poor: A comparative and contemporary analysis of interorganizational politics*. Studies in Social Welfare Policies and Programs, Number 6. New York: Greenwood Press.

Kramer, J. C. 1984. Is corporate crime serious crime? Criminal justice and corporate crime control. *Journal of Contemporary Criminal Justice* 2: 2-10.

Law, S. 1973. *The rights of the poor*. American Civil Liberties Union Handbook Series. New York: E. P. Dutton.

Lawrence, S. E. 1990. *The poor in court: The Legal Services Program and Supreme Court decision making*. Princeton, NJ: Princeton University Press.

Lewis, A. 1964. *Gideon's trumpet*. New York: Random House.

Liebow, E. 1967. *Tally's corner*. Boston: Little, Brown.

Mashaw, J. L. 1983. *Bureaucratic justice: Managing social security disability claims*. New Haven, CT: Yale University Press.

Mencher, S. 1967. *Poor law to poverty program: Economic security policy in Britain and the United States*. Pittsburgh: University of Pittsburgh Press.

Piven, F. F., & Cloward, R. A. 1971. *Regulating the poor: The functions of public welfare*. New York: Vintage Books.

Regan, J. J. 1990. *The aged client and the law*. Columbia Studies of Social Gerontology and Aging. New York: Columbia University Press.

Report of the National Advisory Commission on Civil Disorders. 1968. Washington, DC: U.S. Government Printing Office (Pr 36.8:C 49/R29).

Rowan, C. T. 1993. *Dream makers, dream breakers: The world of Justice Thurgood Marshall*. Boston: Little, Brown.

Rowley, C. K. 1992. *The right to justice: The political economy of legal services in the United States*. Brookfield, VT: Edward Elgar.

Silberman, C. E. 1978. *Criminal violence, criminal justice*. New York: Vintage Books.

Silberstein, L. 1965. *Defense of the poor in criminal cases in American state courts: A field study and report*. Chicago: American Bar Foundation.

Smith, C. E. 1991. *Courts and the poor*. Chicago: Nelson-Hall.

Smith, R. H. 1919. *Justice and the poor: A study of the present denial of justice to the poor and of the agencies making more equal their position before the law with particular reference to legal aid work in the United States*. New York: Carnegie Foundation for the Advancement of Teaching.

Staff of the Duke Law Journal. 1969. *The legal problems of the rural poor*. American Bar Foundation Series on Legal Services for the Poor. Chicago: American Bar Foundation.

Stern, G. M. 1976. *The Buffalo Creek disaster: The story of the survivors' unprecedented lawsuit*. New York: Random House.

Ten Broek, J. 1966. *The law of the poor*. Chandler Publications in Political Science. San Francisco, CA: Chandler.

Tomasic, R., & Feeley, M. M. 1982. *Neighborhood justice: Assessment of an emerging idea*. New York: Longman.

U.S. Bureau of the Census. 1994. *1990 Census of population: Social and economic characteristics: United States* (CT-2-1). Washington, DC: Government Printing Office.

Walker, S. 1989. *Sense and nonsense about crime*. 2nd ed. Contemporary Issues in Crime and Justice Series. Pacific Grove, CA: Brooks/Cole.

Wasserman, D. T. 1990. *A sword for the convicted: Representing indigent defendants on appeal*. Contributions in Criminology and Penology, No 30. New York: Greenwood Press.

Westen, P. 1990. *Speaking of equality: An analysis of the rhetorical force of "equality" in moral and legal discourse*. Studies in Moral, Political, and Legal Philosophy. Princeton, NJ: Princeton University Press.

Wilson, J. Q., & Herrnstein, R. J. 1985. *Crime and human nature*. New York: Simon & Schuster.

Wilson, W. J. 1980. *The declining significance of race: Blacks and changing American institutions*. 2nd ed. Chicago: University of Chicago Press.

————. 1987. *The truly disadvantaged: The inner city, the underclass, and public policy*. Chicago: University of Chicago Press.

SOURCES OF
ADDITIONAL INFORMATION

Bibliographies and Guides

Aday, R. H. 1988. *Crime and the elderly: An annotated bibliography.* Bibliographies and Indexes in Gerontology, No. 8. New York: Greenwood Press.

Berens, J. F. 1987. *Criminal justice documents: A selective, annotated bibliography of U.S. government publications since 1975.* Bibliographies and Indexes in Law and Political Science, No 7. New York: Greenwood Press.

Christianson, S., ed. 1981. *Index to minorities & criminal justice: An index to periodicals and books relating to minorities and criminal justice in the United States.* Albany: Center on Minorities and Criminal Justice, School of Criminal Justice, State University of New York at Albany.

Cordasco, F., & Alloway, D. N. 1985. *Crime in America: Historical patterns and contemporary realities, an annotated bibliography.* Garland Reference Library of Social Science, Vol. 264. New York: Garland.

Crime and punishment in America: A historical bibliography. 1984. Santa Barbara, CA: ABC-CLIO.

Davis, B. L. 1978. *Criminological bibliographies: Uniform citations to bibliographies, indexes, and review articles of the literature of crime study in the United States.* Westport, CT: Greenwood Press.

Hewitt, J. D., Poole, E. D., & Regoli, R. M. 1985. *Criminal justice in America 1959-1984: An annotated bibliography.* Applied Social Science Bibliographies. New York: Garland.

Jacobstein, J. M., & Mersky, R. M. 1985. *Fundamentals of legal research.* University Textbook Series. Mineola, NY: Foundation Press.

Lutzker, M., & Ferrall, E. 1986. *Criminal justice research in libraries: Strategies and resources.* New York: Greenwood Press.

O'Block, R. L. 1986. *Criminal justice research sources.* 2nd ed. Cincinnati, OH: Anderson.

U.S. Department of Justice. Bureau of Justice Statistics. 1991. *Sourcebook of criminal justice statistics.* Washington, DC: U.S. Government Printing Office.

Dictionaries and Encyclopedias

American jurisprudence: A modern comprehensive text restatement of American law, state and federal. 1962 to date. 2nd ed. Rochester, NY: Lawyers Co-operative.

Black's law dictionary. 1990. 6th ed. Minneapolis: West.

Corpus Juris Secundum. 1936 to date. Brooklyn: American Law Book.

Periodicals

Clearinghouse Review
National Clearinghouse for Legal
Services, Inc.
407 South Dearborn, Suite 400
Chicago, Illinois 60605-1113
312-939-3838
Monthly

Indexes/Databases

Criminal Justice Abstracts
Willow Tree Press, Inc.
124 Willow Tree Road
Monsey, NY 10952
914-354-9139
Print and CD-ROM formats

Criminal Justice Periodical Index
University Microfilms International
300 North Zeeb Road
Ann Arbor, MI 48106-1346
800-521-0600
Print and online formats

Index to Legal Periodicals
H. W. Wilson Company
950 University Avenue
Bronx, NY 10452
215-588-8400
Print, online, and CD-ROM formats

*Index to Periodical Articles Related to
Law*
Glanville Publishers, Inc.
75 Main Street
Dobbs Ferry, NY 10522
914-693-8100
Print format

Legal Resources Index
Information Access Company
362 Lakeside Drive
Foster City, CA 94404
800-227-8431
Online and CD-ROM formats

LEXIS-NEXIS
Mead Data Central
9393 Springboro Pike
P.O. Box 933
Dayton, OH 45401-933
800-227-4908
Online format

*National Criminal Justice Reference
Service*
The National Institute of Justice/
NCJRS
Box 6000
Rockville, MD 20850
800-851-3420
Microfiche, online, and CD-ROM
formats. A microfiche set that corre-
sponds to the NCJRS database is also
available.

PAIS INTERNATIONAL
Public Affairs Information Service, Inc.
521 West 43rd Street
New York, NY 10036-4396
212-736-6629
Print, online, and CD-ROM formats

WESTLAW
West Services, Inc.
Westlaw Division
58 West Kellogg Boulevard
P.O. Box 64779
St. Paul, MN 55164-9990
612-687-6643
Online format

Useful Library of Congress
Subject Headings

Almshouses—Law and Legislation
Domicile in Public Welfare
Equality Before the Law
Food Stamp Fraud
In forma Pauperis
Legal Aid
Legal Assistance to the Poor

Legal Assistance to the Rural Poor
Pro Se Representation
Public Defenders
Public Welfare—Law and Legislation
Right to Counsel
Welfare Fraud

If a free society cannot keep the many who are poor, it cannot save the few who are rich.
John F. Kennedy, 1961

4

Poverty, Welfare, and Unemployment

Christine Avery

This chapter is concerned with the problems of poverty, welfare, and unemployment in the United States. These social problems are not new, but despite years of attention their resolution remains elusive. Poverty, welfare, and unemployment will be considered separately and as they relate to each other. The demographic aspects of each issue will be emphasized as a means of indicating relationships between social problems. The success of future efforts to lessen poverty, reform the welfare system, and reduce unemployment depends upon a clearer understanding of the interactions not only between these problems, but also between them and other issues dealt with in this book, such as changing family structures, homelessness, and the health care system.

POVERTY

Poverty in the United States is a pervasive problem despite decades of efforts to eliminate it. Consider the following statistics:

1. The poverty rate in the United States in 1990 was approximately 13.5 percent, representing about 34 million people.

Christine Avery has been a business reference librarian at The Pennsylvania State University, University Park, since 1990. Before that she was a business reference librarian and Head of Reference at the University of Wyoming. Ms. Avery is actively involved in the acquisition of machine-readable data in the Social Sciences for faculty and students at Penn State. Current research interests include a number of library-based surveys. Ms. Avery holds an M.S. in Applied social research from Texas Christian University and an M.L.S. from the University of Texas at Austin.

2. The poverty rate for children is higher than any other age group; 20 percent of all children under the age of 18 are poor, and children made up 40 percent of the total number of poor people in 1990.

3. In 1990 at least one person worked in 60 percent of all poor families.

4. In 1990 28 percent of the population living below the poverty level received no benefits of any kind from government assistance programs. (U.S. Bureau of the Census, 1991b)

Governmental Definition of Poverty

Poverty in the United States can be defined in many different ways, but poverty levels as reported by the Bureau of the Census are the statistics most frequently encountered. The definition of poverty used by the bureau is based on an index developed by the Social Security Administration in 1964 (Orshansky, 1969) and last revised in 1981 (U.S. Bureau of the Census, 1982). The index provides a range of income cutoff points that take into account the size of a household and the number of related children under the age of eighteen. The index was originally based on the assumption that families of three or more individuals spent approximately one third of their income on food, and the subsistence-level food budgets for families of three, four, etc. were multiplied by three to arrive at poverty thresholds for different families. Only money income is used to determine if a family is above or below a poverty cutoff point. The market value of benefits such as food stamps or rent subsidies is not taken into account.

This overall methodology used to define poverty has been criticized on a number of fronts. First, and most importantly, poverty cutoff points are no longer tied to the actual amount of money spent on food. Instead, the poverty thresholds are merely increased annually by the same percentage as the annual average consumer price index to compensate for inflation. As Schwarz and Volgy (1992, p. 35) point out, "changes in the consumption patterns of the average American family and the relatively rapid rise in the costs of other necessities, such as housing and medical care, reduced the proportion of the budget that the typical family spent on food and increased the proportion it spent on other needs." Thus, the official poverty threshold no longer has any tie to the concept of poverty and the inability to afford basic necessities. There is fairly general agreement that the "poverty line" is set considerably lower than it should be, although there has been some criticism of the definition of income as money income only (*Economic report of the president,* 1992).

Additionally, the poverty thresholds do not take into account such issues as regional differences in the cost of living, differing tax burdens

(Winnick, 1989), and the fact that the initial food budget that served as the basis for the poverty index was considered to be inadequate if used as more than a temporary subsistence-level food budget (Lauer, 1986, p. 236). Further, many believe that poverty should not be defined in absolute terms, as it is now, but rather that it should be a relative measure taking into account overall changes in a society's standard of living (Galbraith, 1958).

The Bureau of the Census began publishing statistics on poverty in the United States in 1959. Current Population Reports, Series P-60, published by the Bureau of the Census, are the best source of official data on poverty from 1959 to the present time. After 1978, information on poverty thresholds that includes estimates of the value of noncash benefits (such as food stamps and Medicaid) is available (U.S. Bureau of the Census, 1988), and, beginning in 1986, the bureau has published reports that estimate the effects of noncash benefits as well as taxes on income and poverty (U.S. Bureau of the Census, 1991a).

Pattern of Income Distribution

Much attention has focused on the overall pattern of income distribution in the United States. Winnick (1989) presents a concise description of income distribution changes from 1960 onwards. Maxwell (1990), in an empirical study of income from 1947 to 1985, concludes that income inequality has increased and is likely to continue to increase as a result of shifting industrial employment. The theme of an increasing gulf between the rich and the poor in the United States is repeated in an analysis of data collected annually since 1968 by the Survey Research Center at the University of Michigan. The data indicate a decline in the size of the middle class between 1968 and 1989. To put it succinctly, "the rich got richer and the poor got poorer" (Duncan, Smeeding, & Rodgers, 1992). A significant percentage of middle-class adults moved into upper-income brackets, but an even larger percentage of middle-income adults moved into the ranks of the poor.

This shift in income distribution becomes even more evident in examining data collected by the Bureau of the Census in 1990 (U.S. Bureau of the Census, 1991b). In 1990, the poorest fifth of American households accounted for only 4.6 percent of total income in the United States (down from 5.2 percent in 1980), whereas the richest fifth had 44.3 percent of total income in 1990 (up from 41.5 percent in 1980). This growing inequality is validated in research based on the bureau's Current Population Surveys and Consumer Expenditure Surveys (Cutler & Katz, 1992). Just as the poor received a smaller share of total income, they also consumed a smaller percentage of economic resources, as indicated by changes in the distribution of consumption in the 1980s.

Somewhat related to the topic of income distribution is the growing wage and salary inequality found in the United States. Tilly, Bluestone, and Harrison (1987) found that increasing numbers of part-time workers and changes in percentages of workers in various employment sectors are related to this trend. Despite the narrowing of male-female wage differences, Grubb and Wilson (1992) found inequality in wages and salaries increased between 1967 and 1988. This inequality is linked to the greater diversity of jobs available, with a large gap between highly skilled jobs and the expanding low-skilled and poorly paid work in retail trade and the service sector.

Demographics of Poverty

Research on the demographic aspects of poverty indicate that age, gender, educational attainment, and ethnic background are all strongly correlated with the likelihood of being poor. In the United States in 1990, children accounted for 40 percent of all people living in poverty, 53 percent of all poor families were headed by a female with no spouse present, poverty rates decreased as years of school completed increased, and about 50 percent of all persons below the poverty level were either of Hispanic or African-American background (U.S. Bureau of the Census, 1991c).

The number of children living in poverty in America is of great concern. The Children's Defense Fund is a source of annual information on the extent of child poverty, the long-term effects of such poverty, and strategies for combating the problems affecting children (*The state of America's children*, 1992). This annual report on children also summarizes key developments over the past year that affected prospects for children in the United States. Evidence indicates that as the number of poor children has grown, changes in eligibility requirements for social programs have meant that fewer children are able to receive benefits (Danziger, 1989). The Children's Defense Fund estimated that government assistance helped one in five poor families with children rise above the poverty level in 1979, but only one in eight by 1991 (*The state of America's children*, 1992).

On the other hand, it is interesting to note what has happened to the poverty rate among elderly Americans. The poverty rate among persons aged 65 and older was nearly 30 percent in 1967. The poverty rate for the elderly was greater than the poverty rate for children until 1973. By 1990, slightly less than 11 percent of those aged 65 or older in the United States were poor (U.S. Bureau of the Census, 1991c). Much of this substantial change can be attributed to government spending on such programs for the elderly as social security and Medicare (Danziger, 1989). However, as Estes, Gerard, and Clark (1984) demonstrate, elderly women are a particularly disadvantaged group economically. The number of elderly women as a percentage of the total population is growing rapidly in the United States; thus, the proportion of elderly women among the poor remains a critical problem.

Over the past twenty years, the percentage of poor families headed by women with no spouse present has increased from 36 percent to 53 percent of all poor families (Pearce, 1990, p. 266). Data from the 1990 Census of Population and Housing indicate that Pearce's (1978) notion of the "feminization of poverty" is likely to continue, given that between

1989 and 1990 the increase in the number of poor families headed by a female accounted for 84 percent of the net increase in poor families. (U.S. Bureau of the Census, 1991c). Figures for 1992 indicate that 35 percent of all female-led households were poor and that almost 50 percent of all black female-led households fell below the poverty line (*America's poor showing*, 1993). Duncan (1984) found that a change in family structure, such as divorce, marriage, or birth, is the most important factor in determining the economic well-being of a family. Duncan found women to be far more vulnerable to the effects of changes in family composition than men. Garfinkel and McLanahan (1988) examined the reasons for poverty among female-headed families, focusing on labor force participation rates as well as lack of child support. Children in the United States are increasingly likely to live in a family headed by only one parent, thus reinforcing the importance of the relationship between poverty and single parent households. A bibliography focusing on the feminization of poverty has been compiled by Feinberg and Knox (1990).

Poverty in the United States also has a geographic dimension. Poverty tends to be highest in the southern states and lowest in the Northeast. Roughly 40 percent of the poor live in the South. Poverty rates in 1990 ranged from 6 percent in Connecticut to 26 percent in Mississippi. Regional differences in poverty, including the differing concentrations of poverty in metropolitan areas, are described by the Bureau of the Census on an annual basis (Current Population Reports, Series P-60, No. 175, 1991), while comparisons between farm and nonfarm poverty are documented by the Bureau of the Census in another series (Current Population Reports, Series P-20, No. 457, 1992).

A significant number of the poor in America are employed. In 1990, about 40 percent of all poor persons aged 15 years or older worked, and a little over 9 percent of them worked full time. Individuals who worked full time at a job year-round for the minimum wage in 1992 would still be unable to support a family of three without falling substantially below the poverty line (*The state of America's children*, 1992). In looking at the problem of the working poor, Gardner and Herz (1992, p. 27) found that the number of workers living in poverty, "despite substantial labor force efforts," increased slightly in 1990. Poverty was linked most often to low earnings, followed by spells of unemployment and involuntary part-time work. Winnick (1989, pp. 81-82) found that two-thirds of the individuals earning the minimum wage were adults, whereas only one-third were teenagers. In his examination of employment data for the poor, Winnick argued convincingly that if the effects of teenage unemployment and the work patterns of the elderly were removed from the picture, then "more than two-thirds of poor white males, a majority of poor black males, and more than a third of poor females, were indeed working—and were poor anyhow."

The Underclass

A substantial body of work has developed in conjunction with the study of the persistence of poverty, particularly with regard to what has become known as the "underclass." See Aponte (1990) for a history of the term. Research on the underclass has tended to focus on trends in social and economic conditions that contribute to entrenched poverty. Duncan (1984, p. 48) finds that "The persistently poor are heavily concentrated into two overlapping groups: black households and female-headed households." Duncan also found a greater proportion of entrenched poverty occurring in rural areas and the South.

Glasgow (1980) and Cottingham (1982) concentrated on the interaction between race and poverty in an urban environment. Wilson (1987; 1991) examined both the role that neighborhoods play in the outcomes of the lives of the urban poor and the changes in the U.S. economy that have adversely affected the economic situation of young black men and argued that economic marginality coupled with social isolation in high-poverty areas have led to the underclass. Criticism of the concept of the underclass has come from Jencks (1991). However, in examining the paradox of the continuance of poverty after decades of attempts to eliminate it, Jencks (1991) and Peterson (1991) concluded that such issues as low wages and joblessness among males and the increasing number of low-income, female-headed households contribute most to enduring poverty. Under such conditions, too many children are left with inadequate support and limited chances of ever escaping from poverty.

In spite of extensive research on poverty, aided by our ability to accurately count and describe the poor, poverty rates have not changed much since 1970. The face of poverty has changed in that more children and fewer of the elderly are now poor, but the proportion of poor Americans has remained fairly stable. The eloquent warnings on the nature of poverty in the United States that began to appear in the late 1950s and early 1960s remain relevant. Galbraith's (1958) discussion of a new kind of poverty in the United States has been criticized on a number of points over the years, but his depiction of the invisibility of the poor as due to their lack of political importance remains compelling. Similarly Harrington's (1962) description of the destruction of aspiration among the poor and his characterization of poverty as a social product of our times as opposed to a result of personal or moral failure remain relevant thirty years later.

WELFARE

Many attempts have been made to reduce poverty in America. The most familiar is the welfare system. Welfare refers to government assistance programs in which eligibility for those programs is based on demonstrated need. In 1990 over $210 billion was spent on such programs: $152 billion by the federal government and $58 billion by state and local governments (*Statistical abstract of the United States*, 1992).

There are several excellent works that discuss from different perspectives the historical development of social welfare programs in the United

States and efforts to deal with poverty. Among them are works by Bremner (1956), Katz (1986), Leiby (1978), and Trattner (1984). A feminist perspective on the development of the welfare state in the United States is available in an anthology compiled by Gordon (1990). Berkowitz and McQuaid (1988) trace the development of private and public welfare systems in the United States and discuss the influence of private sector programs on federal programs. A concise historical chronology of legislative and other developments concerned with welfare in the United States can be found in a work by Gronbjerg, Street, and Suttles (1980).

A History of U.S. Welfare

Although private attempts to help those deserving of assistance, such as widows, orphans, the aged, and the sick, have always existed in some measure in this country, it was not until the period following the Civil War that the federal government first played a role in directly addressing the problem of economic hardship through creation of the short-lived Bureau of Refugees, Freedmen, and Abandoned Lands. The beginning of widespread concern with poverty and efforts to alleviate it in America is usually associated with the late nineteenth century. As Critchlow and Hawley (1989, p. viii) express it, "Many Americans came to believe their traditional system was working badly.... The economic and demographic changes under way were widening the gap between welfare needs and the capacity of families, churches, poorhouses, and the other components of the traditional system to meet them."

The period between 1870 and the First World War is important for its "Progressive Era" legislation, which introduced workmen's compensation and standards for working conditions. Another significant development was the interest in child welfare, which led to the mothers' aid movement. Prevailing thought held that in the case of widowed mothers, poverty should not break up families (through institutionalization of children whose mothers could not afford to feed and house them). Support for the provision of cash assistance to mothers with dependent children grew steadily, and the first widows' pension law was enacted in Missouri in 1911 (Trattner, 1984). The popularity of widows' pensions grew rapidly, and by 1935 most states had passed legislation aiding widows with children. Most statutes were eventually amended to cover all needy mothers, including those with illegitimate children. Widows' pension laws were the direct precursor of the Aid to Dependent Children (later Aid to Families with Dependent Children, or AFDC) section of the Social Security Act of 1935 (Trattner, 1984).

The Great Depression marks the point at which social welfare policy in the United States was completely transformed. The federal government assumed both responsibility for and leadership of public welfare programs. Piven and Cloward (1972) have written on the functions served by public welfare during the New Deal and subsequent periods, and examined relief as an institution of social control. In his review of the New Deal and social welfare programs, Bremner (1985, p. 80) noted that the

Social Security Act of 1935 marked the passage of the first permanent relief program and "inaugurated a lasting commitment, as well as a significant involvement on the part of the federal government in social welfare." The aforementioned Aid to Dependent Children section of the Social Security Act provided matching funds to states for widows' pensions or mothers' aid programs. Additionally, the act created a system of unemployment compensation funded by both state and federal government.

Following World War II, which had effectively ended the Depression in the United States, additional legislation was passed that had a general impact on social welfare (primarily amendments that expanded the Social Security Act). But it was not until the 1960s that another major social upheaval occurred with a resulting expansion of public welfare programs. Poverty in America was "rediscovered" in the 1960s when many Americans insisted that the United States live up to its image as the land of prosperity and equality. The reasons for the "War on Poverty," declared in 1964, are beyond the scope of this chapter, but Brauer (1982) can be consulted for a clear summarization. Most important is that the elimination of poverty in the richest nation in the world became a goal accompanied by new welfare legislation. Among the major pieces of legislation were laws that amended the Social Security Act to create Medicare and Medicaid, expanded the benefits available through the Aid to Families with Dependent Children program, provided work incentives, established SSI (Supplemental Security Income), instituted automatic cost of living increases in social security benefits, and established a permanent food stamp program. Other legislation included the Older Americans Act, the Child Nutrition Act, and the Housing and Urban Development Act.

Types of Programs and Who Participates

Most of the money spent by state and federal government on welfare is earmarked for "in-kind assistance," which is not cash aid. Medicaid; food stamps; the school lunch program; subsidies for public and rental housing; educational aid, which includes such programs as Head Start, Pell grants, and the College Work-Study Program; the Special Supplemental Food Program for Women, Infants, and Children (WIC Program); and jobs and training programs are the principal in-kind assistance programs. Spending on in-kind assistance amounted to approximately $155 billion in 1990, three-fourths of the welfare budget. Cash grants are received by the poor as a result of such programs as AFDC, SSI (which assists the elderly, blind, and disabled), pensions for needy veterans, unemployment compensation, and the Earned Income Tax Credit. In 1990, cash assistance amounted to roughly $55 billion, with $37 billion in federal money and $18 billion in state and local funds. Expenditures for the AFDC program amounted to $21 billion, with $12 billion provided by the federal government and $9 billion by the states (*Statistical abstract of the United States*, 1992).

Program costs, as well as statistics on the number of individuals served by assistance programs, can be found in a number of sources that update their information on an annual basis. A concise summary appears each year in the *Economic Report of the President*. With considerably more detail, the Annual Statistical Supplement of the Social Security Bulletin contains a report on the benefits provided by Medicaid, SSI, and other public welfare programs and the characteristics of their recipients. The Committee on Ways and Means, United States House of Representatives, issues an annual report known as the *Green Book*, which details state-by-state statistics on benefit levels, eligibility requirements, and expenditures for the AFDC program. Additionally, the *Statistical Abstract of the United States* has a fairly lengthy section dealing with social insurance and human services at the federal, state, and local levels. Some information is presented to allow comparisons between states and regions. Ginsberg (1992) has prepared an almanac of statistics and facts of relevance to social work and social services that serves as a valuable reference. Other useful sources include Stanley and Niemi (1990), who provide statistics on poverty, unemployment, and social welfare expenditures by program type, and Shea (1992), who gives detailed information on the characteristics of recipients based on an analysis of the ongoing Survey of Income and Program Participation conducted by the Bureau of the Census.

In 1990, an average of 11.4 million people received AFDC benefits each month, nearly 5 million people per month received SSI benefits, 25 million people used Medicaid, over 11 million children participated in the school lunch program, and 21 million people used food stamps in an average month. Each state defines eligibility requirements for AFDC benefits and sets its own benefit levels. The average payment per family was $396 in the United States in 1990, although state averages ranged from $720 in Alaska to $121 in Alabama (*Statistical abstract of the United States*, 1992).

Shea's research (1992) reveals a strong association between race and likelihood of receiving assistance. Roughly 33 percent of all blacks in the United States participated in a major program, as compared to 22 percent of all individuals of Hispanic origin and 8 percent of all whites. This corroborates the earlier work of Duncan (1984). Not surprisingly, children have higher participation rates than any other age group in the United States, and women are more likely to receive assistance than men (although this discrepancy is partly due to eligibility requirements).

In addition to interest in the demographic characteristics of welfare recipients, much research has focused on the length of time an individual or family receives assistance. Duncan (1984) reports that most poverty and use of public assistance programs is short term. However, additional research indicates that, although the use of welfare may be short term, multiple "spells" of welfare use are fairly common (O'Neill et al., 1984). Ellwood (1986) looked at multiple spells of receipt of AFDC benefits over a twenty-five-year period and found that AFDC users can be grouped into roughly equivalent groups of short-term users (one to three years), medium (four to seven years), and long-term users (eight years or longer). Shea (1992) has found that households headed by a single female had longer spells of welfare use than married-couple users of assistance, and that the median length of spells for blacks and persons of Hispanic origin was significantly longer than that of whites. In short, this research indicates a general difficulty in exiting poverty.

Welfare Reform

Piven and Cloward (1982), Katz (1986), and Skocpol (1991) are among those who offer explanations of the means through which the war on poverty eventually became a war on welfare. Public support for social service programs steadily eroded after 1968. Some of the reasons appear to have been politically motivated; however, the failure of the poverty rate to decrease among the non-elderly, and factors such as increasing out-of-wedlock births also played a role. Part of the difficulty with welfare reform, as the outline of the development of welfare programs in the United States has indicated, is that "the U.S. welfare system is no system at all, but rather a conglomeration of assistance programs established at different times, funded and operated by different levels of government and built on differing—and sometimes conflicting—political philosophies" (Jost, 1992, p. 319). Or, as Gronbjerg, Street, and Suttles (1980, p.13) observe, our welfare programs are based upon two differing philosophies: "a progressive one emphasizing reform, and a regressive one stressing deservedness. In short, we have theories of both the carrot and the stick . . . neither has been uniformly successful." There appear to be no unified goals for our current welfare system.

Satisfaction with welfare programs in the United States appears to be nonexistent. The only point in common appears to be the desire to change the welfare system. The AFDC program and other cash-assistance programs consistently attract the most criticism, yet spending on AFDC represents only 10 percent of the welfare budget (Marmor, Mashaw, & Harvey, 1990). Public perceptions regarding characteristics of welfare recipients are frequently biased (Spitzer, 1977; Auclaire, 1984; Coughlin, 1989a) and inaccurate. Common misconceptions are that most of the welfare budget is spent on blacks or that women receiving AFDC benefits have more children than women not receiving welfare benefits. Statistics from the Committee on Ways and Means, United States House of Representatives (1991), revealed that in 1989 only 40 percent of AFDC recipients were black (38 percent white, 16 percent Hispanic, 6 percent other) and that average family sizes were equal.

Overviews of current and historical efforts at welfare reform can be found in Coughlin (1989b), Cottingham and Ellwood (1989), Colby (1989), and Mead (1992). Of particular importance is the evaluation of welfare-to-work programs because future reform efforts will likely include expanded work and training programs. Under the Family Support Act of 1988, each state was required to implement a Job Opportunities and Basic Skills Training Program for welfare recipients by 1990. The federal government pays 60 percent of the cost of the program (which includes education, job training, and support services). Budget problems in most states have limited the ability of states to participate, and much of the federal share of money available is not used. However, the emphasis on work is likely to remain a priority (Jost, 1992).

Part of the difficulty with welfare reform is the lack of agreement over the nature of the relationship between poverty rates and welfare benefits. Murray (1984), Gottschalk and Danziger (1984), Darity and Myers (1987), and Moffitt (1990) have done research in this area. Considerable debate continues over the effect of general economic conditions on the poverty rate, as opposed to the effect of benefit levels, amount of participation in the welfare system, and demographic trends.

Conservatives, most notably Murray (1984), argue that public welfare assistance is responsible for a large share of the poverty that exists in the United States and that if the United States were to do away with welfare, poverty would be reduced. Conversely, many with more liberal tendencies contend that major increases in welfare benefits and program expansion are the only means of eradicating poverty (Schwarz, 1988). Reimer (1988) believes the current welfare system is incapable of eliminating poverty, is impossible to reform, and should be scrapped in favor of a combination of cash benefits for those who cannot work, community service jobs for those who can, and wage supplements for low-income workers. Others, such as Rodgers (1986), are concerned with the increasing feminization of poverty and associated problems with the AFDC program. Recent research by Hoffman (1991) on whether receipt of AFDC benefits "causes" poverty indicates weak statistical evidence for that position, but strong evidence linking the number of poor female-headed households with the number of AFDC recipients. Hoffman suggested that an increase in AFDC benefits would be likely to reduce the poverty rate of female-headed households with children present.

Gueron and Pauly (1991) summarized and interpreted research on welfare-to-work programs and concluded that, although they have not eliminated poverty or welfare use among individuals who have participated so far, such programs did succeed in increasing the earnings of the poor and if improved may reduce dependency in the future. Peterson (1992) evaluated problems associated with the Job Opportunities and Basic Skills Training Program. Also of interest is the collection edited by Manski and Garfinkel (1992) that investigated the challenges of evaluating welfare and training programs. Rose (1990) compared goals and restraints on government work programs from the 1930s through the 1980s and offered suggestions for future programs.

Attempts at welfare reform to date have produced little real change. Reform efforts in the 1970s under Presidents Nixon and Carter focused on the provision of a guaranteed minimum family income and requiring recipients to work, but failed. Welfare benefits under President Nixon were actually expanded when the food stamp program became mandatory for all states in 1972 and eligibility was expanded. The most significant changes that have occurred since 1980 have not been actual changes to programs (although some AFDC benefits have been reduced, eligibility requirements have become more stringent, and the actual number of families receiving AFDC benefits has declined), but rather changes to federal policies that have had the effect of shifting more of the burden for paying for public welfare from the federal government to the state governments (Critchlow & Hawley, 1989).

In addition to liberal and conservative critiques of welfare and ideas for welfare reform, another body of research is emerging that presents a feminist perspective on the issue. Pearce (1990) and Miller (1990) contended that welfare reform must address gender inequality in employment as well as deal fairly with the economic burdens women bear in raising children. Meucci (1992) reviewed changes to AFDC requirements and concluded that welfare reform is being shaped by attitudes that blame single mothers on welfare for their economic dependence. Reform efforts are better described as mandates that female recipients find jobs and exit the welfare rolls. Sawhill (1992) looked at reform efforts linking welfare benefits to marriage, job training, and having fewer children.

Recent reform proposals have included some common goals. As summarized by Burtless (1989) they are, first, to reduce long-term dependency among single mothers on welfare by raising employment and earnings levels. Second, earnings gains should offset any effects of benefit losses once welfare recipients become employed. That is, the standard of living should be better when working than when receiving welfare. A major problem noted in many studies of welfare recipients is that "because most welfare mothers' potential earnings are so low, work seldom has much economic payoff. . . . Though welfare pays badly, low-wage jobs pay even worse" (Edin & Jencks, 1992, pp. 223-25). A third goal is that reforms should eventually lead to less money spent on able-bodied, working-age recipients. It is acknowledged that training and education may be expensive, but the reasoning is that such investments would eventually pay for themselves. Last, better enforcement and collection of child support from absent fathers is a goal in many programs.

The analysis of what works and what doesn't work in welfare reform is far from complete. Part of the problem, as noted by Ellwood (1989) in reviewing a number of proposals, is that the goal of reform is unclear. Is it poverty or dependency that is to be reduced? Although both goals are desired, many feel such possibilities are unrealistic. Ellwood separated reform efforts into three groups of ideas and summarized the possibilities for each. The first set of ideas would fix the welfare system through mixing work and welfare, improving education and training, targeting prospective long-term welfare recipients for intervention strategies, imposing responsibilities on recipients, and increasing support services. The second set would approach reform through nonwelfare approaches such as wage subsidies, an increased minimum wage, expanded tax credits, and child-support payments. The third set of ideas would involve a reorientation of economic, educational, and social policies.

UNEMPLOYMENT

Employment is clearly viewed as a prime means of reducing both poverty and long-term dependence, but a better understanding of the relationship between poverty and unemployment is necessary. Saks (1983) points out that unemployment does not necessarily lead to poverty. Many households are able to handle periods of unemployment without becoming poor. However, in looking at the four groups of individuals Saks identified as quite likely to experience unemployment problems, it is clear that a relationship does exist between the probability of experiencing unemployment and the likelihood of also being poor. The four groups described by Saks are disadvantaged youth, disadvantaged adults whose normal wages are not enough to support a family above a poverty threshold, dislocated middle-aged workers having trouble adjusting to changes in the labor market, and older workers without retirement income who may also be in poor health or have other barriers to employment.

Official unemployment statistics and unemployment rates are understated in the United States (Baumer & Van Horn, 1985). This is because individuals are only considered to be part of the labor force if they are over 16 years of age and either have a job, are actively looking for a job, or are awaiting recall from a layoff. This approach excludes two types of people from the labor force: discouraged workers who have given up looking for work even though they want to work, and underemployed workers who involuntarily work part-time. Only those who are considered to be part of the labor force are included in calculations of the unemployment rate, hence the feeling that unemployment is a more serious problem than the official statistics might indicate. Sources of current statistics dealing with employment and unemployment are available in the *Monthly Labor Review* as well as *Employment and Earnings*, both publications of the Bureau of Labor Statistics.

In 1993, the Labor Department acknowledged the fact that unemployment has been underestimated for at least a decade as a result of undercounting the number of jobless women and miscounting laid-off and discouraged workers (Hershey, 1993). A substantially redesigned questionnaire has been used by the Labor Department beginning in January 1994. The official unemployment rates rose as a result of the revisions to the survey, which removed several sources of bias.

An examination of unemployment rates between 1980 and 1992 reveals considerable fluctuation, with an annual rate at the end of 1992 of approximately 7.4 percent. More important than the yearly averages, however, are unemployment rates for individuals with demographic characteristics most likely to be observed among the poor. For example, the annual unemployment rate in 1991 for women who maintain families was 9.1 percent, as opposed to a rate of only 4.5 percent among married women with a spouse present. The unemployment rate for blacks as a group averaged 12.4 percent in 1991, as compared to only 6.0 percent for all whites (Bureau of Labor Statistics, 1993).

Causes

Considerable research has been done on the various causes of unemployment. Among the poor a lack of education and skills is frequently cited. Johnston and Packer (1987) concluded that in the future even fewer jobs will be available for those who cannot read, follow directions, or use basic mathematics. Yet over half of 17-year-old students are deficient in reading ability, and almost half have limited math skills. They reported that the situation is worse among minority youth and that increased joblessness is likely to result without intervention. Although Wilson (1987) also addressed the lack of skills among poor urban workers, he was much more concerned about social isolation and the lack of role models from whom unemployed youth could learn work habits. The inability to envision a different sort of life is a prime barrier to leaving poverty.

Inability to find work can also result from discrimination (Kirschenman & Neckerman, 1991; Ruhm, 1989). Although Kletzer's research (1991) on the effects of worker displacement (e.g., loss of employment due to a plant closing or layoff from which a worker was not recalled) did not uncover overt discrimination, the findings did indicate that black workers were more likely to have been displaced than white workers during the 1980s, less likely to be reemployed, and out of work longer. Kletzer contended that these differences were most probably a result of the particular industries and occupations in which blacks were likely to be concentrated.

Unemployment as a result of increased competition in the labor market for available jobs was noted by Peterson (1991) and Winnick (1989). Bluestone and Harrison (1982) examined the role that the "deindustrialization" of the United States has played in the loss of manufacturing jobs. They analyzed the diversion of financial and manufacturing resources into wasteful speculation, mergers and acquisitions, and shifting of manufacturing to foreign countries. Mattera (1990) and Goldsmith and Blakely (1992) examined industrial restructuring as it affects unemployment and increased poverty. In his discussion of the extent of the employment problem in the United States, Chisman (1989) made the point that workers who lose their jobs in a recession frequently find jobs again as the economy improves, but they are often paid less than they were previously and are still employed in basic industries where jobs are likely to continue to decline (thus being at great risk of being displaced again).

Reducing Unemployment

The outlook for reducing poverty or lessening welfare dependence through increased employment is further complicated by evidence that clearly indicates a shift in the United States from a manufacturing to service industry base (Eitzen & Zinn, 1989). New jobs created tend to be at the low end of the wage scale (Bluestone & Harrison, 1986). Although Chisman (1989) concluded that there is growth in high-paying jobs in the service sector (nursing, for example), without high levels of specialized training such jobs are out of reach for most individuals.

Reich (1983) was particularly concerned with the economic and social costs of the creation of "dead-end" jobs and what he saw as a decline in the skills of workers entering the labor market. As this trend continues, the problems of the working poor described by Schwarz and Volgy (1992) will intensify. Levitan and Shapiro (1987) foresaw an increase in social problems if the poor are continually blocked from advancing. Bane and Ellwood (1991) argued persuasively that the working poor pose problems for American business and its ability to compete in the long run. They contended that a generation of future workers is growing up under conditions where failure and instability are common due to the economic insecurity caused by the increase in low-wage jobs. They saw poor morale and a passive attitude toward work as likely consequences. Another example of the way in which the poor are actually penalized for working (in comparing potential earnings to welfare benefits) was also included.

The availability of reliable child care is seen as central to the success of women in the labor market. Given the trend toward more female-headed households, any improvement in the employment status of women depends upon better child care. Kahn and Kamerman (1987) described the inadequate child care situation that currently exists, and Miller (1990) summarized child care issues and problems from a feminist perspective. Sidel (1992, p. 131) concluded, "There is little doubt that the absence of a high-quality, coherent, comprehensive day-care policy is a key factor in the perpetuation of poverty among women and children. Without access to affordable day care, women with young children are frequently unable to enter the labor force. Without day care, how can a mother receiving AFDC hope to acquire skills or get a job in order to get off welfare?"

At this point it should be clear that no progress can be made in reducing poverty or welfare dependency or unemployment unless the interrelatedness of these problems is acknowledged. Those who are poor are the most likely to become unemployed, those who are on welfare are the most likely to lack skills that would enable them to get jobs paying enough to escape poverty, and of course those who are chronically unemployed or underemployed are the most likely to be poor and in need of assistance. In addition, there are complicating social problems. For example, the high rate of teenage motherhood in the United States (Henshaw et al., 1989) has an impact on the number of female-headed families, which is of course closely connected to the number of households below the poverty threshold. Additionally, dropping out of school to care for a baby is linked to poor employment prospects and also to putting another generation at risk for poverty and unemployment (Sidel, 1992).

Although many suggestions have been offered to deal with what appears to be a vicious circle, most plans involve targeting programs to those individuals who can benefit most from intervention and expanding the scale of programs, as most programs reach only a fraction of the eligible population (Sawhill, 1989; Danziger & Weinberg, 1986). There is also agreement that a long-term effort is needed to deal with the inter-connected problems of poverty, welfare, and unemployment. There are no short-term solutions. At the beginning of 1993 it is encouraging to see a growing consensus that investment in the people of the United States is critical to our strength as a nation. As Reich (1983, p. 233) stated so eloquently over ten years earlier, "sums spent by government on health care and education are investments in America's future productivity. . . . The government deficits that result from productive social investments should cause us no more concern than the debt that private businesses incur in order to invest in productive assets." The will and the expertise to realistically address some of our most pressing domestic problems finally appear to be present together.

REFERENCES

America's poor showing. 1993. *Newsweek*, 18 October, 44.

Aponte, R. 1990. Definitions of the underclass: A critical analysis. In Gans, H., ed., *Sociology in America*. Newbury Park: Sage, 117-37.

Auclaire, P. A. 1984. Public attitudes toward social welfare expenditures. *Social Work* 29(2): 139-44.

Bane, M. J., & Ellwood, D. T. 1991. Is American business working for the poor? *Harvard Business Review* 69(5): 58-66.

Baumer, D. C., & Van Horn, C. E. 1985. *The politics of unemployment*. Washington, DC: CQ Press.

Berkowitz, E., & McQuaid, K. 1988. *Creating the welfare state: The political economy of twentieth-century reform*. New York: Praeger.

Bluestone, B., & Harrison, B. 1982. *The deindustrialization of America: Plant closings, community abandonment, and the dismantling of basic industry*. New York: Basic Books.

———. 1989. The great American job machine: The proliferation of low wage employment in the U.S. economy. In Eitzen, D. S., and Zinn, M. B., eds., *The reshaping of America: Social consequences of the changing economy*. Englewood Cliffs, NJ: Prentice-Hall, 103-8.

Brauer, C. M. 1982. Kennedy, Johnson, and the war on poverty. *Journal of American History* 69(1): 95-119.

Bremner, R. H. 1956. *From the depths: The discovery of poverty in the United States*. New York: New York University Press.

———. 1985. The new deal and social welfare. In Sitkoff, H., ed., *Fifty years later: The New Deal evaluated*. New York: Knopf, 69-92.

Bureau of Labor Statistics. 1992. *Employment and Earnings* 39(11).

———. 1993. Current labor statistics. *Monthly Labor Review* 116(2): 69-119.

Burtless, G. 1989. The effect of reform on employment, earnings, and income. In Cottingham, P. H., and Ellwood, D. T., eds., *Welfare policy for the 1990s*. Cambridge: Harvard University Press, 103-40.

Chisman, F. 1989. Effective employment policy: The missing middle. In Bawden, D. L., and Skidmore, F., eds., *Rethinking employment policy*. Washington, DC: Urban Institute Press, 249-64.

Colby, I. C., ed. 1989. *Social welfare policy: Perspectives, patterns, insights.* Chicago: Dorsey Press.

Committee on Ways and Means, U.S. House of Representatives. *Overview of entitlement programs: 1991 green book.* Washington, DC: U.S. Government Printing Office.

Cottingham, C. C., ed. 1982. *Race, poverty, and the urban underclass.* Lexington, MA: Lexington Books.

Cottingham, P. H., & Ellwood, D. T., eds. 1989. *Welfare policy for the 1990s.* Cambridge: Harvard University Press.

Coughlin, R. M. 1989a. Welfare myths and stereotypes. In Coughlin, R. M., ed., *Reforming welfare: Lessons, limits, and choices.* Albuquerque: University of New Mexico, 79-106.

Coughlin, R. M., ed. 1989b. *Reforming welfare: Lessons, limits, and choices.* Albuquerque: University of New Mexico.

Critchlow, D. T., & Hawley, E. W., eds. 1989. *Poverty and public policy in modern America.* Chicago: Dorsey Press.

Cutler, D. M., & Katz, L. F. 1992. Rising inequality? Changes in the distribution of income and consumption in the 1980s. *American Economic Review* 82(2): 546-51.

Danziger, S. 1989. Fighting poverty and reducing welfare dependency. In Cottingham, P. H., and Ellwood, D. T., eds., *Welfare policy for the 1990s.* Cambridge: Harvard University Press, 41-69.

Danziger, S. H., & Weinberg, D. H., eds. 1986. *Fighting poverty: What works and what doesn't?* Cambridge: Harvard University Press.

Darity, W. A., & Myers, S. L. 1987. Do transfer payments keep the poor in poverty? *American Economic Review* 77(2): 216-22.

Duncan, G. J. 1984. *Years of poverty, years of plenty.* Ann Arbor, MI: Institute for Social Research.

Duncan, G. J.; Smeeding, T. M.; & Rodgers, W. 1992. The incredible shrinking middle class. *American Demographics* 14(5): 34-38.

Economic report of the president. 1992. Washington, DC: Government Printing Office.

Edin, K., & Jencks, C. 1992. Reforming welfare. In Jencks, C., ed., *Rethinking social policy: Race, poverty, and the underclass.* Cambridge: Harvard University Press, 204-35.

Eitzen, D. S., & Zinn, M. B. 1989. The forces reshaping America. In Eitzen, D. S., and Zinn, M. B., eds., *The reshaping of America: Social consequences of the changing economy.* Englewood Cliffs, NJ: Prentice-Hall, 1-13.

Ellwood, D. 1986. *Targeting the "would-be" long-term welfare recipient: Report.* Princeton, NJ: Mathematica Policy Research.

———. 1989. Conclusion. In Cottingham, P. H., and Ellwood, D. T., eds., *Welfare policy for the 1990s.* Cambridge: Harvard University Press, 269-89.

Estes, C. L.; Gerard, L.; & Clark, A. 1984. Women and the economics of aging. *International Journal of Health Services* 14: 55-68.

Feinberg, R., & Knox, K. E. 1990. *The feminization of poverty in the United States: A selected, annotated bibliography of the issues, 1978-1989*. New York: Garland.

Galbraith, J. K. 1958. *The affluent society*. Boston: Houghton Mifflin.

Gardner, J. M., & Herz, D. E. 1992. Working and poor in 1990. *Monthly Labor Review* 115(12): 20-28.

Garfinkel, I., & McLanahan, S. 1988. The feminization of poverty: Nature, causes, and a partial cure. In Tomaskovic-Devey, D., ed., *Poverty and social welfare in the United States*. Boulder, CO: Westview Press, 27-52.

Ginsberg, L. 1992. *Social work almanac*. Washington, DC: NASW Press.

Glasgow, D. G. 1980. *The black underclass: Poverty, unemployment, and entrapment of ghetto youth*. San Francisco: Jossey-Bass.

Goldsmith, W. W., & Blakely, E. J. 1992. *Separate societies: Poverty and inequality in U.S. cities*. Philadelphia: Temple University Press.

Gordon, L., ed. 1990. *Women, the state, and welfare*. Madison: University of Wisconsin Press.

Gottschalk, P., & Danziger, S. 1984. Macroeconomic conditions, income transfers, and the trend in poverty. In Bawden, D. L., ed., *The social contract revisited*. Bawden. Washington, DC: Urban Institute Press, 185-215.

Gronbjerg, K.; Street, D.; & Suttles, G. D. 1980. *Poverty and social change*. Chicago: University of Chicago Press.

Grubb, W. N., & Wilson, R. H. 1992. Trends in wage and salary inequality, 1967-88. *Monthly Labor Review* 115(6): 23-39.

Gueron, J. M., & Pauly, E. 1991. *From welfare to work*. New York: Russell Sage Foundation.

Harrington, M. 1964. *The other America: Poverty in the United States*. New York: Macmillan.

Henshaw, S. K., et al. 1989. *Teenage pregnancy in the United States: The scope of the problem and state responses*. New York: Alan Guttmacher Institute.

Hershey, R. D. 1993. Jobless rate underestimated, U.S. says, citing survey bias. *New York Times*, 17 November.

Hoffman, E. P. 1991. Aid to families with dependent children and female poverty. *Growth and Change* 22(2): 36-47.

Jencks, C. 1991. Is the American underclass growing? In Jencks, C., and Peterson, P. E., eds., *The urban underclass*. Washington, DC: Brookings Institution, 28-100.

Johnston, W. B., & Packer, A. E. 1987. *Workforce 2000: Work and workers for the twenty-first century*. Indianapolis: Hudson Institute.

Jost, K. 1992. Welfare reform. *CQ Researcher* 2(14): 313-36.

Kahn, A. J., & Kamerman, S. B. 1987. *Child care: Facing the hard choices*. Dover, MA: Auburn House.

Katz, M. B. 1986. *In the shadow of the poorhouse: A social history of welfare in America*. New York: Basic Books.

Kirschenman, J., & Neckerman, K. M. 1991. We'd love to hire them, but . . . : The meaning of race for employers. In Jencks, C., and Peterson, P. E., eds., *The urban underclass*. Washington, DC: Urban Institute Press, 203-32.

Kletzer, L. G. 1991. Job displacement, 1979-86: How blacks fared relative to whites. *Monthly Labor Review* 114(7): 17-25.

Lauer, R. H. 1986. *Social problems and the quality of life*. Dubuque, IA: William C. Brown.

Leiby, J. 1978. *A history of social welfare and social work in the U.S.* New York: Columbia University Press.

Levitan, S. A., & Shapiro, I. 1987. *Working but poor: America's contradiction*. Baltimore: Johns Hopkins University Press.

Manski, C. F., & Garfinkel, I., eds. 1992. *Evaluating welfare and training programs*. Cambridge: Harvard University Press.

Marmor, T. R.; Mashaw, J. L.; & Harvey, P. L. 1990. *America's misunderstood welfare state: Persistent myths, enduring realities*. New York: Basic Books.

Mattera, P. 1990. *Prosperity lost*. Reading, MA: Addison-Wesley.

Maxwell, N. L. 1990. *Income inequality in the United States, 1947-1985*. New York: Greenwood.

Mead, L. M. 1992. *The new politics of poverty: The nonworking poor in America*. New York: Basic Books.

Meucci, S. 1992. The moral context of welfare mothers: A study of U.S. welfare reform in the 1980s. *Critical Social Policy* 12 (Summer): 52-74.

Miller, D. C. 1990. *Women and social welfare: A feminist analysis*. New York: Praeger.

Moffitt, R. 1990. *Incentive effects of the U.S. welfare system: A review*. Madison, WI: Institute for Research on Poverty.

Murray, C. 1984. *Losing ground: American social policy, 1959-1980*. New York: Basic Books.

O'Neill, J. A.; Wolf, D. A.; Bassi, L. J.; & Hannan, M. T. 1984. *An analysis of time on welfare*. Washington, DC: Urban Institute Press.

Orshansky, M. 1969. How poverty is measured. *Monthly Labor Review* 92: 37-41.

Pearce, D. 1978. The feminization of poverty: Women, work, and welfare. *Urban and Social Change Review* (Winter-Spring): 28-36.

———. 1990. Welfare is not for women: Why the war on poverty cannot conquer the feminization of poverty. In Gordon, L., ed., *Women, the state, and welfare*. Madison: University of Wisconsin Press, 265-79.

Peterson, C. D. 1992. JOBS for welfare recipients: A promising program faces many problems. *Journal of Economic Issues* 26: 449-56.

Peterson, P. E. 1991. The urban underclass and the poverty paradox. In Jencks, C., and Peterson, P. E., eds., *The urban underclass*. Washington, DC: Brookings Institution, 3-27.

Piven, F. F., & Cloward, R. A. 1972. *Regulating the poor: The functions of public welfare*. New York: Vintage Books.

———. 1982. *The new class war*. New York: Pantheon Books.

Reich, R. B. 1983. *The next American frontier*. New York: Times Books.

Riemer, D. R. 1988. *The prisoners of welfare: Liberating America's poor from unemployment and low wages*. New York: Praeger.

Rodgers, H. R. 1986. *Poor women, poor families: The economic plight of America's female-headed households.* Armonk, NY: M. E. Sharpe.

Rose, N. E. 1990. From the WPA to workfare: It's time for a truly progressive government work program. *Journal of Progressive Human Services* 1(2): 17-42.

Ruhm, C. J. 1989. Labor market discrimination in the United States. In Blanchard, F. A., and Crosby, F. J., eds., *Affirmative action in perspective.* New York: Springer-Verlag, 149-58.

Saks, D. H. 1983. *Distressed workers in the eighties.* Washington, DC: Brookings Institution.

Sawhill, I. V. 1989. Rethinking employment policy. In Bawden, D. L., and Skedmore, F., eds., *Rethinking employment policy.* Washington, DC: Urban Institute Press, 9-36.

———. 1992. The new paternalism: Earned welfare. *The Responsive Community* 2: 26-35.

Schwarz, J. E. 1988. *America's hidden success: A reassessment of public policy from Kennedy to Reagan.* New York: W. W. Norton.

Schwarz, J. E., & Volgy, T. J. 1992. *The forgotten Americans.* New York: W. W. Norton.

Shea, M. 1992. U.S. Bureau of the Census. Current population reports, P70-31. *Characteristics of recipients and the dynamics of program participation: 1987-1988* (Selected data from the survey of income and program participation). Washington, DC: Government Printing Office.

Sidel, R. 1992. *Women and children last.* New York: Penguin Books.

Skocpol, T. 1991. Targeting within universalism: Politically viable policies to combat poverty in the United States. In Jencks, C., and Peterson, P. E., eds., *The urban underclass.* Washington, DC: Brookings Institution, 411-36.

Spitzer, C. T. 1977. Welfare's bad image and how to change it. *Public Welfare* 35(3): 42-48.

Stanley, H. W., & Niemi, R. G. 1990. *Vital statistics on American politics.* Washington, DC: CQ Press.

The state of America's children. 1992. Washington, DC: Children's Defense Fund.

Statistical abstract of the United States. 1992. 112th ed. Washington, DC: Government Printing Office.

Tilly, C.; Bluestone, B.; & Harrison, B. 1987. *The reasons for increasing wage and salary inequality, 1978-1984.* University of Massachusetts at Boston: John W. McCormack Institute of Public Affairs.

Trattner, W. I. 1984. *From poor law to welfare state: A history of social welfare in America.* New York: New York University Press.

U.S. Bureau of the Census. 1982. *Characteristics of the population below the poverty level: 1980.* Current population reports, Series P-60, No. 133. Washington, DC: Government Printing Office.

———. 1988. *Estimates of poverty including the value of noncash benefits: 1987.* Technical paper No. 58. Washington, DC: Government Printing Office.

———. 1991a. *Measuring the effect of benefits and taxes on income and poverty: 1990.* Current population reports, Series P-60, No. 176-RD. Washington, DC: U.S. Government Printing Office.

———. 1991b. *Money income of households, families, and persons in the United States, 1990.* Current population reports, Series P-60, No. 174. Washington, DC: U.S. Government Printing Office.

———. 1991c. *Poverty in the United States: 1990.* Current population reports, Series P-60, No. 175. Washington, DC: Government Printing Office.

———. 1992. *Residents of farms and rural areas: 1990.* Current population reports, Series P-20, No. 457. Washington, DC: Government Printing Office.

U.S. Department of Health and Human Services. 1991. *Social security bulletin, annual statistical supplement, 1991.* Washington, DC: Government Printing Office.

Wilson, W. J. 1987. *The truly disadvantaged.* Chicago: University of Chicago Press.

———. 1991. Public policy research and the truly disadvantaged. In Jencks, C., and Peterson, P. E., eds., *The urban underclass.* Washington, DC: Brookings Institution, 460-81.

Winnick, A. J. 1989. *Toward two societies: The changing distributions of income and wealth in the U.S. since 1960.* New York: Praeger.

SOURCES OF ADDITIONAL INFORMATION

Indexes/Databases

American Statistics Index
Congressional Information Service
4520 East-West Hwy.
Bethesda, MD 20814-3387
301-654-1550
Print, online, and CD-ROM formats

Social Sciences Index
H. W. Wilson Company
950 University Ave.
Bronx, NY 10452
215-588-8900
Print, online, and CD-ROM formats

PAIS INTERNATIONAL
Public Affairs Information Service, Inc.
521 W. 43rd St.
New York, NY 10036
212-736-6629
Print, online, and CD-ROM formats

Statistical Reference Index
Congressional Information Service
4520 East-West Hwy.
Bethesda, MD 20814-3387
301-654-1550
Print, online, and CD-ROM formats

Useful Library of Congress Subject Headings

Cost and Standard of Living—United States
Discrimination in Employment—United States
Economic Assistance, Domestic—United States
Employment (Economic Theory)
Family—Economic Aspects—United States
Family Policy—United States
Federal Aid to Public Welfare—United States
Income—United States—Statistics
Income Distribution—United States
Manpower Policy—United States

Poor—Government Policy—United States
Poor—United States
Poor Women—United States
Poverty
Poverty—United States
Public Welfare—United States
Unemployment—United States
United States—Economic Conditions
United States—Social Conditions
United States—Social Policy
Urban Poor—Government Policy—United States
Welfare Recipients—United States
Women Heads of Households—United States

A government's responsibility to its young citizens does not magically begin at the age of six.
Gloria Steinem, 1974

5

Caregiving and Caregivers

Diane Zabel

Traditionally, women have assumed primary responsibility for dependent care, ministering to both children and elderly relatives. These family responsibilities have become public policy issues with the entry of more women into the workforce. Two of the most pressing work and family issues of the 1990s and beyond are child care and elder care.

The U.S. Bureau of Labor Statistics has projected that women will compose sixty-two percent of the workforce by the year 2000 (*Statistical abstract of the United States,* 1992). Many of these women will be the mothers of preschool and school age children or the daughters of elderly parents. Some of these women will be caught in the middle, caring for both their young children and aging parents simultaneously. Many employers have become more sensitive to these conflicts between work and family and have developed benefits and programs to help workers balance these demands. At the same time, family-leave laws have been debated by legislators at both the state and federal levels.

Diane Zabel has been the Social Science Reference Librarian at The Pennsylvania State University, University Park, since 1986. She has written several book chapters, including "Sociology" and "Psychology" in *The Social Sciences: A Cross-Disciplinary Guide to Selected Sources* (Libraries Unlimited, 1989); "Psychology and Psychiatry" in *Topical Reference Books* (Bowker, 1991); and "The Travel and Tourism Literature" in *The Leisure Literature: A Guide to Sources in Leisure Studies, Fitness, Sports, and Travel* (Libraries Unlimited, 1992). Her current research interests include flexible work arrangements and total quality management. She coauthored *Flexible Work Arrangements in ARL Libraries* (Association for Research Libraries, 1992) and "Total Management: A Primer" (*RQ*, Winter 1992). She also reviews reference books for *RQ* frequently. Diane Zabel holds a Master of Urban Planning degree and a Master of Science in Library and Information Science from the University of Illinois.

Changing demographics have forced employers and government to consider family-friendly work policies and profamily legislation. *Workforce 2000*, the landmark report issued by the Hudson Institute in 1987, projected that competition for talented workers will increase in a twenty-first-century workforce, one that will be more female and more diverse. The recent concern shown by businesses and government over family issues indicates that dependent care is no longer perceived as a private matter but as a public one.

CHILD CARE

The makeup of the U.S. labor force has changed dramatically in the past four decades. The most significant trend has been the increased participation of women, particularly mothers of young children. The percentage of working mothers of preschoolers increased from 12 percent in 1950 to 53 percent in 1985 (O'Connell & Bloom, 1987). These women share a common problem—locating affordable, quality child care.

Who cares for the preschool children of working mothers? A 1992 report issued by the U.S. Census Bureau indicates that an increasing number of these children are being cared for in day care centers. Whereas only 13 percent of these preschoolers were in organized care facilities in 1977, this percentage doubled to 26 percent in 1988 (U.S. Bureau of the Census, 1992). This same report found that many couples work different shifts so they can trade off caring for their children at home. This arrangement has become a necessity for many American families, given the high cost of day care and the absence of nearby relatives to lend a hand. These data are consistent with the findings of the 1990 National Child Care Survey. This study gathered data on child care trends and practices by surveying a nationally representative sample of U.S. families with children under age thirteen. It found an increase in care by parents and an increase in day care enrollments between 1985 and 1990. In fact, an equal proportion (28 percent) of preschoolers of employed mothers were cared for in centers or by parents in 1990 (Hofferth et al., 1991).

Working mothers use a range of child care options. These arrangements generally include care by relatives or nonrelatives in their own home, care in someone else's home, or care in an organized child care facility. A small percentage of mothers care for their children at work. The highly publicized case in 1992 of an Illinois couple who left their two young children to care for themselves while they vacationed in Mexico dramatized the shocking reality that an unreported number of children are left home alone every day to care for themselves. This chapter focuses on care arrangements outside a child's home, either in a center or in the home of another family—an arrangement typically referred to as family day care. Twenty percent of preschoolers of working mothers were cared for in family day care homes in 1990 (Hofferth et al., 1991).

MAJOR CHILD CARE ISSUES

Inadequate Supply

An increasing number of parents are turning to care outside their home, and the demand for affordable, quality care exceeds the supply of it. No source provides comprehensive data on the availability of child care. This lack of uniform data relates to the nature of child care. Many child care arrangements are informal; that is, children are cared for by relatives, friends, or siblings. Other children are cared for in facilities that are not licensed or regulated. Estimates of the number of licensed care facilities range from 60,000 to 80,000 centers and 118,000 to 168,000 family care homes (Reeves, 1992; Zigler & Lang, 1991). These numbers represent a range of fewer than 3 million to slightly more than 5 million child care slots. Although there are wide discrepancies in the data relating to regulated child care facilities, obviously a shortfall exists, given the sheer numbers of children in need of care. In 1988, there were 10.2 million children younger than six and 16.1 million children between the ages of six and thirteen with employed mothers (*The state of America's children*, 1991). The inadequate supply of care will continue to be a major national crisis given the projected increase of employed mothers. Researchers have estimated that more than three-fourths of school-age children and two-thirds of preschoolers, 49 million children in total, will have a mother in the workforce by the year 1995 (Hofferth & Phillips, 1987). Child care is particularly in short supply for infants, toddlers, and school age children. (Zigler & Lang, 1991).

This limited access to child care contributes to the feminization of poverty. Ruth Sidel has argued that child care is a two-class system in this country (Sidel, 1992). Those with means are able to purchase quality child care, whereas the poor and working poor are often on long waiting lists for subsidized child care. Low-income families with children will not be able to move out of poverty until there is an adequate supply of affordable child care. Studies have consistently shown that an inadequate supply of child care keeps one-quarter to one-half of low-income women from being employed (Adlin, 1988). Moreover, it has been demonstrated that it is more cost, effective to provide child care to low-income families than welfare benefits (Adlin, 1988).

Parental Cost and Caregiver Compensation

What does child care cost? Working parents spent $21 billion on child care in 1988 (U.S. Bureau of the Census, 1992). There are regional variations in cost. When the Children's Defense Fund analyzed 1990 cost data, it found that the average annual cost for infant care in a licensed center ranged from nearly $4,000 in Dallas to nearly $11,000 in Boston

(*The state of America's children*, 1991). Infant and toddler care is typically more expensive than care for preschool-aged children. When this same study analyzed annual child care costs for a four year old, it found that fees ranged from slightly more than $3,000 in Orlando to nearly $5,000 in Oakland. Child care is a major household expenditure, especially for low and moderate-income families. It is the fourth greatest expenditure after food, housing, and taxes (Zigler & Lang, 1991; Di Canio, 1989). Census Bureau data indicate that families spend 6.8 percent of their income on child care (U.S. Bureau of the Census, 1992). The 1990 National Child Care Study found that mothers of preschoolers spend 10 percent of their family income on child care (Hofferth et al., 1991). The proportion of family income spent on child care is a critical measure. Low-income parents spend a greater portion of their income on child care. It is estimated that two-parent poor families spend almost one-quarter of their income on child care, and poor single-parent families headed by women spend almost one-third of their income on child care (Zigler & Lang, 1991).

Although many parents are paying all, or more, than they can afford to pay for child care, the wages of caregivers are deplorably low. The National Child Care Staffing, one of the most comprehensive studies conducted in the 1980s on center-based child care, collected data on more than 200 care centers in five metropolitan areas (Whitebook, Howes, & Phillips, 1989). This 1988 study looked at several staffing issues, including: education and training, wages and benefits, working conditions, job satisfaction, and turnover. Here is a profile of the child care profession based on these findings: It is almost an exclusively female profession—97 percent of the teaching staff surveyed were women. They are well educated. More than half of the assistant teachers and nearly three-fourths of the teachers in the survey had completed some college. Subsequently, they have more formal education than the typical American worker. Almost one-fifth had worked in child care for a decade or more. Two-thirds considered child care as a career rather than a job. Despite their formal education and experience, teachers received on average an hourly wage of $5.35, a wage that resulted in an annual income of less than $10,000. In fact, this average annual income was below the established poverty level. The majority of teachers received no compensation for overtime and they worked without the benefit of a written contract. Health care and other benefits were minimal. Only two out of five teachers were offered health benefits and only one out of five had a retirement plan. Although teachers were unhappy about their poor compensation, they were generally satisfied with their jobs.

Quality and Regulations

However, these low wages contributed to a high turnover rate. The National Child Care Staffing Study found an annual turnover rate of 41 percent. Turnover rates reached 54 percent in centers paying four dollars or less per hour.

Research has shown that turnover has serious consequences for young children. The study found that children enrolled in centers with high turnover were more likely to wander aimlessly, spend less time engaged in play with their peers, and score lower on the Peabody Picture Vocabulary Test, a developmental test (Whitebook, Howes, & Phillips, 1989). A study of child care centers in Bermuda found that higher-quality programs were associated with lower rates of caregiver turnover (Phillips, Scarr, & McCartney, 1987). There is evidence that the stability of care can have a long-term impact. The number of prior child care arrangements was one of the variables examined by Carollee Howes in a study designed to assess the relationship between early child care and school adjustment. Howes found that greater stability in early care predicted better school adjustment (1988).

The National Child Care Staffing Study also found that centers with high staff turnover were less likely to meet the provisions of the Federal Interagency Day Care Requirements (Whitebook, Howes, & Phillips, 1989). This set of standards for federally funded child care programs was developed in 1968, revised in 1980, and suspended in 1981 (Hayes, Palmer, & Zaslow, 1990). They addressed staff/child ratios, group size, and caregiver training. Although these standards were supported by many child care experts, they were opposed by the National Association of Child Care Management, an association representing for-profit child care centers (Klein, 1992). Lobbying and opposition from the for-profit sector has kept federal child care regulations from being adopted. Because there are no federal guidelines regulating child care, regulation is left to the individual states. This situation is cause for concern because child care regulations vary widely from state to state.

Diane Lindsey Reeves has pulled together basic information about current child care regulations in each of the fifty states (1992). Her state-by-state comparisons for center-based and family day care look at child/staff ratios, required staff training, the number of annual inspections, and whether child care providers are screened for criminal or child abuse records. Many of these state regulations do not even meet the minimum standards for quality recommended by such authorities as the Child Welfare League of America and the National Association for the Education of Young Children. The Children's Defense Fund has outlined several inadequacies in these state-mandated standards (*The state of America's children,* 1991). For example, some states allow caregivers to care for as many as twelve infants, even though child care experts recommend ratios that do not exceed three or four babies per caregiver. Staff training requirements also vary widely. More than thirty states require no training at all for staff in family day care homes, and an almost equal number of states do not require specific levels of formal education for teachers employed in child care centers. The Children's Defense Fund has also found that most states do not have the resources to monitor and enforce regulations. In addition, there are serious gaps in regulation. More than twenty states exempt from regulation facilities that care for five or fewer children. As a result, many family day care homes are not regulated or inspected. Overall, the Children's Defense Fund estimates that 43 percent of all children cared for outside the home are in unregulated programs.

What factors influence the quality of care? The National Day Care Study concluded that the following three variables are the major determinants of quality in day care centers: caregiver/child ratio, group size, and caregiver qualifications (Ruopp et al., 1979). This ground-breaking study, conducted between 1974 and 1978, observed children and caregivers in 64 federally subsidized day care centers located in Atlanta, Detroit, and Seattle. The study found that smaller groups and, to a lesser degree, higher caregiver/child ratios were associated with more desirable child behavior and better performance on the Preschool Inventory and the revised Peabody Picture Vocabulary Test, two standardized tests that are used to predict later school achievement. Children also scored better on the Preschool Inventory in centers where a greater proportion of the staff had education and training in child development. Lead teachers with education and training relating to young children spent more time interacting socially with children. Children in their classrooms were more cooperative and more engaged in learning activities.

The three indicators of quality identified by the National Day Care Study have been integrated into various sets of child care standards. They form what has been referred to as the "iron triangle" (Reeves, 1992, p. 42). In addition to these variables, standards for quality child care have addressed interactions between caregivers and children, curriculum, parental involvement, and the physical environment. Six major sets of standards have been developed (Hayes, Palmer, & Zaslow, 1990). Two of the six were developed for federally funded programs: the Federal Interagency Day Care Requirements and Head Start Performance Standards. Although the former are no longer in effect, the latter requirements apply to all Head Start programs. Head Start has provided early childhood programs for low-income families since 1965. Three sets of voluntary standards have been developed by professional associations. The National Association for the Education of Young Children developed standards for the accreditation of center-based early childhood programs. The Child Welfare League of America's Standards for Day Care Service apply to day care centers and family day care homes. The National Black Child Development Institute developed guidelines for public-school-based early childhood programs serving minority children. T. Harms and R. M. Clifford, researchers at the University of North Carolina, developed the Early Childhood Environment Rating Scale, voluntary standards applying to center-based care.

Although there are differences among these six sets of standards, there is also agreement over what constitutes quality child care (Hayes, Palmer, & Zaslow, 1990). For example, they agree across the board that the caregiver/child ratio for infants and toddlers should not exceed one to four. Four of the standards stress the importance of training in early child development for teachers and staff. A high-quality curriculum is one that is both structured and flexible, with a range of developmentally appropriate activities.

There should be a balance of indoor and outdoor activities, active and quiet play, and staff-initiated and child-initiated activity. The physical environment should be designed for children, with clearly defined activity areas and a variety of attractive and developmentally suitable toys, books, games, and other materials. A quality program welcomes parental involvement and encourages parents to drop in any time.

The Effects on Children

Although many child care experts agree on the indicators of quality child care, there has been less consensus among researchers about the impact of nonparental care on children. This issue is more complex than determining that nonparental care is good or bad for children. Research has indicated that many factors, not just the quality of care, contribute to a positive or negative outcome, including the amount of weekly care, parental education, parental marital status, family social class, and gender of child (Vandell & Corasaniti, 1990). Many experts do not view child care in or by itself as a developmental risk (Scarr, Phillips, & McCartney, 1989). Rather, poor quality child care combined with a poor home environment places a child at risk.

Much of the early literature on the effects of child care is linked to the literature on maternal deprivation (Hayes, Palmer, & Zaslow, 1990). In 1951, the World Health Organization published John Bowlby's influential report on maternal care and maternal health (Bowlby, 1951). Bowlby, a psychologist, studied children who had been institutionalized or were living in residential facilities for children. He described the maternal deprivation syndrome resulting from this long-term mother-child separation. His research had a profound effect on attitudes towards child care because it suggested that day nurseries constituted a milder form of institutionalization.

Three decades later, Michael Rutter reversed this early conclusion, arguing that institutional care cannot be the basis for the assessment of child day care (Rutter, 1981a). Sandra Scarr, a prominent child care expert, challenged Bowlby's notion of exclusive maternal attachment in *Mother Care, Other Care*, characterizing it as "a psychology to keep mothers at home" (Scarr, 1984, p. 81). She also disputed this theory of attachment since it denies the role that fathers and other caregivers play. Bowlby maintained that the infant-mother bond is an exclusive relationship essential to normal emotional development. Scarr's review of the literature suggested that babies are capable of forming multiple simultaneous attachments and that babies with several attachments can be well adjusted. Sandra Scarr, Deborah Phillips, and Kathleen McCartney have written that the terms *maternal deprivation* and *maternal absence* evoke images of neglected and institutionalized children. Children in nonmaternal care are not neglected by their parents. The authors calculated that typical working parents spend more time caring for their child over the course of a year than a caregiver, precisely 2,831 hours to a caregiver's 1,715 (Scarr, Phillips, & McCartney, 1989).

Researchers have studied how child care impacts a child's intellectual, social, and emotional development. A panel of child care experts has outlined three waves in child care research (Hayes, Palmer, & Zaslow, 1990). According to these authorities, research from the late 1970s through the early 1980s focused on the difference between home-reared children and those in day care. The second wave of research, conducted from the mid- to late 1980s, centered on the relationship between quality of care and children's development. Recent research has studied the connection between child care quality and family variables (i.e., social, psychological, and economic characteristics).

What conclusions emerged from this evolving body of research? Three major reviews of child care research were published in the late 1970s and early 1980s (Belsky & Steinberg, 1978; Rutter, 1981b; Clarke-Stewart & Fein, 1983). Belsky and Steinberg concluded that child care had neither a positive nor negative effect on a child's intellectual development; that child care does not disrupt a child's emotional bond with his or her mother; and that child care results in greater peer interaction, both positive and negative. The subsequent reviews by Rutter and Clarke-Stewart and Fein supported many of these conclusions. However, Clarke-Stewart and Fein concluded that in the case of intellectual development, children in day care do as well as, or better than, children reared at home. All three reviews of research included evidence that child care may enhance the intellectual development of disadvantaged children from poor families. In addition, the reviews by Rutter and Clarke-Stewart and Fein found that children in day care developed greater social competencies such as self-confidence, self-sufficiency, and friendliness.

Overall, these early reviews were reassuring, indicating that day care was not detrimental to children. However, this complacency was shattered when respected Pennsylvania State University psychologist Jay Belsky reversed his position on day care. Belsky concluded that infants placed in day care for more than twenty hours a week before the age of one were at risk for developing emotional insecurities (Belsky, 1986, 1988a, 1988b; Belsky & Rovine, 1988). He also argued that these children were likely to be more aggressive and noncompliant as preschoolers (Belsky, 1986, 1988a, 1988b). *Early Childhood Research Quarterly*, the journal that published Belsky's controversial 1988 article (an extension of his 1986 article in *Zero to Three*), devoted two special issues, edited by Greta Fein and Nathan Fox, to the ensuing debate over infant day care (Fein & Fox, 1988). The articles published in this important two-part series were subsequently published as a monograph (Fox & Fein, 1990). Belsky's critics questioned the method he used to assess infant security attachment, in particular an assessment known as the Strange Situation. Belsky later defended the validity of this methodology and reiterated his view that babies should be cared for by parents during the first year of life when there is a "window of vulnerability" (Belsky, 1989, p. 46). The continuing debate over infant day care has been chronicled by Ross Thompson (1991).

Infant day care is an emotionally charged issue. However, the reality is that more women than ever are returning to work soon after the births of their babies. The fastest growing group of working mothers are those with babies. Sixty-one percent of women with firstborn babies under the age of one are in the workforce (Chase-Lansdale, Michael, & Desai, 1991). There is no large-scale longitudinal study on which to base firm conclusions about the effects of infant day care (Zigler & Lang, 1991). However, more will be known about the impact of day care on babies when the National Institute of Child Health and Human Development's Study of Early Child Care is completed (Clarke-Stewart, 1993). This study involves 1,200 babies from a wide range of socioeconomic backgrounds. These infants are being studied from birth through age three. Researchers will assess the impact of both day care and family environment on children's development.

The second wave of child care research links child care quality to children's development. There is evidence that high-quality day care is associated with positive developmental outcomes for babies and preschoolers (Thompson, 1991). A longitudinal study conducted in Sweden evaluated the impact of early center care. A researcher studied 119 Swedish children from infancy to the age of eight. He found that children who began day care before the age of one performed better on cognitive tests than children who began day care after the age of one or who stayed at home with their mothers. They also had more social skills, a greater facility with language, and made an easier transition from preschool to school. This researcher concluded that these outcomes were related to the universally high quality of care that characterizes Swedish child care (Andersson, 1989).

One of the best sources on the relationship between quality of care and children's development is a monograph published by the National Association for the Education of Young Children (Phillips, 1987). This book describes five different studies of child care in and outside the United States in a variety of settings. These studies were conducted in the following locations: Pennsylvania; Chicago; Los Angeles; Bermuda; and Victoria, British Columbia. Each study looked at center-based care and studied samples of comparable size and age. Each measured children's intellectual and social development. Children in centers did better developmentally than children cared for at home or in unregulated family day care homes. The following five predictors of quality were identified: A quality program is licensed; child-caregiver interactions are frequent, verbal, and educational; children have structured activities; there is an adequate caregiver/child ratio and a reasonable group size; and stable caregivers have training in child development and professional experience in child care. These five studies also found that families influence children's development.

Several studies have shown an association between quality of care and family variables. Children from families with low levels of education and income are more likely to be enrolled in low-quality family day care homes (Goelman & Pence, 1987). It is generally assumed that high-quality care is more expensive than poor-quality care (Zigler & Lang, 1991). This means that middle- and upper-class families can afford to purchase better care for their children. The result of this two-tiered system is that children in the greatest need of high-quality care are more likely to receive low-quality care (Schorr & Schorr, 1988; Hayes, Palmer, & Zaslow, 1990).

The need for child care does not end when a child begins school. A shortage of before- and after-school care creates major problems for many working parents. Estimates of the number of children (between the ages of five and thirteen) left to care for themselves before or after school range from 2 million to 15 million (Zigler & Lang, 1991; Hayes, Palmer, & Zaslow, 1990; Galambos & Maggs, 1991). It is difficult to determine the number of latchkey children nationally because many parents are reluctant to admit that they have left their children unsupervised. A review of the existing research on latchkey children indicates mixed findings about the impact of self-care (Seligson, Gannett, & Cotlin, 1992). However, most studies suggest negative outcomes. There is evidence that latchkey children are more likely to be lonely, fearful, and susceptible to negative peer influences than children who are supervised. Care for special-needs children is also in short supply. This group includes children who are handicapped, chronically ill, bilingual, or from migrant families (Zigler & Lang, 1991).

SOCIETY'S RESPONSE TO CHILD CARE NEEDS

The United States is the only industrialized nation without a national policy on child care. Ruth Sidel has argued that this is because child care is perceived as a service for the poor (1992). This perception reflects the historical development of day care in America. In the nineteenth century, wealthy Victorian women established day nurseries for the children of working mothers in mill and factory cities (Di Canio, 1989). During the Great Depression, the Works Progress Administration funded child care centers for the children of the unemployed (Zigler & Lang, 1991; Sidel, 1992). Child care became an issue during World War II when women replaced men in defense plants, factories, and other wartime industries. The Lanham Act of 1942 provided federal funding for day care (Zigler & Lang, 1991; Sidel, 1992). Federal and matching state monies funded more than 3,000 centers that cared for 600,000 children, 40 percent of the children in need of care (Sidel, 1992). These so-called Lanham centers were closed after the war in all states with the exception of California, where the state continued to fund them (Zigler & Lang, 1991; Sidel, 1992).

The federal government took little notice of child care until the 1960s when several Great Society programs (such as Head Start, Aid to Families with Dependent Children, and Work Incentive Now) supported day care directly or indirectly (Marver & Larson, 1978). These programs tied day care to welfare, reinforcing the perception that day care is primarily a service for the poor (Sidel, 1992). Abbie Gordon Klein has recorded the legislative history of child care from 1969 to 1990 (Klein, 1992). Although hundreds of child care bills have been introduced in the past 25 years, most have failed to pass both houses of Congress or they have been vetoed by a president (Watkins & Durant, 1987). The Lanham Act was the last comprehensive national child care program to be enacted in this country (Reeves, 1992).

Child care resurfaced as a national issue during the 1988 presidential campaign. Despite this political interest in child care, two significant bills failed to become law during the Bush administration. The Act for Better Child Care (the ABC Bill), which President Bush threatened to veto, failed to pass the Senate in 1989 (Reeves, 1992). This bill would have subsidized child care for low-income families. It also included provisions for federally mandated standards for states and would have established hiring, licensing, inspection, and training requirements. The Family and Medical Leave Act was vetoed twice by former president Bush. This bill would have allowed workers to take up to twelve weeks of unpaid leave for family emergencies or the birth or adoption of a child. One major child care bill was enacted during the Bush administration. The Omnibus Reconciliation Act of 1990, authorizing $2.5 billion for states over a three-year period, will help states improve and expand the supply of day care, before- and after-school care, and early childhood education programs (Reeves, 1992).

President Bill Clinton has promised to make the needs of families a top priority. On February 5, 1993, he signed the Family and Medical Leave Act. This landmark legislation, which became effective August 1993, does not apply to companies that employ fewer than fifty people, workers who have been with a company less than a year, part-timers, or 10 percent of a company's highest-paid workers. This legislation is only a beginning. Many workers will not be able to afford an unpaid leave. However, this legislation will guarantee workers who can afford it a job to return to and continued health benefits while they are on leave from work. President Clinton has pledged full funding for the Head Start program. In 1993 he proposed a $10 billion increase in funding for Head Start over four years, the single largest requested increase for any government program (Kramer, 1993). The $500 million increase Congress approved for the Head Start program fell short of President Clinton's request (Fuller, 1993). Funding for Head Start will continue to be a critical issue. The Advisory Committee on Head Start Quality and Expansion recommended that the Clinton administration expand eligibility to children as young as a few months old and that federal oversight of the project be strengthened (Jordan, 1993; Panel is seeking bigger Head Start, 1993).

The federal government has generally limited its involvement in child care to policies and programs benefiting disadvantaged families. One exception is the Child and Dependent Care Federal Income Tax Credit. Middle- and upper-class families have been the primary beneficiaries of this tax credit. This credit allows families to deduct 20 to 30 percent of their child care expenses from their federal income tax, up to an annual maximum of $2,400 for one child and $4,800 for two or more children (Olmsted, 1989; Hayes, Palmer, & Zaslow, 1990). It's been estimated that 50 percent of all families with working mothers claim this credit and that half of the families claiming this credit have annual incomes exceeding $25,000 (Hayes, Palmer, & Zaslow, 1990). This benefit is of no or little value to the many low-income families who are exempt from paying federal income taxes or who pay only a small amount in taxes (Olmsted, 1989).

The federal tax code also allows employers to offer employees a child care allowance under the Dependent Care Assistance Program. This tax provision allows employees to set aside up to $5,000 of their annual pretax salaries for child care (Saltzman, 1993; Reeves, 1992; Zigler & Lang, 1991). The advantage for employees is that they do not pay federal income tax or social security tax on the amount withheld. Employers benefit because they do not pay unemployment insurance or social security on this amount. There are minimal administrative costs for employers, making this an attractive fringe benefit. Families may use either of these federal tax benefits, but not both. This benefit favors moderate- and high-income families who have more to gain by sheltering their income and who can afford to set aside money for child care (Levitan & Conway, 1990; Klein, 1992).

The implementation of a Dependent Care Assistance Program is just one way employers can help employees with child care. A recent survey conducted by Hewitt Associates, a benefits consulting firm, found that almost three-quarters of large companies have some type of child care program in place (Saltzman, 1993). However, this survey found that employer involvement in child care is most often in the form of a Dependent Care Assistance Program or a resource and referral service offering information about local child care. Some corporations have established other types of programs, such as on-site or near-site day care, financial assistance for off-site child care, parental leave plans, and flexible work arrangements (Auerbach, 1988; Nollen, 1989; Solomon, 1991; Losey, 1992; Reeves, 1992; Tarrant, 1992). How successful has corporate America been in establishing a family-friendly workplace? A 1985 survey conducted by the Conference Board found that only 2 percent of employers offered on-site or near-site day care (Nollen, 1989). It found that only 1,350 employers offered financial assistance for off-site child care. In contrast, the Conference Board found that a large majority of companies offered unpaid maternity leaves and one-third offered unpaid paternity leaves. Flexible work arrangements are also typical. Flexible work arrangements encompass a range of options including the following: flexible work schedules; compressed work weeks; job sharing; voluntary part-time work; and telecommuting. A survey of 521 of the largest American companies found that 93 percent of the companies surveyed provide some form of alternative work arrangements with part-time work and flexible scheduling being the most common options (Christensen, 1990). Unfortunately, a recent study sponsored by the Employee Benefit Research Institute indicates that not all working mothers have access to family-friendly work benefits (*Which moms fare best?*, 1993). This research group found that women who are highly educated, higher paid, and in professional occupations are more likely to be offered at least one benefit such as a flexible schedule or child care assistance than women who are less educated, lower paid, and in service, manufacturing, or agricultural occupations.

In 1989 the CEOs of 200 major companies convened at the Business Roundtable and advocated reforming the nation's public education system (Zigler & Lang, 1991). It is inevitable that the public school system will play an expanded role in child care and early education. Edward Zigler, a prominent early childhood education advocate, has proposed the "School of the 21st Century" (Zigler & Lang, 1991, p. 190). Under this system, federal, state, and local funding for child care would be transferred to local public school systems. Public schools would then be responsible for the care of all preschoolers. Schools would provide before-school, after-school, and vacation care for children from kindergarten through grade six. A range of social and community services would also be delivered through local school systems. Private child care providers would be restricted to providing care for infants and toddlers.

Different versions or pieces of Zigler's plan have been implemented in six different states: Wyoming, Missouri, Colorado, Connecticut, Oklahoma, and North Carolina (Klein, 1992). Several other states are considering Zigler's model. Zigler's proposal has been controversial. Critics have argued that it would force private child care providers out of business, be too expensive to implement, limit parents choice in selecting child care, and harm children's development (Klein, 1992). Roger Neugebauer maintains that the national implementation of Zigler's proposal is unlikely given recent trends in public school involvement in preschool programs and opposition to it by both nonprofit and for-profit child care providers (Neugebauer, 1992). Neugebauer envisions that child care in the year 2000 will continue to be a mosaic of care provided by for-profit and nonprofit centers, employers, and public schools.

SUMMARY OF TRENDS AND ISSUES

Child care has become a mainstream issue. Although researchers debate the impact of nonmaternal care, economic reality has made it necessary for the majority of mothers to enter the workforce before their children reach school age. Good-quality child care is expensive and in short supply. In the absence of federal guidelines, quality of care varies from state to state and many facilities are unregulated and unlicensed. American child care has been best characterized as a "patchwork system," with care being provided by public and private nonprofit agencies, religious organizations, for-profit enterprises, employers, and public schools (Klein, 1992, p. 8).

Roger Neugebauer has identified five trends that will impact child care in the twenty-first century (1992). The first trend is continued growth in center-based care. Neugebauer estimates that by the year 2000, one-half of working mothers of preschool children will enroll them in child care centers. He predicts that child care will continue to be a political issue, especially since more middle-class voters will become consumers of child care. However, Neugebauer expresses concern that elder care may replace child care as the issue of the 1990s, given the formidable political clout of the elderly as a voting block. Another trend identified by Neugebauer is the increased involvement of public schools in the area of early childhood education. There will also be a growing emphasis on the quality of care. Finally, Neugebauer predicts that parents will view themselves as consumers of child care and become more involved in their child care arrangements. Neugebauer concludes that the implementation of high-quality child care in the future is dependent upon improved wages and working conditions for child care providers. A recent survey updating the 1988 National Child Care Staffing Study confirms Neugebauer's concern over salary issues. Four years after the original study, Whitebrook, Phillips, and Howes (1993) found that wages of teachers in child care centers continue to be low, turnover continues to be high, and that the vast majority of teachers are offered no or limited health insurance.

A national panel of child care experts has recommended that the following three goals direct the future development of child care: improved quality; improved accessibility; and an increased affordability for low- and moderate-income families (Hayes, Palmer, & Zaslow, 1990). Who should be responsible for providing an adequate supply of affordable quality care? According to Deborah Phillips, this question will shape the future direction of child care (Phillips, 1989). Most experts agree that child care will continue to be provided by nonprofit and for-profit providers, employers, the government, and public schools. A national commission on child care has recommended that the responsibility for child care be shared among individuals, families, employers, voluntary organizations, communities, and federal, state, and local governments (Hayes, Palmer, & Zaslow, 1990).

ELDER CARE

The elderly are the fastest-growing segment of the population in the United States. It is estimated that 13 percent of the population will be age 65 or over by the year 2000 and by 2050 one out of every five Americans will be elderly (Biegel & Blum, 1990). The fastest growth will occur among the subpopulation referred to as the "old old" or "oldest old"—the elderly aged 85 and over. Demographers predict that there will be more than 5 million old elderly by the year 2000 and that this subgroup will swell to more than 16 million by 2050 (Bould, Sanborn, & Reif, 1989; Biegel & Blum, 1990).

Many of these elderly will need assistance with bathing, dressing, toileting, eating, and other basic activities. Contrary to popular belief, the majority of elderly do not live in nursing homes. Only about 5 percent of the elderly reside in long-term care facilities at any given time (Norris, 1988). Most elderly live independently or semi-independently in their communities. It has been estimated that the number of community elderly requiring assistance with daily living will increase from 2.5 million in 1984 to 6.5 million in 2025 (Kovar, Hendershot, & Mathis, 1989). Substantial numbers of less impaired elderly need assistance with cooking, housework, laundry, home repairs, shopping, managing money, and errands. It is estimated that almost 8 million elderly have difficulty performing personal care and household tasks (Levitan & Conway, 1990).

Frail elderly depend on assistance from their families. More than 4 million family members care for an elderly relative on a daily basis (Abel, 1991). A 1988 national survey sponsored by the American Association of Retired Persons (AARP) and The Travelers Foundation found that 7 million households assisted a disabled older person in a twelve-month period (Scharlach, Lowe, & Schneider, 1991). These informal caregivers provide 70 to 80 percent of long-term care (Abel, 1990; Biegel & Blum, 1990). Women have assumed primary responsibility for elder care. More than 70 percent of caregivers are women (Biegel & Blum, 1990; Levitan & Conway, 1990; Abel, 1991; McLanahan & Monson, 1990). Although the number of elderly in need of care is rising, the number of available caregivers is declining. Many women are no longer able to care for a dependent family member around the clock because they are working outside the home. Women have entered the workforce in record numbers. In 1985, 53 percent of adult women were employed (Abel, 1991). This means that many women combine caring for an elderly relative with part-time or full-time employment. In addition, many of these women are wives, mothers, and grandmothers. These multiple responsibilities often result in physical and emotional strain.

Caring for an elderly family member is not the same as caring for a child (Fernandez, 1990; Roy & Russell, 1992a). Whereas a young child becomes more independent, an aging relative becomes more dependent. An elderly dependent is likely to suffer from chronic health problems. Declining health is inevitable for most frail elderly. The risk of developing one or more disabling disorders such as dementia, Alzheimer's, blindness, deafness, osteoarthritis, or Parkinson's disease increases with age (Scharlach, Lowe, & Schneider, 1991). Some women spend more years caring for an aging parent than for a dependent child (U.S. House Select Committee on Aging, 1987). Caring for an elderly parent is more complicated, however, because it is often done at a distance. Many adult children live apart from their aging parents. It is estimated that 30 percent of elder care is long-distance care (Lefkovich, 1992). Long-distance caregivers often have difficulty locating and arranging services for an elderly relative and traveling to provide care can be expensive (Roy & Russell, 1992b).

FAMILY CAREGIVERS

This chapter focuses on informal care; that is, the network of family, neighbors, and friends that help the elderly avoid institutionalization. Who cares for the elderly? Several surveys indicate that approximately 80 percent of caregivers are family members (Stephens & Christianson, 1986; Stone, Cafferata, & Sangl, 1987). Almost 75 percent of caregivers are women, and they are generally adult daughters, wives, or daughters-in-law (Levitan & Conway, 1990). Women caregivers are most likely to be middle aged or older (Morris & Bass, 1988). Elaine Brody and her colleagues at the Philadelphia Geriatric Center coined the term "women in the middle" to describe the typical caregiver (1981). These women are not only middle aged but caught in the middle between the competing demands of marriage, motherhood, paid employment, and caring for elderly parents or other relatives. A large body of literature focuses on female caregivers, especially caregiving daughters (Brody, 1981; Lang & Brody, 1983; Archbold, 1983; Horowitz, 1985; Abel, 1986; Hooyman & Ryan, 1987; Norris, 1988; Walker et al., 1989; Abel, 1990a; Brody, 1990; Hooyman, 1990; Abel, 1991; Dwyer & Coward, 1992a; Franks & Stephens, 1992). Although researchers know more about female than male caregivers, one book has been published on men who care for a frail spouse, parent, or other relative (Kay & Applegate, 1990). However, the reality is that wives, daughters, and sisters are much more likely to care for an elderly relative than husbands, sons, and brothers (Dwyer & Coward, 1992b). There is also a gender difference in the type of care provided. Studies have consistently shown that female caregivers are more likely to perform personal care and household tasks than male caregivers (Stoller, 1983; Horowitz, 1985; Montgomery & Kamo, 1989; Brody, 1990; Hooyman, 1990; Abel, 1991; Montgomery, 1992a). This sexual division of labor is important since there is evidence that caregivers who are responsible for performing personal care tasks experience greater levels of stress (Brody, 1990; Montgomery, 1992a). In fact, many studies have found that female caregivers experience more stress than male caregivers (Horowitz, 1985; Hooyman & Ryan, 1987; Brody, 1990; Montgomery, 1992a).

What are the impacts of caring? Many studies have found that caregivers experience a range of physical, emotional, social, and financial problems. Caregivers may be old or in frail health themselves. One-third of caregivers are age 65 or older and one-third characterize their own health as fair or poor (Sanborn & Bould, 1989). Studies have estimated that between 15 and 33 percent of adult children experience physical problems such as back pain and ulcers as a result of their caregiving responsibilities (Brody, 1990). One study found that employed caregivers were 20 percent more likely to have visited a physician recently than noncaregivers, suggesting that caregiving can mean increased health costs for employers and reduced employee productivity (Gadon & Serwin, 1989). Although caregiving can be physically demanding, studies have consistently shown that the greatest burden experienced by caregivers is emotional strain (Cantor, 1983; Brody, 1985; Brody et al., 1987). Many studies and literature reviews have focused on the emotional burdens of caregivers. Researchers have found that some caregivers experience one or more of the following emotional problems: anger, anxiety, depression, frustration, guilt, helplessness, irritability, lowered morale, sleeplessness, emotional exhaustion, substance abuse, and marital or family conflicts (Archbold, 1983; Brody, 1985; Gallagher, 1985; Pratt et al., 1985; Chenoweth & Spencer, 1986; Drinka, Smith, & Drinka, 1987; Hooyman & Ryan, 1987; Azarnoff & Scharlach, 1988; Gibeau, 1988; Silliman & Sternberg, 1988; Tennstedt & McKinlay, 1989; Bass, 1990; Noelker, 1990; Schulz, Visintaines, & Williamson, 1990; Googins, 1991; Scharlach, Lowe, & Schneider, 1991; Walker & Allen, 1991; Abel, 1991).

Caregiving also imposes personal limitations. Many studies have indicated that caregiving is particularly stressful because it can mean a loss of freedom, a lack of privacy, a diminished social life, and a forfeit of leisure and recreation (Archbold, 1983; Cantor, 1983; Brody, 1985; Gallagher, 1985; Horowitz, 1985; Montgomery, Gonyea, & Hooyman, 1985; Pratt et al., 1985; Chenoweth & Spencer, 1986; Stephens & Christianson, 1986; Brody et al., 1987; Hooyman & Ryan, 1987; Tennstedt & McKinlay, 1987; Azarnoff & Scharlach, 1988; Gibeau, 1988; Silliman & Sternberg, 1988; Bass, 1990; Brody, 1990; Noelker, 1990; Abel, 1990b; Abel, 1991). *The 36-Hour Day* captures the arduousness of caring for a loved one with Alzheimer's or a related disorder (Mace & Rabins, 1981). Caregiving can also create a financial hardship. It is estimated that 15 to 20 percent of caregivers experience financial problems as a result of their caregiving responsibilities (Brody, 1990; Scharlach, Lowe, & Schneider, 1991). These accumulated stresses can have serious consequences for the care recipient as well. In a study of 104 caregiving families, Steinmetz found that approximately 23 percent of caregivers engaged in some form of physical, psychological, or verbal abuse and neglect (Steinmetz, 1988).

Adult children of the elderly have often been referred to as the "sandwich generation" since they often care for their own children and elderly parents simultaneously (Miller, 1981, p. 419). An estimated 30 to 50 percent of employed caregivers have at least one dependent child at home (Azarnoff & Scharlach, 1988). One employee survey found that more than half (53 percent) of the 341 employees who cared for an elderly person had at least one child living at home (Scharlach & Boyd, 1989). This "sandwich generation" is expected to grow rapidly as more women delay having children until their 30s and 40s (Azarnoff & Scharlach, 1988). Elaine Brody, an eminent gerontologist, has emphasized that many women have "caregiving careers" as they sequentially care for their own children, an elderly parent, other aging relatives, and finally a dependent spouse (Brody, 1985, p. 25).

Several types of intervention programs have been developed to decrease caregiver burden. The major intervention strategies include: educational and support programs, respite programs, and counseling and psychotherapy. There are several excellent literature reviews on these intervention strategies (Gallagher, 1985; Gallagher, 1987; Gallagher, Lovett, & Zeiss, 1989). A variety of agencies and organizations, including the local chapters of such national groups as the Alzheimer's Disease and Related Disorders Association, the American Cancer Society, and the Arthritis Foundation, often sponsor lectures, workshops, and support groups. These types of programs can provide caregivers with information about a particular disease, teach practical coping strategies, and offer emotional support. The most comprehensive directory of caregiver support groups in the United States lists 750 support groups for family caregivers of the frail elderly (Lidoff, 1990). The goal of respite programs is to offer caregivers a temporary break from their responsibilities. This intervention strategy includes a range of programs: homemaker services, home health aides, visiting nurses, adult day care, and inpatient or overnight respite care (short-term stays in hospitals, nursing homes, and other out-of-home facilities). The third major intervention, counseling and psychotherapy, is used to treat depressed caregivers and to improve their coping skills.

How successful are these intervention strategies? There is a proliferation of literature on caregiver interventions. However, Gallagher's excellent synthesis of the literature revealed that much of it is based on pilot studies and is anecdotal in nature (1985). Biegel, Sales, and Schulz reviewed the findings of more than 50 studies of caregiver interventions (1991). Although caregivers responded positively to a variety of interventions, the authors concluded that there is a critical need for additional research in this area because most existing studies have not been longitudinal and are based on a small number of subjects.

SOCIETY'S RESPONSE TO ELDER CARE NEEDS

Although family caregivers have expressed a high level of interest in respite programs, these programs are in short supply in the United States (Abel, 1991; Montgomery, 1992b). This lack of availability is due to limited funding. Funding for respite programs comes from a variety of private and public sources (Lawton, Brody, & Saperstein, 1991). Most respite programs have been financed by foundations, religious institutions, and government funds. Family caregivers and care recipients have also shared the cost. Government funding through Title III of the Older Americans Act, the Social Services Block Grant (formerly Title XX of the Social Security Act), Medicare, and Medicaid has been modest and generally limited to demonstration projects. The majority of caregivers have to pay for outside help (homemaker services, chore services, home health aides, etc.) out of their own pockets, meaning that those with means are better able to purchase supplementary care (Googins, 1991). Studies of employed caregivers found that low-income caregivers experienced higher stress levels than high-income caregivers and that full-time workers who were not able to pay for outside help were stressed (Googins, 1991).

Although the federal government has been slow to implement policies to assist family caregivers, employers have become increasingly interested in developing programs to help employees who care for an elderly relative. Dana Friedman of the Conference Board predicted that elder care would probably be "the new pioneering benefit of the 1990s" (1986, p. 51). Corporations have been motivated to assist caregivers because of evidence that these responsibilities can negatively affect job performance and productivity. In addition to taking a physical and emotional toll on employees, these responsibilities can force them to miss work, arrive late, reduce their working hours, rearrange their schedules, and even quit their jobs (Friedman, 1986; Azarnoff & Scharlach, 1988; Brody, 1988; Gibeau, 1988; Gadon & Serwin, 1989; Scharlach & Boyd, 1989; Bass, 1990; Fernandez, 1990; Levitan & Conway, 1990; Neal et al., 1990; Googins, 1991; Scharlach, Lowe, & Schneider, 1991; Seccombe, 1992).

How has corporate America responded to the problems of caregiving employees? When Hewitt Associates surveyed 1,006 employers in 1991, they found that 36 percent offered elder care benefits (Lefkovich, 1992). A high percentage of employers (87 percent) reported that they offered a Dependent Care Assistance Program. This benefit allows employees to set aside a portion of their pretax salary to pay for dependent care expenses. Other benefits reported were resource and referral services (28 percent); counseling (11 percent); long-term insurance (5 percent); and other programs such as financial contributions to community agencies serving the elderly (3 percent). A few companies have on-site or contracted adult day care centers. Other policies that help employed caregivers include flexible work arrangements and family leave. The recently enacted Family and Medical Leave Act allows workers to take an unpaid leave in order to care for a frail spouse or parent.

SUMMARY OF TRENDS AND ISSUES

The elderly population will increase dramatically in the next several decades. The projected growth in the number of old elderly is even more significant. A large number of these elderly will need assistance from family members in order to avoid hospitalization or nursing home care. Research has shown that families are "the first line of defense" for frail elderly as family care constitutes 80 percent of all long-term care (Googins, 1991, p. 221). Caregiving responsibilities can be equivalent to a part-time job. Family caregivers spend an average of 28 hours weekly helping an elderly relative with personal care and household tasks (Googins, 1991). Given the trend toward containment of health care costs, it is unlikely that formal services would replace this informal system of care. Although some states financially compensate family caregivers, the level of compensation is low and strict criteria regarding eligibility keep the number of eligible caregivers small (Linsk et al., 1992). It has been estimated that family caregivers save taxpayers almost $10 billion a year (Googins, 1991).

However, families need some help if they are to continue to be primarily responsible for the care of the noninstitutionalized elderly. Studies have documented that caring for an elderly relative can be physically and emotionally exhausting. Many caregivers must adjust their vacation, retirement, and career plans. The strain of providing care can cause some caregivers to seek medical attention, reduce their working hours, or quit their jobs. The resulting loss of productivity has motivated corporations to look at ways to help their caregiving employees. However, the private sector alone cannot be responsible for elder care. Like child care, elder care solutions will require a partnership by government, industry, individuals, and families. The problem also requires a range of options. Research has indicated that several types of caregiver interventions are needed (education, support groups, respite services, and counseling) in order to meet the diverse needs of family caregivers (Blieszner & Alley, 1990).

REFERENCES

Abel, E. K. 1986. Adult daughters and care for the elderly. *Feminist Studies* 12: 479-97.

———. 1990a. Daughters caring for elderly parents. In Gubrium, J. F., & Sankar, A., eds., *The home care experience: Ethnography and policy.* Newbury Park, CA: Sage, 189-206.

———. 1990b. Family care of the frail elderly. In Abel, E. K., & Nelson, M. K., eds., *Circles of care: Work and identity in women's lives.* Albany: State University of New York Press, 65-91.

———. 1991. *Who cares for the elderly?: Public policy and the experiences of adult daughters.* Philadelphia: Temple University Press.

Adlin, S. 1988. Can welfare reform be a vehicle for the development of early childhood programs? In Schweinhart, L. J., & De Pietro, L., eds., *Shaping the future for early childhood programs.* Ypsilanti, MI: High/Scope Press, 48-51.

Andersson, B. 1989. Effects of public day-care: A longitudinal study. *Child Development* 60: 857-66.

Archbold, P. G. 1983. Impact of parent-caring women. *Family Relations* 32: 39-45.

Auerbach, J. D. 1988. *In the business of child care: Employer initiatives and working women.* New York: Praeger.

Azarnoff, R. S., & Scharlach, A. E. 1988. Can employees carry the eldercare burden? *Personnel Journal* 67: 60-65 (September).

Bass, D. S. 1990. *Caring families: Supports and interventions.* Silver Spring, MD: NASW Press.

Belsky, J. 1986. Infant day care: A cause for concern? *Zero to Three* 6: 1-7.

———. 1988a. Infant day care and socioemotional development: The United States. *Journal of Child Psychology and Psychiatry and Allied Disciplines* 29: 397-406.

———. 1988b. The effects of infant day care reconsidered. *Early Childhood Research Quarterly* 3: 235-72.

———. 1989. Infant-parent attachment and day care: In defense of the strange situation. In Lande, J. S.; Scarr, S.; & Gunzenhauser, N.; eds.; *Caring for children: Challenge to America.* Hillsdale, NJ: Lawrence Erlbaum, 23-47.

Belsky, J., & Rovine, M. J. 1988. Nonmaternal care in the first year of life and the security of infant-parent attachment. *Child Development* 59: 157-67.

Belsky, J., & Steinberg, L. D. 1978. The effects of day care: A critical review. *Child Development* 49: 929-49.

Biegel, D. E., & Blum, A. 1990. *Aging and caregiving: Theory, research, and policy.* Newbury Park, CA: Sage.

Biegel, D. E.; Sales, E.; & Schulz, R. 1991. *Family caregiving in chronic illness: Alzheimer's disease, cancer, heart disease, mental illness, and stroke.* Newbury Park, CA: Sage.

Blieszner, R., & Alley, J. M. 1990. Family caregiving for the elderly: An overview of resources. *Family Relations* 39: 97-102.

Bould, S.; Sanborn, B.; & Reif, L. 1989. *Eighty-five plus: The oldest old.* Belmont, CA: Wadsworth.

Bowlby, J. 1951. *Maternal care and mental health: A report prepared on behalf of the World Health Organization as a contribution to the United Nations Programme for the Welfare of Homeless Children.* Geneva, Switzerland: World Health Organization.

Brody, E. M. 1981. "Women in the middle" and family help to older people. *The Gerontologist* 21: 471-80.

———. 1985. Parent care as a normative family stress. *The Gerontologist* 25: 19-29.

———. 1988. Family responsibilities. In Friedman, D. E., ed., *Issues for an aging America: Elder care, highlights of a conference.* New York: Conference Board, 16-18.

———. 1990. *Women in the middle: Their parent-care years.* New York: Springer.

Brody, E. M.; Kleban, M. H.; Johnsen, P.; Hoffman, C.; & Schoonover, C. B. 1987. Work status and parent care: A comparison of four groups of women. *The Gerontologist* 27: 201-8.

Cantor, M. H. 1983. Strain among caregivers: A study of the experience in the United States. *The Gerontologist* 23: 597-604.

Chase-Lansdale, P. L., Michael, R. T., & Desai, S. 1991. Maternal employment during infancy: An analysis of children of the National Longitudinal Survey of Youth (NLYS). In Lerner, J. V., & Galambos, N. L., eds., *Employed mothers and their children.* New York: Garland, 37-61.

Chenoweth, B., & Spencer, B. 1986. Dementia: The experience of family caregivers. *The Gerontologist* 26: 267-72.

Christensen, K. 1990. Here we go into the "high-flex" era. *Across the Board* 27: 22-23.

Clarke-Stewart, A. 1993. *Day care.* Rev. ed. Cambridge: Harvard University Press.

Clarke-Stewart, K. A., & Fein, G. G. 1983. Early childhood programs. In Mussen, P. H. ed., *Handbook of child psychology,* vol. 2. New York: Wiley, 917-99.

Di Canio, M. 1989. Day care. In *Encyclopedia of marriage, divorce, and the family.* New York: Facts on File, 148-50.

Drinka, T.; Smith, J. C.; & Drinka, P. 1987. Correlates of depression and burden for informal patients in a geriatrics referral clinic. *Journal of the American Geriatrics Society* 35: 522-25.

Dwyer, J. W., & Coward, R. T. 1992a. Gender, family, and long-term care of the elderly. In Dwyer, J. W., & Coward, R. T., eds., *Gender, families, and elder care.* Newbury Park, CA: Sage, 3-17.

Dwyer, J. W., & Coward, R. T., eds. 1992b. *Gender, families, and elder care.* Newbury Park, CA: Sage.

Fein, G., & Fox, N., guest eds. 1988. *Early Childhood Research Quarterly. Special issue: Infant day care, 3 and 4.*

Fernandez, J. P. 1990. *The politics and reality of family care in corporate America.* Lexington, MA: Lexington Books.

Fox, N., & Fein, G. G. 1990. *Infant day care: The current debate.* Norwood, NJ: Ablex.

Franks, M, & Stephens, M. A. P. 1992. Multiple roles of middle-generation caregivers: Contextual effects and psychological mechanisms. *Journal of Gerontology* 47: S123-S129.

Friedman, D. E. 1986. Eldercare: The employee benefit of the 1990s? *Across the Board* 23: 45-51.

Fuller, B. 1993. Should Head Start be sacred? *Boston Globe,* 14 July.

Gadon, B., & Serwin, S. 1989. Eldercare: Its impact in the workplace. *EAP Digest* 9: 25-28, 65.

Galambos, N. L., & Maggs, J. L. 1991. Children in self-care: Figures, facts, and fiction. In Lerner, J. V., & Galambos, N. L., *Employed mothers and their children.* New York: Garland, 131-57.

Gallagher, D. 1985. Intervention strategies to assist caregivers of frail elders: Current research status and future research directions. *Annual Review of Gerontology and Geriatrics* 5: 249-82.

———. 1987. Caregivers of chronically ill elders. In Maddox, G., ed. *The encyclopedia of aging.* New York: Springer, 89-91.

Gallagher, D.; Lovett, S.; & Zeiss, A. 1989. Interventions with caregivers of frail elderly persons. In Ory, M. G., & Bond, K., eds. *Aging and health care: Social science and policy perspective.* New York: Routledge Kegan Paul, 167-90.

Gibeau, J. 1988. Working caregivers: Family conflicts and adaptations of older workers. In Morris, R., & Bass, S. A., eds., *Retirement reconsidered: Economic and social roles for older people.* New York: Springer, 185-201.

Goelman, H., & Pence, A. R. 1987. Effects of child care, family, and individual characteristics on children's language development: The Victoria day care research project. In Phillips, D. A., ed., *Quality in child care: What does research tell us?* Washington, DC: National Association for the Education of Young Children, 89-104.

Googins, B. K. 1991. *Work/family conflicts: Private lives, public responses.* New York: Auburn House.

Hayes, C. D.; Palmer, J. L.; & Zaslow, M. J.; eds. 1990. *Who cares for America's children?: Child care policy for the 1990s.* Washington, DC: National Academy Press.

Hofferth, S. L., et al. 1991. *National child care survey, 1990.* Washington, DC: Urban Institute Press.

Hofferth, S. L., & Phillips, D. A. 1987. Child care in the United States, 1970 to 1995. *Journal of Marriage and the Family* 49: 559-71.

Hooyman, N. R. 1990. Women as caregivers to the elderly: Implications for social welfare policy and practice. In Biegel, D. E., & Blum, A., eds., *Aging and caregiving: Theory, research, and policy.* Newbury Park, CA: Sage, 221-41.

Hooyman, N. R., & Ryan, R. 1987. Women as caregivers of the elderly: Catch 22 dilemmas. In Figueira-McDonough, J., & Sarri, R., eds., *The trapped woman: Catch-22 in deviance and control.* Newbury Park, CA: Sage, 143-71.

Horowitz, A. 1985. Sons and daughters as caregivers to older parents: Differences in role performance and consequences. *The Gerontologist* 25: 612-17.

Howes, C. 1988. Relations between early child care and schooling. *Developmental Psychology* 24: 53-57.

Jordan, M. 1993. Head Start Commission to recommend lower ages, higher quality. *Washington Post*, 30 October.

Kay, L. W., & Applegate, J. S. 1990. *Men as caregivers to the elderly: Understanding and aiding unrecognized family support.* Lexington, MA: Lexington Books, 1990.

Klein, A. G. 1992. *The debate over child care, 1969-1990: A sociohistorical analysis.* Albany: State University of New York Press.

Kovar, M. G.; Hendershot, G.; & Mathis, E. 1989. Older people in the United States who receive help with basic activities of daily living. *American Journal of Public Health* 79: 778-79.

Kramer, M. 1993. Getting smart about Head Start. *Time Magazine*, 8 March, 43.

Lang, A. M., & Brody, E. M. 1983. Characteristics of middle-aged daughters and help to their elderly mothers. *Journal of Marriage and the Family* 45: 193-201.

Lawton, M. P.; Brody, E. M.; & Saperstein, A. R. 1991. *Respite for caregivers of Alzheimer's patients: Research and practice.* New York: Springer.

Lefkovich, J. L. 1992. Business responds to elder-care needs. *HR Magazine* 37: 103-8.

Levitan, S. A., & Conway, E. A. 1990. *Families in flux: New approaches to meeting workforce challenges for child, elder, and health care in the 1990s.* Washington, DC: Bureau of National Affairs.

Lidoff, L. 1990. *Caregiver support groups in America.* Washington, DC: National Council on the Aging.

Linsk, N. L.; Keigher, S. M.; Simon-Rusinowitz, L.; & England, S. E. 1992. *Wages for caring: Compensating family care.* New York: Praeger.

Losey, M. R. 1992. Workplace policies should be family-friendly. *Modern Office Technology* (May): 84-85.

Mace, N. L., & Rabins, P. V. 1981. *The 36-hour day: A family guide to caring for persons with Alzheimer's desease, related dementing illnesses, and memory loss in later life.* Baltimore: Johns Hopkins University Press.

Marver, J. D., & Larson, M. A. 1978. Public policy toward child care in America: A historical perspective. In Robins, P. K., & Weiner, S., eds., *Child care and public policy: Studies of the economic issues.* Lexington, MA: D. C. Heath, 17-42.

McLanahan, S. A., & Monson, R. A. 1990. *Caring for the elderly: Prevalence and consequences.* Madison: University of Wisconsin, Center for Demography and Ecology.

Miller, D. A. 1981. The "sandwich generation": Adult children of the aging. *Social Work* 26: 419-23.

Montgomery, R. J. V. 1992a. Gender differences in patterns of child-parent caregiving relationships. In Dwyer, J. W., & Coward, R. T., eds., *Gender, families, and elder care.* Newbury Park, CA: Sage, 65-83.

————. 1992b. Long-term care. In *Encyclopedia of sociology,* vol. 3. New York: Maxwell Macmillan, 1158-64.

Montgomery, R. J. V.; Gonyea, J. G.; & Hooyman, N. R. 1985. Caregiving and the experience of subjective and objective burden. *Family Relations* 34: 19-26.

Montgomery, R. J. V., & Kamo, Y. 1989. Parent care by sons and daughters. In Mancini, J. A., ed., *Aging parents and adult children.* Lexington, MA: Lexington Books, 213-30.

Morris, R., & Bass, S. A. 1988. *Retirement reconsidered: Economic and social roles for older people.* New York: Springer.

Neal, M. B.; Chapman, N. J.; Ingersoll-Dayton, B.; Emlen, A. C.; & Boise, L. 1990. Absenteeism and stress among employed caregivers of the elderly, disabled adults, and children. In Biegel, D. E., & Blum. A., eds., *Aging and caregiving: Theory, research, and policy.* Newbury Park, CA: Sage, 160-83.

Neugebauer, R. 1992. Child care 2000: Five trends shaping the future for early childhood centers. In Spodek, B., & Saracho, O., eds., *Issues in child care.* New York: Teachers College Press, 1-8.

Noelker, L. S. 1990. Family caregivers: A valuable but vulnerable resource. In Harel, Z.; Ehrlich, P.; & Hubbard, R., eds., *The vulnerable aged: People, services, and policies.* New York: Springer, 189-204.

Nollen, S. D. 1989. The work-family dilemma: How HR managers can help. *Personnel* 66: 25-30.

Norris, J., ed. 1988. *Daughters of the elderly: Building partnerships in caregiving.* Bloomington: Indiana University Press.

O'Connell, M., & Bloom, D. E. 1987. *Juggling jobs and babies: America's child care challenge.* Washington, DC: Population Reference Bureau.

Olmsted, P. P. 1989. Early childhood care and education in the United States. In Olmsted, P. P., & Weikart, D. P., eds., *How nations serve young children: Profiles of child care and education in 14 countries.* Ypsilanti, MI: High/Scope Press, 365-400.

Panel is seeking bigger Head Start. 1993. *New York Times,* 31 October.

Phillips, D. A. 1989. Future directions and need for child care in the United States. In Lande, J. S.; Scarr, S.; & Gunzenhauser, N., eds., *Caring for children: Challenge to America.* Hillsdale, NJ: Lawrence Erlbaum, 257-73.

Phillips, D. A., ed. 1987. *Quality in child care: What does research tell us?* Washington, DC: National Association for the Education of Young Children.

Phillips, D. A.; Scarr, S.; & McCartney, K. 1987. Dimensions and effects of child care quality: The Bermuda study. In Phillips, D. A., ed., *Quality in child care: What does research tell us?* Washington, DC: National Association for the Education of Young Children, 43-56.

Pratt, C.; Schmall, V. L.; Wright, S.; & Cleland, M. 1985. Burden and coping strategies of caregivers to Alzhiemer's patients. *Family Relations* 34: 27-33.

Reeves, D. L. 1992. *Child care crisis: A reference handbook.* Santa Barbara: ABC-CLIO.

Roy, F. H., & Russell, C. 1992a. Caregiver. In *The encyclopedia of aging and the elderly.* New York: Facts on File, 42-43.

Roy, F. H., & Russell, C. 1992b. Caregiving, long-distance. In *The encyclopedia of aging and the elderly.* New York: Facts on File, 43-44.

Ruopp, R.; Travers, J.; Glantz, F.; & Coelen, C. 1979. *Children at the center: Summary findings and their implications.* Cambridge, MA: Abt Books.

Rutter, M. 1981a. *Maternal deprivation reassessed.* 2nd ed. New York: Penguin.

———. 1981b. Socio-emotional consequences of daycare for preschool children. *American Journal of Orthopsychiatry* 5: 4-28.

Saltzman, A. 1993. Family friendliness. *U.S. News & World Report,* 22 February, 59-60, 63-64, 66.

Sanborn, B., & Bould, S. 1989. Caregivers of the oldest old. In Bould, S.; Sanborn, B.; & Reif, L., *Eighty-five plus: The oldest old.* Belmont, CA: Wadsworth, 99-123.

Scarr, S. 1984. *Mother care, other care.* New York: Basic Books.

Scarr, S.; Phillips, D.; & McCartney, K. 1989. Working mothers and their families. *American Psychologist* 44: 1402-9.

Scharlach, A. E., & Boyd, S. L. 1989. Caregiving and employment: Results of an employee survey. *The Gerontologist* 29: 382-87.

Scharlach, A. E.; Lowe, B. F.; & Schneider, E. L. 1991. *Elder care and the workforce: Blueprint for action.* Lexington, MA: Lexington Books.

Schorr, L. B., & Schorr, D. 1988. *Within our reach: Breaking the cycle of disadvantage.* New York: Doubleday.

Schulz, R.; Visintaines, P.; & Williamson, G. M. 1990. Psychiatric and physical morbidity effects of caregiving. *Journal of Gerontology: Psychological Sciences* 45: 181-91.

Seccombe, K. 1992. Employment, the family, and employer-based policies. In Dwyer, J. W., & Coward, R. T., eds., *Gender, families, and eldercare.* Newbury Park, CA: Sage, 165-80.

Seligson, M.; Gannett, E.; & Cotlin, L. 1992. Before-and-after-school child care for elementary school children. In Spodek, B., & Saracho, N., eds., *Issues in child care.* New York: Teachers College Press, 125-42.

Sidel, Ruth. 1992. *Women and children last: The plight of poor women in affluent America.* Rev. ed. New York: Penguin.

Silliman, R. A., & Sternberg, J. 1988. Family caregiving: Impact of patient functioning and underlying causes of dependency. *The Gerontologist* 28: 377-82.

Solomon, C. M. 1991. 24-hour employees. *Personnel Journal* 70 (August): 56-63.

The state of America's children. 1991. Washington, DC: Children's Defense Fund.

Statistical abstract of the United States. 1992. 112th ed. Washington, DC: Government Printing Office.

Steinmetz, S. K. 1988. *Duty bound: Elder abuse and family care.* Newbury Park, CA: Sage.

Stephens, S. A., & Christianson, J. B. 1986. *Informal care of the elderly.* Lexington, MA: Lexington Books.

Stoller, E. P. 1983. Parental caregiving by adult children. *Journal of Marriage and the Family* 45: 851-58.

Stone, R.; Cafferata, G. L.; & Sangl, J. 1987. Caregivers of the frail elderly. *The Gerontologist* 27: 616-26.

Tarrant, S. M. 1992. How companies can become more family friendly. *Journal of Compensation and Benefits* 7: 18-21.

Tennstedt, S. L., & McKinlay, J. B. 1989. Informal care of frail older persons. In Ory, M. G., & Bond, K., eds., *Aging and health care: Social science and policy perspectives.* New York: Routledge Kegan Paul, 145-66.

Thompson, R. A. 1991. Infant day care: Concerns, controversies, choices. In Lerner, J. V., & Galambos, N. L., *Employed mothers and their children.* New York: Garland, 9-36.

U.S. Bureau of the Census. 1992. *Who's minding the kids?: Child care arrangements, fall 1988.* Washington, DC: Government Printing Office.

U.S. Congress. House. Select Committee on Aging. 1987. *Exploding the myths: Caregiving in America.* Comm. Pub. 99-611. Washington, DC: Government Printing Office.

Vandell, D. L., & Corasaniti, M. A. 1990. Child care and the family: Complex contributors to child development. In McCartney, K., ed., *Maternal employment: A social ecology approach.* San Francisco: Jossey-Bass, 23-37.

Walker, A. J., & Allen, K. R. 1991. Relationships between caregiving daughters and their elderly mothers. *The Gerontologist* 31: 389-96.

Walker, A. J.; Pratt, C. C.; Shin, H.; & Jones, L. L. 1989. Why daughters care: Perspectives of mothers and daughters in a caregiving situation. In Mancini, J., ed., *Aging parents and adult children.* Lexington, MA: Lexington Books, 199-212.

Watkins, K. P., & Durant, L. 1987. *Day care: A source book.* New York: Garland.

Which moms fare best? 1993. *Working Mother* (April): 6.

Whitebrook, M.; Howes, C.; & Phillips, D. 1989. *Who cares? Child care teachers and the quality of care in America, executive summary: National Child Care Staffing Study.* Oakland, CA: Child Care Employee Project.

Whitebrook, M., Phillips, D., & Howes, C. 1993. *The National Child Care Staffing Study revisited: Four years in the life of center-based child care.* San Francisco: Child Care Employee Project.

Workforce 2000: Work and workers for the 21st century. 1987. Indianapolis, IN: Hudson Institute.

Zigler, E. F., & Lang, M. E. 1991. *Child care choices: Balancing the needs of children, families, and society.* New York: Free Press.

SOURCES OF
ADDITIONAL INFORMATION

Juvenile Literature

Kleeberg, I. C. 1985. *Latchkey kid.* New York: Franklin Watts.

Rogers, F. 1984. *Going to day care.* New York: Putnam.

Swan, H. L., & Houston, V. 1987. *Alone after school: A self-care guide for latchkey children and their parents.* Englewood Cliffs, NJ: Prentice-Hall.

Valens, A. 1990. *Jesse's daycare.* Boston: Houghton Mifflin.

Van Zwanberg, F. 1989. *Caring for the aged.* New York: Franklin Watts.

Nonprint Materials

Caregiving: The challenge of elder care. 1987. Carlisle, MA: Southwestern Bell Telephone. Includes a 28-minute videotape, a 45-minute audiocassette, and a manual.

Caring for the elderly. 1987. Princeton, NJ: Films for the Humanities. 19-minute videotape.

Child care alternatives. 1990. Bloomington, IN: Meridian Education Corporation. 14-minute videotape.

Child care choices. 1985. Evanston, IL: Perennial Education. 14-minute videotape.

Child care: Everybody's baby. Boston, MA: WLVI-TV. 57-minute videotape.

Eldercare: Issues & answers. 1987. Westport, CT: Developmental Child Care. 27-minute videotape.

Families in the balance. 1989. Ithaca, NY: Cornell University, Audio Visual Center. 23-minute videotape.

How to find and evaluate high quality eldercare. 1987. Westport, CT: Developmental Child Care. 42-minute videotape.

In care of families and their elders. 1987. New York: Brookdale Center on Aging of Hunter College. 55-minute videotape.

McGruff's self-care alert. Van Nuys, CA: AIMS Media. 14-minute film or video.

My mother, my father. 1985. Chicago, IL: Terra Nova Films. 33-minute film or videotape.

Parent's guide to quality child care. Los Angeles: Eyemedia. 56-minute videotape.

People with aging parents. 1990. Nashville, TN: Ecufilm. 28-minute videotape.

Safe and sound: Choosing quality child care. 1991. Urbana, IL: Carle Medical Communications. 30-minute videotape.

School-age child care: Caring enough. Urbana, IL: University of Illinois, Cooperative Extension. 22-minute videotape.

Selecting day care for your child. 1990. Danielsville, GA: Sperling Video & Film. 70-minute videotape.

Sharing the caring: Adult day care. 1991. Washington, DC: National Council on the Aging. 18-minute videotape.

What is quality child care? 1983. Washington, D. C: National Association for the Education of Young Children. Two videotapes totalling 110 minutes.

You and your aging parent. St. Louis, MO: Applied Gerontology/Geriatrics Educational Seminars. Six 60-minute videotapes.

Resources for Working Parents and Family Caregivers

Carlin, V. F., & Greenburg, V. E. 1992. *Should mom live with us?, and is happiness possible if she does?* New York: Maxwell-Macmillan.

Dolan, M. J. 1992. *How to care for your aging parents . . . and still have a life of your own!* Los Angeles: Mulholland Pacific.

Flating, S. 1991. *Child care: A parent's guide.* New York: Facts on File.

Mall, E. J. 1990. *Caregiving: How to care for your elderly mother and stay sane.* New York: Ballantine Books.

Moskowitz, F., & Moskowitz, R. 1991. *Parenting your aging parents.* Traverse City, MI: Key Publications.

Shell, E. R. 1992. *A child's place: A year in the life of a day care center.* Boston: Little, Brown.

Indexes/Databases

ABI / INFORM
UMI/Data Courier
620 South Third St.
Louisville, KY 40202-2475
800-626-2823
Online and CD-ROM formats

Abstracts in Social Gerontology: Current Literature on Aging
Sage Publications
2455 Teller Rd.
Newbury Park, CA 91320
805-499-0721
Print format

AgeLine
American Association of Retired Persons
601 East St., NW
Washington, DC 20049
202-434-2277
Online format

Business Periodicals Index
H. W. Wilson Company
950 University Ave.
Bronx, NY 10452
212-588-8400
Print, online, and CD-ROM formats

Child Development Abstracts and Bibliography
University of Chicago Press
5720 S. Woodlawn Ave.
Chicago, IL 60637
312-753-3347
Print format

CIS
Congressional Information Service
4520 East-West Hwy.
Bethesda, MD 20814-3387
301-654-1550
Print, online, and CD-ROM formats

Current Index to Journals in Education (CIJE)
Oryx Press
4041 N. Central Ave. at Indian
School Rd.
Phoenix, AZ 85012-3397
602-265-2651
Print, online, and CD-ROM formats

Education Index
H. W. Wilson Company
950 University Ave.
Bronx, NY 10452
212-588-8400
Print, online, and CD-ROM formats

Employee Benefits Info Source
International Foundation of Employee
Benefit Plans
P.O. Box 69
Brookfield, WI 53008-0069
414-786-6700, ext. 360
Online format

ERIC
U.S. Department of Education
2440 Research Blvd., 5th Fl.
Rockville, MD 20850
301-656-9723
Online and CD-ROM formats

Family Resources
Database Information
National Council on Family Relations
3989 Central Ave., NE, Ste. 550
Minneapolis, MN 55421
612-781-9331
Online format

Index Medicus
U.S. National Library of Medicine
8600 Rockville Pike
Bethesda, MD 20894-0001
301-496-6308
Print, online, and CD-ROM formats

Inventory of Marriage & Family Literature
Corwin Press, Inc.
2455 Teller Rd.
Newbury Park, CA 91320
805-499-0721
Print format

Management Contents
Information Access Company
362 Lakeside Dr.
Foster City, CA 94404
800-227-8431
Online format

PAIS INTERNATIONAL
Public Affairs Information Service, Inc.
521 W. 43rd St.
New York, NY 10036
212-736-6629
Print, online, and CD-ROM formats

Personnel Management Abstracts
704 Island Lake Rd.
Chelsea, MI 48118
313-475-1979
Print format

Psychological Abstracts
American Psychological Association
750 First St. NE
Washington, DC 2002-4242
202-336-5500
Print, online, and CD-ROM formats

Resources in Education
Oryx Press
4041 N. Central Ave., Ste. 700
Phoenix, AZ 85012-3397
602-265-2651
Print, online, and CD-ROM formats

Sage Family Studies Abstracts
Sage Publications
2455 Teller Rd.
Newbury Park, CA 91320
805-499-0721
Print format

Social Sciences Index
H. W. Wilson Company
950 University Ave.
Bronx, NY 10452
215-588-8400
Print, online, and CD-ROM formats

Social Work Abstracts
National Association of Social Workers
7981 Eastern Ave.
Silver Spring, MD 20910
301-565-0333
Print, online, and CD-ROM formats

Sociological Abstracts
Sociological Abstracts, Inc.
P.O. Box 22206
San Diego. CA 92122
619-695-8803
Print, online, and CD-ROM formats

Work Related Abstracts
Harmonie Park Press
23630 Pinewood
Warren, MI 48091
313-755-3080
Print format

Women Studies Abstracts
Transaction Periodicals Consortium
Rutgers University
New Brunswick, NJ 08903
908-932-2280
Print format

Periodicals

ADRDA Newsletter
Alzheimer's Disease & Related
Disorders, Inc.
70 E. Lake St., Ste. 600
Chicago, IL 60601
Quarterly

Ageing and Society
Cambridge University Press
40 W. 20th St.
New York, NY 10011
Quarterly

Aging
Administration on Aging
U.S. GPO
Washington, DC 20402
Quarterly

Behavior, Health, and Aging
Springer
536 Broadway
New York, NY 10012-9904
3 issues per year

CAPsule
Children of Aging Parents
Woodburne Office Campus
1509 Woodburne Rd.
Levittown, PA 19057
Bimonthly

Caregiving
Creative Publishing Group, Inc.
30 Moran St.
Newton, NJ 07860
Bimonthly

Child and Youth Care Quarterly
Human Sciences Press
72 Fifth Ave.
New York, NY 10011
Quarterly

Child Care ActioNews
Child Care Action Campaign
330 Seventh Ave., 17th Fl.
New York, NY 10001
Bimonthly

Child Care Information Exchange
Exchange Press, Inc.
17916 N.E. 103rd St.
Redmond, WA 98052
Bimonthly

Child Development
Society for Research in Child
Development
University of Chicago Press
5720 S. Woodlawn Ave.
Chicago, IL 60637
Bimonthly

Childhood Education
Association for Childhood Education
International
11141 Georgia Ave., Ste. 200
Wheaton, MD 20902
5 issues per year

Compensation and Benefits Review
American Management Association
135 W. 50th St.
New York, NY 10020
Bimonthly

Day Care and Early Education
Human Sciences Press, Inc.
72 Fifth Ave.
New York, NY 10011
Quarterly

Developmental Psychology
American Psychological Association
750 First St. NE
Washington, DC 20002-4242
Bimonthly

EAP Digest
Performance Resource Press, Inc.
2145 Crooks Rd., Ste. 103
Troy, MI 48084
Bimonthly

Family Day Caring
Redleaf Press
450 N. Syndicate, Ste. 5
St. Paul, MN 55104-4125
Bimonthly

*Family Relations: Journal of Applied
Family and Child Studies*
National Council on Family Relations
3938 Central Ave. NE, Ste. 550
Minneapolis, MN 55421
Quarterly

Generations
American Society on Aging
833 Market St., Ste. 512
San Francisco, CA 94103
Quarterly

Gerontologist
Gerontological Society of America
1275 K St. NW, Ste. 350
Washington, DC 20005-40006
Bimonthly

HR Magazine: On Human Resource Mgmt.
Society for Human Resource Mgmt.
606 N. Washington St.
Alexandria, VA 22314
Monthly

*Journal of Aging & Social Policy: A Jour-
nal Devoted to Aging and Social Policy*
Haworth Press
10 Alice St.
Binghamton, NY 13904
Quarterly

*Journal of Applied Gerontology: The
Official Journal of the Southern Geron-
tological Society*
Sage Publications
2455 Teller Rd.
Newbury Park, CA 91320
Quarterly

Journal of Marriage and the Family
National Council on Family Relations
3989 Central Ave. NE, Ste. 550
Minneapolis, MN 55421
Quarterly

*Journal of the American Geriatrics
Society*
Williams & Wilkins
428 E. Preston St.
Baltimore, MD 21202
Monthly

Journals of Gerontology
Gerontological Society of America
1411 K St. NW, Ste. 250
Washington, DC 20005-4036
Bimonthly

National Report on Work and Family
Bureau of National Affairs
1231 25th St. NW
Washington, DC 20037
Biweekly

New National Perspective
National Association for Family Day
Care
725 Fifteenth St. NW, Ste. 505
Washington, DC 20005
Bimonthly

*Parent Care: Resources to Assist
Family Caregivers*
University of Kansas Gerontology
Center
Lawrence, KS 66045
Bimonthly

Personnel
American Management Association
135 W. 50th St.
New York, NY 10020
Monthly

Personnel Journal
ACC Communications
245 Fischer Ave., B-2
Costa Mesa, CA 92626
Monthly

Research on Aging: A Quarterly of
Social Gerontology and Adult
Development
Sage Publications
2455 Teller Rd.
Newbury Park, CA 91320
Quarterly

Work and Family Life
Bank Street College
610 W. 112th St.
New York, NY 10025
Monthly

Working Mother
WWT Partnership
230 Park Ave.
New York, NY 10169
Monthly

Organizations

Administration on Aging
330 Independence Ave. SW, Rm. 4146
Washington, DC 20201
202-619-0556

American Association of Retired
Persons (AARP)
1909 K St. NW
Washington, DC 20049
202-434-2277

American Child Care Foundation
1801 Robert Fulton Dr., Ste. 400
Reston, VA 22091
703-758-3583

American Geriatrics Society
770 Lexington Ave.
New York, NY 10021
212-308-1414

American Society on Aging
833 Market St., Ste. 516
San Francisco, CA 94103
415-882-2910

Bank Street College
Work and Family Life Studies
610 W. 112th St.
New York, NY 10025
212-875-4651

Catalyst
250 Park Ave. South
New York, NY 10003-1459
212-777-8900

Child Care Action Campaign
330 Seventh Ave., 17th Fl.
New York, NY 10001
212-239-0138

Child Care Employee Project
6536 Telegraph Ave., Ste. A-201
Oakland, CA 94609
510-653-9889

Child Care Law Center
22 Second St., 5th Fl.
San Francisco, CA 94105
415-495-5498

Child Welfare League of America
440 First St. NW, Ste. 310
Washington, DC 20001-2085
202-638-2952

Children of Aging Parents
Woodburn Office Campus, Ste. 302A
1609 Woodburne Rd.
Levittown, PA 19057
215-945-6900

Children's Defense Fund
122 C St. NW
Washington, DC 20001
202-628-8787

Children's Foundation
725 Fifteenth St. NW, Ste. 505
Washington, DC 20005
202-347-3300

Clearinghouse on Implementation of
Child Care and Eldercare Services
U.S. Department of Labor, Women's
Bureau
200 Constitution Ave. NW, Rm. 53306
Washington, DC 20210
1-800-827-5335

Conference Board Work and Family
Center
845 Third Ave.
New York, NY 10022-6601
212-759-0900

Council for Early Childhood Professional Recognition
1718 Connecticut Ave. NW, Ste. 500
Washington, DC 20009
800-424-4310

Daughters of the Elderly Bridging the
Unknown Together
710 Concord St.
Ellettsville, IN 47429
812-876-5319

Families and Work Institute
330 Seventh Ave.
New York, NY 10001
212-465-2044

Gerontological Society of America
1275 K. St. NW, Ste. 350
Washington, DC 20005
202-842-1257

Head Start
P.O. Box 1182
Washington, DC 20013
202-245-0572

High/Scope Educational Resource
Foundation
600 N. River St.
Ypsilanti, MI 48198
313-485-2000

International Federation on Ageing
601 East St. NW, Bldg. A, Fl. 10,
Rm. 200
Washington, DC 20049
202-434-2430

National Association for the Education
of Young children
1834 Connecticut Ave. NW
Washington, DC 20009-5786
800-424-2460

National Association of Area Agencies
on Aging
600 Maryland Ave. SW, West Wing 208
Washington, DC 20024
202-296-8130

National Association of Child Care Resource and Referral Agencies
2116 Campus Drive, SE
Rochester, MN 53904
800-462-1660

National Association of Family Day
Care
725 Fifteenth St. NW, Ste. 505
Washington, DC 20005
202-347-3356

National Association of State Units on
Aging
600 Maryland Ave. SW, West Wing 208
Washington, DC 20024
202-785-0707

National Child Care Association
1029 Railroad St.
Conyers, GA 30207
800-543-7161

National Council on Rural Aging
409 3rd St. SW, 2nd Fl.
Washington, DC 20024
202-479-6683

National Council on the Aging, Inc.
600 Maryland Ave. SW, West Wing 100
Washington, DC 20024
202-479-6665

National Institute of Senior Centers
409 3rd St. SW, 2nd Fl.
Washington, DC 20024
202-479-6683

National Institute on Adult Day Care
409 3rd. St. SW, 2nd Fl.
Washington, DC 20024
202-479-6680

Older Women's League
730 11th St. NW
Washington, DC 20001
202-783-6686

Parent Action
2 Hopkins Plaza, Ste. 2100
Baltimore, MD 21201
410-752-1790

School-Age Child Care Project
Wellesley College
Center for Research on Women
Wellesley, MA 02181-8259
617-283-2500

Work/Family Directions
930 Commonwealth Ave. South
Boston, MA 02215
800-346-1535

Yale University
Bush Center on Child Development
and Social Policy
P.O. Box 11A
Yale Station
New Haven, CT 06520
203-432-4575

Useful Library of Congress
Subject Headings

Adult Children—Family Relationships
Aged—Home Care—United States
Aged—Medical Care—Government
   Policy—United States
Aged—Medical Care—Social Aspects—
   United States
Aged—Psychology
Aged—Respite Care—United States
Aged—Services for—United States
Aged—United States—Family
   Relationships
Aged-Care—United States
Aged-Care—United States—Case Studies
Aging Parents—Care
Aging Parents—Care—United States
Aging Parents—Home Care—United
   States
Alzheimer's Disease—Patients—Home
   Care
Alzheimer's Disease—Patients—
   Respite Care
Caregivers—United States
Caregivers—United States—Case
   Studies
Caregivers—United States—Psychology
Child Care—United States
Child Care—United States—Statistics
Child Care Services—Government
   Policy—United States

Child Care Services—United States
Children of Working Mothers—United
   States
Children of Working Mothers—United
   States—Statistics
Day Care Centers—United States
Day Care Centers—United States—
   Statistics
Day Care Centers and Industry
Day Care Centers and Industry—
   United States
Day Care Centers for the Aged—
   United States
Employee Assistance Programs—
   United States
Employer Supported Day Care
Employer Supported Day Care—
   United States
Infants—Care—United States
Mothers—Employment—United States
Old Age Assistance—United States
Parent and Adult Child—United States
Senile Dementia—Patients—Home Care
Work and Family—United States
Working Mothers—United States
Working Mothers—United States—
   Statistics

Sometimes I get several meals in a row. Other times I don't have anything for a few days. Sometimes—I just don't really know.
Living Hungry in America, p. 47

6

Hunger and Malnutrition in America

Helen M. Sheehy

When Americans think of hungry or starving people, they most often think of the underdeveloped countries of the world; of countries such as Somalia where a combination of drought and social upheaval has resulted in millions of starving children. The United States gives large quantities of aid to alleviate hunger and malnutrition in foreign countries. Concern for the hungry has even resulted in military operations, such as Operation Restore Hope in Somalia, which provided food aid to that country.

In a society as affluent as America in the late twentieth century, however, it seems unlikely that hunger should be an appreciable problem. Although hunger and starvation on the scale found in many developing countries may not exist in America, evidence from many sources suggests that hunger is a problem, by some accounts a growing problem, for poor people in the United States (Brown & Pizer, 1987; Cohen & Burt, 1989; Food Research and Action Center, 1984; U.S. Conference of Mayors, 1992). Some experts (Citizens' Commission on Hunger in New England, 1984; Food Research and Action Center, 1984; Bread for the World Educational Fund, 1985; Brown, 1989; Maney, 1989) maintain that in the

Helen M. Sheehy is a government documents librarian at The Pennsylvania State University and has worked with government information since 1981. She holds a Bachelor of Science degree in Nutrition Education and a Master of Science in Library Science from Clarion University of Pennsylvania. She spent three years working for the Honduran government and CARE Honduras, teaching nutrition and supervising food distribution programs and clinics for severely malnourished children. She is a member of The Government Documents Roundtable of ALA and 1992/93 Chair of The International Documents Task Force. She has contributed chapters to "Citing Government Information" (Congressional Information Service, 1993) and the *Deskbook of Government Information* (Random House, in press).

past thirteen years, beginning with the implementation of the Reagan administration's budget cuts, there has been an increase in hunger, erasing gains made in the late 1960s and 1970s. Reports from church groups and private charities, soup kitchens and food banks all indicate that the numbers of persons they serve rise annually (U.S. Conference of Mayors, 1992).

Critics who dispute claims of widespread hunger maintain that reports of hunger are anecdotal at best, politically motivated, and that no hard evidence supports the claims (Rector, 1991, 1992; Kondratas, 1985; Leepson, 1983). Those who dispute the existence of hunger point to the increased spending in many federal and state programs, as well as private sources of relief available to feed the poor (Rector, 1991). These food assistance programs, coupled with other entitlement programs such as Aid to Families with Dependent Children (AFDC) and Medicaid, are the "safety net" designed to shield the poor from the worst effects of poverty.

Does hunger exist in America and to what extent? How is hunger measured? Who are the hungry? What are the short- and long-term effects of hunger on individuals and society? What government programs exist to alleviate hunger? Why haven't these programs eliminated the problem of hunger? What is the current direction of government action?

DEFINITIONS

Understanding some basic definitions is useful for comprehending the problem of hunger in America. Although some definitions are provided below, for detailed discussion of terms such as hunger, food security, homeless, low birth weight, and so on, see Leidenfrost, 1993.

Malnutrition. Dietary deficiencies or excesses can cause measurable damage to the health of the victim (Bread for the World Institute, 1991, p. 197). Prolonged dietary deficiencies can lead to overt diseases such as rickets, kwashiorkor, or marasmus, or malnutrition may have more subtle consequences such as anemia, low birth weight, growth failure, or decreased resistance to disease (Citizens' Commission on Hunger in New England, 1985).

Undernutrition. Undernutrition is the measurable change in a person's nutritional status as a consequence of a prolonged deficiency of nutritionally adequate food (Citizens' Commission on Hunger in New England, 1985).

Hunger. Various definitions of hunger exist, some focusing on the physiology of hunger and others on the social aspects. The American Dietetic Association (Hinton, Heimindinger, & Foerster, 1990) defines hunger in terms of its physical effects as "discomfort, weakness, or pain caused by lack of food." Others have defined it in terms of its duration, focusing on hunger as a chronic or recurring problem. Leinwand (1985) defines hunger as "going for extended periods without a full meal, never satisfying your need for food." The Citizens' Commission on Hunger in

New England (1984) defines hunger simply as the "chronic underconsumption of food and nutrients." Linda Randolph of the New York Office of Public Health defines hunger as "involuntarily going without food due to lack of resources" (U.S. House. Select Committee on Hunger, 1989a, p. 15). Allen (1990) defines hunger as an "acute, current food shortage," which may, if it exists over a prolonged period, result in undernutrition.

Food Security and Food Insecurity. More recently, hunger has been defined in terms of food security or insecurity. The U.S. House Select Committee on Hunger (1990, p. 4) defines food security as "access by all people at all times through normal food channels to enough nutritionally adequate food for an active healthy life." Conversely, food insecurity is lack of access to adequate food through normal channels, often requiring people to resort to food banks, soup kitchens, or scavenging. This definition separates hunger from incidences of clinical malnutrition and describes it in terms of its social consequences. Defined this way, hunger need not result in frank malnutrition or undernutrition.

THE PROBLEM: ASSESSING HUNGER

Assessing the extent of hunger in the United States has perplexed many experts and resulted in conflicting estimates of hunger among the nation's poor. Anthropometric measurements, clinical indicators, and food intake surveys have all been used (Paige, 1993; Radimer, Olson, & Campbell, 1990; Habicht & Meyers, 1991). Because frank nutritional diseases, such as kwashiorkor or marasmus, result from prolonged food deprivation, episodic hunger is more difficult to document (Radimer, Olson, & Campbell, 1990).

Various nutrition surveys are conducted by the federal and state governments as well as by private organizations in an attempt to assess the nutritional status of Americans. On the federal level, the National Nutritional Monitoring System, a combined effort of the Department of Agriculture and the Department of Health and Human Services, monitors the clinical indicators of nutritional status through such surveys as the National Health and Nutrition Examination Survey (NHANES), the Nationwide Food Consumption Survey, and the Pediatric Nutrition Surveillance System (U.S. Public Health Service, 1986). However, these surveys were primarily designed to measure the symptoms of malnutrition through clinical indicators, such as low birth weight, anemia, and growth failure in children, and do not effectively address issues of food security. Concern for the inadequacy of current methods led the House Select Committee on Hunger to convene hearings to discuss possible methods for assessing the extent of hunger in the United States (U.S. House. Select Committee on Hunger, 1989a).

Surveys to assess hunger in the United States have shifted focus in recent years and now include food security issues, in addition to signs of clinical malnutrition, as a measure of hunger. Questions related to the adequacy of resources for food were included in the most recent NHANES III questionnaire (U.S. House. Select Committee on Hunger, 1989a). The U.S. Conference of Mayors' annual survey on hunger and homelessness tracks the use of emergency food sources as a measure of hunger (1992). It is the use of these indirect indicators for assessing hunger that has opened the estimates by advocacy groups, such as Food Research and Action Center, to criticism that reports of hunger are "anecdotal" (Demkovich, 1983a; Kondratas, 1986; Rector, 1991, 1992).

One of the most recent attempts to determine food security and insecurity among low-income Americans was the Food Research and Action Center's Community Childhood Hunger Identification Project (CCHIP). The survey questions were designed to determine the number of families who were forced to limit food intake or to skip meals because of inadequate resources. They also examined family income and participation in food assistance programs, such as food stamps, WIC, and school lunch programs, to determine the impact of programs. Using the data gathered from the surveyed sites and extrapolating to the U.S. population as a whole, the researchers concluded that approximately 5.5 million children under twelve were hungry. An additional 12 million were considered to be at risk (Food Research and Action Center, 1991). The House Committee on Agriculture held hearings (1991) to discuss the results of the survey and its value as a method of assessing hunger.

There have also been a number of state and local initiatives designed to determine the incidence of hunger. Surveys have been carried out in Utah, South Carolina, Minnesota, and New York (U.S. House. Select Committee on Hunger, 1989a). On a smaller scale, an ongoing survey of hospital patients in New York tracked the incidence of hunger between 1985 and 1989 (Rosenberg & Bernabo, 1992).

Poverty and adequate nutrition are directly related, and despite some controversy over appropriate measurement techniques, the nutritional status of a population has often been used as a measure of poverty. (Osmani, 1993). Conversely, the U.S. government has considered poverty an accepted measure for the risk of hunger since the Johnson administration began its war on poverty. At that time the method for calculating the poverty line was directly linked to the cost of food (Beeghley, 1983).

To help the poor, it was first necessary to count them, and the President's Council of Economic Advisors (CEA) developed the methodology. Based on a 1955 survey that showed that the average family spent approximately one-third of their income on food, the CEA calculated the cost of an "economy food plan," designed to provide adequate nutrition at low cost, and then multiplied the cost by three. The calculated figure was considered the poverty threshold (Beeghly, 1983). The same baseline figure, adjusted for inflation, is used today to calculate poverty levels. Unfortunately, no attempt has been made to determine if the overall proportion of family income spent on food has changed over time. Thus the higher costs of housing, medical care, and other household expenses are not reflected in poverty-level calculation (Beeghley, 1983; U.S. General Accounting Office, 1992c).

In 1992, the Census Bureau classified 36.9 million Americans (14.5 percent) as poor, 1.2 million more than in 1991. This change represents an increase of 5.4 million Americans since 1989. Of these, approximately 40 percent were children, and 10.8 percent were older Americans (U.S. Bureau of the Census, 1993). Families or individuals who are below the poverty threshold have available to them a number of cash and in-kind transfer assistance programs designed to alleviate the consequences of poverty. Among those assistance programs are Aid to Families with Dependent Children and a number of food assistance programs, such as food stamps, commodity food assistance, school lunch and breakfast programs, summer meals programs, child care programs, etc. (Palmer, 1992). However, socioeconomic indicators should be adjusted to set the food basket as a reasonable percentage of income and to take into account such local variations as high housing costs and the rising costs of medical care (Mayer, 1990).

The 1980s saw a significant shift in the makeup of the poor. The number of poor reached 14.2 percent of the population by 1991 (U.S. House, 1993); the level of poverty deepened; and more single parents and children became poor (U.S. General Accounting Office, 1992c). In addition, changes in public assistance benefits and eligibility criteria meant that these programs were less effective in lifting households out of poverty (General Accounting Office, 1989; U.S. House. Committee on Ways and Means, 1993). The recessions of the early 1980s and 1990s dramatically increased unemployment and threw many formerly middle-class families into the ranks of the "new poor" (U.S. House. Committee on Ways and Means, 1993).

In outlining some of the causes of hunger in the United States, the House Select Committee on Hunger (1993) noted poverty levels as a key issue. The committee focused on the increase in the number of poor persons, especially children, and compared U.S. poverty rates unfavorably with those in other industrialized countries. The committee also noted the increased demand for food stamps and emergency food assistance.

The House Committee on Ways and Means studied the reasons for the increases in poverty as well as the overall effectiveness of government programs in reducing poverty. With the increase in the number of persons living in poverty, per person expenditures (excluding Medicaid) declined by 2 percent between 1979 and 1991 (U.S. House. Committee on Ways and Means, 1993).

THE COSTS OF HUNGER
AND MALNUTRITION

Hunger and malnutrition have significant medical consequences. Numerous studies show that the effects of prolonged malnutrition are severe. Studies range from the classic study of hunger and starvation in the Warsaw Ghetto in 1940 (American Jewish Joint Distribution Committee, 1979) to numerous studies in third world countries (Greene, 1977; Scrimshaw & Wallerstein, 1982).

Productivity

It is generally accepted that well-fed people have the energy to work and are needed for a productive society (Wolanski, 1979; Reed, 1977; Greene, 1977; Scrimshaw & Wallerstein, 1982). The connection between nutrition and health status was the central theme of the government-sponsored National Nutrition Conference for Defense (U.S. Federal Security Agency, 1942).

Iron-deficiency anemias have been proven to reduce work performance in both children and adults (Greene, 1977; Dallman, 1993). Viteri (1982) also studied the relationship between physical labor and nutritional status among highland Guatemalan agricultural workers. He concluded that anemia and inadequate energy consumption in adults had a substantial negative impact on productivity. Adults compensate for inadequate energy intake by reducing activity and thus reducing energy expenditures. He also established that poor nutrition during childhood, which results in impaired growth, affects an adult's ability to perform work. Chronic undernutrition also causes noticeable psychological changes, including listlessness, depression, and other personality changes (Buskirk & Mendez, 1980). Undernutrition also has a significant effect on immunological functions, causing increased susceptibility to disease and increase in the severity of any diseases contracted (Chandra, 1972, 1982; Lewinter-Suskind et al., 1993).

Effects on Learning

Maternal malnutrition is known to have significant effects on the physical and mental development of a fetus. Physically, malnutrition in pregnant women has a significant effect on fetal growth (Pollitt, 1988; Chez, 1993) and results in infants with lower birth weights and significantly lower brain weights (Rush, 1988). Animal studies (Lewis et al., 1988) and studies of human populations indicate that malnutrition, especially if prolonged and severe, has a marked effect on the developing brain (Galler & Ross, 1993). Nutrition is also a factor in conditions such as eclampsia, preeclampsia, and neural tube defects (Davis, 1988). Other physical and mental handicaps may result, at least in part, from nutritional deficiencies (Crawford, 1992).

Hunger and malnutrition have also been shown to affect child behavior (Scrimshaw, 1968; U.S. Public Health Service, 1973; Levitsky, 1979). Some studies show that hunger affects a child's attentiveness and thus learning ability (U.S. Public Health Service, 1973; Conners, 1989; Galler, 1984; Pollitt, 1990). Specific deficiencies, such as anemia, have been shown to have a significant impact on a child's cognitive development (Pollitt, 1990; Dallman, 1993). Even temporary hunger, such as skipping breakfast, impacts a child's ability to learn (Simeon & Grantham-McGregor, 1989; Pollitt, 1988; Meyers et al., 1989). Surgeon General Antonia Novello considered improving nutritional status for children as a key element in the federal education initiative "Healthy Children Ready to Learn" (Novello, Degraw, & Kleinman, 1992).

Studies point out, however, that hunger and malnutrition are not the only factors affecting the learning abilities of children who are hungry. Other environmental factors, such as parental nurturing, also factor heavily into cognitive development (Evans et al., 1980; Lewis et al., 1988; Pollitt, 1990; Galler & Ross, 1993). Improved nutrition coupled with better social and psychological conditions ameliorates many of the effects of malnutrition (Pollitt, 1990).

Given the short- and long-term health consequences, the economic costs of hunger and malnutrition are evident. Decreased productivity, increased frequency of illness and lost work, increased health care costs, and the decreased ability of children to learn all have economic consequences (Scrimshaw & Wallerstein, 1982; Leidenfrost, 1993b).

HISTORICAL PERSPECTIVE

Milbauer and Leinwand (1971) point out that hunger was commonplace in early America, as evidenced in accounts from Jamestown, Virginia, to the settlement of the West. In a society based primarily on subsistence agriculture, however, hunger and malnutrition were most often related to the vagaries of weather, crop failure, or wars; as such, they were temporary or individual problems. The major exception to this was black slaves, who often suffered severe hunger and deprivation with little opportunity to better their living conditions (Hollings, 1970). With the advent of the industrial revolution, the nature of agricultural production in the United States began to change from a subsistence base, where most farm produce was grown and consumed locally, to larger commercial operations with broader markets. The commercial farms often produced large surpluses of foods (Poppendieck, 1986).

The industrial revolution also brought an influx of people to the cities, including large numbers of immigrants in the late 1800s. Those who worked in industrialized cities suffered hunger because of low wages. Economic depression and inflation compounded problems and contributed to breadlines and soup kitchens throughout the country. Unfortunately, government had little motivation to provide aid, and the plight of the poor was considered to be a consequence of their own behavior (Hollings, 1970). The development of the labor unions helped to raise wages and mitigate some of the most devastating effects of poverty, including hunger (Milbauer & Leinwald, 1971).

The surplus of foods resulting from the mechanization of agriculture, especially during the 1910s and early 1920s, caused a major drop in farm prices and drove many farmers from the land into the cities (Poppendieck, 1986).

Still little was done to address hunger as a social problem until the Depression accelerated the crisis. As more farmers lost their land because of high debts and low farm prices, unemployment began to soar in the cities. By 1933, one-third of American workers, approximately 15 million people, were unemployed (Poppendieck, 1986). Breadlines became commonplace, food riots broke out in Oklahoma and Arkansas, and there were reports of Americans scavenging in garbage dumps for food (Poppendieck, 1986; Levenstein, 1993). Even those families living on farms were not immune to hunger. The change from a subsistence farming base to cash cropping left farm families without food to meet their own daily needs. The low crop prices meant they lacked the means to purchase adequate food (Poppendieck, 1986).

Despite the evidence of severe deprivation, the Hoover administration opposed implementation of federal relief programs, maintaining that local governments and private relief agencies, such as the American Red Cross, were best able to meet emergency food needs in their communities (Levenstein, 1993). It was not until the Roosevelt era and the advent of the New Deal programs that the first food-relief programs were instituted (Palmer, 1992).

The first federal food assistance program, the Commodity Distribution Program, was established under the Federal Surplus Relief Corporation in 1933 and was designed primarily to support farm prices through government purchases of surplus agricultural commodities. It was later reorganized under Section 32 of the Agricultural Adjustment Act Amendment of 1935 and administered by the Department of Agriculture (MacDonald, 1977; Jones, 1992). (Public laws cited here may be located at the end of this chapter under "Selected Food Assistance Legislation.") What was essentially begun as a farm price support program eventually provided food to hungry Americans by disposing of surplus commodities through food assistance programs, such as the School Lunch Program, donations to charitable organizations, and direct distribution to the needy (Lipsky & Thibodeau, 1990; Levenstein, 1993; Poppendieck, 1986). Later, in the face of criticism from food retailers that the free distribution program cut into sales of foods, distribution of surplus foods to individuals was modified into a food stamp program, although the foods were still limited to surplus commodities (Lipsky & Thibodeau, 1992). The program required the poor to purchase stamps equivalent to their usual food expenditures and provided additional free stamps to supplement food-purchasing power in local groceries (Maney, 1989).

As America prepared for war, health concerns focused interest on assuring that all Americans had access to an adequate and nutritionally balanced diet. In 1940 the Committee on Food and Nutrition of the National Research Council was established to study the relationship between nutrition and national defense. On May 25, 1941, the committee released the first set of Recommended Dietary Allowances, setting recommended levels of nutrient intakes for the general population. The following day President Roosevelt convened the National Nutrition Conference for Defense, charging participants with the development of a nationwide plan for improving Americans' nutritional status (U.S. Federal Security Agency, 1942).

World War II had several effects on federal food assistance programs. Demand for food to feed the U.S. troops increased along with overseas exports. As a result, agricultural surpluses diminished, thus driving up agricultural prices. Without the need for price supports, the government no longer purchased agricultural commodities in large quantities for distribution to the poor. Also, as the unemployment rate dropped, the perceived need for food assistance diminished (Lipsky & Thibodeau, 1990). Commodity distribution to the needy was largely halted and the food stamp program was discontinued.

The school lunch program survived and was permanently authorized under the National School Lunch Act of 1946. However, what was originally part of the direct commodity distribution program became a cash-subsidy program. Payments were made to states on a matching-funds basis, with the funds to be used to purchase surplus commodities and other foods (Jones, 1992).

During the Truman and Eisenhower administrations, with a postwar economic boom fueled by defense spending and a conservative executive branch, there was little support for extending food assistance programs (Hollings, 1970). There was some expansion of the School Lunch Program (Maney, 1989; Jones 1992), and the scaled-back commodity distribution program continued (Maney, 1989).

Despite a lack of interest from the executive branch, Congress continued to show an interest in increasing food aid. Congress enacted the Agricultural Act of 1954, authorizing the Special Milk Program to provide additional milk to schoolchildren (U.S. Senate. Committee on Agriculture, Nutrition and Forestry, 1983; Jones, 1992). Expansion of the commodity distribution system, food stamps, and food allotment programs were all proposed as means of providing additional food assistance to the poor. In 1959, P.L. 86-341 passed (78 Stat. 608), providing authority to the Department of Agriculture to establish pilot food stamp projects (Maney 1989; Jones, 1992). However, the Eisenhower administration never implemented the legislation.

The Kennedy administration showed more interest in food assistance policy, in part because of conditions Kennedy encountered while campaigning in West Virginia (Lipsky & Thibodeau, 1990). On the first day of his administration, Kennedy signed Executive Order 10914 enlarging surplus commodity distribution. He quickly announced the first sites for food stamp projects authorized under P.L. 86-341 (Maney, 1989). The School Lunch Program was also expanded under Section 11 of the National School Lunch Act Amendments (Jones, 1992).

As a result of several factors, there was a dramatic expansion in food assistance during the Johnson administration. Johnson launched his Great Society War on Poverty, and the civil rights movement focused attention on the plight of minorities, especially in the South (Maney, 1989; Mayer, 1990; Davis, 1969).

The Food Stamp Act of 1964, an initiative of the Kennedy administration, was passed, offering states a choice between food stamps and the commodity-distribution program (Jones, 1992). The Child Nutrition Act of 1966 established the School Breakfast Program. This was followed by the 1968 amendments to the National School Lunch Act and the Child Nutrition Act of 1966, which further broadened programs by establishing the summer and child care food programs (U.S. Senate. Committee on Agriculture, Nutrition, and Forestry 1983; Jones, 1992).

In the late 1960s news reports and surveys highlighting the extent of poverty, hunger, and malnutrition shocked the nation and focused further attention on the problem. The report *Hunger, USA* (Citizens' Board of Inquiry into Hunger and Malnutrition in the United States, 1968) was released in April of 1968, identifying 266 "hunger counties" where conditions were especially critical. In May of the same year, CBS News broadcast *Hunger in America* (see "Sources of Additional Information" at the end of this chapter for details on availability of this program). The Ten State Nutrition Survey authorized by Congress in 1967 verified that hunger was having a significant impact on poor Americans, documenting cases of growth retardation, kwashiorkor, marasmus, anemia, goiter, and other vitamin and mineral deficiencies in large numbers (Hollings 1970; Schlossberg, 1978; U.S. Dept. of Health, Education and Welfare, 1970).

Programs begun under other administrations continued to expand under Richard Nixon. He convened the White House Conference on Food, Nutrition and Health (1969) to develop a series of recommendations for combating hunger and malnutrition. The following year he convened the White House Conference on Children, which again addressed some of the issues related to child nutrition, particularly in the background paper prepared by Leverton (1971). The National Nutrition Policy Study was also conducted during this period (U.S. Senate. Select Committee on Nutrition in Human Needs, 1974a; 1974b).

Other legislative initiatives created a nutrition program for the elderly (P.L. 92-258, 88 Stat. 286), which was extended and expanded in subsequent years. The Nutrition Education and Training Program (NET) provided funds to state educational agencies for programs to teach nutrition to children (Jones, 1992).

By the end of the Nixon administration, expansion of food assistance programs had significantly reduced the level of malnutrition among poor Americans. In a 1976 survey requested by President Nixon, the Department of Agriculture determined that the increased food assistance had reached the most needy, accounting for a substantial increase in food purchases in the poorest counties (Boehm, Nelson, & Longen, 1980).

The Carter administration proposed fundamental changes to the food stamp program (P.L. 95-113, 91 Stat. 958) (Jones, 1992). The elimination of the purchase requirement combined with more restrictive eligibility standards resulted in a significant increase in the number of participants. Hunger advocates suffered a setback late in the Carter administration, however, when child nutrition programs were cut (Maney, 1989).

THE REAGAN-BUSH YEARS

The Reagan administration came to office with an agenda designed to reduce the size of government. As a result, much of the expansion of food assistance programs during the late 1960s and 1970s was reversed as eligibility standards for food assistance tightened and commodity distributions were reduced (Demkovich, 1983b). Although actual dollar amounts for many programs continued to rise, the growth rate slowed substantially (Maney, 1989; U.S. House. Committee on Ways and Means, 1993). Antihunger advocates claimed that, at the same time programs contracted, the increases in unemployment and poverty rates resulted in greater need. Many families, especially the working poor, were now ineligible for food assistance (Food Research and Action Center, 1984; Demkovich, 1983b).

As the recession of the early 1980s deepened, unemployment rose and requests for food assistance increased. Perceptions of the Reagan administration as insensitive to the needs of poor Americans mounted when administration officials dismissed accounts of growing hunger problems as exaggerated (*Do liberals bloat the hunger problem?*, 1984; Wehr, 1983, 1984; Demkovich; 1983a). Presidential Chief of Staff Edwin Meese went so far as to suggest that increased use of emergency food sources, such as food pantries and soup kitchens, did not necessarily indicate increased hunger, but that people used these facilities because the food was free or more convenient (Meese, 1983). Ultimately, concern over increasing hunger prompted the passage of the Temporary Emergency Food Assistance Program (TEFAP). Under the law, additional money was appropriated to distribute commodity foods to states for use by public or nonprofit organizations, such as food banks and soup kitchens, who assisted low-income persons (Jones, 1992).

The controversy over the extent of hunger prompted Reagan to appoint the President's Task Force on Food Assistance to study the adequacy of food assistance programs (Reagan, 1983). The report (*President's Task Force on Food Assistance*, 1984), although acknowledging some problem areas, concluded there was little evidence of widespread hunger. This report was met with skepticism by hunger advocates who charged that task force members were picked primarily for political views that were hostile to increased food assistance (*Do liberals bloat the hunger problem?*, 1984). The Food Research and Action Center (1984) issued a report challenging the conclusions, and Congress convened a joint hearing to discuss the report (U.S. House Committee on Agriculture, House Committee on Education and Labor, and Senate Committee on Agriculture, Nutrition, and Forestry, 1984).

In 1985-1986 Congress was divided over funding for food assistance programs. Studies by such groups as the Physician Task Force on Hunger (1985, 1986), the Citizens' Commission on Hunger in New England (1984), Bread for the World Foundation (1985), and the Food Research and Action Center (1984) continued to surface. Democrats, concerned over continued news stories of widespread hunger (Brown & Pizer, 1987), attempted to expand funding for food programs, while Republicans and the Reagan administration sought to cut programs (Rothman, 1985).

The Bush administration was confronted by a major recession in 1990, 1991, and 1992. Unemployment again rose, poverty figures continued to climb, and reports of hunger by such groups as the Food Research and Action Center (1991) and U.S. Conference of Mayors (1992) continued to appear. Unlike the previous recession, food assistance benefits were not cut, mitigating some of the effects of unemployment (U.S. House. Committee on Ways and Means, 1993).

Despite efforts to control government spending, some food assistance legislation was introduced in the 101st and 102nd Congresses. The Mickey Leland Memorial Domestic Hunger Relief Act was passed as Title XVII of the Food, Agriculture, Conservation, and Trade Act of 1990 (Dumas, 1991; Jones, 1992). The Freedom from Want Act and the Mickey Leland Childhood Hunger Relief Act were introduced in 1991, but did not pass. Food assistance for the homeless was reauthorized under the Stewart B. McKinney Homeless Assistance Act Amendments. Additionally, TEFAP was renamed the Emergency Food Assistance Program and extended through 1995 (Jones, 1992).

In 1992, after holding hearings (U.S. House. Select Committee on Hunger, 1992b), House Concurrent Resolution 302 was introduced, proposing a fourteen-step plan for alleviating hunger problems at the community level. The steps ranged from better coordination among public and private food assistance efforts to needs assessment, outreach programs, and nutrition education (U.S. House, 1992).

THE CLINTON ADMINISTRATION

Hunger made the headlines again in early 1993. When restructuring of House Congressional Committees eliminated the House Select Committee on Hunger, former committee chair Rep. Tony Hall (Ohio) began a hunger strike to attract the attention of the Congress, the Clinton administration, and the American public. He ended the hunger strike twenty-two days later when the Agriculture Department and the World

Bank announced upcoming conferences on both domestic and international hunger problems (*Hall ends fast*, 1993). More recently, the Tufts University Center on Hunger, Poverty, and Nutrition Policy released a study concluding that 30 million Americans, including 12 million children, are hungry. The release of the report prompted Mike Espy, the current Secretary of Agriculture and former member of the House Select Committee on Hunger, to declare that eliminating hunger in America is a high priority in his department (Rakowsky, 1993).

Several initiatives began during the Clinton administration's first year. The budget proposal, both as introduced and as finally passed in the 1993 Omnibus Budget and Reconciliation Act, contained funds for programs under the Mickey Leland Childhood Hunger Relief Act (*Mickey Leland Childhood Hunger Relief Act passes!*, 1993; *Leland hunger bill becomes law*, 1993). This act combined with additional appropriations for food stamps and WIC funding levels designed to provide full funding by fiscal year 1996, which was passed as part of the Agriculture, Rural Development, Food and Drug Administration, and Related Appropriations Act of 1994, significantly increased food program resources (*Congress approves FY 1994 Agriculture Appropriations Act; WIC funds increased*, 1993).

In other Legislative initiatives, Rep. Tony Hall (D-OH) and Rep. Bill Emerson (R-MO) will be the senior member of the new Congressional Hunger Caucus. The caucus will be affiliated with a new nonprofit organization, set up by seed money from a New England hunger activist and entrepreneur. Hall will be the president of the foundation (Jacoby, 1993).

Mike Espy, Secretary of Agriculture, acknowledged the key role of government in combatting hunger (*Government and private sector join forces to end hunger in the United States*, 1993). He also convened the National Hunger Forum in Washington, D.C., on June 17, 1993. The forum, one of the largest since the late 1960's, brought together food advocates, government officials, and food program recipients to discuss actions to reduce hunger (*Espy, Haas host USDA' National Hunger Forum*, 1993).

These actions have encouraged hunger activists, who see greater potential for government involvement in hunger relief (*Government and private sector join forces to end hunger in the United States*, 1993).

THE POLITICS OF HUNGER

Most Americans believe that access to adequate food for a healthy life is a fundamental right for all citizens (U.S. House. Select Committee on Hunger, 1990). However, there is disagreement as to the extent of actual hunger in the United States and the effectiveness of current programs to address any existing problems.

Analysis of congressional debate suggests that views on the extent of hunger and solutions to the problem divide largely along party lines, with Republicans less likely to concede that there are significant hunger problems (Cohen, 1986). Many conservatives dispute the existence of high levels of poverty as well as the inadequacy of food assistance programs (Kondratas, 1985; Rector, 1992; Graham, 1985; Bovard, 1983). Some maintain that the combined income from such programs as AFDC, food stamps, and Medicaid raise most Americans above the poverty line. Rector, of the conservative Heritage Foundation, suggests that the "real" poverty is not insufficient income but "behavioral poverty" or "a breakdown in the values and conduct which lead to the formation of healthy families, stable personalities and self-sufficiency . . ." (Rector, 1992).

POPULATIONS AT RISK

Hunger Among the Homeless

One sector of the population that is particularly vulnerable to hunger and that often falls through the cracks in federal programs is the homeless. (For estimates on the number of homeless, see chapter 7.) In an attempt to gather concrete data on the extent of hunger among the homeless, the House Select Committee on Hunger (1987) surveyed shelters across the country and received responses from 140 shelter managers. Shelters responding ranged in size from those serving under 20 persons to large shelters serving over 100. Although minority members of the committee criticized the methodology of the survey (U.S. House. Select Committee on Hunger, 1987a), the report provides some alarming statistics. Most homeless people rely on shelters for meals, although the majority of shelters do not provide two meals per day. This forces the homeless to rely on soup kitchens, dumpsters, and other free food sites. Also, shelter managers estimated that, although most people in shelters were eligible for food assistance, approximately 49 percent of shelter residents did not receive food stamps.

The report also contained data from the New York City Department of Health on health problems among homeless women and children. Infant mortality, low birth weight, serious growth failure, and hunger-related diseases, such as anemia, as well as repeated respiratory and ear infections, were significantly higher among homeless children than the general population. The department documented an increased incidence of respiratory infections, skin infections, and pulmonary tuberculosis among homeless adults. Other studies have shown similar results (Drake, 1992; Rafferty & Shinn, 1991).

Minorities, the Rural Poor, and Single Persons

Minorities are often among the poorest of Americans. The 1991 poverty rate for blacks was 32.7 percent compared with 28.7 percent for Hispanics and 11.3 percent for whites. Nutrition problems for minorities such as blacks and Hispanics are significantly higher, corresponding to higher rates of poverty (U.S. Senate. Select Committee on Nutrition and Human Needs, 1974a, 1974b). Congress has studied the extent of hunger and nutrition problems of various minority groups during a number of hearings (U.S. House Select Committee on Hunger, 1987a, 1988a, 1991a, 1991b). Migrant workers also have significant health and nutrition problems (Austin & Hitt, 1979). Rural areas also have a high incidence of hunger and health problems, due in large part to high unemployment rates and few job opportunities (Austin & Hitt, 1979; Shotland, Loonin, & Haas, 1988; U.S. House. Select Committee on Hunger, 1987a, 1991a, 1991b, 1991c). The special problems of poor single persons who do not qualify for many welfare programs have also been studied by Congress (U.S. House. Select Committee on Hunger, 1989b).

The Elderly

As a group the elderly are particularly susceptible to hunger problems. The Census Bureau classified 5.7 million elderly Americans as poor or near poor in 1991 (U.S. General Accounting Office, 1992b). Psychological factors play a role (Kohrs et al., 1989). As a result of fixed incomes, as well as high health care and housing costs, the elderly poor often have less disposable income than the nonpoor and consume less than the recommended levels of many nutrients (U.S. General Accounting Office, 1992b). Poor nutrition adversely affects health and increases the costs for medical care among the elderly (Kohrs et al., 1989). Food stamps are a primary source of assistance with over 2 million older Americans having participated in 1987. Congregate meals programs, such as meals on wheels and meals served in community centers authorized under the Older Americans Act and the Child and Adult Care Food Programs, are the second group of programs providing food assistance to the elderly (Kaufman, 1990; Jones, 1989, 1992). In 1991 an estimated 22,600 meals were served each month (Matsumoto, 1991).

A November 1993 report issued by the Urban Institute (Burt, 1993) attempted to measure hunger and food insecurity among the elderly. The study concluded that, depending on how food security was measured, approximately 2.5 to 4.9 million senior citizens suffered food insecurity. The report also indicated that food insecurity is an issue not only for the elderly who fall below the official poverty line but also for the elderly whose income measured 150 percent of poverty.

Women and Children

Among those most vulnerable to the detrimental effects of hunger and malnutrition are pregnant or lactating women, young children, and adolescents. For the developing fetus or child, growth is often rapid and nutrient requirements are correspondingly high (Chez, 1993). Early nutritional deficits can impact a person's health for the remainder of his or her life. The importance of nutrition for women and children was highlighted in the report *Better Health for Our Children*, in which the Select Panel for the Promotion of Child Health stated, "nutrition is [a] major, not marginal, component of efforts to promote health and prevent disease, especially during pregnancy, infancy, childhood, and adolescence when the human organism is growing and developing" (U.S. Public Health Service, 1981, p. 6).

Research indicates that maternal nutrition at conception and during pregnancy can have a significant impact on pregnancy outcomes (Crawford, 1992). A pregnant woman requires an overall higher intake of calories, proteins, vitamins, and minerals for the fetus to maintain optimal growth (Chez, 1993). Poor maternal nutrition can result in a premature or low birth weight infant with health problems. Among the most significant problems are higher rates of infant mortality, mental retardation, and other physical handicaps (Lechtig et al., 1979). Lactating women also require higher food intakes. Dietary inadequacies can lead to maternal health problems as well as decreased milk production (U.S. Public Health Service, 1981).

Young children are easily susceptible to nutritional deficiencies as they grow and develop. Inadequate nutrition during childhood can lead to growth failure, increased susceptibility to disease, and can impact a child's behavior and ability to learn (Galler, 1984; Galler & Ross, 1993; Allen, 1990; Brozek, 1982). One common problem is iron deficiency anemia, which has a marked effect on behavior and intellectual development (Levitsky & Strupp, 1993; U.S. Public Health Service, 1973).

The Department of Health and Human Services set objectives for improving the health of women and children in their report *Healthy Children 2000* (1991). Among the concerns addressed were improvements in the nutritional status of low-income women and children, especially child growth retardation, iron deficiency, infant mortality, and low birth weights. Factors that increase the risk of nutritional and health problems among children are socioeconomic and minority status (U.S. Public Health Service, 1981). Recent surveys of low-income families confirm the children's poor nutritional status by the increased incidence of growth retardation (Yip et al., 1993).

FOOD ASSISTANCE PROGRAMS

Food Stamps

The most important of the food assistance programs, and the program that accounts for more than half of total domestic food assistance expenditures, is the Food Stamp Program (Scheffler, 1988). As of December 1991, program participation had risen to 24.8 million (U.S. House, 1993). In 1988 more than 60 percent of food stamp recipients were children (Pidel, 1988). The program provides coupons that can be used to purchase food items. The amount allotted an individual is designed to provide enough purchasing power to secure a nutritionally adequate diet based on USDA's least expensive Thrifty Food Plan. Benefits in the program average 70 cents per person per meal (Lipsky & Thibodeau, 1990; U.S. House, 1993). Unlike other welfare programs, which specifically target children, women, or the unemployed, the working poor are also eligible for assistance if they meet income requirements, asset limits, and work or job search requirements (U.S. House. Select Committee on Hunger, 1993).

Child Nutrition Programs: Early Intervention

In addition to the Food Stamp Program, there are ten programs designed to provide food assistance specifically to children. They are the School Lunch Program, School Breakfast Program, Child Care Food Program, Summer Foods Service Program, Commodity Assistance, Nutrition Education and Training Program, State Administrative Expenses, Special Milk Program, Commodity Supplemental Foods Program (CSFP), and the Special Supplemental Foods Program for Women, Infants, and Children (WIC) (Jones, 1989).

*School Lunch Program.*The oldest and largest program is the School Lunch Program, established during the Roosevelt administration. In fiscal year 1989, 24.8 million children participated in the program (Jones, 1989). The program provides a basic cash and commodity subsidy for all lunches served, with additional reimbursement for free or reduced-price lunches served to children who meet specified poverty guidelines (Jones, 1989). Meals served under the program are designed to provide approximately one-third of the nutritional requirements of participants (Rush, 1984). Four additional school-based programs supplement the School Lunch Program.

Special Milk Program. Those schools, child care programs, and non-profit institutions that do not participate in the School Lunch Program can receive benefits under the Special Milk Program. Established in 1954 under P.L. 83-690 (68 Stat. 897), participating institutions receive cash reimbursements for milk served (U.S. House. Committee on Agriculture, Nutrition and Forestry, 1983; Jones, 1989).

School Breakfast Program. Begun in 1967 (P.L. 89-642, 80 Stat. 885), this program provides free and reduced-price breakfasts to needy children, with the majority of programs in elementary schools. Eligibility is linked to eligibility for the School Lunch Program (U.S. House. Committee on Agriculture, Nutrition and Forestry, 1983; Jones, 1989) and provides breakfast either free or at a reduced cost for low-income students. Considerably smaller than the School Lunch Program, the Breakfast Program provided meals to approximately 4.4 million schoolchildren in 1991 (Matsumoto, 1991). School breakfasts are designed to provide a high-quality breakfast to participating children and have been shown to affect positively daily food intake (Devaney & Fraker, 1989; Rush, 1988).

Summer Foods Service Program. The summer food program was authorized by Public Law 90-302. The program is designed to serve children during the summer months (U.S. House. Committee on Agriculture, 1983; Jones, 1989). The program provides one to two meals per day to children through public and private schools or local municipal and county government programs in areas where 50 percent or more of school children are eligible for free or reduced-price lunches (U.S. House. Committee on Agriculture 1983; Kauffman 1990; Jones, 1989).

Commodity Assistance. Commodity assistance is available to institutions participating in other meal service programs, such as the Child Care Food and School Lunch programs. Commodities or cash reimbursements allow the purchase of commodity foods for the school feeding programs.

Child Care Food Program. Authorized under the National School Lunch Act, this program provides subsidized breakfasts, lunches, and snacks for children in child care facilities (Jones, 1989).

Services for Women and Children

There are two programs that target both women and young children. They are the Commodity Supplemental Foods Program (CSFP) and the Supplemental Foods Program for Women, Infants, and Children (WIC).

CSFP. The first and smaller program is the CSFP. This program is designed to aid at-risk women and young children by providing USDA surplus commodities at no cost. The program was established in 1969 by USDA regulations under the Agricultural Adjustment Act of 1935. Benefits consist of food packages tailored to meet the specific nutritional needs of the recipient (U.S. Senate. Committee of Agriculture, Nutrition, and Forestry, 1983). In the second quarter of 1991 the CSFP served 282,500 participants at a cost of $17.5 million.

WIC. The larger of the two programs, WIC is designed to reduce the consequences of malnutrition in pregnant or lactating women and young children. The program was established on an experimental basis in 1972 and later authorized as a national program by the National School Lunch

Act and Child Nutrition Act Amendments of 1975 (P.L. 94-105, 89 Stat. 511). Benefits under the program consist of three components: nutritional supplementation, nutrition education, and prenatal care (Shotland, Loonin, & Haas, 1988; Food Research and Action Center, 1988).

To be eligible for participation in WIC a woman must be pregnant, postpartum, or breast-feeding. A child may be up to five years of age. Participants must also meet income eligibility criteria and be certified by a health professional to be at risk nutritionally as determined by a physical examination and laboratory test for iron deficiency (Food Research and Action Center, 1989). Participants in the program receive supplemental food packages (Food Research and Action Center, 1988; Jones, 1990).

It is widely accepted that the WIC program is an effective method of nutritional intervention and that it has a significant impact on birth outcomes. Among the most important studies was the National WIC Evaluation study contracted by USDA (U.S. Dept. of Agriculture, 1987). The study was designed to assess diets and health of women and children enrolled in WIC and compare them with low-income nonparticipants.

The study concluded that the WIC program reduced fetal death rates, prematurity, and low birth weights, as well as increased head circumference in infants. It also stressed the need for follow-up studies to determine the long-term effects of the WIC program (Brown, 1989; Brown, Gershoff, & Cook, 1992; U.S. Dept. of Agriculture, 1987; Rush, 1988; U.S. House. Select Committee on Hunger, 1990; U.S. General Accounting Office, 1989).

The report was surrounded by controversy even before its release. Originally authorized in 1979 and scheduled to be completed in two and one-half years, it was not published until 1986. When the report was finally released, original material written by the research team had been replaced by a compendium of results written by USDA administrators that understated the benefits of WIC. Congress requested that the General Accounting Office investigate the USDA's handling of the report (U.S. General Accounting Office, 1989). After the investigation, the House Select Committee on Hunger held hearings in which the USDA was strongly criticized. Those testifying underscored the purely political motivations for the changes in the report (U.S. House. Select Committee on Hunger, 1990). Rush, principal investigator on the National WIC Evaluation study, also felt it necessary to publish the results of the study independently (1988). In addition, the follow-up studies proposed by the report were never carried out (U.S. House. Select Committee on Hunger, 1990).

Other studies have also pointed to the improvements in the health of low-income women and children enrolled in the WIC program (Mathematica Policy Research, Inc., 1990; Kennedy & Kotelchuck, 1984). In a 1992 study, the General Accounting Office reviewed the results of seventeen separate studies and determined that WIC reduced low birth weights and estimated that substantial cost savings are achieved among WIC participants, particularly in reduced medical costs during an infant's first year (U.S. General Accounting Office, 1992a).

Not everyone has been complimentary to the WIC program. George Graham (1991) of Johns Hopkins University has questioned the positive effects ascribed to the WIC program. Other experts have questioned the methodology Graham used to conclude WIC was a failure and have attributed his opposition to political motivations (Brown, Gershoff, & Cook, 1992).

Despite its critics, WIC has strong support among antihunger advocacy groups (Food Research and Action Center, 1988, 1989; Shotland, Loonin, & Haas, 1988; Children's Defense Fund, 1988). Although the program has generally strong bipartisan support in Congress, it has not been made an entitlement program, which must provide services to all eligible applicants. The WIC program must live within budget appropriations, and the program is underfunded. As a result an estimated 40 to 50 percent of eligible women and children do not receive benefits (Food Research and Action Center, 1988; U.S. House. Select Committee on Hunger, 1988; Jones, 1992). During 1990 unexpected increases in food prices increased the cost of WIC packages, causing some states to scale back program participation and benefits in order to stay within appropriations (Jones, 1990; U.S. House. Committee on the Budget, Task Force on Human Resources, 1990). The Congressional Budget Office estimated the cost of fully funding WIC for 1989 at $3.8 billion, or $1.9 billion more than was appropriated (U.S. House. Select Committee on Hunger, 1988b).

WHY HAVE GOVERNMENT PROGRAMS FAILED?

In the second quarter of fiscal year 1991 government expenditures for food assistance programs reached $7 million (Matsumoto, 1991). Why, despite this, do reports of hungry Americans continue to increase? Advocates for the hungry point to a number of reasons. Programs such as WIC are underfunded (Food Research and Action Center, 1989). Other programs such as the School Lunch, School Breakfast, and Summer Foods Programs are not available to all children and not all eligible children participate in the programs (U.S. Public Health Service, 1981; Jones 1989; Jones 1990).

Food stamps, the largest food assistance program, is estimated to reach only half of the families who are eligible. The General Accounting Office (1988, 1989) studied the reasons for nonparticipation and found that, although some eligible people felt they did not need assistance, lack of adequate outreach programs and other administrative problems were obstacles to participation.

Advocates for the poor also question the method by which food stamp benefit levels are calculated. They point to surveys that show that increased costs for shelter, medical care, and other basic necessities mean individuals have less money available for food purchases than current calculations assume (Food Research and Action Committee, 1991). They also point out that the poor often must rely on small neighborhood stores with higher food costs (U.S. House. Select Committee on Hunger, 1987b). The fact that many households who receive food stamps also regularly use other emergency food services when benefits run out at the end of the month is cited as evidence of program inadequacies. Private efforts have also been inadequate to meet the needs of hungry Americans, with many food banks limiting the number of times a family can request assistance, regardless of need (U.S. Conference of Mayors, 1992).

PRIVATE SECTOR INITIATIVES

Private sector agencies and businesses have also joined the effort to eliminate hunger in America. Food banks and soup kitchens can be found throughout the United States. Antihunger advocacy groups such as the Food Research and Action Center lobby the government and the private sector to develop programs combatting hunger. In addition programs such as Reinvesting in America and Handsnet seek to link private agencies and grassroots organizations and to provide information on innovative and successful programs to fight hunger and poverty. Reinvesting in America (RIA) is an initiative of the World Hunger Year (WHY) foundation created in 1975 by entertainer Harry Chapin. It has cited as model programs efforts such as the Alabama Coalition Against Hunger, Baltimore's Midtown Churches Community Association, and the Seattle Food Committee Resource Networks. RIA is developing a database containing information on model programs such as these to facilitate other grassroot efforts to design antihunger programs (U.S. House. Select Committee on Hunger, 1993). The Handsnet communications network was a joint initiative of Hands Across America and Apple Computer and is designed to link nonprofit organization and state and local government working on antihunger initiatives (*Linking resources to fight hunger and homelessness*, 1989).

Businesses are also taking action to reduce hunger. American Express's "Charge Against Hunger" program proposed to raise $5 million to fight hunger in the United States by contributing two cents to the Share Our Strength organization for every American Express charge transaction made between October 5 and December 31, 1993. American Express donated the first $1 million in October and promoted the program widely on radio and television (*American Express and SOS launch "Charge Against Hunger,"* 1993). Restaurants are also joining the fight against hunger, donating leftover foods to local food assistance programs in an effort to reduce hunger (Zuckerman, 1988; Wiesendanger, 1991; Cheney, 1993).

Church groups are also active on the national level. For example, church organizations such as Catholic Charities, the National Council of

Churches, and Council of Jewish Federation, along with service organizations such as the Red Cross, Salvation Army, and United Way serve on the Emergency Food and Shelter National Board, which assists local organizations with needs assessment and distribution of community resources to hungry and homeless Americans (U.S. House. Select Committee on Hunger, 1992b).

CONCLUSION

Food assistance programs for eliminating hunger in the United States are in place. Groups such as the American Dietetic Association have called for more involvement of dietitians as advocates for the hungry and have stressed that strengthening existing programs is the solution (Hinton, Heimindinger, & Foerster, 1990). The Medford Declaration on Hunger in the United States, developed by a national hunger organization and endorsed by many government officials, businesses, religious leaders, and advocacy groups, proposes a similar strategy (The Medford Declaration, 1992). Perhaps the focus on hunger and current discussions of reform in the welfare system (U.S. House. Select Committee on Hunger, 1991, 1992b) will result in a consensus on how the problem of hunger in America should be addressed.

REFERENCES

Allen, L. H. 1990. Functional indicators and outcomes of undernutrition. *Journal of Nutrition* 120: 924-32.

American Express and SOS launch "Charge Against Hunger." 1993. *Foodlines* 10(4): 8.

American Jewish Joint Distribution Committee. 1979. *Hunger disease: Studies by the Jewish physicians in the Warsaw ghetto.* Current Concepts in Nutrition, vol. 7. New York: John Wiley.

Austin, J. E., & Hitt, C. 1979. *Nutrition intervention in the United States, cases and concepts.* Cambridge: Ballinger.

Beeghley, L. 1983. *Living poorly in America.* New York: Praeger.

Boehm, W. T.; Nelson, P. E.; & Longen, K. A. 1980. *Progress toward eliminating hunger in America.* U.S. Dept. of Agriculture. Agricultural Econcomic Report No. 446. Washington, DC: Government Printing Office.

Bovard, J. 1983. Feeding everybody: How federal food programs grew and grew. *Policy Review* 26: 42-51.

Bread for the World Educational Fund. 1985. *Unfed America '85: Report of hunger watch U.S.A. surveys.* Washington, DC.

Bread for the World Institute on Hunger and Development. 1991. *Hunger, 1992.* Washington, DC.

Brown, J. L. 1989. When violence has a benevolent face: The paradox of hunger in the world's wealthiest democracy. *International Journal of Health Services* 19(2): 257-77.

Brown, J. L., Gershoff, S. N., & Cook, J. T. 1992. The politics of hunger: When science and ideology clash. *International Journal of Health Services* 22(2): 221-37.

Brown, J. L., & Pizer, H. F. 1987. *Living hungry in America*. New York: Macmillan.

Brozek, J. 1982. The impact of nutrition on behavior. In Scrimsahaw, N.S. & Wallerstein, M.B., eds., *Nutrition policy implementation: Issues and experience*. New York: Plenum Press, 21-36.

Burt, M.R. 1993. *Hunger among the elderly: Local and national comparisons. Final report of a national study of the extent and nature of food insecurity among American seniors*. Washington, DC: Urban Institute.

Buskirk, E. R., & Mendez, J. 1980. Energy: Caloric requirements. In Alfin-Slater, R. B., & Kritchevsky, D., eds., *Nutrition and the adult: Macronutrients*. New York: Plenum Press, 49-95.

Chandra, R. K. 1972. Immunocompetence in undernutrition. *Journal of Pediatrics* 18: 1194-1200.

————. 1982. Malnutrition and infection. In Scrimshaw, N. S., & Wallerstein, M. B., eds., *Nutrition policy implementation: Issues and experience*. New York: Plenum Press, 41-52.

Cheney, K. 1993. "Neighbors in Need" takes recession to task. *Restaurants & Institutions* 1033(15): 19-22.

Chez, R. A. 1993. Nutritional factors in pregnancy affecting fetal growth and subsequent infant development. In Suskind, R. M., & Lewinter-Suskind, L., eds., *Textbook of pediatric nutrition*. 2nd ed. New York: Raven Press, 1-7.

Children's Defense Fund. 1988. *A children's defense budget, FY 1989: An analysis of our nation's investment in children*. Washington, DC.

Citizens' Board of Inquiry into Hunger and Malnutrition in the United States. 1968. *Hunger U.S.A*. Boston: Beacon Press.

Citizens' Commission on Hunger in New England. 1984. *American hunger crisis: Poverty and health in New England*. Cambridge: Harvard University, School of Public Health.

Cohen, B. E. 1986. *Hunger in America: Legislative attitudes in food assistance program*. Doctoral dissertation, Brandeis University.

Cohen, B. E., & Burt, M. R. 1989. *Eliminating hunger: Food security policy for the 1990's*. Washington, DC: Urban Institute Press.

Congress approves FY 1994 Agriculture Appropriations Act; WIC funds increased. 1993. *Foodlines* 10(3): 3.

Conners, C. K. 1989. *Feeding the brain: How foods affect children*. New York: Plenum Press.

Crawford. M. A. 1992. Conference review: A think-tank on nutrition in the primary prevention of low birthweight, cerebral palsey, and related handicaps. *Nutrition and Health* 8: 45-55.

Dallman, P. R. 1993. Nutritional anemias in childhood: Iron, folate, and vitamin B12. In Suskind, R. M., & Lewinter-Suskind, L., eds., *Textbook of pediatric nutrition*. 2nd ed. New York: Raven Press, 91-100.

Davis, D. R. 1988. Nutrition in the prevention and reversal of mental retardation. In Menolascino, F. J. & Stark, J. A., eds., *Preventative and curative intervention in mental retardation.* Baltimore: Brookes, 177-219.

Davis, K. S. 1969. *Paradox of poverty in America.* New York: H. W. Wilson.

Demkovich, L. E. 1983a. Hunger in America—Is its resurgence real or is the evidence exaggerated? *National Journal* 15: 2048-52.

———. 1983b. The hungry poor may be the casualties of this year's battle of the budget. *National Journal* 15: 329-32.

Devaney, B., & Fraker, T. 1989. The dietary impacts of the School Breakfast Program. *American Journal of Agricultural Economics* 71: 932-48.

Do liberals bloat the hunger problem? 1984. *Business and Society Review,* 49: 60-64.

Drake, M. A. 1992. The nutritional status and dietary adequacy of single homeless women and their children in shelters. *Public Health Reports* 107: 312-19.

Dumas, K. 1991. Democrats offer major plan on childhood hunger. *Congressional Quarterly Weekly Report* 49: 1058-60.

Espy, Haas host USDA's National Hunger Forum. 1993. *Foodlines* 10(2): 5.

Evans, D.; Bowie, M. D.; Hansen, J. D. L.; Moodie, A. D.; & van de Spuy, H. I. J. 1980. Intellectual development and nutrition. *Journal of Pediatrics* 97: 358-63.

Food Research and Action Center. 1984. *Responses to major findings of Presidential Task Force on Food Assistance.* Washington, DC: FRAC.

———. 1988. National and state profiles of the Special Supplemental Food Program for Women, Infants, and Children. Washington, DC: FRAC.

———. 1989. *Feeding the other half: Mothers and children left out of WIC.* Washington, DC: FRAC.

———. 1991. *Community childhood hunger identification project: A survey of childhood hunger in the United States.* Washington, DC: FRAC. (ERIC ED340798).

Galler, J. R., ed. 1984. *Nutrition and behavior.* Human Nutrition: A Comprehensive Treatise, vol. 5. New York: Plenum Press.

Galler, J. R., & Ross, R. N. 1993. Malnutrition and Mental Development. In Suskind, R. M., & Lewinter-Suskind, L., eds., *Textbook of pediatric nutrition.* 2nd ed. New York: Raven Press, 173-79.

Government and private sector join forces to end hunger in the United States. 1993. *Foodlines* 10(2): 1, 4.

Graham, G. G. 1985. Searching for hunger in America. *Public Interest* 78: 3-17.

———. 1991. WIC: A food program that failed. *Public Interest* 103: 66-75.

Greene, L. S., ed. 1977. *Malnutrition, behavior, and social organization.* New York: Academic Press.

Habicht, J., & Meyers, L. D. 1991. Principles for effective surveys of hunger and malnutrition in the United States. *Journal of Nutrition* 121: 403-7.

Hall ends fast after 22 days. 1993. *CQ Weekly Reports* 51: 1063.

Hinton, A. W.; Heimindinger, J.; & Foerster, S. B. 1990. Position of the American Dietetic Association: Domestic hunger and inadequate access to food. *Journal of the American Dietetic Association* 90: 1437-41.

Hollings, E. F. 1970. *The case against hunger: A demand for a national policy.* New York: Cowles.

Jacoby, M. 1993. Former hunger chair Hall is back in business. *Roll Call,* 17 June, 1993. Text from: CMPGN (Library) ROLLCL (File). (Online database). Referenced 1/6/93. Available on: Lexis/Nexis, Mead Data Central, Dayton, OH.

Jones, J. Y. 1989. *Child nutrition program information and data.* (Major Studies and Issues Briefs of the Congressional Research Service, Reel 10, p. 164). Bethesda, MD: University Publications of America.

———. 1990. *The WIC program: Funding and issues.* (Major Studies and Issue Briefs of the Congressional Research Service, Reel 9, p. 907). Frederick, MD: University Publications of America.

———. 1992. *Federal food assistance legislation, 1935-1991: Chronology and brief description.* (Major Studies and Issues Briefs of the Congressional Research Service, 1992, Reel 2, p. 583). Bethesda, MD: University Publications of America.

Kaufman, M. 1990. Assuring nutrition services for older Americans. In Kaufman, M., ed., *Nutrition in public health: A handbook for developing programs and services.* Rockville, MD: Aspen, 200-19.

Kennedy, E. T., & Kotelchuck, M. 1984. The effect of WIC supplemental feeding on birthweight: A case control analysis. *American Journal of Clinical Nutrition* 40: 579-85.

Kohrs, M. B.; Czajaka-Narins, D. M.; & Nordstrom, J. W. 1989. Factors affecting nutritional status of the elderly. In Munro, H. N., & Danford, D. E., eds., *Nutrition, aging, and the elderly.* Human Nutrition: A Comprehensive Treatise, vol. 6. New York: Plenum Press, 305-33.

Kondratas, S. A. 1985. *Holding hands against hunger: How Americans are being conned.* Backgrounder, no. 512. Washington, DC: Heritage Foundation.

Lechtig, A., et al. 1979. Maternofetal nutrition. In Jelliffe, D. B., and Jelliffe, E. F. P., eds., *Nutrition and growth.* Human nutrition: A comprehensive treatise, vol. 2. New York: Plenum Press, 79-127.

Leepson, M. 1983. Hunger in America. In *Editorial Research Reports,* vol. 2. Washington, DC: Congressional Quarterly, 723-40.

Leidenfrost, N. B. 1993a. *Definitions concerned with food security, hunger, undernutrition, and poverty.* Text from USDA, Extension Service Gopher. Referenced 1/13/94. Available on Internet Gopher Information Client v.2.0-11 (Gopher Server). Follow path Education Base Program-Extension Service (ES), USDA/Nutrition Diet and Health/Poverty, Food Security, Hunger, Undernutrition. Internet address: esusda.gov.

———. 1993b. *An examination of the impact of poverty on health.* Text from USDA, Extension Service Gopher. Referenced 1/13/94. Available on Internet Gopher Information Client v.2.0-11 (Gopher Server). Follow path Education Base Program-Extension Service (ES), USDA/Nutrition Diet and Health/ Poverty, Food Security, Hunger, Undernutrition. Internet address: esusda.gov.

Leinwand, G. 1985. *Hunger and malnutrition in America.* New York: Franklin Watts.

Levenstein, H. 1993. *Paradox of plenty: A social history of eating in modern America.* New York: Oxford University Press.

Leverton, R. M. 1971. Background paper on food and nutrition for the 1970-71 White House Conference on Children and Youth. In U.S. Senate. Committee on Government Operations, *Government research on the problems of children and youth*. Washington, DC: Government Printing Office, 431-84.

Levitsky, D. A., & Strupp, B. J. 1993. The effects of iron deficiency, food additives, and other nutrients on behavior. In Suskind, R. M., and Lewinter-Suskind, L., eds., *Textbook of pediatric nutrition*. 2nd ed. New York: Raven Press, 107-14.

Lewinter-Suskind, L.; Suskind, L. D.; Murthy, K. K.; & Suskind, R. M. 1993. The malnourished child. In Suskind, R. M., and Lewinter-Suskind, L., eds., *Textbook of pediatric nutrition*. 2nd ed. New York: Raven Press, 127-39.

Lewis, P. D.; Jordan, T. C.; Patel, A. J.; & Balazs, R. 1988. Nutrition and brain development. In Meisami, E., & Timiras, P. S., eds., *Handbook of human growth and developmental biology. Vol. I: Neural, sensory, motor and integrative development. Part C: Factors influencing brain development.* Boca Raton, FL: CRC Press, 83-100.

Linking resources to fight hunger and homelessness. 1989. *Nonprofit World* 7(3): 16-19.

Lipsky, M., & Thibodeau, M. A. 1990. Domestic food policy in the United States. *Journal of Health Politics, Policy and Law* 15: 319-39.

MacDonald, M. 1977. *Food, stamps, and income maintenance*. New York: Academic Press.

MacEwan, V. B., & Richardson, J. 1987. *Federal food assistance programs and a brief bibliography on hunger in the United States.* (Major Studies and Issue Briefs of the Congressional Research Service, vol. 1986/87, Reel 9, p 421). Frederick, MD: University Publications of America.

Maney, A. L. 1989. *Still hungry after all these years: Food assistance from Kennedy to Reagan.* Studies in Social Welfare Policies and Programs, no. 11. New York: Greenwood.

Mathematica Policy Research, Inc. 1990. *The savings in Medicaid costs for newborns and their mothers from prenatal participation in the WIC program.* Washington, DC: U.S. Dept. of Agriculture.

Matsumoto, M. 1991. Domestic food assistance costs are rising. *Food Review* 14(4): 40-42.

Mayer, J. 1990. Hunger and undernutrition in the United States. *Journal of Nutrition* 120: 919-23.

The Medford Declaration to end hunger in the United States. 1992. *Nutrition Reviews* 50: 240-42.

Meese, E. 1983. What Meese said to reporters. *New York Times,* 15 December, B3.

Meyers, A. F.; Sampson, A. E.; Weitzman, M.; Rogers, B. L.; & Kayne, H. 1989. School Breakfast Program and school performance. *American Journal of Diseases in Childhood* 143: 1239.

Mickey Leland Childhood Hunger Relief Act passes! 1993. *WHY* 13: 42.

Milbauer, B., & Leinwand, G. 1971. *Hunger*. Problems of American Society. New York: Pocket Books.

Novello, A. C.; Degraw, C.; & Kleinman, D. V. 1992. Healthy children ready to learn. *Public Health Reports* 107: 3-15.

Office of the President. 1969. *White House Conference on food, nutrition and health: Final report*. Washington, DC: Government Printing Office.

Osmani, S. R., ed. 1992. *Nutrition and poverty.* WIDER Studies in Development Economics. Oxford: Clarendon Press.

Paige, D. M. 1993. Nutritional surveillance and supplemental food programs in the United States. In Suskind, R. M., & Lewinter-Suskind, L., eds., *Textbook of pediatric nutrition.* 2nd ed. New York: Raven Press, 517-29.

Palmer, E. A. 1992. Evolution of anti-poverty programs . . . from President Roosevelt's New Deal. *Congressional Quarterly Weekly Report* 50: 1251-52.

Physician Task Force on Hunger in America. 1985. *Hunger in America: The growing epidemic.* Cambridge: Harvard University Press.

————. 1986. *Hunger counties 1986: The distribution of America's high risk areas.* Cambridge: Harvard University Press.

Pidel, L. 1988. A look at the major food programs: Are we meeting our goals? *Food and Nutrition* 18(2): 2-13.

Pollitt, E. 1988. Developmental impact of nutrition on pregnancy, infancy, and childhood: Public health issues in the United States. In Bray, N. W., ed., *International review of research in mental retardation.* San Diego: Academic Press, 33-80.

————. 1990. *Malnutrition and infection in the classroom.* Paris: UNESCO.

Poppendieck, J. 1986. *Breadlines knee-deep in wheat: Food assistance in the Great Depression.* New Brunswick, NJ: Rutgers University Press.

Porter, J. W. G., & Rolls, B. A., eds. 1973. *Proteins in human nutrition.* New York: Academic Press.

President's Task Force on Food Assistance. 1984. *Report.* Washington, DC.

Radimer, K. L.; Olson, C. M.; & Campbell, C. C. 1990. Development of indications to assess hunger. *Journal of Nutrition* 120 (Suppl. 11): 1544-48.

Rafferty, Y., & Shinn, M. 1991. The impact of homelessness on children. *American Psychologist* 46(11): 1170-79.

Rakowsky, J. 1993. Tufts study finds 12 million children in US go hungry. *Boston Globe,* 16 June 1993, 80.

Reagan, R. 1983. Memorandum on establishing a task force on food assistance. In *Public papers of the presidents of the United States.* Washington, DC: Government Printing Office: 1118-19.

Rector, R. E. 1991. *Hunger and malnutrition among American children.* Backgrounder, no. 843. Washington, DC: Heritage Foundation.

————. 1992. Food fight: How hungry are America's children. In *Federal policy perspectives on welfare reform: Rhetoric, reality, and opportunities. Hearing, 9 April 1992.* Serial 102-25. U.S. House. Select Committee on Hunger. Washington, DC: Government Printing Office: 89-94.

Reed, M. S. 1977. Malnutrition and human performance. In Greene, L. S., ed. *Malnutrition, behavior, and social organization.* New York: Academic Press, pp. 95-107.

Rosenberg, E., & Bernabo, L. 1992. Hunger, a hospital survey. *Social Work in Health Care* 16(3): 83-95.

Rothman, R. 1985. Increased funding for food programs sought. *CQ Weekly Reports* 43 (20 April): 736-38.

Rush, D. 1988. The national WIC evaluation. *American Journal of Clinical Nutrition* 48 (Suppl. 2): 389-519.

Rush, D., ed. 1984. Symposium on national evaluation of the school nutrition programs. *American Journal of Clinical Nutrition* 40(2): 361-464.

Scheffler, W. 1988. A look at the major food programs: Are we meeting our goals? *Food and Nutrition* 18(2): 2-6.

Schlossberg, K. 1978. Nutrition and government policy in the United States. In Winikoff, B., ed., *Nutrition and national policy*. Cambridge: MIT Press, 325-59.

Scrimshaw, N. S., & Gordon, J. E. 1967. *Malnutrition, learning, and behavior: Proceedings of the International Conference on Malnutrition, Learning and Behavior.* Massachusetts Institute of Technology, March 1-3, 1967. Cambridge: MIT Press.

Scrimshaw, N. S, & Wallerstein, Mitchell B., eds. 1982. *Nutrition policy implementation: Issues and experience.* New York: Plenum Press.

Shotland, J.; Loonin, D.; & Haas, E. 1988. *Off to a poor start: Infant health in rural America.* Washington, DC: Public Voice for Food and Health Policy.

Simeon, D. T., & Grantham-McGregor, S. 1989. Effects of missing breakfast on the cognitive functions of school children of differing nutritional status. *American Journal of Clinical Nutrition* 49: 646-53.

U.S. Bureau of the Census. 1993. *Poverty in the United States, 1992.* Current Population Survey. Consumer Income, P-60, No. 185. Washington, DC: Government Printing Office.

U.S. Conference of Mayors. 1992. *Status report on hunger and homelessness in America's cities: 1992.* Washington, DC.

U.S. Dept. of Agriculture. 1987. *National evaluation of the special supplemental food program for women, infants, and children.* ASI 1987: 1368-1. Washington, DC: Government Printing Office.

U.S. Dept. of Health, Education, and Welfare. 1970. *Ten state nutrition survey, highlights.* DHEW Publication No. (HSM) 72-81-34. Atlanta: Center for Disease Control.

U.S. Dept. of Health and Human Services. 1991. *Healthy children 2000.* Washington, DC: Government Printing Office.

U.S. Federal Security Agency. 1942. *Proceedings of the national nutrition conference for defense. May 26-28, 1941.* Pr 32.4502:N 21. Washington, DC: Government Printing Office.

U.S. General Accounting Office. 1988. *Food stamps: Reasons for nonparticipation, 1989.* (GAO/PEMD-89-5BR). Washington, DC: Government Printing Office.

———. 1989. *Food stamp program: Administrative hindrances to participation.* (GAO/RCED-89-4). Washington, DC: Government Printing Office.

———. 1992a. *Early intervention: Federal investments like WIC can produce savings.* (GAO/HRD-92-18). Washington DC: Government Printing Office (GA 1.13:HRD 92-18).

———. 1992b. *Elderly Americans: Health, housing, and nutrition gaps between the poor and nonpoor.* (GAO/PEMD 92-29). Washington, DC: Government Printing Office.

———. 1992c. *Poverty trends, 1980-88: Changes in family composition and income sources among the poor.* (GAO/PEMD 92-34). Washington, DC: Government Printing Office.

U.S. House. 1992. *Communities making the transition to hunger free status.* (House Report 102-616). Washington, DC: Government Printing Office.

———. 1993. *Progress report of the select committee on hunger.* (House Report 102-1099). Washington, DC: Government Printing Office.

———. Committee on Agriculture. 1991. *Hunger in america, its effects on children and families, and implications for the future. Hearing, 8 May 1991.* (Serial No. 102-13). Washington, DC: Government Printing Office.

———. Committee on the Budget. Task Force on Human Resources. 1990. *Women, Infants and Children (WIC): The current crisis, Hearing, 27 June 1990.* Washington, DC: Government Printing Office.

———. Committee on Education and Labor. Committee on Agriculture and U.S. Senate. Committee on Agriculture, Nutrition, and Forestry. 1984. *Review of the report of the President's task force on food assistance. Joint Hearing, 26 Jan. 1984.* (Serial No. 98-54). Washington, DC: Government Printing Office.

———. Committee on Ways and Means. 1993. *Sources of the increases in poverty, work effort, and income distribution data.* (WCMP102-2). Washington, DC: Government Printing Office.

———. Select Committee on Hunger, and U.S. Senate Committee on Agriculture, Nutrition, and Forestry. 1990. *National WIC evaluation: Reporting and follow-up issues. Joint Hearing, 24 January 1990.* (Serial No. 101-13). Washington, DC: Government Printing Office.

———. Select Committee on Hunger. 1984. *Accessibility and effectiveness of anti-hunger programs. Hearings, 23 June 1984.* (Serial No. 98-1). Washington, DC: Government Printing Office.

———. 1987a. *Farm crisis: Growing poverty and hunger among American food producers. Hearing, 24 June 1987.* (Serial No. 100-10). Washington, DC: Government Printing Office.

———. 1987b. *Obtaining food: Shopping constraints on the poor.* Committee Print. Washington, DC: Government Printing Office.

———. 1988a. *Poverty and hunger in Hispanic America: The inadequacy of data for policy planning. Hearings, 10 July 1987.* (Serial No. 100-11). Washington, DC: Government Printing Office.

———. 1988b. *Strategies for expanding the special supplemental food program for women, infants, and children (WIC) participation: A survey of WIC directors.* Committee Print. Washington, DC: Government Printing Office.

———. 1989a. *Food security and methods of assessing hunger in the United States. Hearing, 29 March 1989.* (Serial No. 101-2). Washington, DC: Government Printing Office.

———. 1989b. *Hunger and poverty among single persons: Is there a safety net for them?* (Serial No. 101-8). Washington, DC: Government Printing Office.

———. 1990. *Food security in the United States.* Commitee Print. Washington, DC: Government Printing Office.

———. 1991a. *Food assistance in rural communities: Problems, prospects, and ideas from urban programs. Hearing, 5 April 1991.* (Serial No. 102-1). Washington, DC: Government Printing Office.

———. 1991b. *Hearing on Appalachia: Poverty alleviation strategies. Hearing, 22 July 1991.* (Serial No. 102-7). Washington, DC: Government Printing Office.

———. 1991c. *Mississippi revisited: Poverty and hunger problems and prospects. Hearing, 3 May 1991.* (Serial No. 102-5). Washington, DC: Government Printing Office.

———. 1991d. *Redrawing the poverty line: Implications for fighting hunger and poverty in America. Hearing, 4 October 1990.* (Serial No. 101-24). Washington, DC: Government Printing Office.

———. 1992a. *Beyond public assistance: Where do we go from here?* (Serial No. 102-23). Washington, DC: Government Printing Office.

———. 1992b. *Hunger free communities: A local response to a national problem. Hearing, 2 April 1992.* (Serial No. 102-24.) Washington, DC: Government Printing Office.

———. 1993. *Reinvesting in America: New ideas from around the country for fighting hunger and poverty. Hearing, 24 Sept. 1992.* Washington, DC: Government Printing Office.

U.S. Public Health Service. 1973. *Nutrition development and social behavior,* D. J. Kallen, ed. (DHEW Publication No. (NIH) 73-242). Washington, DC: Government Printing Office.

———. 1981. *Better health for our children: The report of the select panel for the promotion of child health.* (DHHS (PHS) Publication No. 79-55071). Washington, DC: Government Printing Office.

———. 1986. *Nutrition monitoring in the United States.* (DHHS Publication No. (PHS) 86-1255). Hyattsville, MD: Public Health Service.

U.S. Senate. Committee on Agriculture, Nutrition, and Forestry. 1983. *Child nutrition programs: Description, history, issues and options.* (Committee Print, S.Prt. 98-15). Washington, DC: Government Printing Office.

———. Select Committee on Nutrition and Human Needs. 1974a. *Nutrition and special groups, national nutrition policy study—1974. Hearings, 19, 20, 21 June 1974.* Vol. 3A. Washington, DC: Government Printing Office.

———. 1974b. *Nutrition and special groups, national nutritional policy study— 1974. Hearings, 19, 20, 21 June 1974.* Part 3A-Appendix. Washington, DC: Government Printing Office.

Viteri, F. E. 1982. Nutrition and work performance. In Scrimshaw, N. S., & Wallerstein, M. B., eds., *Nutrition policy implementation: Issues and experience.* New York: Plenum Press.

Wehr, E. 1983. Food policy battles ahead: Congress, administration debate need for more help to fight hunger in America. *CQ Weekly Report* 41: 881-86.

———. 1984. Report of task force draws mixed reaction from the Hill. *CQ Weekly Report* 42: 51-52.

Wiesendanger, B. 1991. If they can recycle aluminum, why not lasagna? *Sales and Marketing Management* 143(12): 91-92.

Wolanski, Napoleon. 1979. The adult. In Jelliffe, D. B., & Jelliffe, E. F. P., eds. *Nutrition and growth* (Human Nutrition: A Comprehensive Treatise, vol. 2). New York: Plenum, p. 254-69.

Yip, R.; Parvanta, I.; Scanlon, K.; Berland, E. W.; Russell, C. M.; & Trowbridge, F. L. 1992. Pediatric nutrition surveillance system—United States, 1980-1991. *MMWR, CDC Surveillance Summaries* 41 (SS-7): 1-24.

Zuckerman, D. 1988. Hunger in America: Independents can help, and do. *Restaurant Management* 2(12): 48-54.

SOURCES OF
ADDITIONAL INFORMATION

Bibliographies

Leidenfrost, N. B. *Poverty, food security, hunger, and undernutrition. selected bibliography.* Text from USDA, Extension Service Gopher. Referenced 1/13/94. Available on Internet Gopher Information Client v.20-11 (Gopher Server). Follow path Education Base Program - Extension Service (ES), USDA/Nutrition, Diet and Health/Poverty, Food Security, Hunger, Undernutrition. Internet address: esusda.gov.

Nonprint Materials

Hunger in America. 1968. New York: Carousel Films, Inc. 54-minute film.

Hunger in America. 1989. Concord, MA: Stuart Television Productions.

Selected Food Assistance Legislation

The following is a list of laws that either enacted new food assistance legislation or substantially changed programs already available. It is not a complete list.

Age Discrimination Act of 1975, Amendments (PL 95-65, 11 July 1977). *United States Statutes At Large* 91 pp. 269.

Agricultural Adjustment Act, Amendment Act, Amendments (PL 74-320, 24 Aug. 1935). *United States Statutes At Large* 49 (pt. 1) pp. 774-75.

Agriculture, Rural Development, Food and Drug Administration, and Related Appropriations Act of 1994. (PL 103-111, 21 Oct. 1993) *United States Statutes At Large,* 107, pp. 1046-1081.

Agriculture and Consumer Protection Act of 1973, Amendments (PL 93-347, 12 July 1974). *United States Statutes At Large* 88 pp. 340-41.

Agriculture and Consumer Protection Act of 1973 (PL 93-86, 10 Aug. 1973). *United States Statutes At Large* 87 pp. 221-50.

Child Nutrition Act of 1966 (PL 89-642, 11 Oct. 1966). *United States Statutes At Large* 80 pp. 885-90.

Child Nutrition Amendments of 1987 (PL 95-627, 10 Nov. 1978). *United States Statutes At Large* 92 pp. 3603-26.

Child Nutrition and WIC Reauthorization Act of 1989 (PL 101-147, 10 Nov. 1989). *United States Statutes At Large* 103 pp. 877-919.

Food Security Act of 1985 (PL 99-198, 23 Dec. 1985). *United States Statutes At Large* 99 pp. 1354-1660.

Food Stamp Act Amendments of 1982 (PL 97-253, 8 Sept. 1982). *United States Statutes At Large* 96 pp. 772-89.

Food Stamp Act of 1964 (PL 88-525, 31 Oct. 1964). *United States Statutes At Large* 78 pp. 703-9.

Food Stamp Act of 1964 (PL 91-295, 11 Jan. 1971). *United States Statutes At Large* 84 pp. 2048-52.

Food Stamp Act of 1977 (PL 95-113, 29 Sept. 1977). *United States Statutes At Large* 91 pp. 958-81.

Food Stamp and Commodity Distribution Amendments of 1981 (PL 97-98, 22 Dec. 1981). *United States Statutes At Large* 95 pp. 1282-94.

Mickey Leland Childhood Hunger Relief Act (PL 103-66, 10 Aug. 1993). *United States Statutes at Large* 107 pp. 672-681.

Mickey Leland Memorial Domestic Hunger Relief Act (P.L. 101-624, 28 Nov. 1990) *United States Statutes at Large* 104 pp. 3783-3817.

National School Lunch Act (PL 79-396, 3 June 1946). *United States Statutes At Large* 60 pp. 230-34.

National School Lunch Act, Amendments (PL 92-153, 5 Nov. 1971). *United States Statutes At Large* 85 pp. 419-20.

National School Lunch Act, Amendments (PL 92-433, 26 Sept. 1972). *United States Statutes At Large* 86 pp. 724-31.

National School Lunch Act Amendments (PL 87-823, 15 Oct. 1962). *United States Statutes At Large* 60 pp. 944-47.

National School Lunch Act and Child Nutrition Act, Amendments (PL 90-302, 7 May 1968). *United States Statutes At Large* 82 pp. 117-19.

National School Lunch Act and Child Nutrition Act, Amendments (PL 91-248, 14 May 1970). *United States Statutes At Large* 84 pp. 207-14.

National School Lunch Act and Child Nutrition Act Amendments of 1973 (PL 93-150, 7 Nov. 1973). *United States Statutes At Large* 87 pp. 560-64.

National School Lunch and Child Nutrition Act Amendments of 1974 (PL 93-326, 30 June 1974). *United States Statutes At Large* 88 pp. 286-87.

National School Lunch and Child Nutrition Act Amendments of 1975 (PL 94-105, 7 Oct. 1975). *United States Statutes At Large* 89 pp. 511-30.

Older American Act of 1965, Amendments (PL 92-258, 22 May 1972). *United States Statutes At Large* 88 pp. 88-95.

Older American Act of 1965, Amendments (PL 93-351, 12 July 1974). *United States Statutes At Large* 99 pp. 357-58.

Stuart B. McKinney Homeless Assistance Act (PL 100-77, 22 July 1987). *United States Statutes At Large* 101 pp. 482.

Temporary Emergency Food Assistance Act of 1983 (PL 98-8, 24 May 1983). *United States Statutes At Large* 97 pp. 35-36.

Indexes/Databases

CIS
Congressional Information Service
4520 East-West Hwy.
Bethesda, MD 20814-3398
301-654-1550
Print, online, and CD-ROM formats

*Major Studies and Issue Briefs of the
Congressional Research Service*
University Publications of America
4520 East-West Hwy., Ste. 800
Bethesda, MD 20814-3389
301-657-3200
Print Format

*Monthly Catalog of U.S. Government
Publications*
U.S. Government Printing Office
Superintendent of Documents
Washington, DC 20402-9341
202-783-3238
Print, online, and CD-ROM formats

*Nutrition Abstracts and Reviews.
Series A. Human & Experimental*
C.A.B. International
North American Office
845 N. Park Ave.
Tucson, AZ 85719
800-528-4841
Print format

PAIS INTERNATIONAL
Public Affairs Information Service, Inc.
512 W. 43rd St.
New York, NY 10036
212-736-6629
Print, online, and CD-ROM formats

Reports and Testimony
U.S. General Accounting Office
441 G St. NW
Washington, DC 20548
202-512-6000
Print format

Periodicals

Congressional Quarterly Weekly Report
Congressional Quarterly, Inc.
1414 22nd St. NW
Washington, DC 20037
800-432-2250

Food Review
U.S. Dept. of Agriculture
1301 New York Ave. NW, Rm. 228
Washington, DC 20005-4789
800-999-6779

*Foodlines: A Chronicle of Hunger and
Poverty in America*
Food Research and Action Center
1875 Connecticut Ave. NW, Ste. 540
Washington, DC 20009
Bimonthly

Antihunger Advocacy Groups

Food Research and Action Center and
National Anti-Hunger Coalition
1875 Connecticut Ave. NW, Ste. 540
Washington, DC 20009
202-986-2200

Freedom from Hunger Foundation
1644 DaVinci Ct.
P.O. Box 2000
Davis, CA 95617

National Student Campaign Against
Hunger and Homelessness
29 Temple Pl.
Boston, MA 02111
617-292-4823

Second Harvest, the National Food-
bank Network
116 S. Michigan Ave., Ste. 4
Chicago, IL 60603
312-263-2303

Share Our Strength
c/o Bill Shore
1511 K St. NW, Ste. 600
Washington, DC 20005
202-393-2925

U.S.A. Harvest (USAH)
P.O. Box 1638
Louisville, KY 40201-1628
800-872-4366

Electronic Bulletin Board Services

Pennpages (Electronic Bulletin Board)
Pennsylvania State University
College of Agriculture
University Park, PA 16802
Internet address: psupena.psu.edu

Useful Library of Congress
Subject Headings

Aging—Nutritional Aspects
Children—Nutrition—Government
    Policy—United States
Children—Nutrition—Law and
    Legislation—United States
Children—Nutrition—Psychological
    Aspects
Food Relief—Law and Legislation—
    United States
Food Relief—United States
Food Stamp Program—Law and
    Legislation—United States
Food Stamp Program—United States
Food Supply—Government Policy—
    United States
Food Supply—United States

Human Behavior—Nutritional Aspects
Hunger
Hunger—United States
Infants—Nutrition
Malnutrition—United States
Malnutrition in Children—United
    States
Meals on Wheels Programs
Nutrition—Evaluation
Nutrition Policy—United States
Poor—Nutrition—Government Policy
Pregnancy—Nutritional Aspects
Public Welfare—United States
Special Supplemental Food Program
    for Women, Infants, and Children

*People who are homeless are not social inade-
quates. They are people without homes.*
Sheila McKechnie, 1985

7

The Homeless

Debora Cheney

The homeless, although not new to American society, became a more visible and disturbing presence during the 1980s. Without a doubt, the problem of homelessness spans a wide variety of social, economic, medical, and political issues, including mental illness, unemployment, poverty, housing policy, medical care, substance abuse, and education. Not only is the issue of homelessness affected by each of these areas, it also touches a broad range of Americans. The "new homeless"—women, families, children, youth, the elderly, and minorities (especially blacks and Hispanics)—have become increasingly prevalent during the 1980s. There are now more Americans than at any other time in history who are "at risk" of becoming homeless and who, like those before them, fear that last step between poverty and homelessness.

RESEARCH ON HOMELESSNESS

As the problem of homelessness became increasingly more visible during the 1980s, scholarly and governmental interest reflected this growth and visibility. As a result, most studies and literature on the subject are relatively new, with few studies between the post-World War II period and the beginning of the 1980s. Toward the end of the 1980s a growing volume and variety of literature became available.

Debora Cheney is Head of the Documents/Maps section at The Pennsylvania State University Libraries. From 1990 to 1992, she was the State/Local Documents Librarian and a social science cataloger at Penn State. Prior to that she worked as a reference librarian at Bucknell University. Throughout her professional career, her areas of emphasis have been in reference and the use of technology to meet user needs. She has authored several articles on issues of software and on-line systems and is a frequent speaker on these issues. She has been an active member of ALA/RASD's Machine Assisted Reference Section.

Because of the problems involved in studying a large, geographically dispersed homeless population, much of the literature focuses on a single city or state. Local variations in population and other factors that influence homelessness present some problems when comparing these studies. In addition, the lack of an agreed-upon definition of homelessness, as well as the difficulties of counting the homeless, has led to further debate about the accuracy, comparability, and reliability of many studies.

Studies of the homeless have identified a variety of causes for homelessness and tend to fall into two groups: individual (or internal) causes and institutional (or external) causes. The most widely studied external causes are the decline in the availability of low-cost housing; the growing number of persons falling below the poverty line combined with reductions in federal support services; and deinstitutionalization of the mentally ill. The most widely studied internal causes include substance abuse and mental illness. Research is beginning to expand into new and related areas, such as the ability to educate homeless children and adults; the impact of homelessness on the psychology of children; and its impact on their physical health. A growing body of research is appearing that studies specific homeless subpopulations—children and their families, veterans, rural homeless, and youth. In addition, the homeless subpopulations are increasingly distinguished as episodic (families, for example) or chronic (the mentally ill, for example) homeless. The episodic homeless are those whose homelessness is of relatively short duration, but for whom homelessness may occur repeatedly over time, and the chronic homeless are those whose homeless is long-standing.

Further, because many researchers conclude homelessness is caused by problems inherent in the "system," much of the literature also identifies policy areas that authors believe should be reviewed and provides recommended solutions. Thus, a study of the homeless and homelessness is closely interwoven with the political process and requires some understanding of major government programs, legislation, and statistical sources. For this reason, many federal, state, and local government publications are rich sources of information.

The homeless literature has one characteristic not common to many areas of scholarly research: Even the most scholarly studies frequently include personal stories, vignettes, and photographs of the homeless. Clearly, authors believe that the many and varied stories of the homeless can best illustrate their problems and the lives they lead. Stories are frequently used to illustrate gaps in government funding or services or to refute common assumptions or myths related to the homeless. In fact, much of the literature of the early 1980s is more storylike than scholarly. Thus, researching any area related to the homeless and homelessness, unlike many other areas of scholarly interest, also includes a "real-life" view of the life and living conditions of the people being studied.

Because of the recent boom in literature on homelessness, this chapter will focus primarily on monographic studies. Many major studies, originally appearing in periodical literature, have been published as monographs or are well cited or included in collections of essays. The

"Bibliographies" and "Indexes/Databases" sections at the end of the chapter can be used to locate shorter studies about specific communities, problems, or subpopulations of the homeless.

HISTORY OF HOMELESSNESS

Perhaps one of the most well-known "records" of homelessness in America is John Steinbeck's *The Grapes of Wrath* (Steinbeck, 1939). Steinbeck's novel records only a single period in American history; yet the history of homelessness is both older and more recent than Steinbeck, beginning in the fourteenth century and including "the hippies" of the 1960s (Miller, 1991). In fact, tramps, vagrants, bums, and migrant laborers have always been a part of the American scene. The number of homeless and the reasons for homelessness among these groups have typically varied with the economic conditions of the times (Monkonnen, 1984). Some studies documented the life of specific homeless populations during the 1920s (Anderson, 1923); the Great Depression and the 1930s (Anderson, 1940); the post-World War II period, with the development of Skid Row areas (Bahr & Caplow, 1973); and the 1970s and 1980s (Hopper & Hamberg, 1984).

Studies such as these help to document the changing numbers, living conditions, reasons, and attitudes toward homelessness during each of these periods. They also help to document who made up the homeless population in each of these periods, allowing scholars to compare the current homeless population with previous historical periods. Comparability, however, is difficult, not only between historical periods, but also between communities, states, and regions within the United States. This is, in part, due to the differing definitions used by scholars and government agencies at the federal, state, and local levels.

DEFINITION OF HOMELESSNESS

One of the recurrent problems within the study and analysis of homelessness is the lack of a single definition of what constitutes homelessness that is agreed upon by all scholars, government agencies, and activists. Without a definition of what constitutes homelessness, there can be no agreed-upon figures about the numbers of homeless, who those homeless are, the best services for those homeless, or the amount of money needed to help those homeless. For this reason, nearly every study begins with a discussion of this issue.

The definitions that are used are wide-ranging and can cause dramatic differences in the total numbers of homeless counted. Nearly every definition omits or excludes some part of the homeless population. Ultimately, this contributes to concerns about the reliability of each study's figures. However, with the passage of the Stewart B. McKinney Homeless Assistance Act (P.L. 100-77), a definition is now available that provides a central focus, but not a definitive definition. A homeless individual (1) lacks a fixed, regular, and adequate nighttime residence; and (2) has a primary nighttime residence that is (a) a supervised publicly or privately operated shelter designed to provide temporary living accommodations (including welfare hotels, congregate shelters, and transitional housing for the mentally ill); (b) an institution that provides a temporary residence for individuals intended to be institutionalized; or (c) a public or private place not designed for, or ordinarily used as, a regular sleeping accommodation for human beings. Because the McKinney Act's definition of homelessness largely accounts for the visible homeless, it fails to include many groups who others would argue should be included. For example, such a definition can omit or fail to distinguish between those who are:

- temporarily housed with family or friends;

- not visible in street locations (homeless families, for example);

- temporarily homeless or chronically homeless;

- at risk of homelessness.

For this reason, researchers who rely upon numbers available in most studies will want to be aware of the definition used by the author.

A definition of homelessness results in more than just numbers. It is necessary, some believe, to expand the definition of homelessness to be more inclusive in order to see the relationships between causes and solutions (Marcuse, 1990). It is also necessary to understand who today's homeless are in order to provide appropriate programs and funding levels to assist these people. If millions of Americans are homeless, a better case can be made for federal programs and intervention. However, if the numbers are closer to the Department of Housing and Urban Development (HUD) figures, then the problem is frequently viewed largely as a problem for state and local governments and private organizations (Kondratas, 1985). Yet, the difficulties of counting the homeless are caused by the nature of the homeless themselves—who they are, how they live, and where they live. In many ways, the homeless defy counting (Appelbaum, 1990).

COUNTING THE HOMELESS

One of the earliest attempts to generate a national count of the homeless was undertaken by HUD, who estimated that on an average night 192,000 to 586,000 were homeless, with "the most reliable ranges" being 250,000 to 350,000 (U.S. Department of Housing and Urban

Development, 1984). The figures quoted in this study were rigorously opposed by such activists as Mitch Snyder, who had estimated a dramatically higher homeless population of "approximately 1 percent of the population, or 2.2 million people" (Hombs & Snyder, 1986). The methodologies used by both surveys were dramatically different. James Wright estimated, based on six city-specific studies, that the total national homeless population on any given night is about half a million and the annual homeless population is about one and a half million (Wright 1989). At best most scholars agree the estimated number of homeless persons living in the United States is somewhere between 250,000 (HUD's estimate) and 2 or 3 million (Mitch Snyder's estimate).

The debate over the accuracy of the HUD figures dominated much of the discussion in the early 1980s. The numbers differ, in part, due to differing methodologies for producing the total count. Research methodologies for homeless studies vary from counting a sample of persons visible on the street to surveys of persons in shelters to focusing on specific subpopulations (U.S. National Institute on Alcohol Abuse and Alcoholism, 1987), resulting in dramatically different total figures (Milburn, Watts, & Anderson, 1986). In fact, the General Accounting Office (GAO) has identified many of the problems of estimating the number of homeless by examining 16 studies (U.S. General Accounting Office, 1988) and has acknowledged that the task of estimating the homeless is nearly impossible.

Despite the inherent difficulties, the Census Bureau did count the homeless as part of its 1990 census. During a one-night national "Shelter and Street Night" (S-Night), census enumerators attempted to count persons in emergency shelters and visible in street locations (U.S. Bureau of the Census, 1992). Although everyone agrees the count is not entirely accurate—huge numbers of homeless were missed—it serves as the first attempt to produce a national count of the homeless population (Wright, 1992).

Federal agencies and private groups have found it equally difficult to create a total number for the national homeless population, and the states are also finding it difficult to provide accurate counts of their homeless populations. A wide variety of methodologies are used from state to state, with many relying on shelter counts or some variation to determine their homeless population (Walker, 1989). Some states (Conservation Co., 1987) and cities (Shelter Partnership, 1992) have published figures of total homelessness. However, variations in definitions and methodologies make it difficult to compare these studies or to use them to create a national count.

Behind the total number of homeless are the individuals who make up this population. Some of the problems of counting and defining this population also affect our understanding of who the homeless are. However, a picture has developed that provides a great deal of insight into the problem of homelessness.

WHO ARE TODAY'S HOMELESS?

What is dramatically different about today's homeless population is how diverse it is compared to the population that once lived on Skid Row. A complete picture of the homeless population of the 1990s is available from the annual multiple-city surveys carried out by the U.S. Conference of Mayors (see "Annual Reports" section at the end of the chapter) and the studies completed by The Urban Institute (Burt & Cohen, 1989a, 1989b). What these figures do not always show is how families and individuals become homeless and how they live.

Although many have blamed the disintegration of family social ties for the growth of homelessness (White, 1992), a closer look at the statistics shows that homelessness occurs to those who are least able to sustain the additional burden of unemployment or eviction, the additional expenses of a sick child or family member, or the additional strain that a mentally ill, alcoholic, or drug-dependent family member places on a family with already limited resources. Further, many homeless are forced to leave their homes due to physical or sexual abuse or neglect (Rossi, 1989a). For this reason, the homeless frequently lack family or social ties. It is not uncommon, then, for families and individuals to become homeless when family relationships fail or when temporary arrangements with family or friends are stressed beyond their limits (U.S. Interagency Council on the Homeless, 1991a).

In addition, the homeless are less well educated (51 percent have a high school education, compared to the national average of 81 percent); are less likely to have held a steady job or to have ever worked at the same job for three months or more; and are largely members of minority groups, such as blacks and Hispanics (Burt, 1992). The most common characteristic of all homeless people is extreme poverty. Most exist on income far below the federal poverty level. Yet, surprisingly few (about 20 percent overall) receive general assistance benefits, Aid to Families with Dependent Children (AFDC), or Supplemental Security Income benefits. Social Security, veterans benefits, and unemployment insurance benefits are also rarely received by the eligible homeless (Burt & Cohen, 1989a, 1989b).

Although the intent of the original Food Stamp Act (P.L. 88-225) was to improve the diet of the poor, 45 percent of the homeless, although eligible for food stamps, do not receive them. The transient and unique living arrangements of many homeless are a factor in this low rate of involvement; however, such additional causes as complex application forms and procedures and the lack of an appropriate definition of "household" contribute to lengthy delays in many homeless receiving food stamps (U.S. Congress. House of Representatives. Select Committee on Hunger, 1987a). As a result, Congress passed the Homeless Eligibility Clarification Act (P.L. 99-500) to fine-tune the Food Stamp Program and to make it easier for the homeless to participate (U.S. Congress. House of Representatives. Select Committee on Hunger, 1987b). Still, the majority of the homeless depend on the private sector for food, a source that cannot adequately meet their nutritional needs. Most do not eat three meals a day; three out of five eat two or fewer meals per day (Burt & Cohen, 1989a, 1989b).

The effect of their inadequate diet can be seen, in part, in the health of the homeless, who experience a wide range of health problems, ranging from physical and mental health problems to alcohol and drug dependency at a higher level than the nonhomeless population (Wright & Weber, 1987). Many health problems (anemia, infectious diseases, and diabetes, for example) can be traced to hunger—particularly in homeless children (Brickner et al., 1985). More recently, incidences of tuberculosis and AIDS among the homeless have also increased (Brickner et al., 1990).

The poor health of many homeless is also caused by how they live. Although life within a shelter (Kozol, 1989) or on the street (Liebow, 1993) is little discussed in the literature, many homeless choose to live on the streets, in their cars, or in parks rather than use shelters because of the living conditions in many shelters and welfare hotels. However, in order to prepare appropriate programs for those persons who do use shelters, it is necessary to understand the life and living conditions within the shelter environment or on the street (Gounis & Susser, 1990). Those who live on the streets present a unique challenge to service providers (National Resource Center on Homelessness and Mental Illness, 1991), given their inability or unwillingness to participate in government assistance programs (Baxter & Hopper, 1981).

In general, then, the homeless population is a "snapshot" of the poor population of the United States. Yet within that "snapshot" are a variety of subpopulations that many researchers have identified and have studied in greater detail. Although the exact percentages of each group vary from study to study, these studies show us that, although the homeless population is still largely composed of white, middle-aged males, additional groups make up increasingly larger percentages of the total population. These groups, often called the "new homeless," show a strict departure from the homeless population that once existed on Skid Row. For example, today's homeless population includes greater numbers of:

- children and their families;

- veterans, specifically Vietnam War veterans;

- the elderly;

- rural homeless; and

- youth.

Each of these subpopulations has its own unique characteristics and the causes of the homelessness and appropriate programs or assistance for ending the homelessness may vary from group to group (Schutt & Garret, 1992b).

Children and Their Families

Between 1985 and 1990 there was an average increase of 22 percent in the number of families with children seeking emergency shelter (Waxman, 1991). The number of homeless families with children compose 35 percent of the total homeless population. Of these families, 56 percent were headed by a single parent, usually female (Maza & Hall, 1988). These female-headed families are more likely to be poor due to lower income and less opportunity for full-time employment. The impact of homelessness on children cannot be underestimated. To do so is to jeopardize the future of a growing segment of the American population (*The state of America's children,* 1992).

The growing number of homeless families place an increasing number of children at high mental and physical risk (Bassuk, 1992). Many suffer from serious emotional problems and serious developmental lags. Female-headed families are often without family support relationships, and the mothers themselves may exhibit pervasive and chronic emotional disabilities (Bassuk, 1986). In addition, homeless children are also more likely to be placed into foster care (U.S. Congress. House of Representatives. Select Committee on Children, Youth and Families, 1990).

Homeless children are also more likely to experience barriers to attendance at public schools. It is estimated that 28 percent of homeless school-aged children are not attending school (National Law Center on Homelessness and Poverty, 1990). These barriers include residency, guardianship and immunization requirements, availability of records, and transportation to school. Once in school, homeless children have a variety of special physical, physiological, sociological, and psychological barriers to overcome (Stronge, 1992). The percentage of homeless children receiving education varies from state to state, despite federal monies authorized by the McKinney Act (U.S. Department of Education, 1989). Furthermore, children are not the only homeless in need of education. Adult learning and literacy programs are also necessary to help poorly educated homeless back on the road to self-sufficiency (U.S. Department of Education, 1990).

Families become homeless due to job loss, family breakdown, or lack of available or adequate welfare funds to maintain a home. Many women are forced to leave their homes due to domestic violence (*The state of America's children,* 1992). In general, families are more likely to be among the episodic homeless—those persons for whom some series of events or circumstances has forced them from their homes temporarily. Many feel it is necessary to consider ways to help these families end the homeless episode as quickly as possible by making available to them affordable housing, social service monies, low-interest loans, and transitional housing (Thorman, 1988). In fact, a GAO report shows that, of those homeless using transitional housing projects, 28.9 percent are families headed by single females and 8.2 percent are families headed by couples (U.S. General Accounting Office, 1991b).

Although some families are fortunate to be able to find long-term transitional housing, homeless families are frequently placed in substandard housing or welfare hotels or split up because the available shelters cannot accommodate families. For these reasons, families often prefer parks or even their cars. Homeless families present unique challenges for service providers. The cost of maintaining them in welfare hotels often far exceeds the cost of providing permanent and more appropriate housing. The need to identify funds that can be used by state and local governments to build permanent housing in order to eliminate the waste of costly temporary housing has been identified as being a necessary part of assisting homeless families (U.S. Congress. House of Representatives. Committee on Ways and Means. Subcommittee on Public Assistance and Unemployment Compensation, 1987). Some cities have had to deal with large numbers of homeless families and have developed appropriate transitional housing to help these families end their homelessness as quickly as possible. In 1982, New York City experienced a "shock wave" of growing numbers of homeless families. As a result, it has evaluated how best to provide transitional shelter for homeless families (Bach & Steinhagen, 1987).

Veterans

Veterans make up 28 to 47 percent of the homeless in studies of metropolitan areas. Vietnam War veterans compose a large proportion of these homeless. In general, veterans are largely male, older on average than the rest of the homeless populations (42 years of age compared to 34), include a disproportionate number of blacks, are frequently disabled, and frequently exhibit some form of post-traumatic stress disorder due to their combat experience. Veterans also tend to underutilize many of the services offered by the Department of Veterans Affairs (Robertson, 1987).

In order to address many of the problems of homeless veterans, the Supplemental Appropriations Act of 1987 (P.L. 100-71) authorized the Department of Veterans Affairs to implement the Domiciliary Care for Homeless Veterans Program (DCHV). This program was implemented to provide rehabilitation and treatment for physically or psychiatrically ill veterans. The DCHV Program is established at VA Medical Centers across the United States (U.S. Department of Veterans Affairs, 1989). In addition, this program has seen an increase recently in the number of homeless women veterans it serves and expects greater numbers in the future (Leda, Rosenheck, & Gallup, 1991).

Rural Homeless

The rural homeless are a newly recognized homeless subpopulation. The growing number of rural homeless is closely linked, some believe, to the farm crisis in rural America as poverty rates continue to grow in rural areas at a faster rate than in urban areas (U.S. Commission on Security and Cooperation in Europe, 1990). Many of the rural homeless differ from their urban counterparts; they are more likely to be married, white, younger, and better educated. Many are young families who have fallen victim to the large number of the farm defaults commonly taking place in rural America. Many have a better support network of family and friends, making it difficult for them to be identified. The rural homeless, like all homeless, are in need of services that will address their particular needs and allow them to possess homes and farms once again (Patton, 1988).

Youth

Homeless youth were formally recognized in the Runaway and Homeless Youth Act (P.L. 95-115) and are an increasingly visible part of the homeless population. Despite their numbers, existing services and shelters may not meet their special needs and circumstances. Although difficult to study, homeless youth are a microcosm of the larger homeless population. The lack of a clear distinction between runaway youth and homeless youth results in an inability to gather accurate totals of this subpopulation (U.S. General Accounting Office, 1989a). Like the larger homeless population, the homeless youth population is a diverse group ranging in age from 13 to 17. Many have become homeless due to family problems, neglect, physical or sexual abuse, or are "throwaways"—those who have been told to leave their homes. As a group, they experience many of the same problems as the larger homeless population—alcohol and drug dependency, mental illness, and health problems (Robertson, 1991). Most health problems within the homeless youth population occur at a higher incidence than the general, comparably aged population. Incidences of sexually transmitted disease and AIDS are common among homeless youth (Kennedy et al., 1990).

Pregnancy rates among homeless girls are also high. Pregnancies result from incest; rape (sexual assault on homeless women is reported to be approximately 20 times the rate for women in general); promiscuity (sexually abused girls have a higher pattern of promiscuity, often referred to as "acting out"); survival sex (i.e., prostitution, by both males and females); and heterosexual relationships. Abortion is infrequent; infants born to homeless girls are believed to have a higher morbidity rate, due, in part, to inadequate prenatal care (Athey, 1989).

The National Network of Runaway and Youth Services has recommended that homeless youth are best served in the communities where they live. Furthermore, homeless youth who are perceived as avoiding services require a mix of counseling and other support services to overcome their reluctance to use government or private services (National Network of Runaway and Youth Services, 1985).

The variety of subpopulations that compose the total homeless population reveals the complexity of the problem of homelessness. Studies of a wide variety of health programs funded under the McKinney Act have been found to have varying levels of success. Some subpopulations—women and children, chronically mentally ill, and episodic homeless individuals and families—have been more successfully integrated into local programs. Others—substance abusers and the chronically homeless (i.e., street people)—are more difficult to reach (Miller, 1989). In order to find appropriate solutions for each of these subpopulations, it is also necessary to understand what has caused their homelessness and to realize that the causes can be complex and overlapping.

CAUSES OF HOMELESSNESS

Scholars have identified a variety of causes for the growth of the homeless population in the 1980s (Morse, 1992). Generally, these causes can be grouped into two categories—individual (or internal) causes and institutional (or external) causes.

Internal Causes of Homelessness

The traditional view of homelessness is that the individuals or some attributes of the individual are the cause of their homelessness. A variety of internal causes are usually used as evidence of this view, including substance abuse, mental illness, failure of family support systems or personal relationships, and voluntary social deviance. Each of these causes places the control of the homelessness with the individual rather than with an institutional or external source (Redburn & Buss, 1986). Of these explanations two have been studied in great detail—mental illness and substance abuse—and are shown to occur at a high level among certain subpopulations of the homeless population.

Mental Illness

Mental illness is associated with homeless populations in the minds of most Americans. Although studies have identified that between 25 and 50 percent of the homeless population suffer some form of mental illness, they also show that this incidence level is largely limited to specific subpopulations, including veterans, women, and the elderly.

As early as 1978 a presidential commission identified deficiencies in mental health support systems in the United States and recommended community support be improved to create a responsive service system. The report also discussed mental illness among specific subpopulations, including veterans, women, and the elderly (President's Commission on Mental Health, 1978). More recently, the National Institute of Mental Health has taken the lead in identifying mental health housing and support needs and has funded a series of research projects to identify those needs (U.S. National Institute of Mental Health, 1987). The results of these have been summarized and show that a series of problems exacerbate homelessness among the mentally ill. Most simply, the mentally ill are less able to negotiate the welfare system or to obtain support from family or friends and are more likely to be chronically unemployed (Tessler & Dennis, 1989).

A variety of solutions have been recommended. The American Psychiatric Association has recommended that the complexity of the problem calls for a variety of approaches (Lamb, 1984), and the Senate has proposed outreach teams in Metropolitan Statistical Areas (MSAs) to identify the homeless mentally ill persons and to help them obtain the psychiatric and other services to which they are entitled (U.S. Congress. Senate. Committee on Finance. Subcommittee on Health for Families and the Uninsured, 1991). In the meantime, states have passed their own legislation to address the needs of the homeless mentally ill. California, for example, has given counties the flexibility to tailor local programs to the specific needs of the county population (Vernez et al., 1988).

Alcohol and Drug Dependency

Most Americans believe that alcohol and drug dependency exists at a high level among the homeless population. Studies show substance abuse to be high among the homeless and suggests that abuse may be the most common health concern among the homeless (Wright, 1990). Yet many studies showing high substance abuse among the homeless are of questionable use in providing reliable data or information (Milburn, 1990). The actual figures produced depend, in part, on the type of survey used and the population being studied. Overall, however, the range of substance abuse is usually estimated as between 20 and 43 percent. Yet, like mental illness, alcohol or drug dependency is largely limited to specific subpopulations—single white males, veterans, youth, and, to a lesser extent, women (Schutt & Garrett, 1992a).

This impression of homelessness associated with alcohol or drug dependency continues to influence many Americans' attitudes toward the homeless. Yet without an understanding of the extent of alcohol or drug dependency and the homeless who actually need assistance with this problem, it is difficult to provide appropriate services. However, services for substance-dependent homeless must be tailored to the needs of this special community and require three basic components—a special effort to make services available; emphasis on individual recovery from alcohol problems; and support and follow-up services to help the individual maintain sobriety (Wittman & Arch, 1988).

External Causes of Homelessness

External causes of homelessness include the decline in the availability of low-cost housing; the growing number of persons falling below the poverty level combined with a reduction in federal support services; and deinstitutionalization of the mentally ill.

Decline in the Availability
of Low-Cost Housing

For many scholars, "homelessness is a housing problem" (Rossi, 1989b, p. 31). For that reason, the availability of inexpensive housing is probably the most widely studied cause of homelessness. Using *American Housing Survey* and *Poverty in the United States* data, researchers are able to document that poor households are forced to spend a larger percentage of their income on housing than is considered acceptable by the standards established by the U.S. Department of Housing and Urban Development (HUD). The lack of affordable housing hits black and Hispanic households, the elderly, single-parent households, and young households especially hard (Gornstein, 1990). Lower earning power and incidences of discrimination force these groups to spend an even larger percentage of their income on housing (Leonard, Dolbeare, & Lazere, 1989).

Homelessness has become a housing problem, according to some, because many government-subsidized housing programs during the late 1970s and 1980s have been cut back or held to existing levels although poverty during the same period increased (Wright, 1989). In addition, marginal housing was destroyed or eliminated during the urban renewal movement beginning during the 1970s. The goal of many of these efforts was to replace skid row areas of many cities—forcing a large number of poor out of their homes or single-room-occupancy (SRO) hotels without providing replacement housing. Historically, the SRO, more than any other housing option, provided a last-resort housing for the urban poor (Hoch & Slayton, 1989). Thus, "marginal housing has largely been eliminated, but the marginal segment of the poor has not" (Rossi, 1989b, p. 32).

Another study in four metropolitan areas (Baltimore, Chicago, Houston, and Seattle) corroborates this by showing that the number of homeless increases when the number of persons falling below the poverty line increases. This results in an increased demand for low-cost housing. Yet, at the same time, the availability of low-cost housing has declined. This forces families to pay a larger percentage of their income on housing costs, placing them at higher risk of becoming homeless (Ringheim, 1990).

As part of the McKinney Act, funds were made available to HUD to re-create SRO housing for homeless individuals because SRO housing is a relatively affordable way of housing homeless individuals (U.S. Department of Housing and Urban Development, 1990). However, others recommend more involvement by the federal government in addressing racial segregation and discrimination that influences the availability of low-cost housing to specific homeless subpopulations, including Hispanics, blacks, and women with children. Furthermore, without government intervention it is unlikely that the private sector will ever provide adequate low-cost housing for the homeless (Zarembka, 1990).

Growing Number of Persons Falling Below the Poverty Level Combined with a Reduction in Federal Support Services

Government figures show an increasing number of persons falling below the poverty level during the 1980s. Scholars have identified a variety of reasons, including the decline in social welfare payments to those most likely to become homeless; the economic recession of the 1980s, leading to high unemployment rates; and changes in the labor market resulting in fewer jobs for unskilled labor, making it difficult for those groups of people in danger of becoming homeless to find temporary and manual labor. The collision of all these forces contributed greatly to the growing number of homeless, particularly the "new homeless"—families, single women with children, and the elderly.

The Reagan administration's budget cuts to social services in housing, welfare, and job training are now described as being the root cause of much of the increase in homelessness during the 1980s (U.S. Congress. House of Representatives. Committee on Banking, Finance and Urban Affairs, 1992). More specifically, cuts in five programs (Aid to Families with Dependent Children, Social Security, disability benefits, food stamps, and unemployment insurance) left many poor with less income and fewer resources to fall back on (Blau, 1992). At the same time poverty in the United States was increasing, less low-cost housing was available to the poor. These two circumstances have made it difficult for the poor to maintain their housing situation.

Deinstitutionalization of the Mentally Ill

In 1963 more than 400,000 mentally ill were deinstitutionalized under the authorization of the Community Mental Health Centers Act of 1963 (P.L. 88-164). The intent of this legislation was to release these patients back to their communities and Community Mental Health Centers (CMHCs). Many believe this legislation failed to provide the community services these newly released mentally ill required, resulting in a large number of mentally ill becoming homeless (Peele et al., 1984).

From the beginning, the policy of deinstitutionalization was considered by some to have been less than successful. Early reports documented that the program needed to address several problem areas, including more carefully selecting patients for deinstitutionalization, before the policy could be wholly successful (Bachrach, 1976). More recently, it has been called a disaster with the roots of its failure in the psychiatric profession (Torrey, 1988).

Because many mentally ill exist on the edge of society, they are particularly vulnerable to becoming homeless and are less capable of negotiating the systems needed to help them maintain permanent housing. Thus, others have argued that factors that include lack of affordable housing, poverty, fragmentation of services, and lack of family and social supports contribute to the high number of mentally ill among the homeless (U.S. National Institute of Mental Health, n.d.). Others believe the legal profession has also played a role in the large number of homeless mentally ill by pursuing "right to refuse treatment" cases in the courts. The success of these cases has made it nearly impossible to hospitalize and treat many of the most severely mentally ill on the streets (Isaac & Armat, 1990).

More recently, scholars have been exploring the relationship between external and internal causes of homelessness and their impact on chronic homelessness, specifically (Piliavin, Sosin, & Westerfelt, 1988). External causes, such as a decline in the availability of low-income housing, increased poverty and reduction in federal support, and deinstitutionalization, combined with internal causes, such as mental illness or alcohol or drug dependency, that make it difficult for individuals to negotiate a complex system of assistance can make it nearly impossible for most homeless to ever successfully leave the despair of homelessness (Rossi, 1989b). All of these factors combined with ever-lower public opinion ensure that the homeless have even less help than they might need.

PUBLIC OPINION

As the numbers of homeless have grown, the American public's sympathy and understanding of the homeless and their plight have worn thin. Although scholars and government officials increasingly argue that homelessness is caused by a complex web of government policies and inaction, most Americans still believe homelessness is largely caused by alcoholism or mental illness (Stark, 1987). Most Americans believe, a national survey shows, that the number of homeless will continue to rise in the 1990s, thus giving some insight into the pessimism most feel about federal, state, or local government efforts to provide adequate solutions to what has become an everyday sight for many Americans (Bennack, 1989).

Further evidence of the public's lack of understanding is the growing number of local ordinances that attempt to legislate out of existence a problem that a growing number of government policies and programs, as well as efforts on the part of the private sector, have not been able to solve. Local efforts include loitering and antisleeping laws, neighborhood sweeps, transit system regulations, and antibegging ordinances (National Law Center on Homelessness and Poverty, 1991).

After an initial period of sympathy and support, a wide variety of publications have become more willing to print more conservative views of the causes of and solutions to the problem of homelessness. Like so many social problems, homelessness is not an issue that can be clearly defined or solved. Thus, it is often difficult to distinguish between fact and opinion in much of what is written, particularly in the popular press, about the homeless (Orr, 1990). Without public support for the homeless it is difficult for lawmakers to provide the funding necessary to respond to many of the problems the homeless encounter.

RESPONSES AND SOLUTIONS

The homeless population nearly tripled in the period between 1984 and 1988. This amount of growth leads many to wonder if there are enough shelters to meet the basic needs of the homeless population (U.S. Department of Housing and Urban Development, 1989). It may also be a factor in the growing number of legal cases in which the homeless and their advocates seek to give to the homeless those basic human rights that often are lost by the circumstances of their day-to-day lives.

Until 1979, court cases involving the homeless had largely been disorderly conduct cases with the homeless named as defendants. However, Callahan v. Carey (NYLJ [Dec. 11, 1979] at 10, col. 4 N.Y. Sup. Ct., [Dec 5, 1979]), the first right to shelter case, led to the first shelter opening in New York City (*The homeless*, 1992). Since that date, a number of cases, largely in state courts, have determined shelter standards, intake requirements, due process, status offenses, right to treatment, foster care, right to appropriate housing, right to vote, prevention, First Amendment rights, preservation and displacement, and federal program issues (Hombs, 1990). In addition, they have established a history and pattern of legal advocacy on behalf of the homeless that filled in gaps left open in state and federal laws (Blau, 1992).

Much of the debate surrounding the homeless concerns appropriate and workable solutions to a national problem that is most visible at the state and local levels. The federal government continues to wrestle with appropriate mechanisms and funding levels for programs to assist the homeless. During the 100th Congress, 32 separate bills were introduced to assist the homeless. These bills would have dispersed responsibility to a wide range of agencies and departments, thus diluting their total impact (Wright & Weber, 1987). A recent survey reports that many Americans believe the homeless are not adequately assisted by government (Clements, 1994). For this reason, many believe that a "national agenda" is needed that will focus on the many and varied problems, populations, and solutions for homelessness (Partnership for the Homeless, 1989).

Congress has attempted over the years to appropriate funds to address a wide number of the causes of homelessness (Bennett et al., 1992). The single most comprehensive effort to date has been the Stewart B. McKinney Homeless Assistance Act of 1987. This law authorized funds for a wide range of programs to address a wide range of needs for a number of different homeless subpopulations (U.S. General Accounting Office, 1991a). The effectiveness of the monies authorized by the McKinney Act has been monitored in a series of evaluative reports by the General Accounting Office (U.S. General Accounting Office, 1989b; U.S. General

Accounting Office, 1987). Some agencies have proven to be more effective in the distribution of these funds than others. For this reason, these reports have made recommendations that will enhance assistance planning and effectiveness.

In addition, the McKinney Act established the Interagency Council on the Homeless to include most cabinet secretaries and heads of several independent agencies. The Interagency Council's role is to coordinate all federal programs for homeless persons and to provide technical assistance to states, local governments, and public and private nonprofit organizations that serve the homeless (U.S. Interagency Council on the Homeless, 1991b). The Interagency Council's *Annual Report* documents federal efforts to help end homelessness and includes reports of member agencies (see "Annual Reports" section at the end of the chapter).

However, it is increasingly evident that the federal government will need to use innovative solutions to address a growing problem. Candidate Bill Clinton recognized the need to assist the homeless through innovative approaches in his 1992 economic plan (Clinton & Gore, 1992). The death of Yetta Adams on HUD's doorstep during the winter of 1993 forced President Clinton's administration to seek solutions that will fulfill these promises (DeParle, 1993b). To date, various solutions with many different approaches are being tried. These approaches include selling Resolution Trust Corporation housing to public agencies, not-for-profit organizations, and other property owners who promise to rent at least 35 percent of the units to low- and very-low-income households; eliminating waste at HUD, particularly in the use of welfare hotels where the homeless are frequently housed temporarily at a cost far exceeding the actual cost of permanent housing (Stanfield, 1994); the D.C. Homeless Initiative that would make the District of Columbia a model for serving homeless people (DeParle, 1993a); and doubling the federal budget committed to housing for the homeless. In addition, President Clinton issued an executive order that requires the Interagency Council on the Homeless to "develop a single coordinated Federal plan for breaking the cycle of existing homelessness and for preventing future homelessness" (Clinton, 1993).

Although organizations such as Habitat for Humanity International continue to "change the world one house at a time" (Fuller, 1993), it is clear that the problem of homelessness in America cannot be solved in this manner. The federal government is frequently responsible for providing the funding for many projects and programs that would serve the homeless, and one theme is consistent in the recommendations that appear in many sources: the importance of state and local action to assist the homeless and the need for public and private agencies to work together to address the many complex problems that the homeless face (U.S. Advisory Commission on Intergovernmental Relations, 1988). Although the magnitude of the problem requires state and local governments and the private sector to work together to achieve viable solutions, the result is a patchwork of "safety nets" (Shapiro & Greenstein, 1988). This is not to imply that state and local governments are not acutely aware of the complexity of homelessness. Many are creating policy goals to reform existing practices in order to achieve workable solutions (New York (State). Commission on the Homeless, 1992).

Recently the Interagency Council convened The Federal Task Force on Homelessness and Severe Mental Illness. This task force has recommended an approach that includes the following elements in order to eradicate homelessness in the United States:

- Assertive outreach;

- Integrated care management;

- Safe havens;

- Housing;

- Legal protection;

- Treatment;

- Health care;

- Income support and benefits;

- Rehabilitation, vocational training, and employment assistance; and

- Consumer and family involvement (U.S. Federal Task Force on Homelessness and Severe Mental Illness, 1992).

Clearly it will be necessary for federal, state, and local governments to work with profit and nonprofit organizations to provide all of these elements (Lederman, 1993).

THE FUTURE

As the 1980s came to a close there is some disagreement on whether the homeless population continues to increase. However, most surveys still show that demand for homeless services is increasing. There is a need, some believe, for structural changes—a long-term view of solutions and homelessness. Additionally, there is a need for better jobs, education and training, and better housing combined with services for those homeless with disabilities (Burt, 1992). Without these, the growth of homelessness will continue. Poverty, combined with other causes, will force more families and children, minorities, and the mentally ill into homelessness, and the increasing incidence of AIDS and other diseases caused by HIV virus will become more prevalent. The result will be an American nightmare (National Coalition for the Homeless, 1989).

As 1993 came to a close, President Clinton called together a group of homeless advocates from government and nongovernment agencies to symbolize his administration's commitment to moving beyond emergency care and toward a "continuum of care," including a "complete menu of services from outreach efforts to entice them in from the cold, to social services, to the provision of permanent shelter." However, like many before him, President Clinton also recognized the difficulty of providing homes for each homeless person (DeParle, 1993c).

Although the task may be complex and costly, interviews with low-income people, those likely to become homeless, indicate their desires are no different than those of other Americans—to work and be independent (Coalition on Human Needs, 1987). It will take a great deal of effort on the part of the American people to help the homeless bridge the gap from homelessness to independence.

REFERENCES

Anderson, N. 1923. *The hobo: Sociology of the homeless man*. Chicago: University of Chicago Press.

———. 1940. *Men on the move*. Chicago: University of Chicago Press.

Appelbaum, R. P. 1990. Counting the homeless. In Momeni, J. A., ed., *Homelessness in the United States*, vol. 2. New York: Greenwood, 1-16.

Athey, J., ed. 1989. *Pregnancy and childbearing among homeless adolescents: Report of a workshop*. 1991. ASI microfiche 4108-55. Washington, DC: Department of Health and Human Services and the National Institute of Mental Health.

Bach, V., & Steinhagen, R. 1987. *Alternatives to the welfare hotel: Using emergency assistance to provide decent transitional shelter for homeless families*. New York: Community Service Society of New York.

Bachrach, L. L. 1976. *Deinstitutionalization: An analytical review and sociological perspective*. HE 20.8110:D14. Washington, DC: Government Printing Office.

Bahr, H. M., & Caplow, T. 1973. *Old men drunk and sober*. New York: New York University Press.

Bassuk, E. L. 1986. Homeless families: Single mothers and their children in Boston shelters. In Bassuk, E. L., ed., *The mental health needs of homeless persons*. San Francisco: Jossey-Bass, 45-53.

———. 1992. Women and children without shelter: The characteristics of homeless families. In Robertson, M. J., & Greenblatt, M., eds., *Homelessness: A national perspective*. New York: Plenum Press, 257-64.

Baxter, E., &. Hopper, K. 1981. *Private lives/public spaces: Homeless adults on the streets of New York City*. New York: Community Service Society, Institute for Social Welfare Research.

Bennack, F. A. 1989. *The American public's hopes and fears for the decade of the 1990s: A national survey of public awareness and personal opinion*. New York: Hearst Corp.

Bennett, G.; Shane, P.; Tutunjian, B. A.; & Perl, H. I. 1992. *Job training and employment services for homeless persons with alcohol and other drug problems*. HE20.8302:H75/5. Rockville, MD: Alcohol, Drug Abuse, and Mental Health Administration.

Blau, J. 1992. *The visible poor: Homelessness in the United States*. New York: Oxford University Press.

Brickner, P. W.; Scharer, L. K.; Conanan, B. A.; Elvy, A.; & Savarese, M., eds. 1985. *Health care of homeless people*. New York: Springer.

Brickner, P. W.; Scharer, L. K.; Conanan, B. A.; Savarese, M.; & Scanlan, B. C., eds. 1990. *Under the safety net: The health and social welfare of the homeless in the United States*. New York: W. W. Norton.

Burt, M. R. 1992. *Over the edge: The growth of homelessness in the 1980s*. New York: Russell Sage Foundation.

Burt, M. R., & Cohen, B. E. 1989a. *America's homeless: Numbers, characteristics, and programs that serve them*. Urban Institute Report 89-3. Washington, DC: Urban Institute Press.

————. 1989b. *Feeding the homeless: Does the prepared meals provision help?: Report to Congress on the prepared meal provisions*. Vols. 1-2. Rev. ed. Washington, DC: Urban Institute Press.

Clements, M. 1994. What Americans say about the homeless. *Parade Magazine* January 9, 1994:4-6.

Clinton, B. 1993. Executive order 12848: Federal plan to break the cycle of homelessness. *Weekly Compilation of Presidential Documents* 29: 909-10.

Clinton, B., & Gore, A. 1992. *Putting people first: How we can all change America*. New York: Times Books.

Coalition on Human Needs. 1987. How the poor would remedy poverty: Interviews with low income people in Washington, DC, summer 1986, summary of results. In U.S. Congress. House of Representatives. Committee on Ways and Means. Subcommittee on Public Assistance and Unemployment Compensation, *Use of emergency assistance funds for acquisition of temporary and permanent housing for homeless families*. Serial No. 99-104. Y4.W36:99-104. Washington, DC: Government Printing Office, 118-30.

Conservation Co. 1987. *Homelessness in Pennsylvania: Numbers, needs and services*. Harrisburg, PA: Department of Public Welfare.

Deparle, J. 1993a. U.S. offers "model" plan for capital homeless. *New York Times*, Sept. 21, 1993, Late Edition, Sec. A, p. 15, col. 1.

————. 1993b. Homelessness hitting home: A death on HUD's doorstep. *New York Times*, Nov. 30, 1993, Late Edition, Sec. A, p. 1, col. 5.

————. 1993c. Advocates for homeless meet with Clinton. *New York Times*, Dec. 23, 1993, Late Edition, Sec. A, p. 13, col.1.

Fuller, M. 1993. Habitat for Humanity: Changing the world one house at a time. in Lederman, J., ed. *Housing America: Mobilizing bankers, builders and communities to solve the nation's affordable housing crisis*. Chicago: Probus Publishing Co.

Gornstein, A. 1990. *Living on the edge: The housing crisis facing teen parents and their children*. 1991 SRI Microfiche A3875-3. Gornstein: Citizens' Housing and Planning Association and the Alliance for Young Families.

Gounis, K., &. Susser, E. 1990. Shelterization and its implications for mental health services. In Cohen, N. L., ed., *Psychiatry takes to the streets: Outreach and crisis intervention for the mentally ill.* New York: Guilford Press, 231-55.

Hoch, C., & Slayton, R. A. 1989. *New homeless and old: Community and the skid row hotel.* Philadelphia: Temple University Press.

Hombs, M. E. 1990. *American homelessness: A reference handbook.* Santa Barbara, CA: ABC-CLIO.

Hombs, M. E., & Snyder, M. 1986. *Homelessness in America: A forced march to nowhere.* Washington, DC: Community for Creative Non-Violence.

The homeless. 1992. *CQ Researcher* 2: 665-88.

Hopper, K., &. Hamberg, J. 1984. *The making of America's homeless: From skid row to new poor, 1945-1984.* New York: Community Service Society of New York.

Institute of Medicine. 1988. *Homelessness, health, and human needs.* Washington, DC: National Academy Press.

Isaac, R. J., & Armat, V. C. 1990. *Madness in the streets: How psychiatry and the law abandoned the mentally ill.* New York: Free Press.

Kennedy, J. T.; Petrone, J.; Deisher, R. W.; Emerson, J.; Heslop, P.; Bastible, D.; & Arkovitz, M. 1990. Health care for familyless, runaway street kids. In Brickner, P. W., et al., eds., *Under the safety net: The health and social welfare of the homeless in the United States.* New York: W. W. Norton, 82-117.

Kondratas, S. A. 1985. Strategy for helping America's homeless. *Heritage Foundation Backgrounder* 431: 144-49.

Kozol, J. 1989. *Rachel and her children: Homeless families in America.* New York: Ballantine Books.

Lamb, H. R., ed. 1984. *The homeless mentally ill: A task force report of the American Psychiatric Association.* Washington, DC: American Psychiatric Association.

Leda, C.; Rosenheck, R.; & Gallup, P. 1991. Women in the HCMI program: A new subgroup of the homeless veteran population. In U.S. Department of Veterans Affairs, *The fourth progress report on the homeless chronically mentally ill veterans program.* U.S. Congress. House of Representatives. Committee on Veterans' Affairs. Y4.V64/3:H75/7. Washington, DC: Government Printing Office. (H. Prt. no. 5).

Lederman, J., ed. 1993. *Housing America: Mobilizing bankers, builders and communities to solve the nation's affordable housing crisis.* Chicago: Probus Publishing Co.

Leonard, P. A.; Dolbeare, C. N.; & Lazere, E. B. 1989. *A place to call home: The crisis in housing for the poor.* Washington, DC: Center on Budget and Policy Priorities.

Liebow, E. 1993. *Tell them who I am: The lives of homeless women.* New York: Free Press.

Marcuse, P. 1990. Homelessness and housing policy. In Caton, C. L. M., ed., *Homeless in America.* New York: Oxford University Press, 138-59.

Maza, P. L., & Hall, J. A. 1988. *Homeless children and their families: A preliminary study.* Washington, DC: Child Welfare League.

Milburn, N. G. 1990. Drug abuse among homeless people. In Momeni, J. A., ed., *Homelessness in the United States,* vol. 2. New York: Greenwood Press, 61-79.

Milburn, N. G.; Watts, R. J.; & Anderson, S. L. 1986. *An annotated bibliography of research methods used to study the homeless.* Washington, DC: Howard University, Institute for Urban Affairs and Research, Housing and Community Development Studies Center.

Miller, H. 1989. *Assessment of the implementation of grants to provide health services to the homeless: Final report.* 1990 ASI Microfiche 4108-48. Columbia, MD: Center for Health Policy Studies.

———. 1991. *On the fringe: The disposed in America.* Lexington, MA: Lexington Books.

Monkonnen, E., ed. 1984. *Walking to work: Tramps in America, 1790-1935.* Lincoln: University of Nebraska Press.

Morse, G. A. 1992. Causes of homelessness. In Robertson, M. J., & Greenblatt, M., eds., *Homelessness: A national perspective.* New York: Plenum Press, 3-17.

National Coalition for the Homeless. 1989. *American nightmare: A decade of homelessness in the United States.* New York: The Coalition.

National Law Center on Homelessness and Poverty. 1990. *Shut out: Denial of education to homeless children.* Washington, DC: The Center.

———. 1991. *Go directly to jail: A report analyzing local anti-homeless ordinances.* Washington, DC: The Center.

National Network of Runaway and Youth Services. 1985. *To whom do they belong: A profile of America's runaway and homeless youth and the programs that help them.* 1984 SRI Microfiche A8095-1. Washington, DC: The Network.

National Resource Center on Homelessness and Mental Illness. 1991. *Reaching out: A guide for service providers.* Y3.H75:8R22. Washington, DC: Interagency Council on the Homeless.

New York (State). Commission on the Homeless. 1992. *The way home: A new direction in social policy.* New York: The Commission.

Orr, L., ed.. 1990. *The homeless: Opposing viewpoints.* San Diego, CA: Greenhaven Press.

Partnership for the Homeless. 1989. *Moving forward: A national agenda to address homelessness in 1990 and beyond and a status report on homelessness in America, a 46-city survey, 1988-89.* 1990 SRI Microfiche A8671-1. New York: The Partnership.

Patton, L. T. 1988. The rural homeless. In *Institute of medicine homelessness, health, and human needs.* Washington, DC: National Academy Press.

Peele, R.; Gross, B. H.; Arons, B.; & Jafri, M. 1984. The legal system and the homeless. In Lamb, H. R., ed., *The homeless mentally ill.* Washington, DC: American Psychiatric Association.

Piliavin, I.; Sosin, M.; & Westerfelt, H. 1988. *Conditions contributing to long-term homelessness: An exploratory study.* Institute for Research on Poverty, Discussion Paper, 833-87. 1988 ASI Microfiche 4008-82. Madison: University of Wisconsin.

President's Commission on Mental Health. 1978. *Report to the President from the President's Commission on Mental Health.* Vols. 1-4. PR39.8:M52/R29/v.1-4. Washington, DC: Government Printing Office.

Redburn, F. S., & Buss, T. F. 1986. *Responding to America's homeless public policy alternatives.* New York: Praeger.

Ringheim, K. 1990. *At risk of homelessness: The roles of income and rent.* New York: Praeger.

Robertson, M. J. 1987. Homeless veterans: An emerging problem? In Bingham, R. D.; Green, R. E.; & White, S. B.; eds., *The homeless in contemporary society.* Newbury Park, CA: Sage.

———. 1991. Homeless youth: An overview of recent literature. In Salamon, J. H.; Molnar, L. M.; & Kryder-Coe, J. M.; eds., *Homeless children and youth: A new American dilemma.* New Brunswick, NJ: Transaction, 33-68.

Rossi, P. 1989a. *Down and out in America: The origins of homelessness.* Chicago: University of Chicago Press.

———. 1989b. *Without shelter: Homelessness in the 1980s.* New York: Priority Press.

Schutt, R. K., & Garrett, G. R. 1992a. The homeless alcoholic: Past and present. In Robertson, M. J., & Greenblatt, M., eds., *Homelessness: A national perspective.* New York: Plenum Press, 177-86.

———. 1992b. *Responding to the homeless: Policy and practice.* New York: Plenum Press.

Shapiro, I., & Greenstein, R. 1988. *Holes in the safety nets: National overview, poverty programs and policies in the states.* Washington, DC: Center of Budget and Policy Priorities.

Shelter Partnership. 1992. *The number of homeless people in Los Angeles County.* Los Angeles: Shelter Partnership.

Stanfield, B. 1994. Home Economics. *National Journal.* 25: 2999-3002.

Stark, L. 1987. Blame the system, not its victims. In Kneerim, J., *Homelessness: Critical issues for policy and practice.* Boston: Boston Foundation.

The state of America's children. 1992. Washington, DC: Children's Defense Fund.

Steinbeck, J. 1939. *The grapes of wrath.* New York: Modern Library.

Stronge, J. H., ed. 1992. *Educating homeless children and adolescents: Evaluating policy and practice.* Newbury Park, CA: Sage.

Tessler, R. C., & Dennis, D. L. 1989. *A synthesis of NIMH-funded research concerning persons who are homeless and mentally ill.* Rockville, MD: The Institute.

Thorman, G. 1988. *Homeless families.* Springfield, IL: Charles C. Thomas.

Torrey. E. F. 1988. *Nowhere to go: The tragic odyssey of the homeless mentally ill.* New York: Harper & Row.

U.S. Advisory Commission on Intergovernmental Relations. 1988. *Assisting the homeless: State and local responses in an era of limited resources.* Washington, DC: The Commission.

U.S. Bureau of the Census. 1992. *Fact sheet for 1990 decennial census counts of persons in selected locations where homeless persons are found* (CPH-L-87). Washington, DC: The Bureau.

U.S. Commission on Security and Cooperation in Europe. 1990. *Staff report on homelessness in the United States.* Y4.Se2:H45. Washington, DC: Government Printing Office.

U.S. Congress. House of Representatives. Committee on Banking, Finance and Urban Affairs. 1992. *Economic distress in our cities* . Y4.B22/1:Ec7/5. Washington, DC: Government Printing Office (Comm. Prt. 102-12).

U.S. Congress. House of Representatives. Committee on Ways and Means. Subcommittee on Public Assistance and Unemployment Compensation. 1987. *Use
of emergency assistance funds for acquisition of temporary and permanent
housing for homeless families* (Serial No. 99-104). Y4.W36:99-104. Washington, DC: Government Printing Office.

U.S. Congress. House of Representatives. Select Committee on Children, Youth
and Families. 1990. *No place to call home: Discarded children in America.*
Y 1.1/8:101-395. Washington, DC: Government Printing Office (H. Rpt. 101-
395).

U.S. Congress. House of Representatives. Select Committee on Hunger. 1987a.
*Hunger among the homeless: A survey of 140 shelters, food stamp participation
and recommendations* . Y4.H89:H75. Washington, DC: Government Printing
Office (Committee Print).

———. 1987b. *Hunger and homelessness* (Serial No. 100-1). Y4.H89:100-1. Washington, DC: Government Printing Office.

U.S. Congress. Senate. Committee on Finance. Subcommittee on Health for Families and the Uninsured. 1991. *Problems of homeless mentally ill.* Y4.F49:S.hrg.-
102-210. Washington, DC: Government Printing Office (S.Hrg. 102-210).

U.S. Department of Education. 1989. *Status report, education of homeless children
and youth under the Stewart B. McKinney Act.* 1989 ASI Microfiche 4804-35.
Washington, DC: Department of Education.

———. 1990. *Education for homeless adults: The first year.* ED1.2:H75. Washington, DC: Department of Education, Office of Vocational and Adult Education,
Division of Adult Education and Literacy.

U.S. Department of Housing and Urban Development. 1984. *A report to the
secretary on the homeless and emergency shelter.* Washington, DC: HUD,
Office of Policy Development and Research.

———. 1989. *A report on the 1988 national survey of shelters for the homeless.*
HH1.2:H75/24. Washington, DC: Government Printing Office.

———. 1990. *Report to Congress on SROs for the homeless Section 8 moderate
rehabilitation program.* HH1.2:H75/29. Washington, DC: Government Printing Office.

U.S. Department of Veterans Affairs. 1989. *Healing communities: The second
progress report on domiciliary care for homeless veterans program.* West
Haven, CN: Department of Veterans Affairs, Northeast Program Evaluation
Center, Veterans Affairs Medical Center.

U.S. Federal Task Force on Homelessness and Severe Mental Illness. 1992.
Outcasts on main street. Rockville, MD: National Institute of Mental Health.

U.S. General Accounting Office. 1987. *Homelessness: Implementation of food and
shelter programs under the McKinney Act.* GA1.13:RCED-88-6. Washington,
DC: General Accounting Office.

———. 1988. *Homeless mentally ill: Problems and options in estimating numbers
and trends.* GA1.13:PEMD-88-24. Washington, DC: General Accounting Office.

———. 1989a. *Homelessness: Homeless and runaway youth receiving services at
federally funded shelters.* GA1.13:HRD-90-45. Washington, DC: General Accounting Office.

———. 1989b. *Homelessness: HUD's and FEMA's progress in implementing the McKinney Act.* GA1.13:RCED-89-50. Washington, DC: General Accounting Office.

———. 1991a. *Homelessness: McKinney Act programs and funding through fiscal year 1990.* GA1.13:RCED-91-126. Washington, DC: General Accounting Office.

———. 1991b. *Homelessness: Transitional housing shows initial success but long-term effects unknown.* GA1.13:RCED-91-200. Washington, DC: General Accounting Office.

U.S. Interagency Council on the Homeless. 1991a. *The 1990 annual report of the Interagency Council on the Homeless.* Y3.H75:1/990. Washington, DC: The Council.

———. 1991b. *Federal programs to help homeless people.* Washington, DC: The Council.

U.S. National Institute of Mental Health. n.d. *Deinstitutionalization policy and homelessness: A report to the U.S. Congress.* HE 20.8102:D368. Washington, DC: Government Printing Office.

———. 1987. *The homeless mentally ill: Reports available from the National Institute of Mental Health.* HE20.8113:H75. Rockville, MD: The Institute.

U.S. National Institute on Alcohol Abuse and Alcoholism. 1987. *Research methodologies concerning homeless persons with serious mental illness and/or substance abuse disorders.* HE20.8302:H75/2. Washington, DC: Government Printing Office.

Vernez, G.; Burnam, M. A.; McGlynn, E. A.; Trude, S.; & Mittman, B. S., eds. 1988. *Review of California's program for the homeless mentally disabled.* Santa Monica, CA: Rand Corp.

Walker, L. 1989. *Homelessness in the states.* Lexington, KY: Council of State Governments.

Waxman, L. D. 1991. *A status report on hunger and homelessness in America's cities: 1991, a 28-city survey.* ERIC Microfiche ED343984. Washington, DC: U.S. Conference of Mayors.

White, R. W. 1992. *Rude awakenings: What the homeless crisis tells us.* San Francisco: Institute for Contemporary Studies.

Wittman, F. D., & Arch, M. 1988. *Alcohol recovery programs for homeless people: A survey of current programs in the United States.* HE20.8302:H75. Rockville, MD: National Institute on Alcohol Abuse and Alcoholism.

Wright, J. D. 1989. *Address unknown: The homeless in America.* New York: Aldine de Gruyter.

———. 1990. *Correlates and consequences of alcohol abuse in the national "health care for the homeless" client population: Final results.* 1991 ASI Microfiche 4488-14. Bethesda, MD: U.S. Department of Health and Human Services.

Wright, J. D., ed. 1992. Counting the homeless. *Evaluation Review* 16: 355-438.

Wright, J. D., & Weber, E. 1987. *Homelessness and health.* Washington, DC: McGraw-Hill Healthcare Information Center.

Zarembka, A. 1990. *The urban housing crisis: Social, economic, and legal issues and proposals.* New York: Greenwood.

SOURCES OF ADDITIONAL INFORMATION

Bibliographies

Henslin, J. M. 1993. *Homelessness: An annotated bibliography.* Vols. 1-2. New York: Garland, 1993.

Hombs, M. E. 1990. *American homelessness: A reference handbook.* Contemporary World Issues. Santa Barbara, CA: ABC-CLIO.

Nordquist, J. 1988. *The homeless in America: A bibliography.* Santa Cruz, CA: Reference and Research Services.

Ridgely, M. S.; McNeil, C. T.; & Goldman, H. H. 1988. *Alcohol and other drug abuse among homeless individuals: An annotated bibliography.* HE20.8311:H75. Rockville, MD: National Institute on Alcohol Abuse and Alcoholism.

Overview Sources

Cooper, E. F. 1991. *Homeless: Medical conditions.* CRS report for Congress, 91-201SPR. Washington, DC: Library of Congress, Congressional Research Service.

Foster, C. D.; Siegel, M. A.; & Von Brook, P., eds. 1989- . *Homeless in America: How could it happen here?* Wylie, TX: Information Plus.

The homeless. 1992. *CQ Researcher* 2: 665-88.

Klebe, E. R. 1991. *Homeless mentally ill persons: Problems and programs.* CRS Report for Congress, 91-344 EPW. Washington, DC: Library of Congress, Congressional Research Service.

Vanhorenbeck, S. 1991. *HUD's shelter programs for the homeless.* Rev. ed. CRS Report for Congress, 91-198E. Washington, DC: Library of Congress, Congressional Research Service.

Wasem, R. E. 1991. *Homelessness and the federal response, 1987-1991.* CRS Report for Congress, 91-500EPW. Washington, DC: Library of Congress, Congressional Research Service.

―――. 1992. *Homelessness: Issues and legislation in the 102d Congress in America.* CRS Issue Brief, IB88070. Washington, DC: Library of Congress Congressional Research Service. (Updated regularly.)

Annual Reports

Children's Defense Fund. 1991- . *The state of America's children.* Former title: *Children's defense budget.*

Interagency Council on the Homeless. 1988- . *Annual report of the Interagency Council on the Homeless.*

Each year's report is coordinated by a different member agency of the council. For this reason the authorship and title varies from year to year. For example: Department of Agriculture. 1988. *Nation Concerned: The first annual report of the Interagency Council on the Homeless* (1989 ASI Microfiche 14364-1).

Waxman, L. E., & Reyes, L. M. 1984- . *A status report on hunger and homelessness in America's cities: 1990, a 30-city survey*. Washington, DC: United States Conference of Mayors.

Each year the Conference of Mayors surveys more than a dozen American cities to determine the status of hunger and homelessness in the United States. Titles and authorship of these annual reports vary from year to year.

Children's Literature

Beckelman, L. 1989. *The homeless*. New York: Macmillan/Crestwood House.

Bunting, E. 1991. *Fly away home*. New York: Clarion Books.

Fox, P. 1991. *Monkey Island*. New York: Orchard Books.

Stavsky, L., & Mozeson, I. E. 1991. *The place I call home: Faces and voices of homeless teens*. New York: Shapolsky.

Walsh, M. E. 1992. *"Moving to nowhere": Children's stories of homelessness*. New York: Auburn House.

Homeless in Art

Evans, M. A.W., ed. 1988. *Homeless in America*. Washington, DC: Acropolis Books.

Hubbard, J. 1991. *Shooting back: A photographic view of life by homeless children*. San Francisco: Chronicle Books.

Rosen, M. J., ed. 1992. *Home: A collaboration of thirty distinguished authors and illustrators of children's books to aid the homeless*. 1st ed. New York: HarperCollins.

Shames, S. 1991. *Outside the dream: Child poverty in America*. New York: Aperture.

Indexes/Databases

Because homelessness is an interdisciplinary topic, a great many indexes and databases will provide citations to relevant literature. For that reason, an index or database must be selected based on the type of information needed (e.g., U.S. government sources; statistical sources; state and local sources, etc.) or the particular subtopic (e.g., educating the homeless; health problems related to the homeless, etc.).

U.S. Statistical Sources

American Statistics Index
Congressional Information Service
Washington, DC
Print, online, and CD-ROM formats

State and Local Sources

Index to Urban Documents
Greenwood Press
88 Post Road, West
Westport, CT 06881
Print format

Statistical Reference Index
Congressional Information Service
4520 East-West Highway
Bethesda, MD 20814-3387
301-654-1550
Print, online, and CD-ROM formats

Congressional Sources

CIS Index
Congressional Information Service
4520 East-West Highway
Bethesda, MD 20814-3387
301-654-1550
Print, online, and CD-ROM formats

Major Studies and Issue Briefs of the
Congressional Research Service
University Publications of America
4520 East-West Highway
Bethesda, MD 20814-3387
Print format

U.S. Government Sources

Monthly Catalog of U.S. Government Publications
U.S. Government Printing Office
Superintendent of Documents
Mail Stop 55 OP
Washington, DC 20402-9328
Print, online, and CD-ROM formats

Health and Medical Issues

Index Medicus
National Library of Medicine
8600 Rockville Pike
Bethesda, MD 20894-0001
301-496-6308
Print, online, and CD-ROM formats

Psychological Abstracts
American Psychological Association
750 First Street NE
Washington, DC 20002
202-336-5500
Print, online, and CD-ROM formats

Education Issues

Current Index to Journals in Education (CIJE)
Oryx Press
4041 North Central Avenue at Indian School Road
Phoenix, AZ 85012
Print, online, and CD-ROM formats

Political and Economic Issues

PAIS INTERNATIONAL
Public Affairs Information Service, Inc.
521 W. 43rd Street
New York, NY 10036
212-736-6629
Print, online, and CD-ROM formats

Periodicals

Council Communiqué
Interagency Council on the Homeless
451 Seventh Street, SW, Suite 7274
Washington, DC 20410
Bimonthly

Journal of Social Distress and the Homeless
Human Sciences Press
233 Spring Street
New York, NY 10013
Quarterly

Organizations

Children's Defense Fund
25 E Street NW
Washington, DC 20001
202-638-2952

Community for Creative Non-Violence
(CCNV)
425 2nd Street NW
Washington, DC 20001
202-393-1909

Habitat for Humanity International
121 Habitat Street
Americus, GA 31709-3498
912-924-6935

Homelessness Information Exchange
1830 Connecticut Avenue NW, 4th
Floor
Washington, DC 20009
202-462-7551

National Coalition for the Homeless
(NCH)
1621 Connecticut Avenue NW
Washington, DC 20009

U.S. Conference of Mayors
1620 Eye Street NW, 4th Floor
Washington, DC 20006
202-293-7330

Useful Library of Congress Subject Headings

Homeless Aged
Homeless Children
Homeless Persons
Homeless Persons—Alcohol Use
Homeless Persons—Drug Use
Homeless Persons—Mental Health
    Service

Homeless Persons—Services for
Homeless Persons—Substance Abuse
Homeless Students
Homeless Women
Homeless Youth
Homelessness

Somehow the American public has to get back to the great richness and mystery of learning, the playfulness and seriousness of learning, and how that can be nurtured in schools by teachers in classrooms.

Sara Lawrence Lightfoot, 1989

8

Children and Learning

Steven Herb

This is the country in which a young boy from rural Arkansas, whose father dies before he is born and whose stepfather abuses the family, can go on to attend Yale and Oxford, govern his native state, and be elected president. It is also the country in which a similar young teen would have no trouble buying a handgun, taking it to school, and venting his familial frustration in a barrage of bullets aimed at foes, friends, and teachers. For every disadvantaged child in America who learns to transcend the difficulties of life's circumstances, to pick himself up by the proverbial bootstraps and make something of his life, a dozen more learn that life seems

Steven Herb is the Education Librarian at The Pennsylvania State University. During the 1980s he served as Coordinator of Children's Services for the Dauphin County Library System in Harrisburg, Pennsylvania. A former Head Start director in Pennsylvania, he has also held appointments in the special education departments at both Penn State University and Clarion University of Pennsylvania.

Dr. Herb holds a Ph.D. in Curriculum & Instruction from The Pennsylvania State University and masters degree focusing on children's literature. His baccalaureate degree was awarded in special education.

He is a founder of the Children's Literature Council of Pennsylvania and currently serves on the Board of Directors. In addition, he serves on the Advisory Committee to the Children's Literature Center at the Library of Congress and as a consultant to the national literacy partnership project between the Association for Library Service to Children and Head Start. His work as a radio producer and commentator has won numerous awards, including the International Reading Association's Broadcast Media Award (1984) and the Best Program Series Designed for Children Award for Excellence in Broadcasting from the Pennsylvania Association of Broadcasters (1991, 1992, and 1993).

197

hopeless, that the only ticket out of their dead-end street is to enter the lucrative drug sales network so ever-present in our cities. A Latino youth recently told a CNN reporter that he hoped he could grow up and "go to prison and not be dead" (*The state of America's children*, 1992, p. xii). A choice between prison and death is a far cry from the American dream.

Children learn far more than numbers and colors from their families and caregivers in those important early years. They learn how to solve problems and how to make themselves happy. They learn how to request food and seek comfort. They learn the beauty of our language and have laid before them a foundation of early literacy experiences that will yield huge returns when they reach the formal instruction of the public schools. Those are the lucky children. Less fortunate children learn to solve their problems through aggression and cannot comprehend the pursuit of childhood happiness. They learn that hunger and cries of hunger do not always lead to food and that sometimes there is no one to help them comfort themselves. Their agonies of early childhood can grow and gnaw at them well into their adult lives and, perhaps, throughout their lives. They do not hear songs sung or books read or poetry recited, and arrive at school mystified at the black lines on white paper that seem to make sense to their classmates.

Childhood should be a protected time where learning can take place in an atmosphere of joy. The home or the child care facility should be bright, filled with books, toys, and the time and attention of caring adults. The school should be clean, well funded, and filled with competent teachers using the latest technologies in harmony with successful traditional methodologies. After a 25-year absence from public education, Jonathan Kozol found today's urban schools vastly and depressingly changed from his days as a teacher. "[T]hese urban schools were, by and large, extraordinarily unhappy places. With few exceptions, they reminded me of 'garrisons' or 'outposts' in a foreign nation. Housing projects, bleak and tall, surrounded by perimeter walls lined with barbed wire, often stood adjacent to the schools I visited. The schools were surrounded frequently by signs that indicated DRUG-FREE ZONE. Their doors were guarded. Police sometimes patrolled the halls. The windows of the schools were often covered with steel grates. Taxi drivers flatly refused to take me to some of these schools and would deposit me a dozen blocks away, in border areas beyond which they refused to go. I'd walk the last half-mile on my own" (Kozol, 1991, p. 5).

In the Children's Defense Fund's annual list, "Is This the Best America Can Do?", an alarming picture of childhood in the 1990s emerges (*The state of America's children*, 1992, p. x):

- Every 12 seconds of the school day, an American child drops out (380,000 a year).

- Every 13 seconds, an American child is reported abused or neglected (2.7 million a year).

- Every 26 seconds, an American child runs away from home (1.2 million a year).

- About every minute, an American teenager has a baby.

- Evey nine minutes, an American child is arrested for a drug offense.

- Every 40 minutes, an American child is arrested for drunken driving.

- Every 53 minutes in our rich land, an American child dies from poverty.

- Every three hours, a child is murdered.

In a world where a country is often judged not by its military might, but rather by how it treats its children, the United States has

- A higher infant mortality rate than 19 other nations;

- A higher infant mortality rate for black infants than the overall rates of 31 other nations, including Cuba, Bulgaria, and Kuwait;

- A death rate among preschool children worse than 19 other nations;

- A worse low-birth-weight rate than 30 other nations;

- A low-birth-weight rate among blacks worse than the overall rates of 73 other countries, including many Third World and former Communist eastern bloc countries;

- A ranking of 12 out of 14 among industrialized nations in science achievement among 13 year olds;

- A ranking of 13 out of 14 among industrialized nations in mathematics achievement among 13 year olds;

- A higher child poverty rate than seven other industrialized Western countries. One in five U.S. children—143 million—are poor, making them the poorest group of Americans.

Our nation has

- An estimated 2.4 million children involved in juvenile prostitution each year;

- The highest rate of working children among affluent countries, according to the National Consumers League;

- The highest rate of teen drug use of any nation in the industrialized world, according to the U.S. Department of Health and Human Services;

- The record of being one of only seven countries carrying out the capital punishment of juvenile offenders within the past decade. At least 145 nations ban such executions. "We have executed more juvenile offenders than any nation except Iran and Iraq" (*The state of America's children*, 1992, p. x).

The data from the Children's Defense Fund indicate that all is not well in America for its children. This chapter will examine children and learning in a largely social context. The first section examines the history of childhood and finds that a tough life for many of today's children has historical precedents. Perhaps the major difference between yesterday and today is that yesterday nearly all children had miserable lives, whereas today some live quite well; perhaps making the lives of the "have nots" ever more tragic. The second section examines learning by reviewing the research on child and adolescent development in four skill categories—motor, cognitive, language, and social-emotional. Ideal circumstances for learning are described as well as the consequences for children who face less than ideal environments. Because child care environments (see chapter 5) and the home (see chapter 12) are covered elsewhere in this book, section three will focus on the other environment so influential on a child's learning—the school. The issue of a basic education for all versus a quality education for some has been an argument in America since the colonial days and shows no sign of slowing down, but now the debate contains such terms as school choice, schools for profit, training students for the high-tech workplace, and homeschooling. Section four concludes the chapter with an examination of some issues of importance to children and learning in the 1990s and beyond.

CHILDHOOD

Childhood, as we know it or perhaps idealize it, has not always existed. "Medieval art until about the twelfth century did not know childhood or did not attempt to portray it. It is hard to believe that this neglect was due to incompetence or incapacity; it seems more probable that there was no place for childhood in the medieval world" (Aries, 1962, p. 33). "Although there are always exceptions to the rule, medieval communities dealt with their children as they dealt with their animals—and in the same practical and unsentimental way. Both shared the floor, the worms, the dirt, and every manner of disease that being a dog or a child in this period invited and implied. In perhaps one way alone children were uniquely different from the animals with whom they wallowed: Children were treated as if they were expendable" (Schorsch, 1979, p. 14). Over the next several centuries the life of the child did not rapidly improve. Interpretations in the paintings of the day ranged from the miniature adult to the perfect baby Jesus to the child on the way to heaven. The heaven image was, sadly, not far from historical reality, but "there was never a portrait of him, the portrait of a real child, as he was at a certain moment of his life. . . . The general feeling was, and for a long time remained, that one had several children in order to keep just a few. . . . This is the reason for certain remarks which shock our present-day sensibility, such as Montaigne's observation: 'I have lost two or three children in their infancy, not without regret, but without great sorrow.' Most people felt like Montaigne, that children had 'neither mental activities nor recognizable bodily shape' " (Aries, 1962, pp. 38-39).

It was in the seventeenth century that true portraits of real children appeared in Europe, usually as the focal point of a family portrait. Literary references to young children began to use the jargon of and about young children. "[E]ach reflected the discovery of infancy, of the little child's body, habits and chatter" (Aries, 1962, p. 49). In the eighteenth century childhood became a sorting process for the preparation of adults along gender or class lines. Children of the working class lived the apprenticeship of being working class in habits and dress, but the sons of the middle classes or bourgeoisie were "the first children, as they had to be separated off from working activities and sent to school to undergo a long training in preparation for their adult working lives" (Suransky, 1982, p. 7).

Several psychohistorians question Aries's conclusions about the history of childhood as being too gentle or mythological (Suransky, 1982). DeMause, in particular, claims that Aries's work serves to "cover-up" widespread brutality and cruelty to children, common to the times and cultures in which they took place. "The history of childhood is a nightmare from which we have only recently begun to awaken. The further back in history one goes, the lower the level of childcare, and the more likely children are to be killed, abandoned, beaten, terrorized and sexually abused" (DeMause, 1974, p. 1). DeMause's use of the term abandonment covers the broad historical practice of sending children to wet nurses, sometimes, in the cases of the rich, for years at a time (DeMause, 1974). "Perhaps to offset the horrors of an incredible rate of infant mortality, parents consciously limited affection and attachment to their children by putting them out in infancy [wet-nursing] and again at seven or eight years [to find work, apprenticeship, lodging, or rarely, school]. Ironically, these physical and psychological separations sometimes contributed to the high infant death rate. And since women—breeders of babies, and little more—were almost as dispensable as children, there could always be more babies from where the dead ones had come" (Schorsch, 1979, pp. 14-15).

Once childhood was invented, children were declared wicked sinners. They could be saved, but salvation was not guaranteed. Minister Benjamin Wadsworth wrote in 1721, "Their hearts naturally, are a meer nest, root, fountain of Sin, and wickedness; as evil *Treasure* from whence proceed evil things. . . . Indeed, as sharers in the guilt of Adam's first Sin, they're *Children of Wrath by Nature,* liable to Eternal Vengeance, the Unquenchable Flames of Hell. But besides this, their Hearts (as hath been said) are unspeakably wicked, estranged from God, enmity against

Him, eagerly set in pursuing Vanities, on provoking God by actual Personal transgressions, whereby they deserve *greater measures* of Wrath" (cited in Heininger, 1984, p. 2).

In the mid-nineteenth century America's view toward its children began to soften. Perhaps it was the influence of the 1762 work of Jean-Jacques Rousseau (*Emile; or, On education*, 1979) or perhaps the combined optimism of John Locke's philosophy of viewing the child as a "blank slate" at birth (*An essay concerning human understanding*, 1965), first published in 1689, and the fall from favor of predeterminism. All across America, the middle classes felt that, if they nurtured their children correctly and educated them properly, they would become good citizens. This optimism coincided with the Jackson presidency (elected in 1828) and the extension of voting rights to nearly all states. It was also the start of a more universal governmental responsibility for the education of its children, which was reflected in the concerned attitudes of its population toward its children (Heininger, 1984). It was a time when child-rearing advice became accessible to the masses through often-reprinted manuals, many used by newly transplanted urban couples away from the traditional advice of their elders (Heininger, 1984).

The urban migration of America's rural populations coupled with the nation's open immigration policies led to nearly half of all of the United States' population in the Northeast being located in the cities by 1870 (Green, 1984) and to a diminution of America's optimism for the future. "Here [in the rapidly growing cities] children who were without the sound guidance of family or church were forming what Charles Loring Brace, founder of the Children's Aid Society (1853), called 'the dangerous classes'" (Green, 1984, p. 128). The importance of the positive early development of a child's character, the interpretation of Charles Darwin's theories of evolution (*On the origin of species by means of natural selection*, 1859) against a Protestant backdrop, and America's "anything's possible" attitude combined to form the beginning of the heredity vs. environment argument that still rages in arenas of social and political thought. But even in times of doubt, such as the late nineteenth century's horrors over the effects of industrialization, or the mid-twentieth century's reaction to the Soviets' Sputnik "threat," the American culture rests its hopes upon its children. Green writes about the 1890s: "Childhood and youth were thus often characterized as opposite to the present circumstances of life in America, and the positive metaphor of the healthy, unbridled child took hold of the population, expressing itself in a variety of forms" (1984, p. 133).

An investment of time, attention, and money in children is a sound investment of America's optimism. Unfortunately, that investment is not often made, and even when begun, has been stopped before the payoff. Edward Zigler, one of the founders of Head Start, was asked by a reporter, "Why did Head Start succeed and the rest of the War on Poverty fail?" He thought for a moment and replied that he did not think the War on Poverty failed, but rather that it was prematurely halted. Although Head Start hasn't always measured up to its full potential, it is still the longest-running success of the social programs of the 1960s, both in its results with children and families, and in its spirit of compromise. "It still has the capacity to inspire people as far apart politically as Jesse Jackson and Orin Hatch. High hopes made Head Start possible" (Zigler & Muenchow, 1992, p. 1). America's dreams for its children do not always correspond with America's actions, and it is individual children who pay the price. Even the successful Head Start has never been fully funded.

LEARNING VIA DEVELOPMENT

Despite the myriad theories that account for various aspects of learning in children, it is impossible to describe the whole child as a collection of learned tasks. The interaction of what the child brings to the world and the environment in which the child exists is a complex one, where predictions of the eventual adult outcome are only statistical possibilities, not a blueprint for an individual.

A study of children's learning begins with an understanding of how children typically grow and change across the developmental periods that compose childhood: prenatal, infancy, early childhood, middle childhood, and adolescence periods. What are the major learning tasks that children must accomplish across childhood? From infancy on, these developmental tasks take particular forms, which for purposes of this chapter, will be organized into the learning of perceptual and motor, cognitive, language, and social-emotional skills.

Prenatal Development and Learning

During the prenatal period of development, learning is influenced in two ways. First, prenatal environments and events can either prepare the infant or make the infant vulnerable as a learner. Second, the prenatal environment, though restrictive, provides an opportunity for some kinds of early learning.

Most development during the 38-week prenatal period is physical in nature, and is generally a highly reliable process. Over 97 percent of newborns have no serious developmental deficiencies (Guttmacher & Kaiser, 1984). However, certain conditions influence prenatal development in ways that might have adverse effects on fetal growth, on the newborn's ability, or on later learning potential. These conditions, called risk factors, range from those with biological bases, such as genetic defects, disease, or maternal age, to those with environmental origins, for example, exposure to drugs, alcohol, pollution, or stress (Stechler & Halton, 1982). The influence of these risk factors varies, affecting growth more at certain stages of development than at others, affecting some areas of development more than others (Moore, 1983). Recent research on risk factors focused on the alarming incidence of drug use among pregnant women. Maternal drug use is associated with a range of undesirable behavioral outcomes in newborns: prematurity of birth, low birth weight, small head circumference, abnormal reflexes and muscle tone, and hyper- or hyposensitivity to a range of stimuli (Cole, 1991; Committee on Substance Abuse, 1990; Hutchings, 1989).

Can we identify which newborns will have later learning problems? Although it is difficult to make such predictions based on evaluation of the newborn, the Brazelton Neonatal Behavioral Assessment Scale (Brazelton, 1984) does provide some information related to the infant's learning capacity. It assesses, among other characteristics, the newborn's reflexes, sociability, behavioral organization, orientation, and reactions to various environmental stimuli. It is important to recognize, however, that although most developmental problems present at birth can be attributed to genetic or prenatal risk factors, research shows that over the years of childhood, the causation of learning problems changes (Sameroff & Chandler, 1975). Among school-age children, learning problems are more highly correlated with conditions of the child's environment (socioeconomic factors, parents' education) than with prenatal variables (Werner, Bierman, & French, 1971; Werner & Smith, 1982).

In addition to providing a physical environment that facilitates normal growth of the fetus, there is evidence that the fetus engages in perceptual and motor behaviors in the uterus, and that these abilities develop especially in the last trimester of pregnancy. The fetus moves around, changes position when touched, enjoys sweet tastes, and hears music and voices (Maurer & Maurer, 1988). DeCasper and Fifer devised a series of experiments designed to examine what human infants might learn about sound while in utero. Their results indicate that by the time of birth, infants have learned to recognize their mothers' voices (1980), and that they can even differentiate between two different story books read to them during the last six-and-a-half weeks of pregnancy (Kolata, 1984).

Learning During Infancy

Learning during the first three years of life revolves around infants learning to use their own bodies to explore the immediate environment, and learning about the people and objects within that world. The physical realm of learning appears to dominate the infant's behaviors. An important first task for infants is to learn to regulate their daily activities—to establish eating, sleeping, and waking routines. The regularity in passing through states of deep and restless sleep, waking activity and inactivity, regulates the amount of stimulation the infant receives (Wolff, 1966). Research indicates that the sensory stimulation the infant receives during waking (Berg & Berg, 1979) and sleep (Santrock, 1993) enhances early learning. Developing skills in controlling large and fine motor movements is another important physical task of infancy. During the first two years, infants learn to sit, stand, walk, run, kick, and to follow objects visually; they also learn to reach, grasp, and manipulate during this important time of growth (Frankenburg & Dodds, 1967). There is evidence that both cultural practices in child rearing and opportunities for learning influence when infants develop these kinds of skills (Super, 1982).

Cognitive learning during infancy is highly related to the infant's ability to examine his environment—to his sensory capacities, his motor skills, and his ability to integrate them. Through this exploration the infant learns concepts of spatial relations, object characteristics, and causation (Piaget, 1963; Piaget & Inhelder, 1969). In addition, the infant's capacity to remember and act upon these concepts grows across the months of infancy. The Bayley Scales of Infant Development (Bayley, 1969) and the Uzgiris-Hunt Ordinal Scales (Uzgiris & Hunt, 1975) are both widely used to measure infant learning during the first two to three years of life.

The development of language and the capacity to represent experiences are considered developmental capstones of the infancy period. The infant's capacity to represent is seen through his pretend play, which begins at about one year of age (Bretherton, 1984). Infants begin by using real objects to act out experiences from daily life (e.g., pretend to eat from a spoon), and gradually become more skilled at abstraction and imagining (Fenson & Ramsay, 1980). Language itself progresses from cries, coos, and babbles to a vocabulary of 50 to 300 words and use of short sentences by two years of age (DeVilliers & DeVilliers, 1978). Developmental theorists are intrigued and disagree over how infants learn language (Chomsky, 1976; Skinner, 1957; Stern, 1985). Research, however, indicates that language learning is enhanced by certain parent or caregiver practices: turn-taking in conversation (Ginsberg & Kilbourne, 1988; Kaye, 1982); using short and simple expressions (Kemler-Nelson et al., 1989); use of repetitive, melodic, and emphatic expression (Murray, Johnson, & Peters, 1990); and providing developmentally appropriate feedback (Demetras, Post, & Snow, 1986).

The social-emotional world of infancy also includes some significant learning. Infants acquire a repertoire of emotional expressions (Greenspan & Greenspan, 1985). Primary among these expressions is the development of trust and attachment to their primary caregivers (Ainsworth, 1973; Erikson, 1963; Maccoby, 1984). Over the first months of life, infants learn to communicate their emotions (Stern, 1985) and to interact with a number of persons in their families and environments (Belsky et al., 1984; Clarke-Stewart, 1989). During these interactions, infants learn sophisticated social behaviors, such as responding appropriately to the distress of others (Radke-Yarrow, Zahn-Waxler, & Chapman, 1983) and "reading" cues from a caregiver regarding whether or not they should do something, such as touching an unfamiliar object (Walden & Baxter, 1989). Research on attachment between parents and infants suggests that children who have healthy emotional attachments to their parents are more cooperative learners (Londerville & Main, 1981).

Learning During the Preschool Years

Motor development in the preschool years (ages three to six) is skill-oriented. Children learn specialized tasks, such as jumping, throwing, catching, swimming, and dancing; all of which are learned and improved through direct instruction and practice (Schmidt, 1988). Perceptually, preschoolers show more ability in auditory acuity than in visual acuity (Moores, 1987) though acuity and memory in each area improve across these years. Throughout this period, most children have better distant than near vision (Seifert & Hoffnung, 1991). Therefore, reading and drawing tasks can be difficult for preschoolers. Drawing and writing skills progress from scribbling at three years of age to representational drawing and beginning letter formation by four years of age (Kellog, 1969). As with large motor development, these specialized fine motor skills are learned through guidance and opportunity for experience.

The emergence of symbolic thinking is considered a marker of cognitive learning in preschoolers (Piaget, 1963). These children have improved memories; they are beginning to use pictorial, letter, and number symbols; they can explain, retell, and question; they can follow verbal instructions; and they approach experiences in an orderly manner. Simple problems dealing with color and shape can be thought about and solved (Sugarman, 1983), and number concepts can be identified (Baroody, 1987; Gelman & Gallistel, 1978). Although preschoolers are becoming more skilled in thinking with language, research on teaching indicates that children learn most successfully when contingent teaching is used; that is, when the teacher offers help based on careful observations of the child's understanding and does not leave the young learner overwhelmed by a task or by verbal instructions (Wood, Bruner, & Ross, 1976).

Language skills learned during the preschool period involve gains in vocabulary, syntax, grammar, sentence length, and comprehension (Moskowitz, 1978). Theorists and researchers believe that these growing language skills enhance the preschooler's ability to learn and solve problems, since children talk aloud while investigating and thinking (Berk, 1985; Bruner et al., 1966). Also, Lev Vygotsky (1962) hypothesized that inner speech occurs when children are engaged in learning. In addition to improved oral language skills, preschoolers are also learning to understand printed language. They do this through their own attempts at writing and recognizing letters (Schickedanz, 1989), and through their attempts to read familiar print (Sulzby, 1985). Emergent reading and writing during the preschool period has been correlated with family and teacher practices that model and support these early attempts (Clay, 1976; Garton & Pratt, 1989; Taylor, 1983).

Social-emotional learning during these years focuses on socialization in the world outside the family. For many children this age marks the beginning of significant periods of time spent away from home—at child care, a sitter's, a grandparent's, or at preschool. Everyday life presents the need to learn how to enjoy and care about other people, how to follow rules about fairness and sharing, learning to control one's stronger emotions (e.g., refraining from tantrums), and resisting aggressive impulses. Preschoolers who learn to be purposeful and controlled in social interactions are also learning confidence in themselves. They are learning to trust their own judgements, respect the ideas they have, and take initiative to try some tasks independently (Erikson, 1963). The need to balance one's own initiative against respecting the rules set by others accounts for the real challenge in children's social development at this time. Learning now focuses on three tasks: developing autonomy and a positive sense of initiative (Erikson, 1968); understanding and following prosocial practices, such as helpfulness (Zahn-Waxler & Radke-Yarrow, 1982); and developing friendships (Furman, 1982; Vandell, 1980). Parents and teachers who are most successful in guiding children's social and emotional development are ones who allow children some autonomy, give them guidance in their interactions, and express positive emotions toward the children (Denham, Renwick, & Holt, 1991).

In summary, research on learning during the preschool period suggests several strategies that are effective across varied learning tasks. In considering these strategies, note that continued developmental progress during the preschool years is highly dependent on the child's good fortune to learn in environments peopled by observant, skilled, economically and emotionally stable adults.

- Providing an environment that is predictable, has safe and quiet places, and contains items for cognitive exploration is related to favorable cognitive, language, and social learning outcomes in children (Bradley & Caldwell, 1976).

- Adults engaging in everyday conversation related to the child's experiences facilitates children's learning (Furrow et al., 1979).

- Encouraging children's opportunities to play provides a critical integrative experience that helps children master cognitive (Flavell, 1986) and social skills (Corsaro, 1981).

- Parenting styles that provide models for appropriate behavior enhance children's social learning (Main & George, 1985; Mussen & Eisenberg-Berg, 1977).

- Making judicious choices of new learning tasks for children and choosing ones that children will be able to attain success in, if given support, enables children to learn most effectively (Vygotsky, 1978).

- Providing direct teaching (Howard & Barnett, 1981) and rewards (Orlick, 1981) helps children learn social skills more effectively.

Learning During the Middle School Years

Data indicate that physically, these years are a child's healthiest. Growth slows during this period as compared to the preschool years.

Children continue to improve physical skills and often become active in organized sports involving combinations of skills learned earlier, such as throwing and catching. Children make progress in physical tasks requiring coordination and timing skills (Cratty, 1986). Participation in sports and its resulting skill development can contribute to a child's positive self-image: feeling healthy, learning to interact with a team of peers, developing mastery of skills. Children progress in the learning of fine motor skills during this period also. They gain proficiency in writing and in drawing, painting, and other graphic arts (Carlson & Cunningham, 1990). Again, the development of skills in these areas contributes to a sense of competence.

Across middle childhood children show striking changes in their learning of cognitive skills. They become able to think abstractly, to organize and reorganize information, and to follow logical steps in problem solving (Brown & Kane, 1988; Piaget, 1963). These broad abilities enhance children's learning of traditional school curriculum studies, such as reading, mathematics, science, and social studies. Although they may change as a child grows older, this period marks the beginning of individual differences in learning styles. These differences may influence a wide range of learning task requirements and may require individualized approaches to teaching, for example, field dependence versus field independence (Hardy et al., 1987), reflectivity versus impulsiveness (Messer, 1976), convergent versus divergent approaches to problem solving (Kogan, 1973).

Cognitive learning during this period is also related to important dispositional factors: awareness that individuals can influence their own learning ability (metacognition) and development of the motivation to learn. In terms of metacognition, children become aware of memory and learn ways to enhance that ability (Brown et al., 1983; Weinstein et al., 1988). They learn about learning, for example, that study efforts do pay off (Chen & Stevenson, 1989). Motivation to learn is related to what the middle school child comes to believe about his own competence as a learner (Bandura, 1989; Phillips, 1987). This belief is based not just on success in learning, but on messages received from significant others. For example, Dweck (1978) found that some teachers give male and female students different messages about their learning abilities, encouraging males to believe that they can do anything if they work hard enough, and encouraging females to believe that one cannot develop expertise in every area. Indeed, children's beliefs about the difficulty of subject matter do influence how well they master that content, as evidenced by studies of children's difficulties in learning mathematics (Schoenfeld, 1985).

Although learning to read, write, and spell are clearly landmarks of language learning during middle childhood, these children are still gaining more skill in oral language. Specifically, children learn to understand the complexities and ambiguities of word meaning (Sternberg & Powell, 1983) and usage (Schultz & Pilon, 1973) in spoken language. Because many schoolchildren are bilingual or grow up in families where another dialect of English is spoken, becoming skilled in two or more languages is a necessary educational goal for them. Some schools emphasize learning of a second language for all children. Research on the effects of bilingualism indicates that this can positively influence children's attitudes about themselves, and teach them to think fluently and flexibly (Ben-Zeev, 1984; Berman, 1987; Folb, 1980). However, if children perceive that their native language is not respected, they avoid using it and do not benefit as much from their bilingual opportunities (Gal, 1979; Labov, 1982).

During the middle school years, children develop literacy in reading and writing, which then become avenues for further learning (Atwell, 1990; Goodman et al., 1987). Children's abilities in oral language, reading, and writing also generalize to wider ranges of content as they develop literacy across curricular areas: music, art, mathematics, history, etc. Studies about how children come to learn and be literate in these other content areas demonstrate the continued importance that learning be guided by adults who provide appropriate models, direct instruction, and regular, positive feedback (Wood, 1988).

Social and emotional development during the middle school years has two focus areas: learning about one's self, and continuing to learn about getting along with others. Successful learners begin to define themselves based on positive psychological traits, e.g., as someone who tries hard, is a loving daughter, or is a true friend (Harter, 1982). They are able to integrate facts about their abilities and their disabilities into a self-definition that portrays a person who is basically industrious and able to achieve (Erikson, 1968). However, a child's growing sense of self-esteem is fragile, and depends strongly upon positive feedback from others (Ruhland & Feld, 1977).

Skills in getting along with others are enhanced by a child's emerging ability to understand other points of view and to differentiate among a person's behaviors, intentions, and feelings (Dodge, Murphy, & Buchsbaum, 1984; Miller, & DeMarie-Dreblow, 1990). These skills allow the child to begin interacting effectively with a wider range of persons and to understand behaviors necessitated by one's role (e.g., why a school principal chooses to enforce certain rules). Peers become a strong element in learning during middle childhood, as children are influenced by judgments made by peers (Hartup, 1989). The significance of peers can also be seen in research that shows a relationship between a child's ability to make and maintain friendships and school achievement (Green et al., 1980). Fortunately, research also shows that friendliness can also be taught (Dodge et al., 1984; Oden & Asher, 1977).

Learning During Adolescence

Adolescence begins at 11 or 12 years of age and continues into the early twenties. Physically, this is the last growth spurt the developing child experiences. Growth during adolescence is uneven within and across children, making the challenge of rapid bodily change one of the major problems needing to be dealt with by adolescents (Marshall, 1986). While managing these changes, adolescents are expected to learn significant concepts related to maintaining good health: 1) making good nutritional choices; 2) engaging in physical activity; 3) being responsible in sexual matters; and 4) resisting drug and alcohol use. Body image is a factor that appears to predominate thinking, especially in the early adolescent years, and can cause difficulties, as evidenced by adolescent use of steroids (Johnson, 1990) and a high incidence of anorexia and bulimia (Moses, Banilivy, & Lifshitz, 1989). Research on the relationship between physical development during adolescence and academic learning is unclear, but it does suggest differing effects on males and females and early and later maturers (Buchanan, 1991; Magnusson, Strattin, & Allen, 1985; Sussman et al., 1985). The literature shows that as children work to resolve these many problems related to their physical well-being, parents continue to be powerful influences both in positive and negative ways (Schwartz, Barrett, & Saba, 1985) and in helping children develop a self-esteem based on their own strengths (Harter, 1990).

In the domain of cognitive development, adolescence marks the beginning of learning true abstract thinking, called formal operations by Piaget (Inhelder & Piaget, 1958). This kind of thought is characterized by scientific reasoning, the ability to deal with hypothetical situations, and the ability to connect ideas while logically pursuing a problem. This ability to speculate allows the adolescent to begin to be planful about daily life as well as about the future (Elkind, 1984). The growing ability to think hypothetically rather than out of one's own experiences allows the adolescent to develop social cognition and to make hypotheses about other persons. This enables the individual to develop concern for others and to think and make decisions about such concepts as social justice, politics, and religion (Noddling, 1984).

Unfortunately, research indicates that a majority of adolescents, even adults, do not use formal thinking often or consistently (Byrnes, 1988). Evidence indicates that although the adolescent is capable of systematic abstract thinking, it must be learned. Seiffert and Hoffnung (1991) summarize the research regarding how this critical thinking is best taught. Direct teaching is a necessary condition. Although modeling is important, it is not sufficient. Children need to have many and varied opportunities to practice high-level problem solving. Finally, the learning environment should have certain characteristics: expert teachers who model critical thinking, teachers who give students confidence along with constructive feedback, and ample opportunity for on-the-spot feedback.

Language learning during adolescence is seen in the continuing development of oral language skills, the development of writing skills, and in learning how to learn through language (e.g., while reading, listening to lectures). During this period, individual speaking abilities become more complex. Adolescents learn to express interrelationships (Loban, 1975) and to use and understand figurative and comparative language (Elkind, 1976). Although writing and study skills somewhat mirror these growing abilities in oral language, research studies show that these skills lag behind oral expressive abilities. The National Assessment of Student Progress, conducted by ETS in 1984, indicated that in writing, most adolescent students were unable to present a logical thesis and also had difficulty in creative writing (Applebee, Langer, & Mullis, 1986). Furthermore, the study skills among even the best students appear to be declining in recent years (Singal, 1991). On standardized achievement tests, the number of students scoring at the highest levels on such core subjects as science, math, and reading has declined over the past two decades. This research indicates that schools and families could offset these trends by strongly encouraging students to take on more challenging courses, to spend more time on homework, and to do more productive reading (Mullis, Owen, & Phillips, 1990).

The central social-emotional task of adolescence is to find and define one's unique identity. According to Erikson (1968) adolescents must balance the activities of exploring identity options and of resolving that exploration into a decision that fits the individual. Included in identity decisions are major concepts such as sexual identity, moral and religious beliefs, political affiliations, and occupational decisions. The search for vocational or occupational goals is one of the most significant decisions faced during this period. Researchers have attempted to define the steps young people employ to reach these decisions (Ginzberg, 1972). Once again, although peers have substantial influences over one another during these years (Conger & Peterson, 1984), parents continue to influence learning in important areas of development. In a study of adolescent career choices (Schiamberg & Chin, 1987), researchers found that family variables were second only to achievement motivation in influencing choices. Choices were related to parental education and occupation levels, to the strength of parent-child interactions, and to various parenting practices. As adolescents attempt to define themselves in unique and positive ways and to become autonomous adults, they continue to be strongly influenced by families, teachers, peers, and friends (Elliot, Voss, & Wendling, 1966). When parental and peer influences and supports are not strong enough, or are balanced ineffectively, serious problems, such as drug and alcohol use, dropping out of school, delinquency, running away from home, early pregnancies, and even suicide can occur (Rutter, 1983).

THE SCHOOL

Its History

The previous section examined children and learning in a developmental context. It is clear from the many research studies presented that a demonstration of learning can range from the acquisition of a simple task to the acquiring of complex processes. The common ground is the child—the learner—and the context is most often a social and interactive one. Urie Bronfenbrenner's ecological model of child development acknowledges the powerful influences of the various social contexts in and on a child's life (Bronfenbrenner, 1979, 1986). The child is the center, surrounded by the microsystem (family and peers), the mesosystem (child care, school, neighborhood), the extosystem (government, business, television), and the macrosystem (societal attitudes, cultural values). This section will examine the environment most often associated with children and learning—the school.

The Boston Public Latin School is credited with being the oldest school in the United States. It was founded on April 13, 1635, following the British tradition of teaching the grammar of Latin. Massachusetts led the other colonies by enacting the first law regarding education, the Massachusetts Bay Law of 1642, which required all parents to see that their children were "taught to read, to understand the major laws of the colony, to know the catechism, and to learn a trade (Van Scotter, 1991, p. 48)." Five years later the Old Deluder Law of Massachusetts Bay Colony mandated that towns of more than 50 families had to hire an elementary teacher for reading and writing whereas towns of 100 or more families had to hire a Latin teacher. The Old Deluder Law takes its name from the law's drafters, who were establishing a means of keeping that "old deluder, Satan himself," from working his evil on the uneducated youth (Van Scotter, 1991, p. 48). Despite mandated schools, attendance remained optional for over 200 additional years.

The notion of a public education for most children was put forth in various pockets of the new nation in the late eighteenth century. Thomas Jefferson proposed a comprehensive plan to the Virginia legislature, which, although defeated, had some influence on educators of the day. Massachusetts passed an update of its 1647 law in 1789 that served to institutionalize the school district as the political unit that managed the school. In 1805, De Witt Clinton led the group that established the New York Free School Society to provide education for the poor who were not otherwise schooled by religious societies (Van Scotter, 1991). Although elementary schools were growing more common, high schools were still rare in the mid-nineteenth century. At the time of the Civil War, the United States had about 300 high schools, with over one-fourth of them located in Massachusetts, which had mandated state-supported secondary schools in an 1827 law (Krug, 1966).

Horace Mann's work as secretary of the first state board of education (again, Massachusetts) was instrumental in popularizing the growing public school movement in the United States. His annual reports from 1837 through 1848 were influential when written and remain a clear message of the importance of education. He wrote, "Education, . . . beyond all other devices of human origin, is the great equalizer of the conditions of men,—the balance-wheel of the social machinery . . . [I]t gives each man the independence and means by which he can resist the selfishness of other men. It does better than to disarm the poor of their hostility towards the rich: it prevents being poor" (Mann, 1868, p. 669). Education milestones of the nineteenth century included the first compulsory schooling law (Massachusetts in 1852), the founding of the U.S. Department of Education (1867), and, in 1874, the Michigan Supreme Court decision that allowed the people of a community to use tax funds to support public high schools. This decision, followed by public high school laws in Wisconsin and Minnesota soon after, precipitated the rapid growth of public high schools in the late nineteenth century, which coincided with America's transformation from an agrarian culture to an industrial nation (Van Scotter, 1991).

Although the philosophy of educating the youth of America has changed a great deal since the Boston Public Latin School was founded in 1635, the philosophers can still be divided into two major camps: the classicists or traditionalists and the progressives or pragmatists. The former group has believed over the centuries in some form of a liberal, classical education, well grounded in the humanities. Its European model served to train all who underwent such an education for either further education or the life of good citizenry, and in America that meant democracy. R. Freeman Butts called the era from the 1770s to the 1870s the best example of this movement, with the ideal being some education for all and much education for a few (Butts, 1960). The basic curriculum for all, with an emphasis on the humanities, found a revival during the Reagan presidency through the efforts of then Secretary of Education William Bennett and E. D. Hirsch's popular work, *Cultural Literacy: What Every American Needs to Know* (1987). The progressive philosophy is most often attributed to John Dewey, whose advocacy of practical education was a response to the growing urbanization and industrialization of late nineteenth-century America. The philosophy of Thomas Jefferson and Horace Mann and the notion of education for all, regardless of circumstances, has its roots in the very heart of American democracy. Many educators hasten to point out that gravitating too far into either camp is very limiting; it is a combination of both ideas—a basic curriculum for all with acknowledgement of the importance of practical knowledge and individual learning styles—that leads to the best education. Mortimer Adler, associated with the classical tradition, cites philosophical agreement with Dewey in his discussion of what Dewey meant by "learning is by doing." "What John Dewey had in mind was not exclusively physical doing or even social doing—engagement in practical projects of one kind or another. The most important kind of doing, so far as learning is concerned, is intellectual or mental doing. In other words, one can learn to read or write well only by reading and writing" (Adler, 1982, p. 50).

In the twentieth century, most legislation and court action focused on making education equitable and accessible to more children. The landmark court decision was *Brown* v. *Board of Education of Topeka* (1954) where the U.S. Supreme Court found that separate but equal public school facilities for blacks and whites were inherently unequal, and the modern civil rights movement was born. The National Defense Education Act (1958), which provided financial aid to states to upgrade science, mathematics, and foreign language instruction, and the Elementary and Secondary Education Act (1965), which supported libraries, instructional materials, and reading, both had provisions for improving instruction to culturally disadvantaged or educationally handicapped students. Additional court actions in California (*Serrano* v. *Priest*, 1971) and Texas (*Edgewood* v. *Kirby*, 1989) found that differential tax bases for school districts were inherently unequal. Public Law 94-142, the Education of All Handicapped Children Act, in partnership with Section 504 of the Rehabilitation Act of 1973, guaranteed long-overdue equal access to a public school education for all of America's disabled children in the least restrictive environment possible (P.L. 94-142, 1975). Public Law 99-457 extended the right to public education to disabled children ages three and up, so that needed interventions could begin at a more optimum time in a child's development (P.L. 99-457, 1986).

A single line in the Economic Opportunity Act of 1964, the legislative cornerstone of President Lyndon Johnson's War on Poverty, establishing a preschool program to give children a head start in school, has had a profound effect on preschool education. Concerned with the whole child, Head Start provided for health care and social services as well as education. Although many Head Start programs are not what they once were due to staff reductions at the federal level and some losing sight of the program's original purposes at the local level (Zigler & Muenchow, 1992), the longitudinal study results demonstrated that early childhood education intervention programs did have lasting effects and that Head Start had a positive impact on cognitive development, child health, the family, and the community (Mann, Harrell, & Hurt, 1977). Positive findings included reduced special-education placements and grade retentions, twice the likelihood of participants remaining in age-appropriate grades compared to peers who did not attend preschool (Lazar & Darlington, 1982), and twice the likelihood of participants being employed or enrolled in college or vocational training at age 19 compared to peers who did not attend preschool. In addition, teen pregnancy rates were significantly lower and arrest rates were 40 percent below their non-preschool peers (Berrueta-Clement et al., 1984).

School Quality

Sadly, for all the successes in early intervention and America's long history of struggling for equity in the schools and for access for all children, many in the United States perceive the schools to be failing in their mission. In a report of survey findings, 43 percent of the public rates schools only "fair" or "poor" (Lytle, 1990). In the summer of 1992 the poor and fair ratings had climbed to 59 percent, whereas those ranking the quality of public schools as excellent numbered only 3 percent (Lou Harris poll in Vamos, 1992). The reasons for the decline of public schools are as varied as American schools themselves. Glazar blames unions, bureaucracy, curriculum, and changes in and disintegration of the social order (1992). Jonathan Kozol's powerful book, *Savage Inequalities,* provides a stinging indictment of government looking the other way as children attend schools ravaged by poverty in neighborhoods where the living standards fall below those of many Third World nations (Kozol, 1991). Money, specifically the differential application of money from district to district, is the prime culprit in Kozol's view.

On the brighter side, a Gallup poll found that respondents rated teachers higher than schools they teach in, and that the closer a respondent was to a school (e.g., had more than one child attending school or answered questions geared to the local school), the higher the ratings (Rose, 1991). School quality is not only a dominant theme in education, but at the heart of political thought in the 1990s. School quality was found to positively correspond with further educational opportunities for students (as did education level of teachers) (Card & Krueger, 1992) and specific student achievement (Teddlie & Stringfield, 1993).

Many of the issues facing schools are linked to the issues facing the larger culture. What will be our use of technology in the learning process? Can we meet the needs of our high-tech job market by turning out students whose skills remain unaltered from 10 or even 20 years ago? Can a property-tax-based support structure ever equitably fund America's schools? Will the shifting demographics of America, with the former minority groups reaching majority group status by the end of this decade, be accommodated in curriculum content or teaching approaches? Can we stop our culture's violent tendencies? Will our educational institutions locate and replicate those models of success that exist in America?

In *A Nation at Risk*, the problems and needs for educational reform were clearly specified. "If an unfriendly foreign power had attempted to impose on America the mediocre education performance that exists today, we might well have viewed it as an act of war. As it stands, we have allowed this to happen to ourselves" (U.S. Department of Education, 1983, p. 5). Ten years later we have six national education goals to be accomplished by the turn of the century, but many question how far beyond simply stating them our educational systems have responded. The goals are:

1. All children in the United States of America will start school ready to learn.

2. The high school graduation rate will increase to at least 90 percent.

3. American students will leave grades four, eight, and twelve having demonstrated competency over a challenging curriculum that will enable them to be responsible citizens and compete in the twenty-first century.

4. U.S. students will be first in the world in science and mathematics achievement.

5. Every adult American will be literate and will possess the knowledge and skills necessary to compete in a global economy and exercise the rights and responsibilities of citizenship.

6. Every school in the United States will be free of drugs and violence and will offer a disciplined environment conducive to learning.

Impediments to Improving Quality

In a retrospective look at 25 years of education research, the ERIC Document Reproduction Service selected four areas of our society that have most impacted our schools and, therefore, our learners (Colker, 1993). All four compete for our attention, our tax dollars, and our creative energies. Any of the four can single-handedly stand in the way of achieving the Goals of Education 2000 unless a concerted effort is made to address and resolve these root causes of polarity in our culture.

The Increase in Poverty. The process and progress of normal development and learning is extremely resilient, as are children themselves, but the strains of growing up in today's society are exacting a heavy toll on our nation's youth. Marian Wright Edelman writes in *The State of America's Children*: "While the middle class lost ground [between 1980 and 1989], the already poor became poorer, more desperate, hungry, homeless, and hopeless." Today every seventh American is poor, as is every sixth family with a child under 18. Every fifth child and every fourth preschooler is poor. Every third black and brown child is poor, and every second black preschooler are poor. Two out of every three preschoolers are poor if they live in a female-headed family in the richest nation on earth (1992, p. ix). Poverty is the single most often cited problem when examining the environment's effects on children's learning. In addition to being a risk factor for drastic changes in physical and mental health, poverty is also an established link to educational failure (Zigler & Finn-Stevenson, 1992).

The Increase in Families and Children Whose Primary Language Is Not English. Colker claims that despite the many successes of bilingual programs over the past 25 years, bilingual education remains as "hot" a topic today as it was in 1966, and debate continues over the retention of cultural identity and its relation to the language of instruction (1993). NEA Today considers the 1980s' wave of immigration (the second largest in U.S. history) to be one of the major financial burdens on school district budgets in the 1990s (*The big squeeze*, 1991). If one expands this category to include all children of the traditional minority groups, some of the more glaring disparities in our educational system become apparent. Our urban schools still remain largely nonwhite and, many researchers and education advocates quickly point out, unequal (Kozol, 1991). In 1976, 24 percent of school enrollment in the United States was nonwhite, by the year 2000 projections indicate the numbers will exceed 33 percent, and by 2020 the enrollment will reach 46 percent (Hodgkinson, 1985). The court decisions and legislative acts that opened the door for so many of America's children did not mandate they would find an excellent education when they passed through. Hothschild claims that most of the advances toward desegregation took place from 1968 through 1972 with no lessening of segregation since 1976. The situation is especially bleak in the northeastern United States, where nearly half of black students attend all-minority schools (1985). Not only are the schools in deteriorating physical shape (Kozol, 1991), but these same urban areas find their local tax bases disintegrating as well (*The big squeeze*, 1991).

The High Rate of Teenage Pregnancy and Parenthood. For the 25 years teen pregnancy has been labeled an epidemic, the schools have reacted quite slowly or in an ostrich-like manner (Colker, 1993). In Nash and Dunkle's report, titled *The Need for a Warming Trend*, several major problems cited were: 1) attitudes of administrators—they still do not see pregnancy as a drop-out issue; 2) teachers and administrators viewing pregnant teenage girls and teenage mothers as second-class students, often excluding them from extracurricular and leadership activities; 3) administrative inflexibility with scheduling despite the pregnant student's special medical needs; and 4) little special effort to reach teen fathers (Nash & Dunkle, 1989). Although the number of births to teens peaked in 1970 at 656,000 due to the much higher numbers of teens in the population, the birth rate to unmarried teens has continued to climb through the 1980s. The increase in number has been largely among whites, but the overall rate of teen pregnancies remains highest among black teens (1 of 10 white births vs. 1 of 5 black births). By 1988, nearly two-thirds of teen births were to unmarried girls, five times the ratio of 1950. For most teen mothers, especially those without a partner, the downward slide into poverty begins with the difficulty of finding a job as a high school drop-out and the added problem of finding affordable, quality child care (Simons, Finlay, & Yang, 1991).

Widespread Use of Drugs and Alcohol by Children and Youth. A child's education and life can be lost not only to drugs, but also to the crime that accompanies drug use and the drug trade. Every night the evening news brings disturbing images of drive-by shootings where murderer and victim are children. In 1988 the firearm death rate for males ages 15 to 19 reached an all-time high of 18 per 100,000, a 43 percent increase since 1984 (Simons, Finlay, & Yang, 1991). Despite reports of decreased drug use among 12 to 25 year olds (drugs other than alcohol and tobacco) in recent years (from the National Household Survey on Drug Abuse), almost one-fourth of all 12 to 17 year olds and more than half of all 18 to 25 year olds reported having tried illicit drugs some time in their lives. These results are likely to be very conservative as they do not include populations more likely to be samplers of illicit drugs, including the homeless, youths in jails, prisons, juvenile detention, and long-term health care facilities, and college students living in dormitories (cited in Simons, Finlay, & Yang, 1991).

DEVELOPING ISSUES FOR THE 1990s AND BEYOND

There are several issues to watch through the 1990s that will affect children and learning into the next century. Predictions are tricky in America. It probably has something to do with the optimism we feel that somehow everything will work out, why not wait and see what happens? In a survey of American, Japanese, and Chinese parents, the American mothers and fathers were far more likely to view their children as doing fine in school and doing even better the next year, even when the national facts clearly demonstrated otherwise. Even first graders in America predicted they would be among the best students the next year (Stevenson & Stigler, 1992). Cannell found that all 50 states, using test scores, judge their students to perform above the national average, an obviously impossible feat he has termed the Lake Wobegon syndrome—"All our children are above average!" (1988). Usually our optimism serves us well, but Denis Doyle likens our current problem in schools to the "frog's dilemma." You drop one in boiling water and out he leaps. You place one in tepid water and gradually increase the temperature and he remains, overcome by languor, until it is too late (Doyle, 1992).

School Choice and School Reform

In their landmark report, John Chubb and Terry Moe found that school organization was one of the four highly significant variables affecting student achievement as measured by increases in standardized test scores from the sophomore to the senior year of high school. They found schools to be the root of many of the problems, with their top-heavy bureaucracies and stifling lack of autonomy for the teachers. Their recommendation for institutional reform included an elimination of political and bureaucratic control by administrators and boards and a move toward a market-driven system where parents have choices as to what they want in a school for their children (Chubb & Moe, 1990b). Wells points out that Chubb and Moe ignore the importance of their own findings, that three other variables also affect student achievement, when they focus only on the school organization aspect (Wells, 1991). The other three significant variables are student ability at sophomore year, the socioeconomic status of the family, and the socioeconomic status of the student body (Chubb & Moe, 1990b). Many education administrators, whose jobs would be on the line, consider the school choice plan unworkable as a totally deregulated plan. However, Massachusetts has tried a "controlled-choice" plan in 16 schools in which parents make informed choices and each school maintains a racial balance (Chubb & Moe 1990a; Wells, 1991). Will all children have equitable choices to attend a good school, or will school choice result in another case of "haves" and "have nots"? Voices are ringing in from all over the social sciences. Most in business, not surprisingly, support school choice (Fierman, 1989; Tucker, 1993), whereas the majority of articles in education point out inherent problems. Sosniak and Ethington, in a longitudinal study, examined schools operating under the "choice" model and a matched sample of standard practice schools on several curricular and instructional measures. Contrary to the claims of the proponents of school choice, "the extent to which schools are educationally different and the nature of the differences among schools are the same in typical non-choice schools as in our sample of public schools of choice" (Sosniak & Ethington, 1992, p. 48). Others have examined the issue from an experiential perspective and found problems of equity, cost, and implementation, from perspectives as varied as a social studies teacher (Pearson, 1993), university professors (Brown et al., 1991), and the California Superintendent of Public Instruction (Honig, 1990). School choice success stories also exist in pockets around the country (Yanofsky & Young, 1992). The school choice debate has widened the arena in which the discussion of educational reform takes place, and options other than the status quo are being seriously examined for the first time in decades (Allen, 1992; Beare & Slaughter, 1993; Cobb, 1992).

Schools for Profit and Partnerships with Business

The old argument of a basic humanities education for all versus the job-training model popular at various points in our country's history has taken on a new strength in the 1990s as businesses clamor for a workforce trained to handle their high-tech needs and see the public school not supplying their demand. Not only are some businesses forming partnerships with high schools to help turn out the workforce they need, some are creating on-site elementary schools as a sound education practice that doubles as an excellent employee recruitment strategy (Beales, 1993; Laabs, 1991). Several entrepreneurs are taking the school concept and making it a true business enterprise from start to finish. John T. Golle, the founder of Education Alternatives, Inc., is currently managing several public schools under the auspices of his public company (DeGeorge, 1991). The package includes an integrated system of tested educational programs as well as staff training and implementation support. EAI's biggest experiment is in Baltimore, Maryland, where their contract is worth $130 million over five years with a potential profit of $13 million. Teacher's union president Irene Dandridge says, "Give us $5,400 per student, give us the exclusion from the constant bureaucracy . . . as you've done with EAI, . . . and we'll show you what a school system can really do" (National Public Radio, 1992). The project that will command the greatest amount of attention in the school-for-profit category over the next several years is the Edison Project, founded by education entrepreneur Chris Whittle, already famous for his Channel One program now broadcasting teen-oriented news (and controversial ads) in over 10,000 schools nationwide. Schools get free video equipment in exchange for signing on with Channel One. Whittle plans to open 200 schools in the fall of 1996, to the chagrin of many educators (Rist, 1991); however, his plan received a massive boost and some instant respectability when Yale University President Benno C. Schmidt was hired to head the 100-member team designing the Edison Project (Goodrich, 1992). Recently, Whittle's plans have been redirected from his original goal of opening 1,000 low-tuition private schools to taking over the operation of between "a half dozen and a dozen" public schools by September 1995 (*Private management tried in Baltimore schools,* 1993, p. 28a). The recent hiring of Dr. Stephen Tracy, the Connecticut charter school advocate (Polk, 1993), demonstrates the continued resolve of the Edison Project. Although controversy will follow the project's development, the country is ripe for an idea that works in the schools.

Some business and education leaders believe the missing connection between business and the schools is in the area of technological innovation. Businesses attempt to remain on the cutting edge of communication and information technologies while school classrooms share outdated hardware and software for lack of a realistic technology budget. Lewis Perelman's book, *School's Out: Hyperlearning, the New Technology, and the End of Education,* is a good example of the radical end of the pro-technology/pro-innovation spectrum (1992). In a promising development earlier this year, Bell Atlantic and cable powerhouse TCI announced that public schools would have free connections to the companies' future video network (Gibbons, 1994).

Involving Parents and the Community

The effect of a child's immediate learning environment on the child is inextricably linked to the child's family. The fragmentation and isolation of the American family are frequently cited as the root causes of many of our culture's ills and often fuel political debate, but the statistics do yield alarming trends (see chapter 12). Changes in family structures are not, in and of themselves, negative influences, but many do increase the probability that problems will develop. Increases in step-families, divorce and custody battles, two parents working, single working mothers, latchkey arrangements, and long hours in child care facilities are all potential risk factors in the child's learning environment (Zigler & Finn-Stevenson, 1992). Many educators see flexible schools that seek partnerships with community agencies and parents as having the best chance at success. Parent involvement has always been at the heart of preschool programs like Head Start, and now school-age populations have been placed in the parent/community context as well in New Haven, Connecticut, and Prince Georges County, Maryland. The strategy, designed by James Comer, director of the School Development Program at Yale's Child Study Center, uses a governing council of parents, administrators, and teachers who set goals and map ways to meet them (Del Valle, 1991). Researchers are finding that it is more imperative than ever that parents are brought into the school fold and out of isolation. The extended families are gone and even cohesive neighborhood communities are a thing of the past in many urban, suburban, and rural areas (Lindle & Boyd, 1991).

Even the growth in homeschooling should not be isolated from its community roots. From a period of contention and confrontation in the 1970s, many school districts are finding it easier to cooperate with parents wishing to homeschool. They have found that the legal battles are costly and often find in favor of parents. The consolidation of the movement helped bring like-minded parents together and delivered some political clout to the movement (Knowles, Marlow, & Muchmore, 1992). In an ideal partnership between community and school, the needs of individual children and families would be accommodated via flexible scheduling, acknowledgment of differing styles of parenting and learning, and cooperative administration of both the parents and the professionals—for the benefit of the children.

Two events at the conclusion of 1993 brought a sense of hope to those who work with children in schools. Although there are widely differing interpretations of the results, the report issued in December 1993 by the Organization for Economic Cooperation and Development in Paris contains many positive findings. Among them:

- The fall in college entrance exam scores has stabilized and American students score about average in reading comprehension and above average in science;

- 90.2 percent of all five year olds attend public or private early childhood programs, a percentage that places the United States among the top 5 of the 24 nations surveyed (Celis, 1993);

- Many states that have students competing at or near the top, for example, 13 year olds in Iowa, North Dakota, and Minnesota, are among the world's top performers in mathematics, comparing favorably with 13 year olds in Japan (Sanchez, 1993).

Education Secretary William Riley called the report "full of pluses and minuses" and said the report "confirms why there is an urgent need to press ahead in our continuing efforts to give every American child a world-class education" (Celis, 1993).

Walter Annenberg was certainly paying attention. In a philanthropic gesture of staggering proportions, Mr. Annenberg has donated 500 million dollars to public education over the next five years. Annenberg said he was deeply troubled by school violence and concerned that if it continues unabated it will have a devastating impact on life. "We must ask ourselves whether improving education will halt the violence," he said. "If anyone can think of a better way, we may have to try that. But the way I see this tragedy, education is the most wholesome and effective approach" (*Annenberg offers...*, 1993).

REFERENCES

Adams, M. J. 1990. *Beginning to read: Thinking and learning about print.* Cambridge: MIT Press.

Adler, M. 1982. *The Paideia proposal: An educational manifesto.* New York: Macmillan.

Ainsworth, M. 1973. The development of infant mother attachment. In Caldwell, B. M., & Riciutti, H. N., eds., *Review of child development research,* vol. 3. Chicago: University of Chicago Press.

Allen, D. W. 1992. *Schools for a new century: A conservative approach to radical school reform.* New York: Praeger.

Anderson, G. M.; Shughart, W. F.; & Tollison, R. D. 1991. Educational achievement and the cost of bureaucracy. *Journal of Economic Behavior and Organization* 15: 29-45.

Annenberg offers millions to schools. 1993. *Cleveland Plain Dealer,* 18 December.

Applebee, A. N.; Langer, J. A.; & Mullis, I. V. S. 1986. *The writing report card: Writing achievement in American schools.* Princeton, NJ: Educational Testing Service.

Aries, Philippe. 1962. *Centuries of childhood.* London: Jonathan Cape.

Atwell, N. 1990. *Coming to know: Writing to learn in the intermediate grades.* Portsmouth, NH: Heinemann Educational Books.

Bandura, A. 1989. Human agency in social cognitive theory. *American Psychologist* 44: 1175-84.

Baroody, A. 1987. *Children's mathematical thinking.* New York: Teachers College Press.

Bayley, N. 1969. *Bayley scales of infant development: Manual.* New York: Psychological Corporation.

Beales, J. 1993. Job and school under one roof. *Nation's Business* 81(2): 55-56.

Beare, H., & Slaughter, R. 1993. *Education for the twenty-first century.* London: Routledge Kegan Paul.

Belsky, J.; Gilstrap, B.; & Rovine, M. 1984. The Pennsylvania Infant and Family Development Project, I: Stability and change in mother-infant and father-infant interaction in a family setting at one, three, and nine months. *Child Development* 55: 692-705.

Ben-Zeev, S. 1984. Bilingualism and cognitive development. In Miller, N., ed., *Bilingualism and language disability: Assessment and remediation.* San Diego, CA: College Hill Press.

Berg, K., & Berg, K. 1979. Psychophysiological development in infancy: State, sensory function and attention. In Osofsky, J., ed., *Handbook of infant development.* New York: John Wiley.

Berk, L. 1985. Why children talk to themselves. *Young Children* 40: 46-52.

Berman, R. 1987. Cognitive components of language development. In Pfaff, C., ed., *First and second language acquisition processes.* Cambridge, MA: Newbury House.

Berrueta-Clement, J.; Schweinhart, L.; Barnett, W. S.; Epstein, A.; & Weikart, D. 1984. *Changed lives: The effects of the Perry Preschool Program on youths through age 19.* Monograph 8. Ypsilanti, MI: High/Scope Educational Research Foundation.

The big squeeze: Why your school district can't find quality education. 1991. *NEA Today* 10(1): 4-5.

Bradley, R. H., & Caldwell, B. M. 1976. Early home environment and changes in mental test performance in children from 6 to 36 months. *Developmental Psychology* 12: 93-97.

Brazelton, T. B. 1984. *Neonatal behavioral assessment scale.* 2nd ed. Philadelphia: J. B. Lippincott.

Bretherton, I. 1984. *Symbolic play.* New York: Academic Press.

Bronfenbrenner, U. 1979. Contexts of child rearing: Prospects and problems. *American Psychologist* 34(10): 844-50.

———. 1986. Ecology of the family as a context for human development: Research perspectives. *Developmental Psychology* 22: 723-42.

Brown, A.; Bransford, J.; Ferrara, R.; & Campione, J. 1983: Learning, remembering and understanding. In Flavell, J. H., & Markman, E. M., *Carmichael's manual of child psychology*. New York: John Wiley.

Brown, A. L., & Kane, M. J. 1988. Preschool children can learn to transfer: Learning to learn and learning from example. *Cognitive Psychology* 20: 493-523.

Brown, F., 1991. Issue on school choice plans. *Education and Urban Society* 23(2): 115-230.

Bruner, J. et al. Oliver, R.; & Greenfield, P. 1966. *Studies in cognitive growth*. New York: John Wiley.

Buchanan, C. M. 1991. Pubertal status in early-adolescent girls: Relations to moods, energy, and restlessness. *Journal of Early Adolescence* 11(2): 185-200.

Butts, R. F. 1960. Search for freedom—The story of American education. *NEA Journal* 49: 33-49.

Byrnes, J. P. 1988. Formal operations: A systematic reformulation. *Developmental Review* 8: 66-87.

Cannell, J. J. 1988. The Lake Wobegon effect revisited. *Educational Measurement: Issues and Practice* 7(4): 12-15.

Card, D., & Krueger, A. B. 1992. Does school quality matter? Returns to education and the characteristics of public schools in the United States. *Journal of Political Economy* 100(1): 1-40.

Carlson, K., & Cunningham, J. L. 1990. Effect of pencil diameter on the graphomotor skill of preschoolers. *Early Childhood Research Quarterly* 5: 279-93.

Celis, W. 1993. International report card shows U.S. schools work. *New York Times*, 9 December. Sec. A:1.

Chen, C., & Stevenson, H. W. 1989. Homework: A cross-cultural examination. *Child Development* 60: 551-61.

Chomsky, N. 1976. *Reflections on language*. New York: Pantheon.

Chubb, J. E., & Moe, T. M. 1990a. Choice *is a* panacea. *The Brookings Review* 8(3): 4-12.

———. 1990b. *Politics, markets, and America's schools*. Washington, DC: Brookings Institution.

Clarke-Stewart, K. A. 1989. Infant day care: Maligned or malignant? *American Psychologist* 44(2): 266-73.

Clay, M. M. 1976. *Young fluent readers*. London: Heinemann.

Cobb, C. W. 1992 *Responsive schools, renewed communities*. San Francisco: ICS Press.

Cole, J. G. 1991. High-risk infants: Prenatal drug exposure (PDE), prematurity, and AIDS. In Lauter-Klatell, N., ed., *Readings in child development*. Mountain View, CA: Mayfield, 36-42.

Colker, L. J. 1993. *Beyond reading, writing, and arithmetic: A retrospective look at how schools have responded to changing societal needs. A celebration of ERIC*. Fairfax, VA: Cincinnati Bell Information Systems.

Committee on Substance Abuse. 1990. Drug-exposed infants. *Pediatrics* 86: 639-42.

Conger, J. J., & Petersen, A. C. 1984. *Adolescence and youth: Psychological development in a changing world.* 3rd ed. New York: Harper & Row.

Corsaro, W. 1981. Friendship in the nursery school: Social organization in a peer environment. In Asher, S., & Gottman, J., eds., *The development of children's friendships.* Cambridge: Cambridge University Press.

Cratty, B. 1986. *Perceptual and motor development of infants and pre-school children.* 4th ed. Englewood Cliffs, NJ: Prentice-Hall.

Darwin, C. R. 1859. *On the origin of species by means of natural selection, or Preservation of favoured races in the struggle for life.* London: John Murray.

DeCasper, A. J., & Fifer, W. P. 1980. Of human bonding: Newborns prefer their mothers' voices. *Science* 208: 1174-76.

DeGeorge, G. 1991. The green in the little red schoolhouse. *Business Week,* 14 October, 68-69.

Del Valle, C. D. 1991. Readin', writin', and reform. *Business Week,* 25 October, 140, 142.

DeMause, L. 1974. The evolution of childhood. In DeMause, L., ed., *The history of childhood.* New York: The Psychohistory Press.

Demetras, M. J.; Post, K. N.; & Snow, C. E. 1986. Feedback to first language learners: The role of repetitions and clarification questions. *Journal of Child Language* 13: 275-92.

Denham, S. A.; Renwick, S. M.; & Holt, R. W. 1991. Working and playing together: Prediction of preschool social-emotional competence from mother-child interaction. *Child Development* 62: 242-49.

DeVilliers, J. 1980. The process of rule learning in child speech: A new look. In Nelson, K., ed., *Children's language,* vol. 2. New York: Gardner Press.

DeVilliers, P., & DeVilliers, J. 1978. *Language development.* Cambridge: Harvard University Press.

Dodge, K. A.; Murphy, R. R.; & Buchsbaum, K. 1984. The assessment of intention-cue detection skills in children: Implications for developmental psychopathology. *Child Development* 55: 163-73.

Doyle, D. P. 1992. The challenge, the opportunity. *Phi Delta Kappan* 73(7): 512-20.

Dweck, C. S. 1978. Achievement. In Lamb, M. E., ed., *Social and personality development.* New York: Holt, Rinehart & Winston.

Elkind, D. 1976. *Child development and education: A Piagetian perspective.* New York: Oxford University Press.

———. 1984. *All grown up and no place to go: Teenagers in crisis.* Reading, MA: Addison-Wesley.

Elliot, D.; Voss, H.; & Wendling, A. 1966. Capable dropouts and the social milieu of the high school. *Journal of Educational Research* 60: 180-86.

Erikson, E. 1963. *Childhood and society.* 2nd ed. New York: W. W. Norton.

———. 1968. *Identity: Youth and crisis.* New York: W. W. Norton.

Fenson, L., & Ramsay, D. S. 1980. Decentration and integration of the child's play in the second year. *Child Development* 51: 171-78.

Fierman, J. 1989. Giving parents a choice of schools. *Fortune* 120(14): 147-52.

Flavell, J. 1986. Development of children's knowledge about the appearance-reality distinction. *American Psychologist* 41(4): 418-25.

Folb, E. 1980. *Running down some lines: The language and culture of black teenagers*. Cambridge: Harvard University Press.

Frankenburg, W., & Dodds, J. 1967. The Denver developmental screening test. *Journal of Pediatrics* 71: 181-91.

Furman, W. 1982. Children's friendships. In Field, T., ed., *Review of Human development*. New York: John Wiley.

Furrow, D.; Nelson, K.; & Benedict, H. 1979. Mothers' speech to children and syntactic development. *Journal of Child Language* 6: 423-42.

Gal, S. 1979. *Language shift*. New York: Academic Press.

Garton, A., & Pratt, C. 1989. *Learning to be literate: The development of spoken and written language*. New York: Basil Blackwell.

Garvey, C. 1977. *Play*. Cambridge: Harvard University Press.

Gelman, R., & Gallistel, C. R. 1978. *The child's understanding of number*. Cambridge: Harvard University Press.

Gibbons, K. 1994. Bell Atlantic, TCI promise schools free access. *Washington Times*, 11 January.

Ginsburg, G. P., & Kilbourne, B. K. 1988. Emergence of vocal alternation in mother-infant interchanges. *Journal of Child Language* 15: 221-35.

Ginzberg, E. 1972. Toward a theory of occupational choice: A restatement. *Vocational Guidance Quarterly* 20: 169-76.

Glazer, N. 1992. The real world of urban education. *Public-Interest* 106: 57-75.

Goodman, K. S.; Smith, E. B.; Meredith, R.; & Goodman, Y. 1987. *Language and thinking in school: A whole-language curriculum*. 3rd ed. New York: Richard C. Owen.

Goodrich, C. 1992. Whittle's classroom gamble. *Publishers Weekly* 239(43): 50-53.

Green, H. 1984. Scientific thought and nature of children in America, 1820-1920. In *A century of childhood, 1820-1920*. Rochester, NY: Margaret Woodbury Strong Museum.

Green, K. D.; Beck, S. J.; Forehand, R.; & Vosk, B. 1980. Validity of teacher nomination of child behavior problems. *Journal of Abnormal Child Psychology* 8: 397-404.

Greenspan, S. I., & Greenspan, N. T. 1985. *First feelings: Milestones in the emotional development of your baby and child*. New York: Viking Penguin.

Guttmacher, A., & Kaiser, I. 1984. *Pregnancy, birth, and family planning*. New York: Signet.

Hardy, R. C.; Eliot, J.; & Burlingame, K. 1987. Stability over age and sex of children's responses to embedded figures test. *Perceptual and Motor Skills* 64: 399-406.

Harter, S. 1982. Children's understanding of multiple emotions: A cognitive-developmental approach. In Overton, W., ed., *The relationship between social and cognitive development*. Hillsdale, NJ: Lawrence Erlbaum.

———. 1990. Causes, correlates and the functional role of global self-worth: A life-span perspective. In Sternberg, R., & Kolligian, J., eds., *Competence considered*. New Haven, CT: Yale University Press.

Hartup, W. W. 1989. Social relationships and their developmental significance. *American Psychologist* 44(2): 120-26.

Heininger, M. L. S. 1984. Children, childhood, and change in America. In *A century of childhood, 1820-1920*. Rochester, NY: Margaret Woodbury Strong Museum.

Hirsch, E. D. 1987. *Cultural literacy: What every American needs to know*. Boston: Houghton Mifflin.

Hodgkinson, H. L. 1985. *All one system: Demographics of education—kindergarten through graduate school*. Washington, DC: Institute for Educational Leadership.

Honig, B. 1990. Why privatizing public education is a bad idea. A criticism of John E. Chubb et al.'s, article, "America's Public Schools: Choice Is a Panacea." *The Brookings Review* 9(1): 15-16.

Howard, J. A., & Barnett, M. A. 1981. Arousal of empathy and subsequent generosity in young children. *Journal of Genetic Psychology* 138: 307-8.

Hutchings, D. E. 1989. *Prenatal abuse of licit and illicit drugs*. New York: Annals of the New York Academy of Sciences.

Inhelder, B., & Piaget, J. 1958. *The growth of logical thinking from birth to adolescence*. New York: Basic Books.

Johnson, M. D. 1990. Anabolic steroid use in adolescent athletes. *Pediatric Clinics of North America* 37(5): 1111-23.

Kaye, K. 1982. *The mental and social life of babies. How parents create persons*. Chicago: University of Chicago Press.

Kellog, R. 1969. *Analyzing children's art*. Palo Alto, CA: National Press Books.

Kemler-Nelson, D. G.; Hirsh-Paseck, K.; Jusczyk, P. W.; & Cassidy, K. W. 1989. How the prosodic cues in motherese might assist language learning. *Journal of Child Language* 16: 55-68.

Knowles, J. G.; Marlow, S. E.; & Muchmore, J. A. 1992. From pedagogy to ideology: Origins and phases of home education in the United States, 1970-1990. *American Journal of Education* 100(2): 195-235.

Kogan, N. 1973. Creativity and cognitive style: A lifespan perspective. In Baltes, P., & Schate, K., eds., *Life span developmental psychology, personality, and socialization*. New York: Academic Press.

Kolata, G. 1984. Studying in the womb. *Science* 225: 302-3.

Kozol, J. 1991. *Savage inequalities: Children in America's schools*. New York: Crown.

Krug, E. A. 1966. *Salient dates in American education, 1635-1964*. New York: Harper & Row.

Laabs, J. J. 1991. Schools at work. *Personnel Journal* 70(11): 72-81.

Labov, W. 1982. *Social stratification of English in New York City*. Washington, DC: Center for Applied Linguistics.

Lazar, I., & Darlington, R. B. 1982. *Lasting effects of early education*. Chicago: Society for Research in Child Development.

Lindle, J., & Boyd, W. L. 1991. Parents, professionalism and partnership in school-community relations. Chapter 7. *International Journal of Educational Research* 15(3/4): 323-337.

Loban, W. 1975. *Language development: Kindergarten through grade twelve*. Urbana, IL: National Council of Teachers of English.

Locke, J. 1965. *An essay concerning human understanding*. In two volumes edited with an introduction by John W. Yolton. Rev. Ed. London: Dent.

Londerville, S., & Main, M. 1981. Security of attachment, compliance and maternal training methods in the second year of life. *Developmental Psychology* 17: 289-99.

Lytle, V. 1990. Listen to the public: Rating the schools. *NEA Today* 9(2): 11.

Maccoby, E. 1980. *Social development, psychological growth, and parent-child relations*. New York: Harcourt Brace Jovanovich.

———. 1984. Socialization and developmental change. *Child Development* 55: 317-28.

Magnusson, D.; Strattin, H.; & Allen, V. L. 1985. Biological maturation and social development: A longitudinal study of some adjustment processes from mid-adolescence to adulthood. *Journal of Youth and Adolescence* 14: 267-83.

Main, M., & George, C. 1985. Responses of abused and disadvantaged toddlers to distress in agemates: A study in the day care setting. *Developmental Psychology* 21(3): 407-12.

Mann, A. J.; Harrell, A.; & Hurt, M. 1977. *A review of Head Start research since 1969 and an annotated bibliography*. Washington, DC: Social Research Group, George Washington University.

Mann, H. 1868. *Annual reports on education*. Boston: Horace B. Fuller.

Marshall, W. 1986. Puberty. In Falkner, F., & Tanner, J., eds., *Human growth*, vol. 2. 2nd ed. New York: Plenum Press.

Maurer, D., & Maurer, C. 1988. *The world of the newborn*. New York: Basic Books.

Messer, S. 1976. Reflection-impulsivity: A review. *Psychological Bulletin* 83: 1026-52.

Miller, P. H., & DeMarie-Dreblow, D. 1990. Social-cognitive correlates of children's understanding of displaced aggression. *Journal of Experimental Child Psychology* 49: 488-504.

Moore, K. L. 1983. *Before we are born: Basic embryology and birth defects*. 2nd ed. Philadelphia: W. B. Saunders.

Moores, D. 1987. *Educating the deaf: Psychology, principles, and practices*. Boston: Houghton Mifflin.

Moses, N.; Banilivy, M. M.; & Lifshitz, F. 1989. Fear of obesity among adolescent girls. *Pediatrics* 83: 393-98.

Moskowitz, B. A. 1978. The acquisition of language. *Scientific American* 239: 92-108.

Mullis, I. V. S.; Owen, E.; & Phillips, G. 1990. *America's challenge: Accelerating academic achievement: A summary of findings from 20 years of NAEP*. Princeton, NJ: Educational Testing Service.

Murray, A. D.; Johnson, J.; & Peters, J. 1990. Fine-tuning of utterance length to preverbal infants: Effects on later language development. *Journal of Child Language* 17: 511-25.

Mussen, P., & Eisenberg-Berg, N. 1977. *Roots of caring, sharing and helping: The development of prosocial behavior in children*. San Francisco: W. H. Freeman.

Nash, M. A., & Dunkle, M. 1989. *The need for a warming trend: A survey of the school climate for pregnant and parenting teens*. ERIC Document ED307547.

Nelson, K. 1985. *Making sense: Acquisition of shared meaning*. New York: Academic Press.

Noddling, N. 1984. *Caring*. Berkeley: University of California Press.

Oden, S., & Asher, S. R. 1977. Coaching children in social skills for friendship making. *Child Development* 48: 495-506.

Orlick, T. D. 1981. Positive socialization via cooperative games. *Developmental Psychology* 17(4): 426-29.

Pearson, J. 1993. *Myths of educational choice.* Westport, CT: Praeger.

Perelman, L. J. 1992. *School's out: Hyperlearning, the new technology, and the end of education.* New York: William Morrow.

Phillips, D. A. 1987. Socialization of perceived academic competence among highly competent children. *Child Development* 58: 1308-20.

Piaget, J. 1963. *The origins of intelligence in children.* M. Cook, trans. New York: W. W. Norton.

Piaget, J., & Inhelder, B. 1969. *The psychology of the child.* New York: Basic Books.

Polk, N. 1993. Connecticut Q & A: Dr. Stephen C. Tracy; Expanding choices with charter schools. *New York Times,* 20 November. Section 13CN:3.

Private management tried in baltimore schools, 1993. *The Washington Post,* 29 October.

Radke-Yarrow, M.; Zahn-Waxler, C.; & Chapman, M. 1983. Children's prosocial dispositions and behavior. In Mussen, P. H., ed., *Handbook of child psychology: Vol. 4, Socialization, personality and social development.* 4th ed. New York: John Wiley.

Rist, M. C. 1991. Here comes "McSchool". *The American School Board Journal* 178(9): 30-31.

Rose, L. C. 1991. A vote of confidence for the schools. *Phi Delta Kappan* 73(2): 121-22.

Rousseau, J. J. 1979. *Emile; or, On education.* Introduction, translation, and notes by Allan Bloom. New York: Basil Books.

Ruhland, D., & Feld, S. 1977. The development of achievement motivation in black and white children. *Child Development* 48: 1362-68.

Rutter, M. 1983. School effects on pupil progress: Research findings and policy implications. *Child Development* 54: 1-29.

Saltz, E., & Brodie, J. 1982. Pretend-play training in childhood: A review and critique. In Pepler, D., & Rubin, K., eds., *The play of children: Current theory and research.* Basel, Switzerland: Karger.

Sameroff, A. J., & Chandler, M. J. 1975. Reproductive risk and the continuum of caretaking casualty. In Horowitz, F., ed., *Review of child development research,* vol. 4. Chicago: University of Chicago Press.

Sanchez, C. 1993. New report rates students by state rather than nation. *Morning Edition,* 8 December. Washington, DC: National Public Radio.

Santrock, J. W. 1993. *Children.* 3rd ed. Madison, WI: Brown & Benchmark.

Schiamberg, L. B., & Chin, C. H. 1987. The influence of family on educational and occupational achievement of adolescents in rural low-income areas: An ecological perspective. Paper presented at the Biennial Meeting of the Society for Research in Child Development, Baltimore, MD (April 23-26).

Schickedanz, D. 1989. The place of specific skills in preschool and kindergarten. In Strickland, D. S., & Morrow, L. M., eds., *Emerging literacy.* Newark, DE: International Reading Association.

Schmidt, R. A. 1988. *Motor control and learning:* A behavioral emphasis. 2nd ed. Champaign, IL: Human Kinetics.

Schoenfeld, A. 1985. *Mathematical problem solving.* Orlando, FL: Academic Press.

Schorsch, Anita. 1979. *Images of childhood: An illustrated social history*. New York: Mayflower Books.

Schultz, T. R., & Pilon, R. 1973. Development of the ability to detect linguistic ambiguity. *Child Development* 44: 728-33.

Schwartz, R. C.; Barrett, M. J.; & Saba, G. 1985. Family therapy for bulimia. In Garner, D. M., & Garfinkel, P., eds., *Handbook of psychology for anorexia nervosa and bulimia*. New York: Guilford Press.

Seifert, K. L., & Hoffnung, R. J. 1991. *Child and adolescent development*. Boston: Houghton Mifflin.

Shapiro, H. S., & Purpel, D. E. 1993. *Critical social issues in American education: Toward the 21st century*. New York: Longman.

Simons, J. M.; Finlay, B.; & Yang, A. 1991. *The adolescent & young adult fact book*. Washington, DC: Children's Defense Fund.

Singal, D. 1991. The other crises in American education. *The Atlantic Monthly* 253: 59-74.

Skinner, B. F. 1957. *Verbal behavior*. New York: Appleton-Century-Crofts.

Sosniak, L. A., & Ethington, C. A. 1992. When public school "choice" is not academic: Findings from the National Education Longitudinal Study of 1988. *Educational Evaluation and Policy Analysis* 14(1): 35-52.

The state of America's children. 1992. Washington, DC: Children's Defense Fund.

Stechler, G., & Halton, A. 1982. Prenatal influences on human development. In Wolman, B., ed., *Handbook of developmental psychology*. Englewood Cliffs, NJ: Prentice-Hall.

Stern, D. 1985. *The first relationship: Infant and mother*. 4th ed. Cambridge: Harvard University Press.

Sternberg, R., & Powell, J. 1983. The development of intelligence. In Mussen, P., ed., *Handbook of Child Psychology*, vol. 3. 3rd ed. New York: John Wiley.

Stevenson, H. W., & Stigler, J. W. 1992. *The learning gap: Why our schools are failing and what we can learn from Japanese and Chinese education*. New York: Summit Books.

Sugarman, S. 1983. *Children's early thought: Developments in classification*. New York: Cambridge University Press.

Sulzby, E. 1985. Children's emergent reading of favorite storybooks: A developmental study. *Reading Research Quarterly* 20(4): 458-81.

Super, C. 1982. Behavioral development in infancy. In Munroe, R.; Munroe, R.; & Whiting, B., eds., *Handbook of cross-cultural human development*. New York: Garland.

Suransky, V. P. 1982. *The erosion of childhood*. Chicago: University of Chicago Press.

Susman, E. J.; Nottelmann, E. D.; Inoff-Germain, G. E.; Dorn, L. D.; Cutler, G. B., Jr.; Loriaux, D. L.; & Chrousos, G. P. 1985. The relation of relative hormonal levels and physical development and social-emotional behavior in young adolescents. *Journal of Youth and Adolescence* 14(3): 245-64.

Taylor, D. 1983. *Family literacy: Young children learning to read and write*. London: Heinemann.

Teddlie, C., & Stringfield, S. 1993. *Schools make a difference: Lessons learned from a 10-year study of school effects*. New York: Teachers' College Press.

Tucker, J. A. 1993. Evils of choice. *National Review* 45(4): 44-46.

Tucker, W. Trustbusters. 1991. *Forbes,* 148(12): 180-84.

U.S. Department of Education. National Commission on Excellence in Education. 1983. *A nation at risk, The imperative for educational reform: A report to the nation and the Secretary of Education, United States, Department of Education.* Washington, DC: Government Printing Office.

Uzgiris, I., & Hunt, J. McV. 1975. *Assessment in infancy: Ordinal scales of psychological development.* Urbana: University of Illinois Press.

Vamos, M. N. 1992. How Americans grade the school system. *Business Week,* 14 September, 85.

Vandell, D. L. 1980. Sociability with peer and mother during the first year. *Developmental Psychology* 16(4): 355-61.

Van Scotter, R. D. 1991. *Public schooling in America: A reference handbook.* Santa Barbara, CA: ABC-CLIO.

Vygotsky, L. S. 1962. *Thought and language.* Cambridge: MIT Press.

———. 1978. *Mind in society: The development of higher psychological processes.* Cambridge: Harvard University Press.

Walden, T. A., & Baxter, A. 1989. The effect of context and age on social referencing. *Child Development* 60: 1511-18.

Weinstein, C.; Goetz, E.; & Alexander, P. 1988. *Learning and study strategies, issues in assessment, instruction and evaluation.* San Diego: Academic Press.

Wells, A. S. 1991. Choice in education: Examining the evidence on equity. A symposium on politics, markets, and America's schools by John E. Chubb and Terry M. Moe. *Teachers College Record* 93(1): 137-55.

Werner, E. E.; Bierman, J. M.; & French, F. E. 1971. *The children of Kauai.* Honolulu: University of Hawaii.

Werner, E. E., & Smith, R. S. 1982. *Vulnerable but invincible: A longitudinal study of resilient children and youth.* New York: McGraw-Hill.

Wolff, P. 1966. The causes, controls, and organization of behavior in the neonate. *Psychological Issues* 5: 1-105.

Wood, D. 1988. *How children think and learn.* New York: Basil Blackwell.

Wood, D.; Bruner, J. S.; & Ross, G. 1976. The role of tutoring in problem solving. *Journal of Child Psychology and Psychiatry* 17: 2, 89-100.

Yanofsky, S. M., & Young, L. 1992. A successful parents' choice program. *Phi Delta Kappan* 73(6): 476-79.

Zahn-Waxler, C., & Radke-Yarrow, M. 1982. The development of altruism. In Eisenberg, N., ed., *The development of prosocial behavior.* New York: Academic Press.

Zigler, E., & Finn-Stevenson, M. 1992. Applied developmental psychology. In Bornstein, M. H., & Lamb, M. E., eds., *Developmental psychology: An advanced textbook.* 3rd ed. Hillsdale, NJ: Lawrence Erlbaum.

Zigler, E., & Muenchow, S. 1992. *Head Start: The inside story of America's most successful educational experiment.* New York: Basic Books.

SOURCES OF ADDITIONAL INFORMATION

Juvenile Literature

There is a children's book to teach every topic, to demonstrate every concept, and to help every child over emotional or psychological hurdles. Sometimes, just to see oneself in a book makes children realize they are not alone. The Association for Library Service to Children, a division of the American Library Association, 50 East Huron Street, Chicago, IL 60611, 800-545-2433, is an excellent place to obtain lists of high-quality books on a variety of topics. The *Best of the Best for Children: Librarians Recommend Books, Magazines, Videos, Audio, Software, Toys, and Travel* is an excellent source for quality juvenile books and other media (published by the American Library Association and Random House, 1992).

Indexes/Databases

ABI/INFORM
UMI/Data Courier
620 S. Third St.
Louisville, KY 40202-2475
800-626-2823
Online and CD-ROM formats

Child Development Abstracts and Bibliography
University of Chicago Press
5720 S. Woodlawn Ave.
Chicago, IL 60637
312-753-3347
Print format

CIS
Congressional Information Service
4520 East-West Hwy.
Bethesda, MD 20814-3387
301-654-1550
Print, online, and CD-ROM formats

Current Index to Journals in Education (CIJE)
Oryx Press
4041 N. Central Ave. at Indian School Rd.
Phoenix, AZ 85012-3397
602-265-2651
Print, online, and CD-ROM formats

Dissertation Abstracts
University Microfilms International
300 N. Zeeb Rd.
Ann Arbor, MI 48106
313-761-4700
Print, online, and CD-ROM formats

Education Daily Online
Capitol Publications
1101 King St., #444
Alexandria, VA 22314-2968
Online format

Education Index
H. W. Wilson Company
950 University Ave.
Bronx, NY 10452
212-588-8400
Print, online, and CD-ROM formats

Educational Testing Service Test Collection Database (ETSF)
Educational Testing Service/Princeton, N.J.
Provided by Minnesota Department of Education
725 Capital Square Building
550 Cedar St.
St. Paul, MN 55101
612-296-5078
Online format

ERIC
U.S. Department of Education
2440 Research Blvd., 5th Fl.
Rockville, MD 20850
301-656-9723
Online and CD-ROM formats

Resources in Education
Oryx Press
4041 N. Central Ave., Ste. 700
Phoenix, AZ 85012-3397
602-265-2651
Print, online, and CD-ROM formats

PAIS INTERNATIONAL
Public Affairs Information Service, Inc.
521 W. 43rd St.
New York, NY 10036
212-736-6629
Print, online, and CD-ROM formats

Social Sciences Index
H. W. Wilson Company
950 University Ave.
Bronx, NY 10452
215-588-8400
Print, online, and CD-ROM formats

Psychological Abstracts
American Psychological Association
750 First St. NE
Washington, DC 20002-4242
202-336-5500
Print, online, and CD-ROM formats

Periodicals

American Educational Research Journal
American Educational Research Assoc.
230 17th St. NW
Washington, DC 20036
Quarterly

Arithmetic Teacher
National Council of Teachers of
Mathematics
1906 Association Dr.
Reston, VA 22091
Monthly (9 issues)

Art Education
National Art Education Association
1916 Association Dr.
Reston, VA 22091
Bimonthly

Child and Youth Care Quarterly
Human Sciences Press
72 Fifth Ave.
New York, NY 10011
Quarterly

Child Development
Society for Research in Child Development
University of Chicago Press
5720 S. Woodlawn Ave.
Chicago, IL 60637
Bimonthly

Childhood Education
Association for Childhood Education
International
11141 Georgia Ave., Ste. 200
Wheaton, MD 20902
5 issues per year

Childrens' Defense Fund Reports
Children's Defense Fund
25 E St. NW
Washington, DC 20001
Monthly

Children's Literature in Education: An
International Quarterly
Human Sciences Press, Inc.
233 Spring St.
New York, NY 10013
Quarterly

Day Care and Early Education
Human Sciences Press, Inc.
72 Fifth Ave.
New York, NY 10011
Quarterly

Developmental Psychology
American Psychological Association
750 First St. NE
Washington, DC 20002-4242
Bimonthly

Early Childhood Research Quarterly
National Association for the Education
of Young Children
Ablex Publishing Corporation
355 Chestnut St.
Norwood, NJ 07648
Quarterly

Education and Urban Society
Corwin Press
2455 Teller Rd.
Newbury Park, CA 91320
Quarterly

Education Week
4301 Connecticut Ave. NW,
Ste. 250
Washington, DC 20008
Weekly (40 issues)

The Educational Forum
Kappa Delta Pi
P.O. Box A
West Lafayette, IN 47906
Quarterly

*Elementary School Guidance &
Counseling*
American Association for Counseling
and Development
5999 Stevenson Ave.
Alexandria, VA 22304
Quarterly

Exceptional Children
Council for Exceptional Children
1902 Association Dr.
Reston, VA 22091
Bimonthly

Harvard Education Review
Guttman Library, Ste. 349
6 Appian Way
Cambridge, MA 02138
Quarterly

Journal of Educational Research
Heldref Puplications
4000 Albemarle St. NW
Washington, DC 20016
Bimonthly

Journal of Learning Disabilities
Donald D. Hammill Foundation
8700 Shoal Creek Blvd.
Austin, TX 78758
Monthly

Journal of Reading
International Reading Association
800 Bardsdale Rd.
P.O. Box 8139
Newark, DE 19714
8 issues yearly

Language Arts
National Council of Teachers of
English
1111 Kenyon Rd.
Urbana, IL 61801

Learning
Springhouse Corporation
1111 Bethlehem Pike
Springhouse, PA 19477
Monthly (9 issues)

Mathematics Teacher
National Council of Teachers of
Mathematics
1906 Association Dr.
Reston, VA 22091
Monthly (9 issues)

Merrill-Palmer Quarterly
Merrill-Palmer Institute
Wayne State University Press
Leonard N. Simons Bldg.
5959 Woodward Ave.
Detroit, MI 48202
Quarterly

Phi Delta Kappan
Phi Delta Kappa
P.O. Box 789
Bloomington, IN 47402
Monthly (10 issues)

The Reading Teacher
International Reading Association
800 Bardsdale Rd.
P.O. Box 8139
Newark, DE 19714
Monthly (9 issues)

Rethinking Schools: An Urban Education Journal
1001 E. Keefe Ave.
Milwaukee, WI 53212
Bimonthly

Social Education
National Council for the Social Studies
3501 Newark St. NW
Washington, DC 20016
7 issues per year

Theory Into Practice
College of Education, The Ohio State University
149 Arps Hall
1945 N. High St.
Columbus, Ohio 43210
Quarterly

Vocational Education Journal
American Vocational Association
1410 King St.
Alexandria, VA 22314
8 issues per year

Young Children
National Association for the Education of Young Children
1834 Connecticut Ave. NW
Washington, DC 20009
Bimonthly

Organizations

American Association of Colleges for Teacher Education (AACTE)
One Dupont Cir. NW, Ste. 610
Washington, DC 20036
(202) 293-2450

American Association of School Administrators (AASA)
1801 N. Moore St.
Arlington, VA 22209
703-528-0700

American Council on Education (ACE)
One Dupont Cir. NW
Washington, DC 20036
202-939-9300

American Psychological Association
1200 Seventeenth St. NW
Washington, DC 20036
202-336-5500

American School Counselor Association (ASCA)
5999 Stevenson Ave.
Alexandria, VA 22304
713-823-9800

Children's Defense Fund
122 C St. NW
Washington, DC 20001
202-628-8787

Council for Exceptional Children (CEC)
1920 Association Dr.
Reston, VA 22091
703-620-3660

Head Start
P.O. Box 1182
Washington, DC 20013
202-245-0572

High/Scope Educational Resource Foundation
600 N. River St.
Ypsilanti, MI 48198
313-485-2000

National Association for Bilingual Education (NABE)
Union Center Plaza
810 First St.
Third Floor
Washington, DC 20002
202-898-1829

National Association for the Education
of Young Children
1834 Connecticut Ave. NW
Washington, DC 20009-5786
800-424-2460

National Association of Elementary
School Principals (NAESP)
1615 Duke St.
Alexandria, VA 22314
703-684-3345

National Association of Secondary
School Principals (NASSP)
1904 Association Dr.
Reston, VA 22091
703-860-0200

National Association of State Boards
of Education (NASBE)
701 N. Fairfax St.,
Ste. 340
Alexandria, VA 22314
703-684-4000

National Congress of Parents and
Teachers (PTA)
700 N. Rush St.
Chicago, IL 60611
312-787-0977

National Middle School Association
(NMSA)
4807 Evanswood Dr.
Columbus, OH 43229
614-848-8211

Nonprofit Oranizations

American Federation of Teachers
(AFT)
555 New Jersey NW
Washington, DC 20001
202-879-4400

Carnegie Foundation for the Advancement of Teaching (CFAT)
5 Ivy Ln.
Princeton, NJ 08540
609-452-1780

National Education Association (NEA)
1201 16th St. NW
Washington, DC 20036
202-833-4000

Phi Delta Kappa (PDK)
P.O. Box 789
Bloomington, IN 47402
812-339-1156

Government Agencies

National Center for Education
Statistics
555 New Jersey Ave. NW
Washington, DC 20208
800-424-1616

Office of Civil Rights
U.S. Department of Education
330 C St. SW
Washington, DC 20202
202-732-1213

Electronic Conferences (Interest Groups)

There are 16 subject-oriented ERIC Clearinghouses around the country that organize the data for CIJE and RIE. Their addresses can be obtained in all forms of the indexes.

ALTLEARN: On Alternative Approaches to Learning [Online]. Available e-mail:

listserv@stjohns.edu or

listserv@sjuvm.bitnet

ECENET-L: The ERIC Clearinghouse on Elementary and Early Childhood Education [Online]. Available e-mail:

listserv@vmd.cso.uiuc.edu or

listserv@uiucvmd.bitnet

ECEOL-L: Early Childhood Education Online [Online]. Available e-mail:

listserv@maine.edu or

listserv@maine.bitnet

EDSTYLE: On Learning Styles Theory and Research [online]. Available e-mail:

listserv@stjohns.edu or

listserv@sjuvm.bitnet

ERL-L: On Educational Research, including discussion and updates from Washington on education-related proposals [Online]. Available e-mail:

listserv@asuvm.inre.asu.edu or

listserv@asuacad.bitnet

GC-L: On Global Classroom, International Student E-mail, and debates [Online]. Available e-mail:

listserv@uriacc.uri.edu or

listserv@uriacc.bitnet

THE LEARNING LIST: Forum for discussing child-centered learning [Online]. Available e-mail:

learning-request@sea.east.sun.com

Useful Library of Congress Subject Headings

Adolescence
Adolescent Psychology
Child Development
Child Psychology
Child Rearing
Child Welfare
Children
Children's Literature
Children's Stories
Early Childhood Education
Education
Education—Curricula
Education—Demographic aspects
Education—Evaluation
Education—History
Education, Elementary
Education, Preschool
Education, Primary
Education, Rural
Education, Secondary
Education, Urban

Educational Psychology
Educational Sociology
Educational Technology
Language and Languages—Study and Teaching
Learning
Learning, Psychology of
Learning Disabilities
Mathematics—Study and Teaching
Psychology
Psychology, Applied
Psychology, Comparative
Psychology, Experimental
Reading
Reading, Psychology of
Reading (Early childhood)
Reading (Elementary)
Reading (Preschool)
Reading (Primary)
Reading (Secondary)
Writing

She said that I must always be intolerant of ignorance but understanding of illiteracy.
Maya Angelou, 1969

9

Adult Literacy

Carol Wright

A literate society is essential to a democracy. Literacy is a measure of social progress and is the base from which all other advances in society occur. Problems associated with inadequate levels of adult literacy permeate our total society and are increasingly reflected in the literature of education, business, management, political science, public policy, and economics. Attention to adult literacy in the United States has been sharply focused in the last decade by reports of alarmingly high illiteracy rates, by declining American economic competitiveness, and by the reflection of its human costs throughout our society (Kozol, 1985; Harman, 1987; *Workforce 2000*, 1987). The abundance of literature on adult literacy throughout all social science disciplines reflects the inherent complexity of the issue, indicates the relationship of literacy to broad social issues, and suggests the multiplicity of solutions required to effect sustainable and permanent change.

Several important publications on adult literacy help delineate the critical issues. One of the most comprehensive reports identifying the conditions of adult literacy and illiteracy was a report to the Ford Foundation (Hunter & Harman, 1979). This report profiled the demographics of illiteracy and made a series of recommendations that directed subsequent analysis and research. Fingeret's analysis of literacy definitions,

Carol Wright is a reference librarian at The Pennsylvania State University Libraries, having served in the Undergraduate Library, the Office of Instruction, and the General Reference Section. She is the Basic Skills Instruction Specialist, and works with adult students returning to higher education. She has written on the problems of basic skills instruction in libraries. She also serves as the University Scholars Librarian, and is a member of a university-wide team that teaches use of the Internet to faculty, students, and staff.

the reading process, characteristics of illiterate adults, and the purpose of adult reading programs called for a deep examination of the underlying causes of adult illiteracy (Fingeret, 1984). Public attention was focused in both *Prisoners of Silence* (Kozol, 1980) and *Illiterate America* (Kozol, 1985) by translating abstract concepts into concrete experiences and suggestions. Newman and Beverstock have written a comprehensive review of the literature on literacy (Newman & Beverstock, 1990). Essays edited by Kintgen, Kroll, and Rose discuss literacy's theoretical, historical, educational, and community perspectives; analyze the cognitive, economic, and social consequences of literacy; and trace the development of literacy in Western civilization (Kintgen, Kroll, & Rose, 1988). Essays edited by Taylor discuss broad issues of adult literacy in a global context (Taylor, 1989). Historical and political issues of literacy are discussed in an entire (Spring 1990) issue of *Daedalus*. Within the larger context of "World Literacy in the Year 2000," the March 1992 issue of the *Annals of the American Academy of Political and Social Science* explores the relationship of research to policy making, and places literacy issues within a larger political and social context. The literature on adult literacy is plentiful, and a wide range of resources can be identified in several bibliographies (French, 1987; Dunn-Rankin, 1989; Hladczuk, 1990; Rupp-Serrano, 1993).

DEFINITIONS AND MEASURES OF LITERACY

Scholars, educators, governmental agencies, and business and industry do not agree on what it means to be literate. Definitions carry implicit views of functions (what literacy can do for individuals) and uses (what individuals can do with literacy skills). The range of definitions indicates that there are many types of literacies (Heath, 1980). Definitions of literacy are considered within a specific context, such as school, workplace, or community, and vary widely depending upon the purpose of the assessment (Calfee, 1988; Venezky, 1990; Fingeret, 1990; Mikulecky, 1990a). Changing definitions of literacy reflect advances in societal expectations and carry significant social and political implications. Over the last century, definitions have ranged from a self-reporting approach, which asked if a person can read or write, to linking literacy to years of school completed and grade-level scores on reading tests, to defining literacy as "the ability to read or write in any language" (Newman & Beverstock, 1990). By these vague measures, the United States has consistently reported high literacy levels. But prompted by national concerns about the long-term ability of the American workforce to remain globally competitive, the United States Department of Education in the 1983 report *A Nation at Risk* estimated that 23 million American adults and 13 percent of all 17 year olds (perhaps as high as 40 percent of minority youth) were functionally illiterate by the simplest tests of everyday reading, writing, and comprehension (United States Department of Education, Commission on Excellence in Education, 1983). A subsequent extensive study, *Illiteracy in America: Extent, Causes and Cures* (National Advisory Council on Adult Education, Literacy Committee, 1986), concluded that a lack of uniform definition results in conflicting estimates of literacy. The committee also outlined in detail many social and educational factors responsible for the steady decline in literacy levels in recent years. Complicating the ability to compile reliable estimates is the fact that literacies are not static—they constantly respond to new technologies and changes in the information environment.

During the 1970s surveys to define literacy moved to a competency-based approach. This approach measures performance within the context of specific social settings, such as the workplace or the community at large. This concept of "functional literacy" had its roots in the experiences of soldiers in World War II who could not understand written instructions. "Functional literacy" is considered to be more reliable than school-based measures in predicting performance on literacy tasks in nonschool settings. A significant national attempt to survey adult literacy and define literacy tasks within a set of competencies was the creation of the Adult Performance Level (APL) (University of Texas at Austin, 1977; Newman & Beverstock, 1990). The APL consisted of three levels (APL 1-2-3) that described a hierarchy of skill proficiencies and formed the basis of competency-based adult education. Applying these APL standards, the Office of Education in 1975 estimated that 57 million Americans did not have the skills necessary to perform basic tasks with a minimum degree of competence. Although an important initial study, the APL characterized literacy as being applicable to all types of competencies and did not attempt to identify the factors that contributed to the difficulty of performing specific tasks (Newman & Beverstock, 1990; Campbell, Kirsch, & Kolstad, 1992).

The National Assessment of Educational Progress conducted in 1985 utilized more extensive survey techniques, including the collection of background information and performance data. The Young Adult Literacy Assessment, a study of 21 to 25 year olds, recognized several types of literacies on a continuum of proficiency levels and included interviews of individuals as part of the assessment. It employed several literacy scales: "prose tasks," or understanding and using information from such texts as news stories and editorials; "document tasks," or using information from such materials as indexes, tables, and order forms; and "quantitative tasks," or applying arithmetic operations. Literacy was defined by the NAEP study as "using printed and written information to function in society, to achieve one's goals, and to develop one's knowledge and potential" (Kirsch & Jungeblut, 1986).

The most recent assessment of adult literacy is the National Adult Literacy Survey. Assessments were conducted during 1992 and results were reported in 1993. It was developed in response to directives in the Adult Education Amendments of 1988, an act requiring the United States Department of Education to submit a report to Congress defining literacy and estimating the nature and extent of literacy among adults in the nation. Building on the profile survey approach of the 1985 NAEP, the National Adult Literacy Survey surveyed over 26,000 randomly selected individuals aged 16 and over, including 1,100 inmates from federal and state prisons. Each assessment was to be conducted in a one-hour face-to-face interview that included simulation tasks and background questions. The same literacy scales used in the earlier NAEP survey (prose literacy, document literacy, and quantitative literacy) were applied. The tasks included reading, writing, speaking, and listening. Subjects were also required to demonstrate their ability to recognize, acquire, organize, interpret, produce, and apply information from various printed materials (Campbell, Kirsch, & Kolstad, 1992). Each literacy scale was rated on a proficiency rating of relative difficulty of from 0 to 500. Level 1 (0-225) rated the ability to locate one piece of information in a sports article, or locate the expiration date on a driver's license. Level 5 (376-500) rated the ability either to summarize the way two lawyers may challenge prospective jurors or, using a calculator, to determine the total cost of carpet to cover a room. Twenty-one to 23 percent of the respondents (representing 40-44 million of the 191 million adults in this country) demonstrated skills at Level 1. An additional 25 to 28 percent (about 50 million adults nationwide) performed at Level 2. It is noteworthy that most respondents in these groups described themselves as being able to read "well" or "very well." One-third of the participants (representing 61 million adults) demonstrated performance at Level 3, and only 18 to 21 percent (representing 34 to 40 million adults) performed at Levels 4 and 5 (Kirsch, Jungeblut, Jenkins, & Kolstad, 1993). Similar results were reported in a 1992 study prepared for the U.S. Department of Labor, which concluded that people will need to perform at either Level 4 or 5 in all three literacy scales to be employed in the high-skill workplace of the future (Kirsch, Jungeblut, & Campbell, 1992).

The heart of the question of literacy definition is who decides what constitutes literacy (Fingeret, 1990). Individual needs and desires for literacy are closely linked to one's socioeconomic status, and are not necessarily compatible with a proscribed set of basic skills developed by experts (Kazemek, 1988). Functional literacy assessments are complicated by the constantly changing demands of society (Sticht, 1987; Ehringhaus, 1990). Harman states that illiteracy is situational, that reading has a value beyond a functional skill, and in order to understand the literacy dilemma it is necessary to examine cultures (Harman, 1987). The search for national illiteracy figures, he claims, has neglected analyzing the clustering of illiterate communities—groups living in environments in which literacy plays a minor role and is not encouraged. Ultimately, literacy is measured within an individual not by literacy skills but rather by literacy behaviors such as the ability to compare, sequence, argue, interpret, and create (Heath, 1991; Guthrie & Greaney, 1991). A significant cost of the inability to arrive at literacy definitions and standards is that we are unable to advance on a course of action to assess the problem and move toward solutions (Chall, 1990). The manner in which literacy is conceptualized determines the types of research programs pursued to solve the problem (Sticht, 1978). The language used to describe the lack of literacy skills also alters public opinion and potential political support for literacy programs. Educators need to be aware of the strategic uses of language and metaphors to dramatize illiteracy in the adult literacy context (Stahl, 1993).

TEACHING ADULTS

Because adult illiteracy results largely from failures in the traditional educational process, it is critical to not repeat the same approaches that failed initially. Adult learners have needs and learning styles different from younger learners. They bring a different set of motives, attitudes, status, experiences, and psychological needs that must be accommodated in adult literacy instructional programs. Programs must be sensitive to the learners' self-concepts and their relationships to authority; programs must be pragmatic and selective in what is taught; and they must provide appropriate successes and opportunities for stimulation (Beck, 1990; Knowles, 1980). Theories of andragogy (the science of helping adults learn) contribute to the organization, administration, and evaluation of a comprehensive adult education program. Such comprehensive programs include recruitment and public relations, student orientation, counseling, diagnostic testing and assessment, a variety of instructional materials, student follow-up, and program evaluation (Lerche, 1980). Adminstrators of programs need sufficient managerial skills so they can direct financial, physical, and human resources, develop staff, and perform program evaluations (Lerche, 1980; Crandall et al., 1984). Hunter and Harman contend that adult students must establish their own appropriate literacy needs and merge these personal needs into a larger societal context (Hunter & Harman, 1979). This concept has evolved into the paradigm of participatory literacy education, a philosophy that recognizes the learner's capacities to shape and control the literacy program design and to share power equally with staff members. Case studies of actual participatory programs, providing an historical context, a theoretical framework (Fingeret & Jurmo, 1989), and a psychological model of trait-state for a framework for adult literacy theory (Fagan, 1991), further support the participatory concept.

DELIVERY

For almost three decades education for adults has been delivered through the Adult Basic Education Program (ABE) administered by the United States Department of Education and funded by state and federal governments. ABE instruction, often directed toward the completion of the General Education Development Test (GED), does not consider the special learning needs of adults (Mezirow, Darkenwald, & Knox, 1975). Within this limited approach, only a small percentage of the population has been reached by ABE programs (Hunter & Harman, 1979). Literacy instruction in the United States predominantly relies on methods and materials developed by two volunteer groups: the Laubach Literacy Action (LLA) and Literacy Volunteers of America (LVA) (Medary, 1954; Schild, 1990). Basic differences exist between these two programs. The Laubach method is based on phonics, uses standardized instructional materials, uses key words for consonant and vowel sounds, and is considered a "bottom-up" approach because of its emphasis on decoding and structural analysis. The more eclectic, research-based program offered by LVA is considered more adaptable to student differences, because it uses more extensive evaluation and has a superior published reading series. (Meyer & Keefe, 1988; Unwin, 1989; Fingeret & Jurmo, 1989).

Many community programs are heavily reliant on volunteers for the delivery of literacy instruction. Caution against this heavy dependence is one of the many recommendations in *Turning Illiteracy Around: An Agenda for National Action* sponsored by the Business Council for Effective Literacy (McCune & Alamprese, 1985; Harman, 1985). In addition to high turnover, levels of training and certification among volunteers are often low (Mikulecky, 1989). Effective teaching in literacy programs is complex and can be affected by many external variables, such as open enrollment, irregular attendance, student diversity, and teacher characteristics (Darkenwald, 1986). Use of materials appropriate for adult learners is critical to success (Campbell, 1991). Guides and manuals for both new and experienced literacy tutors that provide worksheets and sample forms can be useful (Rosenthal, 1987; Muir & Wischropp, 1982). Adult educators should be expert in their knowledge of content, learning styles, and teaching methods. Educators must develop teaching styles suitable for the needs of the adult learner, and should be able to assess their own philosophical orientation and teaching styles (Conti, 1991; Galbraith & Knowles, 1990). Adult students with learning disabilities require more flexible teaching approaches that incorporate assessments of learning styles using appropriate diagnostic tools (Ross-Gordon, 1989). An estimated 50 to 80 percent of all adult literacy students may have a form of learning disability. Integrated teaching approaches and specific strategies can be successful with these students (Hellwedge & Sell, 1990; Hagner et al., 1989; Ross & Smith, 1990). Some evidence suggests that teaching methods that are useful for adult students with learning disabilities are useful for all adult learners (Bingman, 1989). A whole-language-oriented instruction is more suited to the adult learner (Roskos, 1990).

Scholars increasingly refer to literacy research in place of either writing or reading research. Within this expanded definition, instruction delivered by computer has many advantages over traditional methods to teach learning, thinking, and problem solving. Computers can lead students to reason inductively, creating linkages and patterns, in contrast to the deductive, linear, and sequential thinking taught through print materials. Students in literacy programs must be prepared for a multiliterate society (Howie, 1990). When reading and writing are taught as problem-solving skills, computer learning should transfer well to print literacy. In a workplace or community environment where computers may be encountered, it is critical to incorporate those skills and knowledge into adult literacy programs. Principles of Adult Literacy System (PALS), an IBM interactive media, is one of several programs designed to promote individualized learning (Turner, 1988).

Computer learning is a prime component of the whole-language teaching approach in the *Complete Theory-to-Practice Handbook of Adult Literacy* (Soifer et al., 1990). Computers can be a means for reading and writing improvement and a vehicle for empowering students with tools of contemporary society. Selection of software appropriate for adult learners is critical for success (Askov, 1989b, 1989c, 1991; Howie, 1990). A comprehensive study conducted by the Office of Technology Assessment stressed that technology has the potential to both improve the existing system of literacy education and to reach people in new ways. It presents opportunities for adults to control the timing and settings for acquiring new skills and knowledge. Computers also offer solutions to perennial problems in adult literacy instruction; issues of recruitment and retention; instructional issues (e.g., curriculum materials, assessment, staff development, and distance teaching to remote learners); and administrative issues concerning funding, coordination, and student record maintenance. The study notes that traditional barriers to technological advances (e.g., inadequate funding and software marketing, inadequate information available to consumers and educators, and institutional obstacles) must be overcome for the promises of technology to be realized (U.S. Congress. Office of Technological Assessment, 1993).

DEMOGRAPHICS OF ILLITERACY

When the demographics of illiteracy are studied closely, the emerging pattern strongly parallels serious social problems—poverty, unemployment, crime, and homelessness. A lack of literacy skills often forms the base of an individual's inability to assimilate and fully participate in society (Hunter & Harman, 1979; Kozol, 1985). Certain populations are at greater risk for experiencing the web of illiteracy and poverty, and the data show an urgent need for public policy reforms. Hispanics are the most undereducated segment of the population. It is estimated that 7 million Hispanics are illiterate, composing one-third of the total of functionally illiterate Americans (Romero, 1987). The Business Council for Effective Literacy (BCEL) estimates that 37 percent of illiterate adults do not speak English at home, and that up to 86 percent of non-English speakers are also illiterate in their native languages (Business Council for Effective Literacy, 1987). In addition, the population speaking limited

English is growing each year, not from new immigrants but from those who have attended U.S. schools (Romero, 1987; Vargas, 1988; DeLaRosa & Maw, 1990). Individuals for whom English is a second language are at particular risk and have special learning needs (Holisky, 1985; Hayes, 1989; *Basic skills,* 1989; Burnaby, 1990; Gaber-Katz, 1990; *Teaching adults with limited English skills,* 1991). African Americans are at risk because there is a strong relationship between illiteracy and crime. A BCEL study indicates that 50 percent of adults in federal and state prisons cannot read or write and that blacks, who compose only 12 percent of the general population, constitute over 50 percent of the prison population (Business Council for Effective Literacy, 1986). Homeless adults have literacy needs that are complicated by their desperate living conditions (McDowell, 1988). The combination of fewer low-skilled jobs, illiteracy, inadequate training opportunities, criminal activity, drugs, and a myriad of other social ills will result in thousands of potential workers lacking basic skills and lacking meaningful commitments to the labor force. Seeds are present for a permanent underclass. (U.S. Congress. Joint Economic Committee, 1988). But illiteracy is not a condition that characterizes only the disadvantaged, the poor, or minority populations. Recent national assessments indicate that literacy issues affect "middle America" as well. Many thousands of gainfully employed individuals compensate for their inability to read and are fearful of being discovered or of being displaced in their jobs.

RESPONDING TO THE NEED

Attention to adult literacy issues in the United States has always been in response to perceived national interests rather than in the intrinsic benefits to individuals. During the great waves of immigration, during wars, and after the Russian Sputnik, a broadly educated, literate populace was considered a national priority. Current national interest in a literate society is directly linked to concerns about America's ability to remain competitive in the global marketplace (*Workforce 2000,* 1987; Askov & Alderman, 1991).

The Comprehensive Employment and Training Act of 1973 (CETA) was an early attempt to achieve a more proficient and literate workforce through combined efforts of governmental, educational, and private agencies. The Job Training Partnership Act (JTPA) had a significant impact on workplace education programs during the 1980s. It was initiated as part of Reagan's "New Federalism," a policy that assigned the administration of federally funded programs to states and localities rather than the federal government. The JTPA was the channel for many state programs and served as a model for partnership initiatives between private and government agencies. The act specified that success was to be measured by decreased unemployment, increased wages, and reduced welfare dependency (National Commission for Employment Policy, 1988). JTPA programs met many of their goals, but did not address the basic issues of adult literacy and workplace literacy. The gap between a strong literate workforce and the numbers of well-prepared individuals was widening. Leaders in education, business, and industry joined forces to mobilize efforts to reverse this trend. *Jump Start,* the final report of the Project on Adult Literacy, an independent, nonpartisan research effort that examined the role the federal government has and should play in promoting adult literacy, found serious flaws in the fundamental approach of existing national policy and proposed a far-reaching plan of action. It found that without government intervention, the existing, fragmented efforts would be insufficient. Workplace literacy programs were singled out as being the highest priority. The six objectives identified by the report were developing clear national goals and measures for tracking them; building intellectual, political, and institutional focal points for adult basic education; focusing on workforce literacy; holding basic skills programs accountable; investing in technology and training; and building on existing services and knowledge. It recommended that literacy issues be addressed by the executive and legislative branches, and that the president establish a cabinet council on adult literacy (Chisman, 1989). Federal legislation for job-related basic skills was included in the Omnibus Trade and Competitiveness Act of 1988, but progress resulting from this act was slow. Federal education legislation also provided for literacy programs in an extension to the Adult Education Act in 1988. This legislation authorized the creation of a National Workplace Literacy Program to be administered by the Department of Education. This program requires joint partnerships between businesses, industries, labor unions, private councils, and educational organizations. No single organization is eligible for a grant under this program (U.S. Department of Education, Office of Vocational and Adult Education, 1992).

The 1989 President's Education Summit with governors was an initiative to consider an enlargement of the federal education role, and the resulting plan included strategies for addressing issues of adult literacy. With a resolve described as the "educational equivalent of war," President Bush declared six National Education Goals. Goal 5 stated that "By the year 2000, every adult American will be literate and will possess the skills necessary to compete in a global economy and to exercise the rights and responsibilities of citizenship" (U.S. Department of Education, 1989; U.S. President [Bush], 1991). Sub-goals include strengthening the connection between education and work; measures to meet these goals include school-to-work transition, adult literacy programs, vocational-technical education, postsecondary assistance, and educating for democracy. Mikulecky acknowledges that although universal literacy within the decade is probably not possible, many of these sub-goals are attainable (Mikulecky, 1990b). In response to the goals established at the Education Summit, the Department of Education prepared the report America 2000 (1991), which is a long-term national strategy, not a federal program, to accomplish the stated goals by the year 2000. America 2000 places heavy emphasis on higher standards, national testing, and the education-work relationship. The America 2000 Excellence in Education Act called for the establishment of Regional Literacy Resource Centers. The National Literacy Act authorized $1.5 billion through 1995; established a National Institute for Literacy to coordinate federal literacy programs, research literacy issues, and evaluate programs; provided grants to states for training; provided technical assistance for state, federal, and local programs; and assured that community groups can compete for literacy funds (U.S. Congress. House. Committee on Education and Labor, 1991). In 1990 the National Education Goals Panel was created and charged with measuring and reporting annual progress toward achieving the six national goals over the ten-year period to the year 2000. The panel's annual goals report, *Building a Nation of Learners*, provides current state-by-state data against baseline indicators for each of the goals.

TWO ARENAS FOR SUCCESS

Two avenues that have been targeted by professional, business, and government leaders as promising the highest degree of success in eradicating adult illiteracy are intergenerational family literacy programs and workplace programs.

Workplace Programs

Studies indicate that the American workforce is at risk. Single women, minorities, and immigrants—populations with historically high illiteracy rates—will represent the largest percent of new entrants to the workforce. In addition, almost 80 percent of the projected workforce for the year 2000 is presently employed. This slower growth of the population and the workforce means a heavier reliance on older workers, who may be less able or inclined to learn new skills and new technologies (*Workforce 2000,* 1987; Vickery, 1990). Failure to confront the dilemma posed by an increasingly less literate workforce threatens to condemn us to Third World, debtor-nation status.

Advancing technologies require a more sophisticated workforce. Escalating fears of America's inability to compete in a global marketplace because of an inadequately prepared workforce are reflected across the literacy literature (Skagen, 1986; National Commission for Employment Policy, 1988; U.S. Department of Education and Labor, 1988; Barton & Kirsch, 1990; Lund, 1990). Congressional testimony offered in *Crisis in the Workplace: The Mismatch of Jobs and Skills* (U.S. Congress. Joint Economic Committee, 1989) paints a dismal picture of conditions. Change from a manufacturing-based to a service-based economy, coupled with changes in the workforce, has focused attention on the workplace as the target for reform (Chisman, 1990a; Crawford & Romero, 1991). Qualified workers are becoming a scarce pool, and business and industry cannot wait for the schools to effect changes that will improve the workforce. Partnerships forged by education and industry must immediately address this problem. Reliance on a school-centered strategy can now be considered only one part of the solution (Campbell, Kirsch, & Kolstad, 1992; U.S. Congress. Office of Technology Assessment, 1993). Future literacy instruction developments will need to recognize that every major American business will be involved in strengthening the connection between education and work (U.S. Department of Education, 1993).

Why do schools fail to produce a proficient and literate workforce? Diehl and Mikulecky concluded that there is little relevance in school curriculum to the workplace, and schoolwork, lacking context and accountability, is easier than workplace demands (Diehl & Mikulecky, 1980). Most reading done in the workplace is for the purpose of doing, assessing, and learning, whereas most reading done by secondary students is to obtain information to answer teachers' questions. The transfer of skills from the classroom to the workplace should not be assumed; it must be taught. Schools fail to emphasize occupational literacy competencies, such as technical vocabulary, locating useful information, following directions, and self-monitoring comprehension and performance (Rush, 1986).

What do employers need? Mikulecky developed a problem-solving model of determining required literacies using a cognitive process theory of writing (Mikulecky, 1987). Carnevale, in conjunction with the American Society for Training and Development, provides a lengthy analysis of the essential skills composing workplace basics (Carnevale et al., 1990). These include learning to learn, reading, writing, computation, oral communication, listening, problem solving, creative thinking, self-esteem, motivation, goal setting, employability, career development, interpersonal skills, teamwork, negotiation, organizational effectiveness, and leadership. These same skills were mentioned in the report *America's Choice: High Skills or Low Wages* (National Center on Education and the Economy, 1990). *What Work Requires of Schools* (1991), a study prepared by the Labor Secretary's Commission on Achieving Necessary Skills (SCANS), examined the demands of the workplace, determined the level of skills required to enter employment, and assessed whether young people were capable of meeting those demands. Two broad generic categories, applicable to most jobs, were identified: competencies and foundations (skills underlying the competencies). A companion study, *Skills and Tasks for Jobs* (U.S. Department of Labor, 1992), analyzes the tasks and skills against 35 model jobs to indicate the rating structure. The SCANS project is of value to curriculum developers, job counselors, and training directors and is a model for cooperation among schools and employers. Many new programs will be supported under the workplace literacy objectives outlined in "Reaching the Goals." Two of the five adult literacy/lifelong learning objectives are specific to the workplace: "Every major American business will be involved in strengthening the connection between education and work"; "All workers will have the opportunity to acquire the knowledge and skills, from basic to highly technical, needed to adapt to emerging technologies, work methods, and markets through public and private educational, vocational, technical, workplace or other programs" (U.S. Department of Education, 1993, p. 2).

Important strategies for successful school-business relationships are offered in *America's Choice: High Skills or Low Wages* (National Center on Education and the Economy, 1990). Recommendations include: a new educational national performance standard to be met by age 16; completion by all students of a Certificate of Initial Mastery (CIM); a comprehensive system of technical and professional certificates; associate degrees for those who do not pursue baccalaureate degrees; employer incentives for employee training and education; and a system of federal and state Employment and Training Boards to organize and oversee the new school-to-work transition programs and training systems. A valuable supplement to SCANS' *America's Choice* and *America 2000* is *Three Strategies,* which summarizes the fundamental ideas of each report, identifies areas of common ground and differences, and establishes a structure for incorporating additional reports (*Three strategies,* 1992).

The content of workplace literacy programs raises important social, political, and philosophical questions. Because national attention to the literacy crisis is placed in the context of competition in the global marketplace, productivity is the implicit goal of workplace literacy efforts. Fingeret argues that the turn away from the literacy goals of the 1960s (which promoted social mobility) to implementation of programs for basic, entry-level employment simply trains people for specific tasks rather than helping them learn how to learn (Fingeret, 1988). Harman supports placing literacy programs within a cultural and social context (Harman, 1985). Instruction should include generic and long-term skills as well as occupational or domain-specific skills (Stasz et al., 1990). Organized labor is taking an active role in sharing responsibility for literacy development with management (Sarmiento, 1990; Collins, Balmuth, & Jean, 1989).

Many excellent programs have been developed by corporations in partnership with education and government (Kutner et al., 1991). Many programs, both developmental and remedial, sponsored by the Job Training Partnership Act and by the National Workplace Literacy Program are described in both the education literature and the business-training literature. Corporations often maintain permanent staffs for continuous training. Some provide incentives, such as allowing employees to keep the computers they used in training. Many programs, such as General Motors' Project TACKLE, offer a complete range of literacy opportunities including adult basic literacy, high school completion, computer literacy and programming, limited English proficiency training, problem-solving skills, PALS, and career counseling (Project Tackle, 1990). Success stories from West Virginia, Arizona, Louisana, Wisconsin, and Washington, D.C., are profiled in *Workplace Literacy* (U.S. Department of Education. Office of Vocational and Adult Education, 1992). Other model programs are described in Campbell (1987) and Rothwell (1990).

Design and Administration of
Workplace Literacy Instruction

Literacy program development is a challenging task. The development and administration of an effective workplace literacy program is complex (Lerche, 1980; Rothwell, 1990). Jurmo cautions against programs using prepackaged "quick fixes" (Jurmo, 1991). Rather, program planners should build on the valuable knowledge their employees possess. Instruction should be designed around the realities of workers' lives rather than relying on preconceived notions of what management thinks workers ought to know. Internal programs may not always be the best choice for an organization. Identification of basic skills and the decision making required to select an in-house program are critical. Once chosen, the development and maintenance of a successful in-house program demands extensive support and commitment. Commercially available program are often a more appropriate choice (Rothwell, 1990). Independent consultants can design custom-made instruction using work-related materials (Askov, 1989c, 1992). Curriculum should be based on needs that have been identified through task analysis and on an understanding of the specific workplace (Taylor, 1990a, 1990b; Taylor & Lewe, 1991; Philippi, 1991). One workable model for introducing academic skills in the workplace is the Work-Education Bridge (WEB) Project, covering communication, mathematics, and computer skills (Pershing, 1988). Planners must consider factors important to their employees beyond the immediate curriculum needs. Dependent care, travel time, expense, and other related employee concerns must be addressed (Seitchik, 1990). Small businesses are less able to offer literacy programs than their larger competitors, but will be aided by provisions of the 1991 Literacy Act, which gives priority to applications from small businesses. Identifying contacts who can consult in the design of workplace literacy projects is facilitated by the Workforce and Workplace Literacy Series. This is a series of directories listing support available for small businesses and for such particular industries as hotel, food service, health care, and commercial drivers (Business Council for Effective Literacy, 1991a, 1991b, 1992a, 1992b).

Evaluation of Workplace
Literacy Programs

The recognition of the need for adult literacy has resulted in a greater awareness by corporate leaders; in curriculum development with a more functional context; in increased collaboration between government, industry and education; and in increased funding (Jurmo, 1991). However, this is just a beginning. Although a thorough set of guidelines for evaluating the effectiveness of preemployment literacy programs is found in the eight-volume Job Training Partnership Act, most of the available reports indicate that existing evaluations are based on inappropriate research designs (Grubb et al., 1991). Assessments are often limited to questionnaire data, participant surveys, and ancedotal reports. The evaluation literature lacks follow-up data on the impact of programs on job performance, job retention, or earning power (Mikulecky & Weinstein, 1991).

Taylor suggests that criterion-referenced tests should be developed for basic workplace training (Taylor, 1990c). Sticht warns that standardized tests need to be used cautiously (Sticht, 1990a, 1990b). Comprehensive assessment must include indicators that measure progress toward goals for learners, programs, and policies, and must consist of needs assessment, skills appraisal, student placement, progress monitoring, and certification. Intake and progress interviews, work samples, and behavioral checklists should be among the assessment tools. One model is the Comprehensive Adult Student Assessment System (CASAS) developed by the California Department of Education (Rickard, 1991). Sticht's description of evaluation as required by the Department of Education is intended to help workplace programs meet these requirements (Sticht, 1991). The Review of the National Workplace Literacy Program analyzed 29 projects and six site visits, identified criteria for successful programs, and made additional recommendations to increase program effectiveness.

Literacy professionals confront political and institutional barriers that sustain demeaning attitudes toward adult literacy learners (Kazemek, 1988). Hinzen warns that literacy campaigns often result in failed policies because of unrealistic goals, misused statistics, inaccurate definitions, and a failure to listen to literacy students (Hinzen, 1989). By overstating goals, we diminish our ability to reach realistic ones.

Intergenerational Programs

Some research indicates that an individual's potential for intellectual growth and development is primarily determined by the social and cultural groups in which the person is raised. The association of illiteracy with social marginality may be rooted in the early stage of life when schools, no matter how excellent, can no longer compensate for the lack of richness in home and community resources (Sticht, 1989; Beverstock, 1991). This conclusion is supported by evidence that children born to illiterate parents do not receive transferred literacy skills in the home and therefore begin school without necessary readiness skills. This persistent cycle of illiteracy spawns school dropout, poverty, unemployment, and a host of related social problems. The intergenerational character of illiteracy is insidious and must be broken to meet national educational goals. The Carnegie Foundation's *Ready to Learn* states that parents must be able to provide their children with a secure environment that encourages language development and one that promotes continuity between home and school (Carnegie Foundation for the Advancement of Teaching, 1991). Family literacy and intergenerational literacy programs are being designed to break this illiteracy cycle. Traditional separate programs for adults and children have been substituted by programs that integrate classes and materials for common use. Use of materials designed for family programs is important for success (Lane et al., 1991). Intergenerational literacy programs assure the readiness of children born into otherwise illiterate families and also prepare mothers for productive employment.

Intergenerational programs also have the significant benefit of an holistic approach using a broader instructional framework, and may therefore ultimately be more successful than more narrowly focused skills-based workplace literacy programs (Reuys, 1992; Edlund, 1992). Even Start, a major federal initiative begun in 1989, is a family-centered, compensatory education program that combines adult literacy, parent education, and childhood education and allows parents to become partners in their children's education.

A private program, sponsored by the Kenan Trust Family Literacy Project, teaches undereducated parents together with their three- and four-year-old children. Instruction includes both shared class time and separate vocational and academic instruction for parents (Darling, 1989). Follow-up studies of the Kenan project revealed that most children were achieving in the top half of their class, were exhibiting appropriate learning behaviors, and that most parents took an active role in the education of their children. Some parents planned to continue their education (Seaman et al., 1991). Most parents in this project were school dropouts. Studies revealed that their reasons for dropping out were not strongly related to grades or attendance, but rather to a persistent sense of alienation, a feeling that was also responsible for their dropping out of adult basic education classes. The findings from the Kenan project reported that this intergenerational approach addressed that sense of alienation (Popp, 1991a). Paratore likewise reported high attendance and low attrition rates from intergenerational programs offered by the Boston University/Chelsea Public schools partnership (Paratore, 1990). Stemming from the success of the Kenan project, the Kenan Trust has funded the establishment of The National Center for Family Literacy in Louisville, Kentucky.

Definitions of family literacy programs are still evolving. Nickse presents a classification of intergenerational programs based on the type of interventions offered (Nickse, 1990). Intergenerational programs are differentiated from other literacy programs in that they are conceptualized around the concerns of the family as a unit, have at least one educational component that impacts the child's literacy, and have at least one adult component that focuses on child-adult interactions. Nickse provides a framework for program development and evaluation. Handbooks are available that describe successful programs and outline guidelines for intergenerational program development (Quintero, 1987, 1988; Thompson, 1988; Nickse, 1989, 1990; Padak, 1990; Ryan et al., 1991). Popp explains important legislation and funding sources and gives suggestions for preparing proposals for family literacy projects (1991b).

FUTURE PROSPECTS

Efforts to increase literacy in the workplace have resulted in interest in apprenticeship programs. During the 1992 election, attention sharpened on these programs. Of the approximately 60 percent of American high school students who do not go on to college, only 2 percent participate in apprenticeship programs. Germany, by contrast, accommodates 66 percent of its students in such programs (Hamilton, 1992; Pritchard, 1992). Apprenticeships differ from other vocational education, cooperation education, or other work experience programs in that they combine supervised, on-the-job training with related instruction; use a training strategy that prepares students for skilled employment with content defined by the industry; may require several years for completion; have requirements that are legally defined and lead to a certification of completion and journeyworker status; pay wages to participants; involve work with masters of the craft; and involve written and social obligations between the program and the apprentice (*Meaning of apprenticeships*, 1992). Careful planning and administration required for successful apprenticeship programs (Cantor, 1990; Roditi, 1991; Marshall, 1989). Parallel to the Job Training Partnership Act, the Carl D. Perkins Vocational and Applied Technical Education Act of 1984 (U.S. Congress, 1984), amended in 1990 (U.S. Congress, 1990), provided for integration of academic and vocational educational opportunities, and provided for the development of "Tech-Prep," vocational education programs that provide preparation for technical careers. In the spring of 1992 President Bush proposed the National Youth Apprenticeship Act of 1992, calling for programs that combine worksite learning and experience, academic instruction, and workbase learning (U.S. President [Bush], 1992). Interest in the apprentice concept has heightened in the Clinton administration, and is a major component of the Clinton economic plan, which additionally calls for employers to spend 1.5 percent of their payroll on employee training. The School-to-Work Opportunities Act of 1993 proposed strong partnerships with the business community to create national high-school and postsecondary apprenticeship programs (U.S. Congress, 1993). Collectively these types of efforts will ensure a literate workforce, help meet the goals of *America 2000*, and provide the stepping stone to a sustainably literate society.

The crisis of adult literacy is one of the major obstacles facing the United States in the 1990s and is inextricably linked to other social and economic problems that threaten to destroy the fabric of our society. A literate society is required for economic and political survival. Government, education, and industry each have responsibilities in remedying the problem. Chisman calls for the creation of centers for basic and applied research, the establishment of more adequate assessment tools, greater investments in teacher training and instructional technology, higher standards for teacher preparation, and better management and planning systems to promote better cooperation among the literacy providers (Chisman, 1990b). Within the government, solutions are required at both the state and the federal levels (Brizius, 1990; Chisman, 1990a). We must soon make progress towards realizing Goal 5 of the Education Summit: "By the year 2000, every adult American will be literate and will possess the knowledge and skills necessary to compete in a global economy and exercise the rights and responsibilities of citizenship."

REFERENCES

America 2000, an education strategy: Sourcebook. 1991. Washington, DC: Government Printing Office.

Apprenticeship 2000: A model for community college collaboration with business and industry. Results of a national study involving three industries. U.S. Educational Resources Information Center ERIC. Document ED341864.

Askov, E. N. 1989a. *Upgrading basic skills for the workplace.* U.S. Educational Resources Information Center. ERIC Document ED309297.

———. 1989b. Using computers for teaching basic skills to adults. *Lifelong Learning* 12: 28-31.

———. 1989c. *Index of workplace and adult basic skills software.* U.S. Educational Resources Information Center. ERIC Document ED333122.

———. 1991. Using computers in adult literacy instruction. *Journal of Reading* 34: 434-38.

———. 1992. Curriculum design for workplace literacy. *Adult Learning* 3: 12-13.

Askov, E. N., & Alderman, B. 1991. Understanding the history and definitions of workplace literacy. In Taylor, M.; Lewe, G. R.; & Draper, J. A., eds., *Basic skills for the workplace.* Toronto: Culture Concepts, 7-20.

Barton, P. L., & Kirsch, I. S. 1990. *Workplace competencies, the need to improve literacy and employment readiness.* U.S. Department of Education, Office of Educational Research and Improvement. Washington, DC: Government Printing Office.

Basic skills, preparation for the GED, and English as a second language. Workplace literacy quarterly report, 1989. U.S. Educational Resources Information Center. ERIC Document ED315563.

Beck, J. A. 1990. *Instructional strategies and resources for literacy and employment training programs, a technical assistance guide.* Washington, DC: Wider Opportunities for Women. ERIC Document ED329754.

Beverstock, C., ed. 1991. *Adult literacies: Intersections with elementary and secondary education.* U.S. Educational Resources Information Center. ERIC Document ED331038.

Bingman, M. B. 1989. *Learning differently: Meeting the needs of adults with learning disabilities.* Knoxville: University of Tennessee, Center for Literacy Studies.

Brizius, J. A. 1990. What states can do about the literacy problem. In Chisman, F., ed., *Leadership for literacy, the agenda for the 1990's.* San Francisco: Jossey-Bass, 198-220.

Burnaby, B. 1990. Materials for ESL literacy teaching. *TESL Talk* 20: 265-87.

Business Council for Effective Literacy. 1986. *Behind bars.* U.S. Educational Resources Information Center. ERIC Document ED300541.

———. 1987. *Literacy in a new language.* United States Educational Resources Information Center. ERIC Document ED300542.

———. 1991a. *Health care industry. Workforce and workplace literacy series.* U.S. Educational Resources Information Center. ERIC Document ED344078.

———. 1991b. U.S. *Commercial Motor Vehicle Safety Act of 1986. Workforce and workplace literacy series.* U.S Educational Resources Information Center. ERIC Document ED344079.

———. 1992a. *National technical assistance organizations. Workforce and workplace literacy series.* U.S. Educational Resources Information Center. ERIC Document ED344076.

———. 1992b. *Small businesses. Workforce and workplace literacy series.* U.S. Educational Resources Information Center. ERIC Document ED344080.

Calfee, R. C. 1988. *Indicators of literacy.* Santa Monica, CA: Rand.

Campbell, A.; Kirsch, I. S.; & Kolstad, A. 1992. *Assessing literacy, the framework for the National Adult Literacy Survey.* U.S. Department of Education, Office of Educational Research and Improvement, National Center for Education Statistics. Washington, DC: Government Printing Office.

Campbell, P. 1991. *An annotated bibliography of adult literacy resources.* 2nd ed. Edmonton, Canada: PROSPECTS Adult Literacy Association. ERIC Document ED333140.

Campbell, R. E. 1987. *Adult literacy, programs and practices.* Columbus, OH: National Center for Research in Vocational Education, Ohio State University.

Cantor, J. A. 1990. *Apprenticeship linkages to secondary education and other training programs.* U.S. Educational Resources Information Center. ERIC Document ED317781.

Carnegie Foundation for the Advancement of Teaching. 1991. *Ready to learn: A mandate for the nation.* Lawrenceville, NJ: Foundation; Princeton University Press.

Carnevale, A. P.; Gainer, L. J.; & Meltzer, A. S. 1990. *Workplace basics: The essential skills employers want.* Alexandria, VA: American Society for Training and Development; San Francisco: Jossey-Bass.

Chall, J. S. 1990. Policy implications of literacy definitions. In Venezky, R.; Wagner, D. A.; & Ciliberti, B. S., eds., *Toward defining literacy.* Newark, DE: International Reading Association, 54-62.

Chisman, F. P. 1989. *Jump start: The federal role in adult literacy. Final report of the project on adult literacy.* Southport, CT: Southport Institute for Policy Analysis. ERIC Document ED302675.

———. 1990a. The federal role in developing an effective adult literacy system. In Chisman, F. P., *Leadership for literacy: The agenda for the 1990s.* San Francisco: Jossey-Bass, 221-27.

———. 1990b. Solving the literacy problem in the 1990s: The leadership agenda. In Chisman, F. P., *Leadership for literacy: The agenda for the 1990s.* San Francisco: Jossey-Bass, 247-64.

Collins, S.; Balmuth, M.; & Jean, P. 1989. So we can use our own names, and write the laws by which we live: Educating the new U.S. labor force. *Harvard Educational Review* 59: 454-69.

Conti, G. J. 1991. Teaching styles and the adult basic educator. In Taylor, M., & Draper, J. A., eds., *Adult literacy perspectives.* Toronto, Canada: Cultural Concepts 311-17.

Crandall, D. P.; Lerche, R. S.; & Marchilonis, B. A. 1984. *Guidebook for effective literacy practice.* U.S. Educational Resources Information Center. ERIC Document ED253776.

Crawford, E., & Romero, C. J. 1991. *A changing nation, its changing labor force.* Washington, DC: National Commission for Employment Policy.

Darkenwald, G. G. 1986. *Effective approaches to teaching basic skills to adults: A research systhesis.* U.S. Educational Resources Information Center. ERIC Document ED325631.

Darling, S. 1989. *Breaking the cycle of illiteracy: The Kenan Family Literacy Model Program.* Chapel Hill, NC: William R. Kenan Jr. Charitable Trust Family Literacy Project, Final Report. ERIC Document ED324496.

DeLaRosa, D., & Maw, C. E. 1990. *Hispanic education: A statistical portrait 1990.* Washington, DC: National Council of LaRaza. ERIC Document ED325562.

Diehl, W. A., & Mikulecky, L. 1980. The nature of reading at work. *Journal of Reading* 24: 221-27.

Dunn-Rankin, P. 1989. *Workplace literacy programs: A review of the literature.* Honolulu: Hawaiian Educational Council. ERIC Document ED309255.

Edlund, J. K. 1992. Breaking the cycle of illiteracy in America: Moving beyond the status quo. *Future Choices* 3: 7-29.

Ehringhaus, C. C. 1990. Functional literacy assessment: Issues of interpretation. *Adult Education Quarterly* 40: 187-96.

Fagan, W. T. 1991. A social psychological conceptualization of adult literacy. Paper presented at the North American Conference on Adolescent and Adult Literacy, March. ED333106.

Fingeret, A. 1984. *Adult literacy education, current and future directions.* U.S. Educational Resources Information Center. ERIC Document ED246308.

Fingeret, A. 1988. The politics of adult literacy education. Address presented to the National Urban Literacy Conference, January 22. ED292053.

———. 1990. Literacy for what purpose? A response. In Venezky, R. L.; Wagner, D. A.; & Ciliberti, B. S., eds., *Toward defining literacy.* Newark, DE: International Reading Association, 35-39.

Fingeret, A., & Jurmo, P., eds. 1989. *Participatory literacy education.* San Francisco: Jossey-Bass.

French, J. N. 1987. *Adult literacy, a source book and guide.* New York: Garland.

Gaber-Katz, E. 1990. *Guide to resources for ESL facilitators.* U.S. Educational Resources Information Center. ERIC Document ED319268.

Galbraith, M. W., & Knowles, M. S., eds. 1990. *Adult learning methods, a guide for effective instruction.* Malabar, FL: R. E. Krieger.

Grubb, W. N.; Kalman, J.; Castellano, M.; Brown, C.; & Bradby, D. 1991. *Readin', writin', and 'rithmetic one more time: The role of remediation in vocational education and job training programs.* Berkeley, CA: National Center for Research in Vocational Education.

Guthrie, J. T., & Greaney, V. 1991. Literacy acts. In *Handbook of reading research,* vol. 2. New York: Longman, 68-96.

Hagner, T.; Hopkins, L.; Marshall, B.; McAdams, D.; Perham, B.; & Tasker, D. 1989. *Learning problems of adult basic education students: Remediation and compensations.* Dover, NH: Dover Adult Learning Center. ERIC Document ED320014.

Hamilton, S. F. 1992. Bridging the work-to-school gap. *School Administrator* 49: 8-15.

Harman, D. 1985. *Turning illiteracy around, an agenda for national action.* Working Paper No. 2. New York: Business Council for Effective Literacy.

———. 1987. *Illiteracy, a national dilemma.* New York: Cambridge University Press.

Hayes, E. 1989. Hispanic adults and ESL programs: Barriers to participation. *TESOL Quarterly* 23: 37-63.

Heath, S. B. 1980. The functions and uses of literacy. *Journal of Communications* 30: 123-33.

———. 1991. The sense of being literate: Historical and cross-cultural features. In *Handbook of reading research,* vol. 2. New York: Longman, 3-25.

Hellwege, N. C., & Sell, I. L. 1990. *Different strokes for different folks.* Miami: Miami-Dade Community College, Southeast Florida Training Center for Adult Literacy Educators. ERIC Document ED329655.

Hinzen, H. 1989. Literacy policy and practice: Issues for debate. *Adult Basic Education* 19: 505-17.

Hladczuk, J. 1990. *General issues in literacy/illiteracy, a bibliography.* New York: Greenwood Press.

Holisky, D. A., ed. 1985. *A guideline for teaching literacy: A competency-based curriculum for use with adult ESL students.* U.S. Educational Resources Information Center. ERIC Document ED312907.

Howie, S. H. 1990. Adult literacy in a multiliterate society. *Journal of Reading* 33: 260-63.

Hunter, C. St. John, & Harman, D. 1979. *Adult illiteracy in the United States, a report to the Ford Foundation.* New York: McGraw-Hill, 1979.

Irwin, P. M. 1988. *Adult literacy issues, programs, and options.* Washington DC: Office of Vocational and Adult Education, Clearinghouse on Adult Education and Literacy. ERIC Document ED317794.

Jurmo, P. 1991. Understanding lessons learned on employee basic skills efforts in the U.S.: No quick fix. In Taylor, M. C.; Lewe, G. R.; & Draper, J. A., eds., *Basic skills for the workplace.* Toronto, Canada: Culture Concepts, 67-83.

Kazemek, F. E. 1988. Necessary changes: Professional involvement in adult literacy programs. *Harvard Educational Review* 58: 464-87.

Kintgen, E. R.; Kroll, B.; & Rose, M., eds. 1988. *Perspectives on literacy.* Carbondale: Southern Illinois University Press.

Kirsch, I. S., & Jungeblut, A. 1986. *Literacy: Profiles of America's big adults.* Princeton, NJ: National Assessment of Educational Progress, Educational Testing Service.

Kirsch, I. S.; Jungeblut, A.; & Campbell, A. 1992. *Beyond the schoo! doors, the literacy needs of job seekers served by the U.S. Department of Labor.* Princeton, NJ: Educational Testing Service.

Kirsch, I. S.; Jungeblut, A.; Jenkins, L.; & Kolstad, A. 1993. *Adult literacy in America, a first look at the results of the National Adult Literacy Survey.* Washington, DC: U.S. Department of Education, Office of Educational Research and Improvement.

Knowles, M. S. 1980. *The modern practice of adult education, from pedagogy to andragogy.* Rev. ed. Chicago: Follett.

Kozol, J. 1980. *Prisoners of silence, breaking the bonds of adult illiteracy in the United States.* New York: Continuum.

———. 1985. *Illiterate America.* New York: Anchor Press.

Kutner, M. A.; Sherman, R. Z.; & Webb, L. 1991. *A review of the national workplace literacy programs.* Washington, DC: Pelavin. ERIC Document ED333199.

Lane, M., Laskowski, N., & McDougall, S. 1991. *Family literacy: Commuity and family life materials. A guide to recent recommended books.* U.S. Educational Resources Information Center. ERIC Document ED343458.

Lerche, R. S. 1980. *Effective adult literacy programs, a practitioner's guide.* New York: Cambridge Books.

Lund, L. 1990. *Literacy in the workforce.* New York: Conference Board.

Marshall, R. 1989. *Workforce policies for the 1990's: A new labor market agenda. The possibilities of employment policy.* U.S. Educational Resources Information Center. ERIC Document ED310014.

McCune, D., & Alamprese, J. 1985. *Turning illiteracy around, an agenda for national action.* Working Paper No. 1. New York: Business Council for Effective Literacy.

McDowell, B. D., ed. 1988. *Assisting the homeless: State and local responses in an era of limited resources.* Papers from a policy conference, Washington, DC, March 10-11. ERIC Document ED313478.

Meaning of apprenticeship: When and how to use the term. A policy recommendation. 1992. U.S. Educational Resources Information Center. ERIC Document ED342924.

Medary, M. 1954. *Each one teach one: Frank Laubach, friend to millions.* New York: Longmans, Green.

Meyer, V., & Keefe, D. 1988. The Laubach way to reading: A review. *Lifelong Learning* 12: 8-10.

Mezirow, J. D.; Darkenwald, G. G.; & Knox, A. B. 1975. *Last gamble on education, dynamics of adult basic education.* Washington, DC: Adult Education Association of the U.S.A.

Mikulecky, L. 1987. *Training for job literacy demands: What research applies to practice.* University Park: Pennsylvania State University. ERIC Document ED284968.

———. 1989. *Second chance basic skills education.* U.S. Educational Resources Information Center. ERIC Document ED317669.

———. 1990a. Literacy for what purpose? In Venezky, L.; Wagner, D. A.; & Ciliberti, B. S., eds. *Toward defining literacy.* Newark, DE: International Reading Association, 24-33.

————. 1990b. National adult literacy and lifelong learning goals. *Phi Delta Kappan* 72: 304-9.

Mikulecky, L., & Weinstein, L. D'Adamo. 1991. Evaluating workplace literacy programs. In Taylor, M., ed., *Basic skills in the workplace.* Toronto, Canada: Culture Concepts, 481-99.

Muir, H. P., & Wischropp, T. W. 1982. *Training manual for experienced ABE / GED instructors.* Manhattan: Kansas State University, Division of Continuing Education. ERIC Document ED229550.

National Advisory Council on Adult Education, Literacy Committee. 1986. *Illiteracy in America: Extent, causes, and suggested solutions.* Washington, DC: Government Printing Office.

National Center on Education and Economy. Commission on the skills of the American workforce. 1990. *America's choice: High skills or low wages, the report.* Rochester, NY: The Center.

National Commission for Employment Policy. 1988. *U.S. employment in an international economy. Report #24.* Washington, DC: The Commission.

National Education Goals Report Panel. 1991. *National Education Goals Report. Building a nation of learners.* Washington, DC: Government Printing Office.

Newman, A. P., & Beverstock, C. 1990. *Adult literacy, contexts and challenges.* Newark, DE: International Reading Association.

Nickse, R. S. 1989. *Noises of literacy: An overview of intergenerational and family literacy programs.* U.S. Educational Resources Information Center. ERIC Document ED308415.

————. 1990. *Family and intergenerational literacy programs: An update of "Noises of literacy."* U.S. Educational Resources Information Center. ERIC Document ED327736.

Padak, N. 1990. *Family literacy programs training manual.* U.S. Educational Resources Information Center. ERIC Document 329731.

Paratore, J. R. 1990. *An investigation of an intergenerational approach to literacy.* U.S. Educational Resources Information Center. ERIC Document 329898.

Pershing, J. A. 1988. *Bridging education and employment with basic academic skills. The work-education bridge.* U.S. Educational Resources Information Center. ERIC Document ED297159.

Philippi, J. W. 1991. How to design instruction: From literacy task analysis to curriculum. In Taylor, M. C.; Lewe, G. R.; & Draper, J. A., eds., *Basic skills for the workplace.* Toronto, Canada: Culture Concepts, 237-61.

Popp, R. J. 1991a. *A guide to funding sources for family literacy.* Chapel Hill, NC: William R. Kenan Charitable Trust. ERIC Document ED340875.

————. 1991b. *Past and present educational experiences of parents who enrolled in Kenan Trust Family Literacy Programs.* U.S. Educational Resources Information Center. ERIC Document ED340874.

Pritchard, R. M. O. 1992. The German dual system: Educational utopia? *Comparative Education* 28: 131-43.

Project T.A.C.K.L.E. [Together Addressing the Challenges of Knowledge and Literacy for Employees]. 1990. *Project TACKLE. Evalation report.* U.S. Educational Resource Information Center. ERIC Document ED329746.

Quintero, E. 1987. *Intergenerational literacy model project handbook*. U.S. Educational Resources Information Center. ERIC Document 290004.

———. 1988. *Intergenerational literacy model handbook*. U.S. Educational Resources Information Center. ERIC Document ED323408.

Reuys, S. 1992. A quest for meaning in adult basic education. *Adult Learning* 3: 22-23.

Rickard, P. L. 1991. *Assessment in adult literacy programs*. U.S. Educational Resources Information Center. ERIC Document ED 337575.

Roditi, H. F. 1991. *How much does a youth apprenticeship program cost, and who will pay for it? Lessons from some long-standing school-to-work programs and youth apprenticeship programs under development. A working paper*. U.S. Educational Resources Information Center. ERIC Document ED337635.

Romero, F. E. 1987. *Literacy in the Hispanic community*. U.S. Educational Resources Information Center. ERIC Document ED318297.

Rosenthal, N. 1987. *Teach someone to read. A step-by-step guide for literacy tutors, including diagnostic phonics and comprehensive assessments*. Belmont, CA: Lake Publishers. ERIC Document ED284051.

Roskos, K. 1990. *A naturalistic study of the ecological differences between whole language and traditional individualized literacy instruction in ABE settings*. Cleveland: John Carroll University. ERIC Document ED329769.

Ross, J. M., & Smith, J. O. 1990. Adult basic educators' perceptions of learning disabilities. *Journal of Reading* 33: 340-47.

Ross-Gordon, J. M. 1989. *Adults with learning disabilities: An overview for the adult educator*. U.S. Educational Resources Information Center. ERIC Document ED315664.

Rothwell, W. J. 1990. *The workplace literacy primer, an action manual for training and development professionals*. Amherst, MA: HRD Press.

Rupp-Serrano, K. 1993. Workplace literacy: A selected bibliography. *Reference Services Review* 1: 79-91.

Rush, R. T. 1986. *Occupational literacy education*. Newark, DE: International Reading Association.

Ryan, K. E.; Knell, S.; & Geissler, B. 1991. *An evaluation framework for family literacy programs*. U.S. Educational Resources Information Center. ERIC Document 331029.

Sarmiento, A. R. 1990. *Worker-centered learning: A union guide to workplace literacy*. U.S. Educational Resources Information Center. ERIC Document ED338863.

Schild, M. 1990. *How to start an effective adult literacy program*. New York: Literacy Volunteers of New York City. ERIC Document ED330873.

Seaman, D.; Popp, B.; & Darling, S. 1991. *Follow-up study of the impact of the Kenan Trust model for family literacy*. U.S. Educational Resources Information Center. ERIC Document ED340479.

Seitchik, A., ed. 1990. *Employer strategies for a changing labor force, a primer on innovative programs and policies*. Washington, DC: National Commission for Employment Policy.

Skagen, A., ed. 1986. *Workplace literacy*. New York: American Management Association.

Soifer, R.; Irwin, M.; Crumrine, B. M.; Honzaki, E.; Simmons, B. K.; & Young, D. L. 1990. *The complete theory-to-practice handbook of adult literacy, curriculum design and teaching approaches.* New York: Columbia University, Teachers College.

Stahl, N. 1993. Reconceptualizing the language of adult literacy. *Journal of Reading* 37: 20-27.

Stasz, C.; McArthur, L. M.; & Ramsey, K. 1990. *Teaching and learning generic skills for the workplace.* Berkeley, CA: National Center for Research in Vocational Education.

Sticht, T. 1978. Basic skills movement: Its impact on literacy. Paper presented at the Right to Read Conference, Washington, DC.

———. 1983. *Literacy and human resources development at work: Investing in the education of adults to improve the educability of children.* U.S. Educational Resources Information Center. ERIC Document ED262201.

———. 1987. *Issues in indexing functional adult literacy.* U.S. Educational Resources Information Center. ERIC Document ED279970.

———. 1989. *Making the nation smarter: The intergenerational transfer of cognitive ability.* San Diego: Applied Behavioral and Cognitive Sciences. ED309279.

———. 1990a. *Teach the mother, reach the child: Literacy issues across generations. Literacy lessons.* Geneva, Switzerland: International Bureau of Education. ERIC Document ED321063.

———. 1990b. *Testing and assessment in adult basic education and English as a second language programs.* San Diego: Applied Behavioral Cognitive Sciences.

———. 1991. *Evaluating national workplace literacy programs.* San Diego: Applied Behavioral and Cognitive Sciences. ERIC Document ED334431.

Taylor, M. C. 1989. *Adult literacy perspectives.* Toronto, Canada: Culture Concepts.

———. 1990a. *Basic skills training: A launchpad for success in the workplace. Literacy Task Analysis Project. Final Technical Report.* U.S. Educational Resources Information Center. ERIC Document ED337579.

———. 1990b. *Literacy task analysis. A how to manual for workplace trainers.* U.S. Educational Resources Information Center. ERIC Document ED337580.

———. 1990c. *Workplace literacy assessment tools.* U.S. Educational Resources Information Center. ERIC Document ED 330885.

Taylor, M. C., & Lewe, G. 1991. How to plan and conduct a literacy task analysis. In Taylor, M. C.; Lewe, G.; & Draper, J. A., eds., *Basic skills for the workplace.* Toronto, Canada: Culture Concepts, 217-35.

Teaching adults with limited English skills: Progress and challenges. 1991. U.S. Educational Resources Information Center. ERIC Document ED341296.

Thompson, L. W. 1988. *Even start: Factors to consider in planning an intergenerational literacy program.* U.S. Educational Resources Information Center. ERIC Document ED321227.

Three strategies . . . one future: A crosswalk among three proposals shaping America's workforce preparation policy. 1992. U.S. Educational Resources Information Center. ERIC Document ED344037.

Turner, T. C. 1988. An overview of computers in adult literacy programs. *Lifelong Learning* 11: 9-12.

U.S. Congress. House of Representatives. 1984. *The Carl D. Perkins Vocational Education Act.* Conference report to accompany H.R. 4164. Report 98-1129. Washington, DC: Government Printing Office.

———. 1990. *The Carl D. Perkins Vocational and Applied Technology Education Act Amendments of 1990.* Conference report to accompany H.R. 7. Report 101-660. Washington, DC: Government Printing Office.

———. Committee on Education and Labor. 1991. *National Literacy Act of 1991, Report 102-23.* 18 March. Washington, DC: Government Printing Office.

———. Joint Economic Committee. 1989. *Crisis in the workplace, the mismatch of jobs and skills.* 31 October. Washington, DC: Government Printing Office.

———. Subcommittee on Investment, Jobs and Prices. 1988. *Employment in the year 2000, a candid look at our future.* S.Hrg. 100-728. Washington, DC: Government Printing Office.

U.S. Congress. Office of Technology Assessment. 1990. *Technologies for literacy.* Washington, DC: Government Printing Office.

———. 1993. *Adult literacy and the new technologies: Tools for a lifetime.* Washington, DC: Government Printing Office.

U.S. Congress. Senate. Committee on Labor and Human Resources. 1993. *School-to-Work Opportunities Act of 1993.* 10 November. Washington, DC: Government Printing Office.

U.S. Department of Education. 1989. *The president's education summit with governors, joint statement.* Washington, DC: Government Printing Office.

———. Division of Adult Education and Literacy. 1990. *Profiles of state programs: Adult education for the homeless.* ERIC Document ED327730.

———. National Commission on Excellence in Education. 1983. *A nation at risk, the imperative for educational reform: A report to the nation and the Secretary of Education, United States Department of Education.* Washington, DC: Government Printing Office.

———. Office of Education Research and Improvement. 1993. *Reaching the goals, goal 5: Adult literacy and lifelong learning.* Washington, DC: Government Printing Office.

———. Office of Vocational and Adult Education. Division of Adult Literacy. 1991. *Teaching adults with limited English skills, progress and challenges.* Washington, DC: Government Printing Office.

———. 1992. *Workplace literacy, reshaping the American workforce.* Washington, DC: Government Printing Office.

U.S. Department of Education and the U.S. Department of Labor. 1988. *The bottom line, basic skills in the workplace.* Washington, DC: Government Printing Office.

U.S. Department of Labor. 1992. *Skills and tasks for jobs. A SCANS report for America 2000.* Washington, DC: Government Printing Office.

U.S. National Advisory Council on Adult Education. Literacy Committee. 1986. *Illiteracy in America, extent, causes and suggested solutions.* Washington, DC: Government Printing Office.

U.S. National Commission for Employment Policy. 1988. *U.S. employment in an international economy*. Washington, DC: Government Printing Office.

U.S. President (Bush). 1991. *Proposed legislation—America 2000 Excellence in Education Act*. Message from the President of the United States transmitting a draft of proposed legislation. House document 102-91. Washington, DC: Government Printing Office.

———. 1992. *Proposed legislation: The National Youth Apprenticeship Act of 1992*. Message from the President of the United States transmitting a draft of proposed legislation to promote youth apprentice, and for other purposes. Washington, DC: Government Printing Office.

University of Texas at Austin. 1977. *Adult Performance Level Study. Final report*. Austin: Adult Performance Level Project.

Unwin, C. G. 1989. Two volunteer programs for instructing adult illiterates: An evaluation. *Adult and Basic Education* 13: 118-26.

Vargas, A. 1988. *Literacy in the Hispanic community*. Washington, DC: National Council of LaRaza. ERIC Document ED296059.

Venezky, R. L. 1990. Definitions of literacy. In Venezky, R. L.; Wagner, D. A.; & Ciliberti, B. S., eds., *Toward defining literacy*. Newark, DE: International Reading Association, 2-15.

Vickery, L. 1990. *An annotated bibliography on basic skills in the workforce and related issues*. Washington, DC: Southport Institute for Policy Analysis.

What work requires of schools: A SCANS report for America 2000. 1991. Washington, DC: Secretary's Commission on Achieving Necessary Skills.

Workforce 2000, work and workers for the 21st century. 1987. Indianapolis, IN: Hudson Institute.

SOURCES OF
ADDITIONAL INFORMATION

Nonprint Materials

The adult learner. 1985. Houston, TX: Gulf Publishing Company Video. 2 videocassettes, 76 minutes, 1/2" VHS.

Adult literacy; don't call me stupid. 1984. Evanston, IL: Beacon. 28 minutes, 16mm.

Adults and learning. Athens, OH: Ohio University Telecommunication Center. 28 minutes, 3/4" or 1/2" video cassette.

Basic education—teaching the adult. (Series). Annapolis: Maryland State Department of Education. Each 30 minutes, 3/4" or 1/2" videocassette.

Titles in the series include:

Articulation of GED	Learners with problems
Basic education—teaching the adult, an overview	Listening and speaking
	Methods and techniques
Can adults learn	Orientation to ABE
Characteristics of the ABE learner	Paraprofessionals and volunteers
A climate for learning	Program planning
Community resources	Recruitment and retention
Developing occupational concepts	Selection and use of materials
Diagnosing for reading placement	Success, needs and interests
Evaluation of reading progress	Teaching basic reading
Goal performance and objectives	Teaching machines
Guiding the ABE learner	Teaching mathematics—basic level
Human relations and interpersonal communications	Teaching reading comprehension
	Teaching word recognition
Individualization of instruction	Teaching writing
Intermediate mathematics	What is the teacher/student role

Can't read, can't write. 1984. Philadelphia, PA: Capital Cities Communications. 60 minutes, 1/2" VHS.

Don't call me stupid. 1983. Bloomington: Indiana University. 28 minutes, 16mm.

Education for adults, if you can't read or write. 1983. San Diego, CA: Media Guild. 24 minutes, 1/2" VHS.

Education for adults: The Wisconsin idea. 1983. San Diego, CA: Media Guild. 23 minutes, 1/2" VHS.

Helping adults learn. 1985. Parts 1, 2, 3. (1-Who are your students; 2-Communicating with your students; 3-Counseling for adults). University Park, PA: Penn State Television WPSX-TX. Each 28 minutes, 1/2" VHS.

———. 1986. Part 4. Students' needs: An instructional resource. University Park, PA: Penn State Television WPSX-TV. 28 minutes, 1/2" VHS.

———. 1986. Part 5. Language experience approach. University Park, PA: Penn State Television WPSX-TV. 28 minutes, 1/2" VHS.

―――. Part 6. 1990. Family literacy: The learning triangle. University Park, PA: Penn State Television, WPSX-TV. 29 minutes, 1/2" VHS.

―――. Part 7. 1991. Learning disabilities. University Park, PA: Penn State Television WPSX-TV. 29 minutes, 1/2" VHS.

Literacy instructor training. (Series). 1978. Bloomington: Indiana University. Each 20 minutes. 16mm, 3/4" or 1/2" video.

Titles in series include:

Comprehension   Talking it over
Language experience approach   Word analysis skills
Patterns in language

Literacy lost. 1986. Princeton, NJ: Films for the Humanities. AV 26 minutes, 1/2" VHS.

Teaching adults to read. 1984. San Francisco: ADAIR Films. 84 minutes, 1/2" VHS.

What if you couldn't read? 1979. New York: Filmmakers Library. 28 minutes, 16mm.

ERIC Descriptors

Adult Basic Education
Adult Dropouts
Adult Education
Adult Learning
Adult Literacy
Adult New Readers
Adult Programs
Adult Reading Programs
Adult Students
Andragogy
Basic Skills
Community Education
Community Influence
Competency-Based Education
Education Work Relationship
Emergent Literacy
Family Influence
Family Literacy
Family Programs
Functional Literacy

Functional Reading
Illiteracy
Industrial Training
Intergenerational Learning
Intergenerational Programs
Job Training
Literacy
Literacy Campaigns
Literacy Education
Literacy Events
Mimimum Competencies
On the Job Training
Program Evaluation
Reading Skills
Teacher Student Relationship
Transfer of Training
Vocational Rehabilitation
Workplace Literacy
Writing Skills

Indexes/Databases

ABI /INFORM
UMI/Data Courier
620 S. Third St.
Louisville, KY 40202
800-626-2823
Online and CD-ROM formats

Business Periodicals Index
H. W. Wilson Company
950 University Ave.
Bronx, NY 10452
212-588-8400
Print, online, and CD-ROM formats

CIS
Congressional Information Service
4520 East-West Hwy.
Bethesda, MD 20814
301-654-1550
Print, online, and CD-ROM formats

Current Index to Journals in Education
Oryx Press
4041 N. Central Ave. at Indian
School Rd.
Phoenix, AZ 85012
602-265-2651
Print, online, and CD-ROM formats

Education Index
H. W. Wilson Company
950 University Ave.
Bronx, NY 10452
212-588-8400
Print, online, and CD-ROM formats

ERIC
U.S. Department of Education
2440 Research Blvd., 5th Fl.
Rockville, MD 20850
301-656-9723
Online and CD-ROM formats

PAIS INTERNATIONAL
Public Affairs Information Service, Inc.
521 W. 43rd St.
New York, NY 10036
212-736-6629
Print, online, and CD-ROM formats

Psychological Abstracts
American Psychological Association
750 First St. NE
Washington, DC 20002
202-336-5500
Print, online, and CD-ROM formats

Social Sciences Index
H. W. Wilson Company
950 University Ave.
Bronx, NY 10452
215-588-8400
Print, online, and CD-ROM formats

Organizations

AFL-CIO Human Resources Development Institute
815 16th St. NW, Rm. 405
Washington, DC 20006
202-638-3912

American Association for Adult and
Continuing Education
1112 16th St. NW, #420
Washington DC 20036
202-463-6333

American Association of Advertising
Agencies
666 Third Ave.
New York, NY 10017
212-682-2500

American Association of Community
Colleges
National Center for Higher Education
One Dupont Cir. NW, Ste. 410
Washington, DC 20036
202-728-0200

American Council on Education
General Educational Development
Training Service
One Dupont Cir. NW, Ste. 20
Washington, DC 20036
202-939-9490

American Library Association
50 E. Huron St.
Chicago, IL 60611
302-944-6780

American Reading Council
20 W. 40th St.
New York, NY 10018
212-462-6333

Association for Community-Based
Education
1805 Florida Ave.
Washington, DC 20009
202-462-6333

B. Dalton Bookseller
7505 Metro Blvd.
Minneapolis, MN 55435

Business Council for Effective Literacy
1221 Avenue of the Americas,
35th Fl.
New York, NY 10020
212-512-2415

Center for Excellence in Education
Indiana University
Poplars Research and Conference
Center, Rm. 805
Bloomington, IN 47405
812-855-4337

Coalition for Literacy
P.O. Box 81826
Lincoln, NE 68501
800-228-8813

Educational Testing Service
Literacy and Learning Assessment
National Adult Literacy Survey
Rosedale Rd.
Princeton, NJ 08541
800-551-1230

Gannett Foundation
Lincoln Tower
Rochester, NY 14604
716-262-3315

Institute for the Study of Adult
Literacy
Penn State University
204 Calder Way, Ste. 209
University Park, PA 16801
814-863-3777

International Association for Continuing Education and Training
1101 Connecticut Ave. NW
Washington, DC 20036
202-857-1122

International Reading Association
800 Barksdale Rd.
P.O. Box 8139
Newark, DE 19714
302-731-1600

Laubach Literacy Action
1320 Jamesville Ave.
Syracuse, NY 13210
315-422-9121

Literacy Volunteers of America (LVA)
404 Oak St.
Syracuse, NY 13210
315-474-7059

National Advisory Council on Adult
Education
2000 L. St. NW, Ste. 570
Washington, DC 29936

National Alliance of Business, Inc.
1201 New York Ave. NW,
Seventh Fl.
Washington, DC 20005
202-289-2888

National Center on Adult Literacy
(NCAL)
University of Pennsylvania
Graduate School of Education
3700 Walnut St.
Philadelphia, PA 19104
215-898-2100

National Center on the Educational
Quality of the Workforce
University of Pennsylvania
4200 Pine St.
Philadelphia, PA 19104

National Center for Family Literacy
(Kenan Project)
401 South Fourth Ave., Ste. 610
Louisville, KY 40202
502-584-1133

National Council of State Directors of
Adult Education
1201 16th St. NW, Ste. 230
Washington, DC 20036

Project Literacy U.S. (PLUS)
4802 Fifth Ave.
Pittsburgh, PA 15213
412-622-1491

U.S. Department of Education
Adult Education and Literacy
330 C St. SW
(mailing address: 400 Maryland Ave.
SW)
Washington, DC 20202
202-732-2270
Literacy Clearinghouse: 202-732-2396

U.S. Department of Education
National Institute for Literacy
800 Connecticut Ave. NW, Ste. 200
(mailing address: 400 Maryland Ave.
SW)
Washington, DC 20006
202-401-1169

U.S. Department of Education
Vocational and Adult Education
330 C St. SW
(mailing address: 400 Maryland Ave.
SW)
Washington, DC 20202
202-732-2251

U.S. Department of Labor
Employment and Training
Administration
Workplace Literacy
200 Constitution Ave. NW
Washington, DC 20210
202-535-0677

U.S. Department of Labor
Secretary's Commission on Achieving
Necessary Skills (SCANS)
200 Constitution Ave. NW,
Rm. C-231B
Washington, DC 20210
202-523-4840

U.S. Department of Labor
Work-Based Learning
200 Constitution Ave. NW
Washington, DC 20210
202-219-5921

Volunteers in Service to America
(VISTA) Literacy Corps
1100 Vermont Ave. NW
Washington, DC 20525
202-606-4845

Useful Library of Congress
Subject Headings

Adult Education—United States
Adult Education Dropouts
Adult Education Teachers
Adult Learning
Basic Education
Dropouts
Elementary Education of Adults
Employees, Training of, United States
Employer Supported Education
Even Start Programs
Functional Literacy
Industry and Education

Libraries and New Literates
Literacy—United States
Literacy Programs
Motivation in Adult Education
Occupational Retraining—United
　States
Occupational Training—United States
Reading—Ability Testing
Reading—Adult Education
Skilled Labor—United States—Supply
　and Demand
Transfer of Training

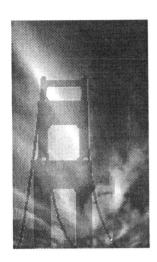

Today, there is a drug and alcohol abuse epidemic in this country. And no one is safe from it—not you, not me and certainly not our children, because this epidemic has their names written on it.
Nancy Reagan, 1986

10

Substance Abuse

Adele Bane

HOW BAD IS IT?

By some accounts, substance abuse is seen as the single biggest problem facing the country today (Iso-Ahola, 1991). In a 1989 poll conducted annually by the *New York Times*/CBS News, 64 percent of those interviewed identified drugs as the nation's leading problem (Gold, 1991). The statistics are alarming. It has been estimated that somewhere between 3 percent and 8 percent of the U.S. adult population is chemically dependent (Clifford, 1985-1986). This may be a conservative figure according to the U.S. Government Office of Technology Assessment (OTA), which estimates that 9 percent of the U.S. adult population are "problematic" drinkers and that the actual prevalence of different forms of substance abuse has probably been underestimated (Clifford & Rene, 1985-1986).

More than once, "epidemic" has been used to describe the extent to which Americans are abusing mood-altering drugs and alcohol. One out of twelve Americans, 21 million people, admit to smoking marijuana on occasion. In 1990, an estimated 15 to 18 million people were classified as alcohol dependent, another 3 million used cocaine, and perhaps another half-a-million were heroin addicts (Gold, 1991).

Currently, Adele Friedrich Bane is the librarian for the Great Valley graduate campus of The Pennsylvania State University. Her career as a librarian has provided a variety of work experiences in the areas of higher education, public education, business, and industry. Both an educator and a librarian, Dr. Bane holds graduate degrees from Carnegie Mellon University in English Literature and from the University of Pittsburgh in Library Science. Her primary research interests are adult learning, educational technology, and health and fitness.

The pattern of substance abuse among the young is of particular concern. Drug abuse by schoolchildren was identified in one Gallup Poll as the number one problem facing schools today (Fox & Forbing, 1991). Records show that over 3 million children between the ages of ten and eighteen get into serious trouble with drugs and alcohol (Falco, 1992).

It is not surprising then to find extensive substance abuse among college students. Studies have indicated that 88 percent to 95 percent of the college population has used alcohol, and that many of these students suffer from alcohol-related problems (Hackett, Henry, & Manke, 1991). The misuse of alcohol and other substances by young people is now recognized as a major public health problem (Arria, 1991).

WHEN DOES USE BECOME ABUSE?

When does the use of alcohol or drugs become problematic and cross over to abuse or addiction? When does a person change from user to addict? Surprisingly, the literature does not have a commonly accepted definition of the complex concept that is addiction. A definition that encompasses the emerging view of addiction suggests that addiction is a disease characterized by repetitive and destructive use of one or more mood-altering substances and stemming from a biological vulnerability influenced by environmental forces (Gold, 1991). This view of addiction builds on the Alcoholics Anonymous (AA) philosophy, which treats chemical dependency as a disease, not a moral failing. Whether a person is at risk for an alcohol or drug-abuse problem depends on how that individual interacts with the environment. Some important lifestyle factors affecting abuse potential are attitude toward drug use, substance availability, occupation, stress levels, setting, and underlying disease (Gold, 1991).

The process by which a user becomes addicted is complex. Researchers have identified a number of behavioral and interpersonal factors that are associated with increased risk for subsequent substance abuse by children and adolescents. They include early antisocial behavior combined with hyperactivity, family history of alcoholism or drug use, family management problems, academic failure, friends who use drugs, alienation, and early first use of drugs (Casemore, 1992).

Much less documented is the influence genetic predisposition plays on later addiction. Little research has been conducted on genetic predisposition and the abuse of drugs other than alcohol (Hawkins et al., 1985). One theory suggests that people have different biological "set points" that determine their vulnerability to drugs or alcohol (Gold, 1991). But a recent study of 356 patients in treatment for alcoholism and their twins found that environmental factors are far stronger than genes in cases of alcoholism in men who develop drinking problems in adulthood and in women (Goleman, 1992).

Commonly accepted symptoms of addiction are compulsion, loss of control, preoccupation with the drug, continued use despite adverse consequences, and denial (Gold, 1991). These characteristics noted by treatment professionals help to clarify when the "occasional user" has become the substance abuser.

HISTORICAL PERSPECTIVE

At the turn of the century, there were virtually no restrictions on opiates, cocaine, or marijuana. These drugs were readily available from mail-order catalogs, pharmacies, and grocery stores. Opium, valued for its soothing effects, was an ingredient in many health remedies, such as laudanum. Morphine, a stronger derivative of opium, was first produced in 1810 and rapidly became popular as a painkiller. Marijuana was widely used in cures for corns and cough preparations (Falco, 1992).

Cocaine, introduced commercially in the 1880s, was initially considered a miracle drug. This extract of the coca leaf was used by Americans both for pleasure and as a medicine. It was used to remedy assorted ailments, including hay fever, seasickness, diphtheria, syphilis, and fatigue. A popular drink of the late 1800s, Coca-Cola, used a tiny dose of cocaine and was promoted as a stimulant and headache remedy. Cocaine became associated with blacks, particularly in the South, working on cotton plantations, railroad work camps, and construction sites (Falco, 1992).

American pharmaceutical companies and patent medicine manufacturers used marijuana, coca, opium, and their more powerful derivatives in a wide variety of products. Marketing was unrestrained, and the American drug industry was highly profitable. By the early 1900s, as the addictive nature of these drugs became evident, public pressure from the middle classes mounted for more stringent controls, particularly over patent medicines. In 1906, the government responded with the passage of the Pure Food and Drug Act, which severely limited the use of cocaine in medicines and elixirs (Falco, 1992).

Opium had been introduced to many western settlements by Chinese immigrants building the transcontinental railroad in the mid-1800s. The influx of Chinese labor and the opium dens associated with them contributed to Americans' labeling the Chinese a "yellow peril." Anti-Chinese feeling culminated in the passing of the Chinese Exclusion Act of 1882, followed by the prohibition on the import of opium in 1909 (Falco, 1992).

Responding to public fears of violence among drug-addicted minorities and criminals, Congress adopted the Harrison Narcotic Act in 1914. This was the first federal law to impose regulation and record-keeping requirements on the production and sale of opiates and cocaine. Medically approved use of these drugs was still permitted. But by 1924, successive amendments and legal interpretations of the act resulted in total prohibition of these drugs. Alcohol was also targeted as a menace to society. In 1920 the Eighteenth Amendment was ratified, launching Prohibition and an age of jazz clubs. This era ended in 1933 when the Eighteenth Amendment was repealed. Marijuana was not outlawed until the adoption of the Marijuana Tax Act in 1937. By this time the drug had become linked with Mexican immigrants numerous in the South and West. It seems that once drugs became linked in the public mind with foreigners and racial minorities, popular dangerous attitudes were formed that persist today. The strategy to combat this "foreign" drug threat through the police power of the state was established (Falco, 1992).

The widespread use of drugs in the 1960s caused a dilemma for many Americans. Millions of young people started experimenting with drugs, many of them from the middle class. Marijuana became the symbol of social protest, particularly against the war in Vietnam. While in Vietnam, many American soldiers turned to heroin for solace. Many young people at home experimented with LSD and other hallucinogens for recreation, spiritual enlightenment, or as a gesture of rebellion against society. The new addict of the sixties was white and middle class (Falco, 1992).

If the 1960s are characterized by widespread experimentation with drugs, the 1970s can be remembered as the decade in which drug use became epidemic. A "softening" in the public attitude toward drug use was evident as its popularity grew among the middle class. Tolerance to alcohol increased as well. Many states lowered the drinking age to eighteen from twenty-one. At the same time, cocaine became the status drug among professionals, sports stars, and entertainers. For many Americans cocaine became the symbol of "fast-track" living, and its glamorous image persisted into the 1980s. During this period of liberalization, only the social consensus against heroin held firm, largely because its dangers were known and its use had long been associated with criminals and social outcasts. Events in the mid-1980s changed the nature of cocaine use in America. Two promising athletes, Len Bias and Don Rodgers, died from cocaine overdose. Their deaths dispelled the myth that occasional use of cocaine was safe (Falco, 1992; Gold, 1991).

The emergence of "crack" cocaine in the mid-1980s created a sense of national crisis. Cheap and rapidly addictive, crack (named for the crackling sound it makes when smoked) produces an intense euphoria lasting ten to fifteen minutes. Unlike heroin or marijuana, crack makes users aggressive, violent, and paranoid (Falco, 1992). It has become the "gateway" drug of choice for a growing number of addicts (Gold, 1991).

In 1981, Ronald Reagan became president and political conservatism resurfaced. The public attitude hardened toward drug use and more punitive responses toward drug use came into favor. The Reagan administration's "War on Drugs" began to combat the destructive impact of drugs on American life. Congress passed major antidrug legislation before the 1986, 1988, and 1990 elections, including large increases in funding. Since 1986, the federal drug budget has grown fivefold, reaching $11.9 billion in 1992. The popular view of drug use as immoral continued to guide our public policy (Falco, 1992).

ABUSE IN THE 1990s

Illicit Drugs

Cocaine, marijuana, and alcohol are the top three hits on today's substance abuse charts, but some "golden oldies," including LSD, are making a comeback (Gold, 1991). The United States has the highest rate of drug abuse of any industrialized country in the world. Twenty-six million Americans used illicit drugs in 1991 (Falco, 1992). The misuse of alcohol and other substances by young people is recognized as a major health problem (Arria, 1991). Cocaine has eclipsed heroin as the main drug of addiction. The Bush administration estimates that there are 1.7 million "hard-core" cocaine users. This estimate from the administration's Office of Drug Control Policy was based on combining several surveys to account for groups of people missed in previous surveys—homeless drug users and those in prisons, colleges, and other institutions (Daley, 1991).

Heroin users number approximately 700,000 (Gold, 1991). Heroin is, however, experiencing a rise in popularity. Traditionally, heroin sold in the United States has been so diluted that it must be injected to maximize its effect, but the heroin available today is so inexpensive and pure that it can be smoked and still provide a powerful high. Since smoking eliminates the need for needles, this "new" heroin may attract users who have previously feared contracting AIDS (Falco, 1992).

Legal Drugs: Alcohol and Nicotine

Alcohol has been an accepted part of human culture since antiquity. Beer and wine were consumed in Mesopotamia as early as 3,000 B.C. Over the centuries, numerous cultures have used alcohol as an integral part of social festivals, religious ceremonies, and medical treatment (Williams, 1992). Alcohol is a drug, and of all the drugs used to excess by Americans, it is the most widely abused (Cory, 1989). Estimates vary, but several sources place the number of alcoholics in this country at 10 million, with another 10-18 million having serious drinking problems. Alcoholism is a primary, progressive, chronic disease characterized by a growing compulsion to drink (Yoder, 1990). Research is being conducted to confirm the role that hereditary factors play in determining who becomes an alcoholic. But all the factors that predispose millions of Americans to become alcoholics are not known to date. Alcoholism has no known cure. Only abstinence can stop the progress of the disease (Gold, 1991).

Although drug use makes the headlines, alcohol abuse is the more serious problem in terms of sheer numbers. Together, drug and alcohol abuse cost the United States economy at least $177 billion a year, including $99 billion in lost productivity, according to Businesses for a Drug Free America. Others estimate the cost to business as closer to $250 billion. Two-thirds of that cost is attributed to alcohol abuse (Staroba, 1990). Alcohol-related injuries cost the nation an estimated $47.5 billion a year. In individual terms, that's about $190 for every man, woman, and child in America. Alcohol use is associated with approximately 41 percent of deaths from unintentional falls; 47 percent of drownings in those younger than fifteen; 69 percent of deaths in boating accidents; 49 percent of episodes of interpersonal violence; 39 percent of partner batterings; 50 percent of reported rapes; and 39 to 58 percent of deaths by fires (Marwick, 1992c).

Alcohol remains the number-one drug of abuse for children and teenagers (Gold, 1991). Everyday over 500 children ages ten to fourteen begin using illegal drugs and over 1,000 start drinking alcohol. Nearly one-half of all middle schoolers abuse drugs or alcohol, or engage in unprotected sex, or live in poverty (Richman, 1992). Because substance abuse is highly correlated with other types of social problems, the "real" cost to individuals and society is impossible to measure.

Cigarettes and other forms of tobacco are addicting. Nicotine is the drug in tobacco that causes addiction. The processes that encourage tobacco addiction are similar to those that predispose people to such drugs as heroin and cocaine. Smoking and alcohol inflict greater damage on society than all illegal drugs combined. The comparative statistics are enlightening: An estimated 18 million Americans are alcoholics, 55 million are regular smokers. Compare this to 5.5 million serious drug abusers. Annual deaths from alcohol are approximately 200,000, and more than 400,000 people die from smoking. By contrast, deaths from all illicit drugs range from 5,000 to 10,000 annually (Falco, 1992). Even with the statistical evidence, most Americans still do not perceive alcohol and tobacco to be as big a threat to society as illegal drugs.

Although the general number of American smokers declines by about 1 million each year, tobacco use among the young has decreased only slightly. Many experts are convinced that the industry is actively promoting nicotine addiction among the young. Because children and teenagers constitute 90 percent of all new smokers, they are an important target market for advertising (DiFranza & Fletcher, 1991). A recent study of RJR-Nabisco's "Old Joe Camel" campaign found that six-year-old children recognize Old Joe Camel as easily as Mickey Mouse. The illegal sale of Camel cigarettes to minors represents $476 million a year, accounting for one-quarter of all Camel sales (Falco, 1992).

SUBSTANCE ABUSE IS BAD BUSINESS

A 1989 survey revealed that 64 percent of management executives now believe that substance abuse is the nation's most critical labor and employment problem (Gold, 1991). A powerful advertising campaign by the Partnership for a Drug-Free America has highlighted the need to get drugs out of the workplace (Falco, 1992). Most substance abusers—73 percent—are employed (Cory, 1989). They account for an average of 15 to 25 percent of the workforce, or 20 million jobs (Gold, 1991). The cost to American employers is about $60 billion a year in absenteeism, accidents, medical benefits, lowered productivity, and employee theft, according to the Institute for a Drug Free Workplace in Washington, D.C. This translates to approximately 3 percent of payroll (Corey, 1989; Staroba, 1990).

Illegal drug use varies by industry, ranging from 13 percent in transportation and 14 percent in retail to 22 percent in construction. Almost half of all employees with alcoholism problems are in professional fields, whereas less than a third are manual laborers, and the rest are white-collar workers (Falco, 1992). To combat this problem, most of the country's large companies have established employee assistance programs (EAPs) to help employees take care of personal problems, which include drug and alcohol abuse (Staroba, 1990). The modern-day concept of an EAP evolved from programs developed during the 1940s that focused on the needs of alcohol abusers. At this point, nearly 30 million workers are employed in businesses that provide EAPs (Gold, 1991). They are cost-effective for companies. In a three year study of the financial impact of its EAP, the McDonnell Douglas Corporation reported a savings of $5.1 million from reduced medical claims, absenteeism, and turnover rates (Falco, 1992). For every dollar invested in an EAP, companies save anywhere from $5 to $16 in medical and other costs. For most companies, the average cost per employee is somewhere between $12 and $20 (Gold, 1991). Companies are taking advantage of this preventive strategy. In 1991, American companies spent an average of $245 on mental-health and substance abuse treatment for each covered employee. That represents 10 percent of a typical company's total health care expense, a figure that is up 5 percent from a decade ago (*Personal briefing*, 1992).

Prevention efforts in the workplace were stimulated by the passage of the Workplace Act of 1988. This federal legislation requires all companies to certify themselves as providing a drug-free workplace if they receive government grants or if they buy property or services worth more than $25,000 from any federal agency (Gold, 1991). The Corporation Against Drug Abuse (CADA) was formed in 1989 by the private sector in metropolitan Washington to develop programs aimed at preventing drug abuse among businesses with fewer than one hundred employees (Singer, 1991; Falco, 1992).

Companies who wish to defend themselves against the high costs of substance abuse are adopting employee drug testing. Though still controversial, drug testing is gaining popularity in both the public and private sectors. In just three years, the number of Fortune 500 companies that screened employees for drug use rose from 3 percent to nearly 30 percent (Gold, 1991). The Greyhound Company is generally credited with pioneering the drug-testing movement in the early 1980s (Gold, 1991). Two-thirds of the largest U.S. companies (those with five thousand employees or more) conduct drug testing, compared to less than a third of all businesses nationwide (Falco, 1992). Of those companies with testing programs, 85 percent test new job applicants (pre-employment) and 64 percent focus on current employee (random or annual) testing (Gold, 1991).

The number of major U.S. companies testing employees and job applicants for drug use rose 18 percent last year, according to the American Management Association (AMA). Three factors encouraged increased testing. One factor was the state and federal laws that mandated testing in the defense and transportation industries. A second was the number of court decisions backing employers' right to test. The third was the growing amount of public opinion that supported workplace testing (*Drug testing* . . . , 1992). Although most employees admit the necessity of testing, a substantial minority have concerns about the practice. Employees are concerned about privacy, confidentiality, and validity (Staroba, 1990). Companies have the responsibility to make sure their drug-testing program respects workers' rights, including the right to privacy. Tests must not be conducted arbitrarily or capriciously (Gold, 1991). Test results should always be confirmed by more than one source and, if necessary, by more than one type of test (Cory, 1989). Companies with a written policy on drug testing face fewer employee objections (*Do you* . . . , 1992). In the future, drug testing may become a "non-issue." Within five years, three-minute computer games are predicted to be widely available that will measure a worker's capacity to concentrate on the task at hand. Conceivably, computers could then replace drug testing as a means of determining a worker's fitness for the job (Falco, 1992).

VICTIMS OF ABUSE

Substance abuse is a symptom and often a cause of a host of other social problems. There is a strong correlation between alcohol and other drug dependence and a number of other social ills, including child abuse, child neglect, domestic violence, sexual abuse, and homelessness (Smith, 1990). The incidence of substance abuse appears to be related to the major socioeconomic forces of poverty, racism, and sexism (Sowers, 1991). In addition, many people see drug abuse at the core of what they think has gone wrong with America's cities, schools, and families (Falco, 1992). Special populations emerge as particularly vulnerable to the effects of substance abuse, including infants and children, adolescents, women, and minorities.

Perinatal Abuse and "Crack" Babies

The newest problem to hit the medical, school, and child welfare communities is substance abuse by pregnant women (Horowitz, 1990). Without support and treatment, women substance abusers who become pregnant pose serious threats to fetal well-being. One estimate is that 375,000 babies born per year have been exposed to illicit substances of all kinds in utero, including cocaine (King, 1991). However, at present, no reliable national estimates of the extent or patterns of cocaine use during pregnancy exist (Mayes, 1992; Chasnoff, 1991; Gittler & McPherson, 1990; Chavkin, Allen, & Oberman, 1991). From a national perspective, the total cost implications of alcohol and drug use—especially cocaine use—during pregnancy are unknown, because we really do not know how many exposed infants there are (Chasnoff, 1991).

Pregnant women who abuse cocaine and other illegal drugs are reluctant to report this fact to health care providers. Society has generally considered this behavior negligent, if not criminal. Pregnant women who abuse alcohol experience less censure than those who abuse drugs. Despite the fetal damage alcohol causes, society allows pregnant women who drink to be responsible for their children. The pregnant drug user may face punishment if she seeks prenatal care. As a result, many women choose not to seek it (Falco, 1992).

Although damaging effects of cocaine on the developing fetus exist, they are not seen universally or consistently, and no one knows how much cocaine is needed to produce what effect (Chavkin, Allen, & Oberman, 1991; Chasnoff, 1991). Preliminary evidence suggests that children exposed to drugs in utero are more at risk for developmental problems that may affect learning. Since widespread crack abuse first started in the late 1980s, public schools are now just beginning to see the first large group of these children in the classroom (Gittler & McPherson, 1990).

As the results of some long-term studies on drug-exposed infants begin to be reported, researchers are predicting that older children who were exposed to drugs prenatally may need specialized educational services beyond the scope of the average day care facility, preschool, or kindergarten (Novello, Degraw, & Kleinman, 1992; Fox & Forbing, 1991). This problem is complicated by the fact that school administrators say they rarely know the children who have been exposed to drugs.

The effects of crack are even more difficult to diagnose because they may mirror and be combined with the symptoms of malnutrition, low birth weight, lead poisoning, child abuse, and many other ills. In addition, the mothers who used crack may have used other drugs as well (Daley, 1991). Research by pediatrician Ira Chasnoff has suggested that drug-exposed children are born with a form of minimal brain dysfunction and are more likely to become hyperactive. Concentrating in school is also difficult for these children (Gold, 1991).

Some teachers, faced with this first large wave of children prenatally exposed to drugs, are referring them to special education classes because of physical, learning, and behavior problems (Daley, 1991). Meeting the needs of this population in early intervention programs and schools will require substantial resource allocation (Gittler & McPherson, 1990). Such programs as Head Start, which concurrently address the health and education needs of children, are examples of an integrated approach to both health and education services that have worked (Novello, Degraw, & Kleinman, 1992). A study conducted by the National Association of Perinatal Addiction Research and Education found that when the mothers and children received early help, many of the children appeared to be normal at the age of three (Daley, 1991).

There is a consensus among caregivers that pregnant women with alcohol and other drug problems need comprehensive treatment services that take into consideration the complexity of addiction as well as the medical, psychological, and economic needs of women and their children. Unfortunately, treatment programs tailored to the needs of women and their children are scarce (Smith, 1990; Chavkin, Allen, & Oberman, 1991; Horowitz, 1990; Falco, 1992). On the federal level, some action has been taken to provide appropriate treatment for women and children. In 1985 Congress amended the alcohol and drug abuse block grant program to require that a percentage of grants be set aside for alcohol and drug abuse programs that serve women, especially pregnant women and women with dependent children. This was followed in 1989 by the Abandoned Infants Act, in which Congress authorized funding for a variety of child welfare and foster care services for drug-exposed newborns (Horowitz, 1990).

Although there are indications that some types of illicit drug use are declining, the number of women of childbearing age who abuse legal and illegal drugs is high. This problem has serious social dimensions, and its impact falls most heavily on those least able to bear it, poor and minority women (King, 1991). Public education programs that help prevent drug use during pregnancy, along with enlightened treatment options, should help reverse this trend.

Adolescents

The high prevalence of alcohol and substance abuse by adolescents poses a significant threat to the wellness of youth (Werner, 1991). Approximately 10 percent of America's high-school-senior-age teens are truly chemical dependent. Chemical dependency is defined as a medical diagnosis of a primary, progressive, chronic, and fatal disease (Casemore, 1992). Some 10,000 teenagers a year are lost in substance-related accidents, not including those who are injured and maimed. One in four teenagers drinks to excess every two weeks, and there are an estimated 2 million alcoholic teenagers in this country (Elkind, 1992).

Although adolescent use of illicit drugs has declined in recent years, overall levels remain high compared to use prior to 1965. Despite the decline in illicit drug use, there has been no change in alcohol and cigarette use. Adolescent substance abuse appears to be part of a syndrome of problem behavior that includes dropping out of school, alcohol and drug use, and precocious sexual activity, rather than specific isolated problems. Problem drug use is, most likely, a symptom, not a cause, of personal and social maladjustment (Werner, 1991; Casemore, 1992).

What are the factors that predispose adolescents toward substance abuse behavior? Psychological and behavioral theorists point to the dominant influences of social factors, such as the environment, peer and parental sanctions, and social competence, in the dynamics of adolescent substance abuse (Caudill, Kantor, & Ungerleider, 1990). The evidence of a positive relationship between childhood antisocial behavior and subsequent drug abuse is relatively consistent (Hawkins et al., 1985). Research on adolescent substance use and abuse has indicated that parents and peers are major influences on adolescent alcohol consumption and drug-use patterns. Peers tend to exert more influence on immediate lifestyle issues, whereas parents exert more influence on long-term goals. Strong social bonds between parent and adolescent may serve a protective function by delaying the initiation of drug use, drinking, and smoking (Windel et al., 1991; Hawkins et al., 1985; Werner, 1991).

An interesting correlation has been shown to exist between parent substance usage and increased adolescent substance usage. Offspring tend to imitate their perception of their parent's drinking, particularly the same-sex parent (Halebsky, 1987). Parental influence is strongest in the early stages of drug involvement, preceding initiation. Peer influence dominates after drug use has begun (Werner, 1991). Results of a survey of 27,335 New York State high school students indicate that adolescents are not likely to seek help from their parents for substance abuse problems (Windel et al., 1991).

Available evidence indicates that most first-time use is initiated through a known peer rather than through a stranger (Werner, 1991; Orlandi, Dozier, & Marta, 1990). The best predictors of adolescents' substance use are the proportion of friends who are users and their friends' tolerance of use. These findings are not influenced by the gender or age of the adolescents (Werner, 1991; Hawkins et al., 1985).

Kandel (1988) has proposed (with varying degrees of acceptance) that adolescents become initiated into substance abuse through a sequence of stages progressing from legal to illegal and less to more serious drugs. Related research suggests that cigarettes play a prominent role as a gateway to marijuana and hard drugs (Werner, 1991). Among the numerous factors that have been implicated in the initiation and maintenance of adolescent drug use are poor academic achievement, early alcohol use, poor self-esteem, depression, dysfunctional family, and lack of social conformity (Werner, 1991). Because school, peers, and family are the primary influences on an adolescent's life, preventive programs should focus on these areas to increase their "prosocial" influences (Wodarski, 1990; Hawkins et al., 1985).

Minorities

Ethnic and minority groups in the United States grow up and live within unique social, cultural, and psychological contexts that shape their knowledge, attitudes, and beliefs, as well as their self-image, value system, and lifestyle. Although substance abuse in minority communities is a well-known problem, relatively few basic research or intervention development research projects have been conducted to validate perceptions. What data are known tend to be grouped around four major ethnic groups: African American, Hispanic American, Native American, and Asian American (Orlandi, 1986).

   In 1991, more than a third of all Americans who reported using drugs at least once a month were African American or Hispanic. Although African Americans constitute only 12 percent of the total population, they account for 41 percent of drug arrests and a third of all criminal drug convictions nationwide. Because minorities are so closely linked with illegal drugs in our society, political leaders with strong popular support have turned to enforcement as the major weapon in the "war on drugs" (Falco, 1992). If the problem of substance abuse, as well as other types of health problems, in the African American community are to be significantly addressed, Americans must also work on the racist and discriminatory practices of the larger society (Clifford & Rene, 1985-1986). Given the disproportionate amounts of poverty, unemployment, and other social ills in the African American community, the negative impact of substance abuse experienced is more severe (Clifford & Rene, 1985-1986; Orlandi, 1986). Empirical data are lacking on the extent of substance abuse in the African American community (Clifford & Rene, 1985-1986). In addition, the negative socioeconomic factors prohibit the majority of African Americans from receiving treatment for alcoholism and drug abuse.
   The Native American population in the United States, including Alaska Natives, is estimated at 1.5 million (Orlandi, 1986). Although unhealthy for all Americans, substance abuse is inordinately harmful for American Indian and Alaska Native people. Whether due to historical, socioeconomic, or biological factors, Indian Health Service officials have rated alcohol, substance abuse, and the diseases associated with alcohol as the most significant health problem affecting Indian communities (Parker, 1990; Moncher, Holden, & Trimble, 1990). Although substance abuse appears to be declining among affluent Americans, this trend is not repeated among minority populations. Samples of seventh- to twelfth-grade American Indian youths obtained from diverse tribal groups between 1975 and 1987 indicate that across the majority of substances reported lifetime incidence of use has increased (Moncher, Holden, & Trimble, 1990). The Indian Health Service estimated in 1985 that nearly one-half of all Indian adolescents were at risk for physical and emotional problems resulting from alcohol and drug use (Parker, 1990).
   It has been suggested that skills deficiencies often lead to stress among youth, and that substance use is a coping response to both environmental and interpersonal stress factors (Moncher, Holden, & Trimble, 1990). In order to address these needs, prevention programs in many Native American communities follow the multifaceted "knowledge, attitudes, and behavior" approach, individualized by incorporating the additional element of teaching cultural traditions to the younger members of the community (Parker, 1990). A core prevention program that provides these cultural elements can act to strengthen bonds and allow access to health-promoting values and norms of the larger society (Parker, 1990).
   Because so little empirical data exist, it is difficult to generalize about minority substance abuse. This is particularly true for Hispanics and Asians. Hispanics are the second largest ethnic group in the United States, estimated at 23 million people. This group is highly heterogeneous

and composed of many subgroups. Valid analysis of the entire population is unavailable because most research has focused on Mexican Americans. The term *Asian American* covers more than 32 nationalities totalling about 3.5 million people in 1980. Incidences of substance use have been reported among these different nationalities, a factor that makes generalizations unreliable (Orlandi, 1986). As in the larger society, prevention is seen to offer the most promise of reducing substance abuse among minorities. However, prevention efforts for these groups must have proven efficacy and address acculturation issues if they are to be successful.

Children of Alcoholics (COA)

The Children of Alcoholics (COA) movement has become a national phenomenon. COAs can be of any age, and older ones are often called Adult Children of Alcoholics (ACOA). Already at risk from having one or more parents that are substance abusers, these children are highly susceptible to the psychological problems that come from living with parents who can't function. One result is that they often fall into the trap of forming similar dysfunctional relationships, known as "codependent" relationships (Gold, 1991). Codependence progresses just as an addiction does, and some experts regard it as an addiction to dysfunctional relationships (Yoder, 1990). The concept of codependence has been evolving for thirty years. Treatment providers first identified traits of codependence in spouses of alcoholics, whom they called coalcoholics. Coalcoholics tended to enable the alcoholic to keep drinking while at the same time making efforts to control the drinkers. Later the same traits were observed in children of alcoholics and in families that were dysfunctional because of mental illness, addiction, domestic violence, or other compulsive behavior (Yoder, 1990). Children of alcoholics tend to experience serious difficulties that interfere with their growth and development. These include psychological difficulties, learning disabilities, anxiety, suicide and attempted suicide, eating disorders, and other compulsive behavior. They are children at risk (Johnson, 1988).

PREVENTION EFFORTS

Prevention is seen as critical to reduce the demand for drugs and to achieve long-term reduction of substance abuse. Traditionally, prevention programs have been classified in public health terms as primary (preventing initial drug use), secondary (stopping the progress of dependency) and tertiary (ending compulsive use). The classification indicates where on the continuum of substance abuse the intervention takes place (*Drug abuse . . .* , 1991; Werner, 1991).

In the past, prevention programs were almost completely informational, but it was found that increased knowledge alone has little effect on subsequent use. Research on smoking prevention led to strategies rooted in social learning and problem behavior theories and a focus on the psychological and social factors involved in the initiation of cigarette smoking. Most recently, peer resistance and life skills training show promise for preparing adolescents to resist substance abuse (*Drug abuse* . . ., 1991).

School-Based Programs

American society and its schools are in the midst of a drug-dependency crisis. Prevention is commonly thought to be the answer. The responsibility for this effort, if supported, will fall upon the schools (Johnson, 1988). During the last thirty years, a variety of prevention approaches have been tried. In the late 1960s, the media was used to deliver hardline antidrug messages. By the 1970s, this scare-tactics approach was replaced by one that focused on more positive values, especially family values. Drugs or alcohol might not even be mentioned directly in ads. Later in the 1970s school-based programs that provided "straight" information on drugs were popular. Although these programs were effective in changing attitudes, they were less successful in changing behavior (Bangert-Drowns, 1988; Caudill, Kantor, & Ungerleider, 1990).

Previous prevention programs failed, in part, because they were based on faulty assumptions about why young people begin using alcohol, tobacco, and drugs (Falco, 1992). By the early 1980s, however, prevention programs began to reflect a broader understanding of the factors that motivate young people to try drugs. This "social influences" model views drug use as something children learn from their environment. Its goal is to help them understand the pressures they feel to use tobacco, alcohol, and drugs and to teach them how to resist these pressures (Falco, 1992).

Effective school prevention programs emphasize both a broad-based community intervention model and cognitive and behavioral intervention at social and individual levels (Caudill, Kantor, & Ungerleider, 1990). Their curricula commonly include strategies to help students define their choice problems, enlarge their response options, identify pertinent information, and implement their desired alternative (Horan, Kerns, & Olson, 1988). The U.S. Department of Education has developed a booklet, "Drug Prevention Curricula: A Guide to Selection and Implementation," for schools choosing an antidrug program.

There are programs that show promise as models for schools to adapt or adopt. An elementary education program, the I'm Special Program (ISP), is a nine-session program directed to fourth graders. Its purpose is either to reduce or delay the onset of student substance abuse by using insights gained from personal growth, social learning, and social development theory (Kim, McLeod, & Palmgren, 1989). Called "the most popular drug education program in America," Project DARE (Drug Abuse Resistance Education) was first offered in 1983 in fifty Los Angeles elementary schools. In this program, police officers enter the classroom and provide factual information on drug abuse, usually in the fourth or fifth grade. The program is now taught in 4,700 communities nationwide in nearly a quarter of all U.S. grade schools. DARE is patterned after a University of Southern California drug education model and discourages drug use by building self-esteem and helping kids develop skills to resist peer pressure (Pereira, 1992). The program is not without critics, who caution that using police officers tends to separate drug prevention education from regular classroom learning (Falco, 1992).

Two popular prevention programs have found that alcohol is more resistant to prevention efforts than drugs. The Life Skills Training Program (LST), designed by Gilbert Botvin at Cornell University Medical College, teaches seventh graders how to make decisions, solve problems, and handle broad social relations in a fifteen-session curriculum. The STAR (Students Taught Awareness and Resistance) program, developed in the early 1980s at the University of Southern California, is built on the social influences approach and combines classroom teaching with a broader outreach involving the family, the media, and the community. Given the importance of social attitudes in adopting a substance abuse habit, it is harder for children to resist alcohol than drugs because alcohol is seen in a more favorable light by society (Falco, 1992).

Continuing evaluation of school-based programs is needed before conclusions can be reached about their effectiveness. Although there is no blueprint for an effective school prevention program, past experience indicates that certain elements appear to be essential: credible information, skills for resisting peer pressure, active involvement of the students, and family and community participation. Experts further agree that these programs should be more comprehensive (Falco, 1992).

Community Involvement

Citizens have been creating their own strategies to combat substance abuse. Washington, D.C., was the site of the first national meeting of community coalitions in November 1990. The goal of this coalition meeting was to develop a long-term comprehensive response to this problem that involved the entire community (Falco, 1992). Experience has shown that the most effective antidrug coalitions draw on the strength of powerful local foundations, businesses, churches, and universities. Since 1990 the Office of Substance Abuse (OSAP) has provided $243 million to support 252 coalitions working on substance abuse prevention (Falco, 1992). The Corporation Against Drug Abuse in Washington, D.C., has been active since 1988. It was created by a group of the city's professional, corporate, and civic leadership to commission independent studies designed to assess Washington's substance abuse problems and devise effective strategies to address them (Falco, 1992).

Coalitions often enlist the local media to expand community awareness of drug and alcohol problems, as well as to build public support for their efforts (Falco, 1992). National media have also been effective in influencing society's attitude toward drugs. In 1986 the Partnership for a Drug-Free America was formed by leading media executives to conduct a public awareness campaign to fight drug abuse. Through this partnership, advertising agencies donate the equivalent of $1 million a day in terms of time and space in print and TV campaigns. The group also sponsors comprehensive surveys that reflect the attitudes of Americans toward drugs.

Another effective mass media campaign is the Harvard Alcohol Project, which was launched in 1987. Its object is to have television writers introduce dialogue into scripts of top-rated television programs to reinforce the "designated driver" concept as a social norm. The targeted audience for the message, "Don't drink and drive," is preteens, adolescents, and high-risk youth (DeJong & Winsten, 1990). Further research indicates that community action groups are most effective when they are composed of "average" people who feel passionate about the issue and are willing to volunteer their time for the effort. These organizations are successful because they focus on prevention, they take into account the environment in which the abuse occurs, and they are able to link substance abuse to broader social problems, such as unemployment, homelessness, inadequate heath care, and crime (Wechsler, 1990).

Ultimately, community prevention efforts work to minimize exposure to abusable substances and to maximize opportunities to adopt an alternative and more healthy lifestyle (Orlandi, 1986). Examples from across the country suggest that societal forces are capable of effecting change. Families, schools, peers, communities, businesses, and media all have the power to eradicate this problem with combined, cooperative effort (Wodarski, 1990).

Federal Prevention Efforts

The current epidemic of abuse of alcohol and other drugs in the United States persists with rates of use exceeding those of all other nations (*Drug abuse . . .* , 1991). Drug dealing continues to be a huge and powerful multinational operation. The U.S. Drug Enforcement Agency (DEA) estimates that a hundred billion dollars' worth of illicit drugs are sold every year in this country alone—twice what is spent on oil (Gold, 1991).

Responding to criticism that his antidrug program has emphasized law enforcement to the detriment of treatment and prevention, President Bush said in 1991 that his plan for controlling drugs contained several new health initiatives. But critics still contended that its dominant focus was on keeping drugs from coming into the country rather than recognizing demand reduction through prevention and treatment as the first priority (Treaster, 1991a). The Bush National Drug Control Strategy provided nearly half a billion dollars to wage war at the international level through a three-tiered approach: eradication, interdiction, and extradition. Eradication aimed at reduction of the supply of drugs; interdiction focused on seizing drugs before they reach the market; and extradition aimed at the legal right to bring foreign criminals to trial in America. At the same time it provided support for local drug prevention efforts, antidrug media events, and efforts to guarantee drug-free work-places (Gold, 1991).

When President Clinton was elected, many expected major changes in the way the federal government would deal with the national drug problem. However, a rational drug policy has not been a hallmark of the Clinton administration. The staff of the Office of National Drug Control Policy was cut from 146 to 25, leading to the resignation of acting drug czar John Walters (Witkin, 1993). At the same time, Mr. Clinton announced that he would elevate the director's position to cabinet-level status. In April, when President Clinton presented his $13.04 billion antidrug budget, critics charged that it was little changed from the approach followed for twelve years by Ronald Reagan and George Bush. That approach relied heavily on law enforcement, instead of emphasizing rehabilitation and prevention efforts (Treaster, 1993a).

Since 1981, Americans have spent over $100 billion in taxes to support drug enforcement. There is growing feeling that the traditional government emphasis on supply reduction has been ineffective. Many law enforcement officials agree that the reduction in supply of drugs cannot succeed as long as the demand for drugs exists in a significant segment of society (*Drug abuse . . .* , 1991). Prevention, not enforcement, is seen as critical to reducing this demand.

The issue of deciding how to reallocate resources among treatment and law enforcement, both at home and abroad, is the primary challenge for President Clinton's director of national drug control policy, Lee P. Brown. Although Brown will have cabinet rank, he is working with a much diminished staff of 24, compared with 146 who worked in President Bush's drug office. In a report to Congress, Brown outlined a national drug strategy that would be presented with further refinements in the February 1994 drug budget. Highlights included an increased focus on providing treatment for hard-core drug users and a reduction of drug-related violence. The proposed strategy also suggested attention to the wider social issues like housing, education, jobs, and health that impact the drug problem (Treaster, 1993b).

TREATMENT OPTIONS

Addiction treatment is a relatively young field. It began with the advent of Alcoholics Anonymous (AA) in 1935, when AA was the primary source of treatment available to alcoholics. Over the years, the "disease" model of addiction was applied to other types of addicts. During the last twenty years, there have been many changes in the treatment field. For example, alcoholism and drug addiction are frequently treated as one illness: chemical dependency (Yoder, 1990).

Improved and increased treatment options are needed for all substance abusers. An effort is under way to provide better care for the patient with alcohol and substance abuse. The Office of Treatment

Improvement, a component of the Alcohol, Drug Abuse, and Mental Health Administration, sponsored a national conference charged with providing strategy and action plans to promote greater access to cost-effective, quality health care for those with substance abuse problems and for those who are infected with the Human Immunodeficiency Virus (HIV) and the Acquired Immunodeficiency Syndrome (AIDS) (Marwick, 1992a). It is widely agreed that any plan for winning the drug war must include wide access to drug treatment programs, and provide programs that are tailored to the individual addict (Gold, 1991). In the United States there are an estimated 4 million addicts (defined as people who use drugs at least 200 times a year) but only 600,000 treatment slots (Gold, 1991).

Treatment programs were unprepared for the massive increase in the number of people needing help, particularly women and teenagers hooked on cocaine in the 1980s. Although the number of women who use addictive substances is substantial, comparatively few programs treat women. Historically, available programs were oriented to the needs of the male addict (King, 1991; Falco, 1992). Given the nature and extent of the service needs of drug-exposed newborns and their families, it is critical that health care delivery systems be developed for addicted women and their children (Gittler & McPherson, 1990).

Since the causes of addiction (whether biochemical, psychological, behavioral, or some combination of these) are not known, exploring different treatment options makes sense (Falco, 1992). Most treatment programs in the United States fall into one of four categories: outpatient clinics, methadone maintenance programs, residential therapeutic communities, and detoxification programs (Gold, 1991). Over the years, experience gained from these treatment programs has provided some guidelines for what "works" in treating drug addiction. It has been shown that treatment must be lengthy, intensive, and highly structured (Falco, 1992).

Experience shows that recovering addicts maintain treatment gains better with continuing participation in Alcoholics Anonymous or other support groups (Falco, 1992). Alcoholics Anonymous (AA) now has 2 million members around the world. The core of AA's philosophy is the Twelve Step program. These twelve steps promote sobriety through self-help, mutual support, and positive reinforcement. The same approach has been adapted successfully to other programs, such as Narcotics Anonymous and Cocaine Anonymous (Gold, 1991; Falco, 1992).

Society has relied heavily on law enforcement to curtail drug abuse. Yet treatment is still scarce in the nation's prisons where 70 percent of the 1.4 million inmates have drug problems (Treaster, 1993b). The General Accounting Office (GAO) reported in 1991 that more than three-quarters of all state prison inmates are drug abusers, but only 10 to 20 percent receive any help. The GAO concluded that most prison treatment, which usually consists of drug education and occasional counseling, is ineffective (Falco, 1992). Just as law enforcement has not been successful in reducing the demand for drugs, jails have not been effective treatment facilities. Because addicts commit 15 times as many robberies and twenty times as many burglaries as criminals not on drugs, it is "folly" to send them back into society untreated (Zuckerman, 1993).

Historically, primary health care and substance abuse treatment have been two separate systems. Now, they are being forced together because of widespread HIV disease and the recent outbreaks of multidrug-resistant tuberculosis. Health care and social service workers are recommending that primary care be provided in the same facility that provides substance abuse treatment (Marwick, 1992a). This approach has particular implications for treating pregnant substance abusers. Providing such key services as pediatric health care, drug treatment, child development, and family planning in one location with one appointment system and the same staff may facilitate use of the services leading to the health and well-being of both mothers and children (Mayes, 1992). A national strategy for helping substance abusers must include easy access to a wide range of treatment options. Clearly, it may cost society more to ignore addiction than to treat it (Marwick, 1992a).

LEGALIZATION ISSUE

A heated debate over drug policy in the United States centers on the issue of legalizing drugs. At the core of the debate lie conflicting beliefs about the health effects of drugs and their economic ramifications under various conditions of regulation and availability (Warner, 1991). The "great unknown" is the question of how much legalization would increase drug consumption, and to what effect (Warner, 1991). Proponents and opponents of legalization diverge radically on both questions. Proponents argue that legalization would "take the crime out of drugs." Potential economic benefits are anticipated from spending less money on law enforcement and from revenue generated from legal drugs. Proponents of legalization generally concede that legalization will increase drug use and addiction, but argue this is a small price to pay for eliminating drug crime (Falco, 1992).

The majority, those against legalization, argue that drug use is kept at a certain level because it is difficult, costly, and illegal to obtain drugs (Gold, 1991). They feel the negative effects of increased drug use and addiction would far outweigh any social benefits. Past experience with alcohol and tobacco suggest strongly that a significant number of users would become abusers—anywhere from 250,000 to 20 million. More importantly, legalization would signal a change in American attitude, suggesting tolerance rather than disapproval of drug use (Falco, 1992). Much of the legalization debate is based on conjecture and emotion. Critical data are needed to arrive at a conclusion on whether drug use would increase and, if so, by how much (Gostin, 1991). When Surgeon General Joycelyn Elders recommended that the government study the idea of legalizing drugs with the intent of reducing the crime rate, she created a furor among the Clinton administration, some Republicans, and public and health care professionals. President Clinton immediately distanced himself from this suggestion saying that he remained firmly against the legalization of drugs. However, Dr. Elder's comments served to revive the perennial debate over the best way to handle our nation's drug problem (Labaton, 1993). The true social costs of drug addiction and drug-related crime are difficult, if not impossible, to measure, even though they may account for the society's greatest drug-related burden (Warner, 1991).

AN ENCOURAGING TREND

Society's attitudes toward drugs are undergoing an upheaval. Drugs are no longer as socially acceptable as they were in the 1960s (Gold, 1991). Mass media campaigns encourage hostility toward marijuana, cocaine, and crack and make drug use, in general, look "pathetic, unattractive and foolish" (Falco, 1992). The illegality of marijuana, heroin, and cocaine conveys a strong message that these drugs are harmful.

Because television and radio advertising are such powerful forces in shaping behavior, tobacco and alcohol commercials (except for beer and wine) have been banned from the air. Warning labels on alcoholic beverages adopted in 1991 have begun to send a larger social message about alcohol. In 1991, 68 percent of Americans aged twelve and over reported drinking in the previous year, compared to 73 percent in 1985. Two-thirds of Americans now believe that smoking a pack of cigarettes a day is very hazardous (Falco, 1992). Mass media campaigns will continue to be a critical component of the nation's long-term effort to encourage more responsible use of alcohol and prescription drugs by adults, to discourage tobacco and illegal drug use, and to promote universal abstinence among youth (DeJong & Winsten, 1990). Even kids are getting the message. From 1990 to 1991, marijuana and other illicit drug use fell among high school seniors and college students surveyed by the University of Michigan. Even alcohol use showed a decline (*Pot shot*, 1992). For most students, alcohol and marijuana are the legal and illegal drugs of choice. Recent surveys show a "significant" downturn in the use of crack for both college and high school students. According to a 1991 study, a health consciousness about drugs has made it "not cool" to "do" them (Marriott, 1991). This attitude may account for growing numbers of Americans who are rejecting marijuana, cocaine, alcohol, and nicotine (Treaster, 1991b).

Federal government studies corroborate declining drug use around the country, identifying the sharpest decline among the middle class. Drug experts attribute decreased use to several factors, including public condemnation (Treaster, 1991b). The demographics of drug use point to the inner city poor as a high-risk population for all types of substance abuse. For the first time, the Partnership for a Drug-Free America is focusing specific antidrug campaigns on the inner city, where the decline in drug use has been less pronounced (Treaster, 1991c). An increasingly divided nation seems to be emerging, with the greatest declines in drug use occurring among the better educated and more affluent, and growing addiction among the poor, the disadvantaged, and racial minorities (Falco, 1992). Those most affected by substance abuse tend to be victims of other social ills like poverty, dysfunctional families, crime, and violence (Murphy et al., 1991). Americans are beginning to realize that the drug problem is "embedded" in every other serious social problem in contemporary society (Falco, 1992). Experts repeatedly underscore that efforts to combat substance abuse will require a deeper understanding of wider social values.

REFERENCES

Arria, A. 1991. The effects of alcohol abuse on the health of adolescents. *Alcohol Health & Research World* 15: 52-57.

Bangert-Drowns, R. L. 1988. The effects of school-based substance abuse education: A meta-analysis. *Journal of Drug Education* 18: 243-64.

Casemore, B. 1992. Teen drug use: Risks and initial response. *Addiction & Recovery* 12: 8-11.

Caudill, B. D.; Kantor, G.; & Ungerleider, S. 1990. Project impact: A national study of high school substance abuse intervention training. *Journal of Alcohol and Drug Education* 35: 61-74.

Chasnoff, I. J. 1991. Drugs, alcohol, pregnancy and the neonate. *Journal of the American Medical Association* 266: 1567-68.

Chavkin, W.; Allen, M. H.; & Oberman, M. 1991. Drug abuse and pregnancy: Some questions on public policy, clinical management, and maternal and fetal rights. *Birth* 18: 107-12.

Clifford, P., & Rene, A. A. 1985-1986. Substance abuse among blacks: An epidemiological perspective. *Urban League Review* 9: 52-58.

Cory, J. 1989. Substance abuse: The facts you need to fight it. *Hardware Age*, 1 June, 59-62.

Daley, S. 1991. Born on crack and coping with kindergarten. *New York Times*, 7 February.

DeJong, W., & Winsten, J. A. 1990. The use of mass media in substance abuse prevention. *Health Affairs* 9: 30-46.

DiFranza, J. R., & Fletcher, C. 1991. RJR Nabisco's cartoon camel promotes camel cigarettes to children. *Journal of the American Medical Association* 266: 3149-63.

Do you have a right to know? 1992. *INC.*, 16 October.

Drug abuse in the United States. 1991. *Journal of the American Medical Association* 265: 2102-7.

Drug testing rose 18% among big companies in 1991, survey says. 1992. *Wall Street Journal*, 3 April.

Elkind, D. 1992. Waaah! Why kids have a lot to cry about. *Psychology Today* 25: 38-41, 80-81.

Falco, M. 1992. *The making of a drug-free America: Programs that work*. New York: Random House.

Fox, C. L., & Forbing, S. E. 1991. Overlapping symptoms of substance abuse and learning handicaps: Implications for educators. *Journal of Learning Disabilities* 24: 24-31.

Gittler, J., & McPherson, M. 1990. Prenatal substance abuse. *Children Today* 19: 3-7.

Gold, M. 1991. *The good news about drugs and alcohol: Curing, treating and preventing substance abuse in the new age of biopsychiatry*. New York: Random House.

Goleman, D. 1992. "Wisdom" on alcoholic's child called stuff of fortune cookies. *New York Times*, 19 February.

Gostin, L. 1991. Compulsory treatment for drug-dependent persons: Justification for a public health approach to drug dependency. *Milbank Quarterly* 69: 561-71.

Hackett, P.; Henry, M.; & Manke, M. P. 1991. Courses in substance abuse use and abuse: A survey of colleges and universities. *Journal of Alcohol and Drug Education* 104: 58-64.

Halebsky, M. A. 1987. Adolescent alcohol and substance abuse: Parent and peer effects. *Adolescence* 22: 961-67.

Hawkins, J. D.; Lishner, M. S. W.; Catalano, R. F.; & Howard, M. O. 1985. Childhood predictors of adolescent substance abuse: Toward an empirically grounded theory. *Journal of Children in Contemporary Society* 18: 11-48.

Horan, J. J.; Kerns, A.; & Olson, C. 1988. Perspectives on substance abuse prevention. *Elementary School Guidance & Counseling* 23: 84-92.

Horowitz, R. 1990. Perinatal substance abuse. *Children Today* 19: 8-12.

Iso-Ahola, S. 1991. Adolescent substance abuse and leisure boredom. *Journal of Leisure Research* 23: 260-71.

Johnson, J. L. 1988. The challenge of substance abuse. *Teaching Exceptional Children* 20: 29-31.

Kandel, D. B. 1988. Issues of sequencing of adolescent drug use and other problem behaviors. *Drugs & Society* 31(1-2): 55-76.

Kim, S.; McLeod, J.; & Palmgren, C. L. 1989. The impact of the "I'm special" program on student substance abuse and other related student problem behavior. *Journal of Drug Education* 19: 83-95.

King, P. A. 1991. Helping women helping children: Drug policy and future generations. *Milbank Quarterly* 69: 595-621.

Labaton, S. 1993. Surgeon General suggests study of legalizing drugs. *New York Times*, 8 December.

Marriott, M. 1991. Raid notwithstanding, campus drug use seems less. *New York Times*, 26 March.

Marwick, C. 1992a. Effort under way to enlist more primary care physicians in treatment of substance abuse. *Journal of the American Medical Association* 267: 1887, 1891.

———. 1992b. Guns, drugs threaten to raise public health problem of violence to epidemic. *Medical News & Perspectives, Journal of the American Medical Association* 267: 2993.

———. 1992c. Counteracting alcohol's "glamour image." *Journal of the American Medical Association* 267: 2289.

Mayes, L. 1992. The problem of prenatal cocaine exposure. *Journal of the American Medical Association* 267: 406-8.

Moncher, M. S.; Holden, G. W.; & Trimble, J. E. 1990. Substance abuse among Native American youth. *Journal of Consulting and Clinical Psychology* 58: 408-15.

Murphy, J. M.; Jellick, M.; Quinn, D.; Smith, G.; Poitrast, F. G.; & Goshko, M. 1991. Substance abuse and serious child mistreatment: Prevalence, risk, and outcome in a court sample. *Child Abuse & Neglect* 15: 171-211.

Novello, A. C.; Degraw, C.; & Kleinman, D. 1992. Healthy children ready to learn: An essential collaboration between health and education. *Public Health Reports* 107: 3-11.

Orlandi, M. A. 1986. Community-based substance abuse prevention: A multicultural perspective. *Journal of School Health* 56: 394-401.

Orlandi, M. A.; Dozier, C. E.; & Marta, M. A. 1990. Computer-assisted strategies for substance abuse prevention: Opportunities and barriers. *Journal of Consulting and Clinical Psychology* 58: 425-31.

Parker, L. 1990. The missing component in substance abuse prevention efforts: A Native American youth. *Contemporary Drug Problems* 17: 251-70.

Pereira, J. 1992. In a drug program, some kids turn in their own parents. *Wall Street Journal*, 20 April.

Personal briefing. 1992. *Philadelphia Inquirer*, 8 September.

Pot shot. 1992. *Psychology Today*, May-June, 8.

Richman, L. S. 1992. Struggling to save our kids. *Fortune*, 10 August, 35-40.

Singer, P. 1991. Small business focus on drugs in the workplace. *New York Times*, 10 November.

Smith, B. V. 1990. Improving substance abuse treatment for women. *Clearinghouse Review* 24: 490-92.

Sowers, J. G. 1991. Preventive strategies in education: History, current practices, and future trends regarding substance abuse and pregnancy prevention. *Bulletin of the New York Academy of Medicine* 67: 256-69.

Staroba, K. 1990. The substance abuse maze. *Association Management* 42: 26-32.

Treaster, J. B. 1991a. Bush proposes more anti-drug spending. *New York Times*, 1 February.

———. 1991b. Costly and scarce, marijuana is a high more are rejecting. *New York Times*, 29 October.

———. 1991c. From toys to TV, drug fight grows. *New York Times*, 16 March.

———. 1993a. Clinton is chided on drug program. *New York Times*, 12 April.

———. 1993b. Clinton altering nation's tactics in drug battle. *New York Times*, 20 October.

Warner, K. 1991. Legalizing drugs: Lessons from (and about) economics. *Milbank Quarterly* 69: 641-61.

Wechsler, R. 1990. Harnessing people power: A community-based approach to preventing alcohol and drug abuse. *Western City* 66: 3-5, 36.

Werner, M. J. 1991. Adolescent substance abuse: Risk factors and prevention strategies. *Maternal and Child Health Technical Information Bulletin*, February, 3-15.

Williams, M. H. 1992. Alcohol and sport performance. *Sports Science Exchange* 4: 1.

Windel, M.; Miller-Tutzauer, C.; Barnes, G. M.; & Welte, J. 1991. Adolescent perceptions of help-seeking resources for substance abuse. *Child Development* 62: 179-89.

Witkin, G. 1993. How politics ruined drug-war planning. *U.S. News & World Report* 114: 29.

Wodarski, J. S. 1990. Adolescent substance abuse: Practice implications. *Adolescence* 25: 667-88.

Yoder, B. 1990. *The recovery resource book*. New York: Simon & Schuster.

Zuckerman, M. B. 1993. Fighting the right drug war. *U.S. News & World Report* 114: 74.

SOURCES OF ADDITIONAL INFORMATION

Indexes/Databases

ABI/INFORM
UMI Data Courier
620 S. Third St.
Louisville, KY 40202-2475
1-800-626-2823
Online and CD-Rom formats

Academic Index
Online Services
Information Access Company
362 Lakeside Dr.
Foster City, CA 94404
415-378-5200
Online and CD-ROM formats

Business Periodicals Index
H. W. Wilson Company
950 University Ave.
Bronx, NY 10452
212-588-8400
Print, online, and CD-ROM formats

*Combined Health Information
Database (CHI)*
BRS Information Technologies
8000 Westpark Dr.
McLean, VA 22102
703-442-0900
800-289-4277
Online format

*Current Index to Journals in
Education (CIJE)*
Oryx Press
2214 N. Central at Encanto
Phoenix, AZ 85004
602-254-6156
Print, online, and CD-ROM formats

Druginfo and Alcohol Use and Abuse
University of Minnesota
Drug Information Services
3-160 Health Sciences Unit F
308 Harvard St. SE
Minneapolis, MN 55455
612-624-6492
Online format

Education Index
H. W. Wilson Company
950 University Ave.
Bronx, NY 10452
212-588-8400
Print, online, and CD-ROM formats

ERIC
U.S. Department of Education
2440 Research Blvd., 5th Fl.
Rockville, MD 20850
301-656-9723
Online and CD-ROM formats

Family Resources Database
Database Information
National Council on Family Relations
3989 Central Ave. NE, Ste. 550
Minneapolis, MN 55421
612-781-9331
Online format

Health Periodicals Database
Information Access Company
362 Lakeside Dr.
Foster City, CA 94404
415-378-5200
Online and CD-ROM formats

Hospital Literature Index
American Hospital Association
840 North Lake Shore Dr.
Chicago, IL 60611
800-621-6902
Print and microform formats

Magazine ASAP
Information Access Company
362 Lakeside Dr.
Foster City, CA 94404
800-227-8431
Online and CD-ROM formats

*Monthly Catalog of United States
Government Publications*
U.S. Government Printing Office
Superintendent of Documents
Mail Stop: SSOP
Washington, DC 20402-9328
Print and online formats

National Newspaper Index
Online Services
Information Access Company
362 Lakeside Dr.
Foster City, CA 94404
800-227-8431
Online and microfiche formats

Readers' Guide to Periodical Literature
H. W. Wilson Company
950 University Ave.
Bronx, NY 10452
212-588-8400
Print, online, and CD-ROM formats

Social Sciences Index
H. W. Wilson Company
950 University Ave.
Bronx, NY 10452
212-588-8400
Print, online, and CD-ROM formats

Periodicals

Addiction and Recovery
Medquest Communications Inc.
629 Euclid Ave., Ste. 500
Cleveland, OH 44114
Bimonthly

Addictive Behaviors
Pergamon Press Inc.
660 White Plains Rd.
Tarrytown, NY 10591-5153
Quarterly

Adolescence
Libra Publishers Inc.
3089C Claremont Dr., Ste. 383
San Diego, CA 92117
Quarterly

Adolescent Counselor
12729 N.E. 20th St., Ste. 12
Bellevue, WA 98005
Bimonthly

Alcohol Health and Research World
National Institute on Alcohol Abuse
and Alcoholism (NIAAA)
CSR Inc.
1400 Eye St. NW, Ste. 600
Washington, DC 20005
Quarterly

Alcoholism and Addiction Magazine
Quantum Publishing Company
23860 Miles Rd.
Cleveland, OH 44128
Bimonthly

*The American Journal of Drug and
Alcohol Abuse*
Marcel Dekker Inc.
270 Madison Avenue
New York, NY 10016
Quarterly

The American Journal of Psychiatry
American Psychiatric Press Inc.
1400 K St. NW
Washington, DC 20005
Monthly

Annual Review of Public Health
Annual Reviews Inc.
Camino Way
Palo Alto, CA 94306
Annual

British Journal of Addiction
Carfax Publishing Company
Box 25 Abingdon
Oxfordshire OX14 3UE England
Monthly

Business and Health
Medical Economics Inc.
680 Kinderkamack Rd.
Oradell, NJ 07649
Monthly

Children Today
Superintendent of Documents
Government Printing Office
Washington, DC 20402
Bimonthly

Contemporary Drug Problems
Federal Legal Publications Inc.
157 Chambers St.
New York, NY 10007
Quarterly

Drug and Alcohol Dependence
Elsevier Scientific Publishers
Ireland Ltd., P.O. Box 85
Limerick, Ireland
Irregular (8 times a year)

EAP Digest
Performance Resource Press Inc.
2145 Crooks Rd., Ste. 103
Troy, MI 48084
Bimonthly

Elementary School Guidance and Counseling
American Association for Counseling Development
5999 Stevenson Ave.
Alexandria, VA 22304
Quarterly

Employee Assistance Quarterly
The Haworth Press Inc.
12 W. 32nd St.
New York, NY 10001
Quarterly

Fortune
Time Inc.
301 E. Ohio St.
Chicago, IL 6 0611
Biweekly

Health Affairs
Project Hope
Millwood, VA 89674
Quarterly

Health Education Research
John Wiley & Sons Inc.
605 3rd Ave.
New York, NY 10158
Quarterly

JAMA: The Journal of the American Medical Association
American Medical Association
535 North Dearborn St.
Chicago, IL 60610
Weekly

Journal of Addictive Diseases
The Haworth Press Inc.
10 Alice St.
Binghamton, NY 13904
Quarterly

Journal of Alcohol and Drug Education
1120 E. Oakland
P.O. Box 10212
Lansing, MI 48901
3 times a year

Journal of Consulting and Clinical Psychology
American Psychological Association
1400 N. Uhle St.
Arlington, VA 22201
Bimonthly

Journal of Drug Education
Baywood Publishing Company
120 Marine St.
P.O. Box D
Farmingdale, NY 11735
Quarterly

Journal of Drug Issues
P.O. Box 4021
Tallahassee, FL 32315
Quarterly

Journal of Public Health Policy
208 Meadowood Dr.
South Burlington, VT 05403
Quarterly

Journal of School Health
ASHA
P.O. Box 708
Kent, OH 44240
Monthly

Journal of Studies on Alcohol
Rutgers Center of Alcohol Studies
P.O. Box 969
Piscataway, NJ 08855
Bimonthly

Journal of Substance Abuse
Ablex Publishing Corp.
355 Chestnut St.
Norwood, NJ 07648
Quarterly

Journal of Substance Abuse Treatment
Pergamon Press Inc.
Maxwell House
Fairview Park
Elmsford, NY 10523
Quarterly

Milbank Quarterly
Cambridge University Press
32 E. 57th St.
New York, NY 10022
Quarterly

Monthly Labor Review
Department of Labor
200 Constitution Ave. NW
Washington, DC 20210
Monthly

New York Times
229 W. 43rd St., 6th Fl.
New York, NY 10036
Daily

Newsweek
Newsweek Building
Livingston, NJ 07039
Weekly

Professional Counselor
12729 N.E. 20th St., Ste. 12
Bellevue, WA 98005
Bimonthly

Psychiatric Annals
Slack Inc.
6900 Grove Rd.
Thorofare, NJ 08086
Monthly

Public Health Reports
U.S. Government Printing Office
Department of Health and Human
Services
200 Independence Ave. SW
Washington, DC 20201
Bimonthly

Student Assistance Journal
Subscribers Service Department
P.O. Box 6282
Syracuse, NY 13217
Quarterly

Time
Time Inc.
301 E. Ohio St.
Chicago, IL 60611
Weekly

*US Journal of Drug and Alcohol
Dependence*
US Journal, Inc.
Enterprise Center
3201 S.W. 15th St.
Deerfield Beach, FL 33442
Monthly

Wall Street Journal
Eastern Edition
The Wall Street Journal, Dow Jones &
Company Inc.
200 Burnett Rd.
Chicopee, MA 01021
Daily

Organizations

Private Organizations and Groups

Alcohol and Drug Problems Association
444 N. Capitol St. NW, Ste. 181
Washington, DC 20001
202-737-4340

American Council for Drug Education
204 Monroe St.
Rockville, MD 20850
800-488-DRUG
301-294-0600

American School Health Association
7263 State Rte. 43
P.O. Box 708
Kent, OH 44240
216-678-1601

American Society of Addiction Medicine (ASAM)
12 W. 21st St.
New York, NY 10010
212-206-6770

Beginning Alcohol and Addiction Basic
Education Studies (BABES)
17330 Northland Park Ct.
Southfield, MI 48075
800-54-BABES
313-443-0888

The Corporation Against Drug Abuse
(CADA)
1010 Wisconsin Ave. NW, Ste. 250
Washington, DC 20007
202-338-0654

Institute for a Drug-Free Workplace
P.O. Box 65708
Washington, DC 20035-5708
202-828-4590

Institute for Social Research
The University of Michigan
Ann Arbor, MI 48106-1248
313-763-5043

Institute on Black Chemical Abuse
(IBCA)
2614 Nicollet Ave. South
Minneapolis, MN 55408
612-871-7878

National Association of Perinatal Addiction Research and Education
11 E. Hubbard St., Ste. 200
Chicago, IL 60611
312-329-2512

National Association of State Alcohol
and Drug Abuse Directors
444 N. Capitol St. NW, Ste. 520
Washington, DC 20001
202-783-6868

National Families in Action
2296 Henderson Mill Rd., Ste. 204
Atlanta, GA 30345
404-934-6364

National Federation of Parents for a
Drug-Free Youth (NFP)
P.O. Box 3878
St. Louis, MO 63122
314-968-1322

National Head Start Association
201 N. Union St., Ste. 320
Alexandria, VA 22314
703-739-0875

Partnership for a Drug-Free America
666 Third Ave.
New York, NY 10017
212-922-1560

PRIDE (Parent's Resource Institute
for Drug Education)
The Hurt Building, Ste. 210
Atlanta, GA 30303
404-577-4500

Substance Abuse Librarians and
Information Specialists (SALIS)
Alcoholism and Drug Abuse Institute
3937 15th Ave. NE
Seattle, WA 98105
206-543-0397

Government Organizations

Alcohol and Drug Abuse Education
Program
United States Department of
Education
400 Maryland Ave. SW
Washington, DC 20202-4101
202-708-5366

Alcohol, Drug Abuse and Mental
Health Administration
(U.S. Department of Health and
Human Services)
5600 Fishers Ln.
Rockville, MD 20857
301-443-4797

Center for Substance Abuse Treatment
Rockwall II, 10th Fl.
5600 Fishers Ln.
Rockville, MD 20857
301-443-6549

National Clearinghouse for Alcohol
and Drug Information (NCADI)
P.O. Box 2345
Department PA
Rockville, MD 20852
800-729-6686

National Institute of Alcohol Abuse
and Alcoholism (NIAAA)
5600 Fishers Ln.
Rockville, MD 20857
301-443-4373

National Institute on Drug Abuse
5600 Fishers Ln.
Rockville, MD 20857
301-443-6487
800-662-HELP(4357) (English)
800-66-AYUDA (Spanish)
Drug Free Workplace Helpline:
800-843-4971

Office for Substance Abuse Prevention
(OSAP)
Communications Division
Parklawn Building, Rm. 13A-54
5600 Fishers Ln.
Rockville, MD 20857
301-443-0373

Office of National Drug Control Policy
The Executive Office of the President
Washington, DC 20500
202-467-9800

Office of Substance Abuse Prevention
Alcohol, Drug Abuse, and Mental
Health Administration
5600 Fishers Ln.
Rockwall II
Rockville, MD 20857
301-443-0365

Office on Smoking and Health
Public Information Branch
Park Building, Rm. 118
5600 Fishers Ln.
Rockville, MD 20857

President's Drug Advisory Council
The Executive Office of the President
Washington, DC 20503
202-466-3100

U.S. General Accounting Office
P.O. Box 6015
Gaithersburg, MD 20877
202-275-6241

Treatment / Self-Help Groups

Alanon Family Group, Inc.
P.O. Box 862
Midtown Station
New York, NY 10018-6106
800-344-2666

Adult Children of Alcoholics (ACOA)
P.O. Box 35623
Los Angeles, CA 90035
213-534-1815

Alcoholics Anonymous (AA)
General Service Office
468 Park Ave. South
New York, NY 10016
212-686-1100

Children of Alcoholics Foundation, Inc.
P.O. Box 4185
Grand Central Station
New York, NY 10163-4185
212-754-0656

Cocaine Anonymous
World Services, Inc.
3740 Overland Ave., Ste. G
Los Angeles, CA 90034
800-347-8998
213-554-2554

Narcotics Anonymous
NA World Services
P.O. Box 9999
Van Nuys, CA 91409
818-780-3951

National Association for Children of
Alcoholics (NACOA)
31706 Coast Hwy., Ste. 201
South Laguna, CA 92677-3044
714-499-3889

Electronic Conferences (Interest Groups)

Addict-L [Online]. Available e-mail:
   listserv@kentvm
   listserv@kentvm.kent.edu

AIDSNewsForum [Online]. Available e-mail:
   aidsnews%rutvm1.bitnet@cunyvm.cuny.edu

ALCOHOL [Online]. Available e-mail:
   alcohol@lmuacad.bitnet

Drug Abuse [Online]. Available e-mail:
   drugabus@mab.umd.edu or
   drugabus@umab.bitnet or
   drugabus%umab.bitnet@vm1.nodak.edu

Health Reform [Online]. Available e-mail:
   HealthRe on listserv@ukcc.bitnet or listserv@ukcc.uky.edu

Minority Health [Online]. Available e-mail:
   minhlth@dawn.hampshire.edu

Smoke-Free [Online]. Available e-mail:
   listserv@ra.msstate.edu

Useful Library of Congress
Subject Headings

Addiction
Addictive Behavior
Adult Children of Alcoholics (ACOA)
AIDS—Prevention
Alcohol
Alcohol Abuse
Alcohol and Athletes
Alcohol and Counselors
Alcohol and Nurses
Alcohol and the Handicapped
Alcohol and Youth
Alcohol Education
Alcohol—Law and Legislation
Alcohol—Physiological Effect
Alcoholic Beverages
Alcoholics
Alcoholics Anonymous (AA)
Alcoholics—Care and Treatment
Alcoholics—Family Relationships
Alcoholics—Psychological Testing
Alcoholism
Alcoholism and Employment
Alcoholism—Counseling
Alcoholism—Diagnosis
Alcoholism—Economics
Alcoholism—Epidemiology
Alcoholism—Etiology
Alcoholism—Physiological Effect
Alcoholism—Prevention and Control
Alcoholism—Psychological Aspects
Alcoholism—Rehabilitation
Alcoholism—Research
Alcoholism—Social Aspects
Alcoholism—Study and Teaching
Alcoholism—Tests and Scales
Alcoholism—Therapy
Alcoholism—Treatment
Children of Alcoholics (COA)
Cocaine
Codependence
DARE America
Drug Abuse
Drug Abuse and Alcoholism
Drug Abuse and Crime
Drug Abuse and Employment
Drug Abuse Control
Drug Abuse Counseling
Drug Abuse—Economic Aspects
Drug Abuse Education
Drug Abuse Etiology

Drug Abuse—Genetic Aspects
Drug Abuse in Pregnancy
Drug Abuse—Law and Legislation
Drug Abuse—Prevention
Drug Abuse—Psychological Aspects
Drug Abuse—Rehabilitation
Drug Abuse—Research
Drug Abuse—Social Aspects
Drug Abuse—Study and Teaching
Drug Abuse Surveys
Drug Abuse—Testing
Drug Abuse—Treatment
Drug Addiction
Drug Addicts
Drug and Alcohol Treatment Centers
Drug Education
Drug Legislation
Drug Prevention
Drug Rehabilitation
Drug Testing
Drug Therapy
Drug Use
Drug Use Testing
Drugs
Drugs and Employment
Drugs and Sex
Drugs and Youth
Drugs—Law and Legislation
Drugs—Physiological Effect
Drugs—Testing
Drunk Driving
Employee Alcohol Problem
Employee Assistance Programs
Fetal Alcohol Syndrome
Grandchildren of Alcoholics
Marijuana
Narcotic Addicts
Narcotics Control
National Institute on Drug Abuse
    (U.S.)
Nicotine
Partnership for a Drug-Free America
Smoking
Student Assistance Programs
Substance Abuse
Substance Abuse—Diagnosis
Substance Abuse—Epidemiology
Substance Abuse—Family
    Relationships
Substance Abuse—Genetic Aspects

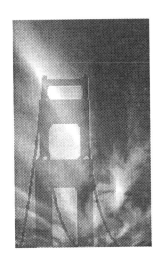

*The truth is, we already have a kind of rationing in
this country. But, no one wants to admit to it. We
stand by and watch people fall through the cracks.
The question is: How much bigger will the cracks
have to get . . . and how many more people will
have to fall through them before we start acknowledging what is happening to health care in
this country?*
Henry A. Waxman, 1986

11

The Health Care System

Nancy Henry

Health care in the United States has become a raging national debate
for many reasons. Americans value their health and are proud of the
technological advancements that provide them with state-of-the-art
medical care. However, in the same moment that an organ transplant
saves a life, another life ceases to exist because of inadequate access to
medical care. It seems contradictory that a nation with such advanced
capabilities is unable to adequately reconcile the gaps that exist within
the health care delivery system itself. The complexity of the health care
system does not lend itself to easy solutions. Experts appear to agree on
two things: first, that there is a health care crisis in the United States
and, second, that reform is inevitable (Coddington et al., 1990; Blendon
& Edwards, 1991). The question of how to implement reform measures
continues to provide fuel for the raging debate.

Nancy Henry has been the Health Sciences Reference Librarian at The Pennsylvania State
University, University Park, since 1991. She is a Registered Nurse with fourteen-years
experience in public health, and a member of the Academy of Health Information Professionals. She holds a Bachelor of Arts degree in Psychology and a Master of Library Science
from the State University of New York at Buffalo. Credits include co-editor and contributor
of two chapters ("Psychology and Psychiatry" and "Area Studies") to an extensive annotated
bibliography, *Prostitution: A Guide to Sources, 1960-1990* (Garland, 1992). In addition, she
co-authored "A Resource Sharing Project Using Ariel Technology" (*Medical Reference Services Quarterly*, Spring 1993) and is currently involved in research comparing several
commercially available software packages that utilize the Internet for document delivery.

Although the current health care system has many positive attributes, there is consensus that several major problems exist. At a very basic level, Relman proposes that three major problems need to be addressed at the national, state, and local levels (Relman, 1989). Kaplan summarizes these problems in three simple words: "Affordability, Access, and Accountability" (Kaplan, 1992). Many sectors of American society recommend reform, but there is no unified voice capable of proclaiming the best method for instituting such reform. This lack of consensus adds to the complexity of the task. The dynamic interactions among social, economic, and political forces have contributed to the development of several major problems in the delivery of health care in the United States. Piecemeal efforts to institute comprehensive reform in these areas have generally proven ineffective, but economic pressures that have resulted in what many view as a health care crisis may force some degree of unified consensus building among the various constituencies.

MAJOR PROBLEMS

Affordability

Of Kaplan's three problems, the foremost is affordability. Why is there so much concern about the cost of health care? Primarily because health care is consuming an excessive and unsustainable portion of public and corporate budgets, as well as individual family incomes. In the annual federal publication *Health United States* (U.S. Department of Health and Human Services, 1992, p. 4) it is estimated that 12.2 percent of the gross national product is expended annually on health care. According to a report issued by the Robert Wood Johnson Foundation, "personal health expenditures in the U.S. increased 10 percent from $434 to $478 billion between 1987 and 1988, a period when economy-wide inflation, as measured by the Consumer Price Index, was only 4.4 percent" (1991, p. 94). Many experts are concerned because the high cost of health care does not translate directly into measures associated with improved health outcomes, such as increased life expectancy and decreased mortality rates for certain populations.

Widespread disagreement exists among economists, politicians, researchers, and members of the health care industry as to the causes of inflationary health care spending. Physician fees, hospital costs, pharmaceuticals, advanced technology, the third-party payment system, fraud, inefficiency, and waste are all blamed for contributing to the current situation. The reality is that any comprehensive reform adopted in the near future must control costs. Coordinated, cooperative efforts to control inflation are the responsibility of all those involved in and associated with the provision of health care services.

Accessibility

Although Americans are spending more on health care, an equitable distribution of health care services does not exist. Access is a problem for the approximately 38 million uninsured or underinsured Americans (Nelson & Short, 1990) who dwell on the edge of the gap, or are already engulfed by the abyss. Those populations denied adequate access include the poor, children, elderly, homeless, and minorities.

Add to these populations rural and urban dwellers who are denied access to adequate care because of lack of health care personnel and technologically advanced facilities. The uninsured, who do not seek adequate care throughout a lifespan, may develop conditions that require costly funding of health services later on. Preventative measures, such as immunizations for children and prenatal care, result in the reduction of costly expenditures for health services at a later date.

For an increasing number of Americans, health insurance provides no guarantee of access to or payment for health care services. As employers and insurers have reduced funding for health care in response to escalating costs, the underinsured population (those with borderline coverage) has been placed at increased risk of financial ruin should they develop any acute or long-term disabilities (O'Keeffe, 1992). Certain insurance policies do not provide coverage for pre-existing conditions or experimental treatments, and others do not place a ceiling on cost sharing or copayments by the insured parties. In light of the problems of accessibility, will American society decide that health care is a basic right for all individuals (Buchanan, 1984)?

Accountability

Although Americans are spending more on health care, there is little empirical evidence to suggest that health care services result in healthier individuals. Do health care services result in healthier individuals? Kaplan argues that the health care industry is not "held accountable for what it produces" (Kaplan, 1992, p. 28). Adequate measures have not been developed to ascertain the correlation between health care and health outcomes. Recently, researchers have been in the process of defining quality (Donabedian, 1988; Roper et al., 1988) and the relationships that exist between cost and quality (Cleverly & Harvey, 1992; Morey et al., 1992; Sulmasy, 1992). Once the construct to be studied is defined, adequate measures can then be developed.

It is apparent that current methods being used to measure health outcomes are grossly inadequate. Infant mortality rates and life expectancy are crude measures that do not relay the entire story. Many health services that are provided to individuals have no effect on either of these measures. The collection of data and establishment of evaluative processes are essential to understanding other important health outcomes, such as the quality of life. Any model that is developed must be flexible enough to apply to diverse socioeconomic groups, provide a basis for understanding the variations in the costs for procedures, and correlate essential resources with specific health outcomes (Kaplan, 1992).

Another area of accountability that has not been adequately addressed is the lack of health research based on populations other than white males. Women have been excluded from clinical trials, and their health issues have in large part been disregarded by researchers (Lewin, 1992).

This is probably also true for minority populations. In addition, the poor do not have access to the same technological advancements that mainstream America takes for granted. Accountability, therefore, extends beyond practitioners to society as a whole, which must address the ethical dilemmas that are increasingly associated with the health care delivery system (Coile, 1990). Will society consider it a moral obligation to provide equity of quality as well as equity of access to health care for all Americans? Are taxpayers willing to pay the price?

Numerous proposals are being made to reform the current system based on the immediacy of the economic situation. Efforts to control costs are viewed as the primary goal, but other aspects of the system are equally important in the decision-making process. Restructuring the current health care delivery system would have major implications for American society. Proposals for reform necessitate a comprehensive understanding of the history of the current system, the major components, societal values regarding health, and the ethical dilemmas that will need to be addressed with the advancement of technology. Health care reform is indeed a complex task.

THE CURRENT
U.S. HEALTH CARE SYSTEM

There are many models that define and identify the current health care system, and some argument that the United States does not really have a system at all, but rather a "non-system," because of the lack of central control. For purposes of this discussion, there is an acknowledgment that some form of structure exists that attempts to provide for health care delivery. A health care system can be defined as "the complete network of agencies, facilities, and all providers of health care in a specified geographic area" (Glanze, Anderson, & Anderson, 1990, p. 546). The underlying philosophy of a system determines what health model will be used in the delivery of health care.

Although the basic premise of health care is to promote health, a much broader conceptualization of health is crucial to understanding the complex nature of the health care system in the United States. Jonas argues that although the health care community sees its role as the promotion of health, "it deals primarily with disease and not with health" (Jonas, 1986, p. 12). Therefore, it is difficult to define health without considering disease. *Black's Medical Dictionary* (Havard, 1990, p. 326) proposes that "the state of health implies much more than freedom from disease," but must also include "the attainment and maintenance of the highest state of mental and bodily vigor of which any given individual is capable." The World Health Organization includes additional factors by postulating that health is "a complete state of physical, mental and social well-being, and not merely the absence of illness or infirmity" (Jacobs, 1991, p. 20).

Two basic models for health care delivery have evolved. The disease model focuses on the diagnosis and treatment of disease and has a basis in altered pathology or biophysiologic function. This model can be further divided into areas of acute and chronic disease processes, which have a direct impact on the amount and length of care required by an individual. Medical care is primarily administered and directly influenced by physician activity.

A second model is concerned with other aspects of human functioning mentioned in the definition of the World Health Organization. This health care model is involved with functions that preserve, maintain, and enhance health status. The preventative model, as it is also known, has gained increasing credibility and influence since the 1970s, focusing on such areas as adequate nutrition, exercise, and dental hygiene (Russell, 1987). Aspects of this model are concerned with public health, research, health planning, and education. Duhl advocates the development of a system that focuses on "healthy development" (Duhl, 1986, p. 298) rather than traditional methods of treating illness. Such a system would promote health as a means of preventing disease and be concerned with environmental influences, including societal interactions.

Governmental efforts to define, plan for, and address the health care issues of the nation are documented in the annual publication *Health United States*. Increasingly, elements of both the disease and preventative models have been integrated into this process. Priorities have been established in an attempt to target areas of concern in the public, private, and individual sectors of society. However, the overwhelming process of addressing the biological, psychological, and societal components of health crystallizes the complexity of developing and maintaining a health care system that effectively meets demands. Jonas reminds us of society's obligation to this process when he writes that "medicine and health must be defined socially, because as society changes, its view of what constitutes health changes as well" (Jonas, 1986, p. 12).

HISTORY

The issues of affordable, accessible, and quality health care in the United States have concerned Americans throughout history. Individual and societal initiatives to address these concerns have fluctuated within a dynamic social, political, and economic arena. Colonial America did not have any formalized means of delivering health care. During this period, most aspects of funding and providing for health care were dependent on voluntarism. Many charitable organizations shouldered the responsibility for meeting the needs of the poor, sick, and homeless in almshouses and hospitals. The first hospital built specifically to care for the needs of the sick was the Pennsylvania Hospital at Philadelphia in 1751 (Rosner, 1993).

Attempts to administer treatment for health problems were instituted by physicians who had been trained outside the United States, by persons literate enough to read and apply their acquired knowledge to a particular situation. The need for health services resulted in the development of informal apprenticeships, though no organized method of testing competence existed for many years. It was not until 1756 that the first medical school was established at the College of Philadelphia, which later became the University of Pennsylvania. The apprenticeship concept became a more formalized method of education by 1773 when hospitals attempted to regulate the system by charging fees for these programs, establishing requirements, and granting certificates at the completion of the training process (Raffel, 1984).

During the 1800s the correlation between illness and social condition was recognized, resulting in widespread sanitary reform and the control of infectious disease. This was accomplished through the combined efforts of private organizations and individuals. Also in the nineteenth century significant advances were made in the organization of health care in the United States. The federal government centralized marine hospitals under a Surgeon General and Congress created a National Board of Health that worked cooperatively with state and local health departments to promote health care. The first American nursing school was established at the New England Hospital of Women and Children in 1872. The American Association of Medical Colleges (AAMC) was established in 1876 and individual states began to mandate the licensure of physicians by empowering state boards of medical examiners.

Although the number of medical schools increased greatly in the nineteenth century, quality remained questionable in many instances. In 1847, the American Medical Association was established and proceeded to address such issues as the quality of medical education, the establishment of medical journals, and a method of communicating accurate, updated knowledge. The standardization of medical education practices in the United States was significantly advanced by the Flexner report (Flexner, 1910). Abraham Flexner, an educator from the Carnegie Foundation for the Advancement of Teaching, was hired by the American Medical Association to inspect, assess, and make recommendations to medical schools and the AMA's Council on Medical Education for reform measures to improve the educational process. He visited 155 schools in the United States as well as Canada, and in the final report recommended that the number of schools be reduced to 31. As a result, the number of schools was reduced to 85 by the end of 1920, and the quality of the remaining schools was significantly improved. The independent, objective nature of the study served to strengthen the platform for medical reform at the local, state, and national levels (Raffel, 1984).

During this period, the National Board of Medical Examiners was established and administered its first exam in 1916. Not all states agreed to accept the test results as an adequate measure of knowledge for licensure, but this changed as the testing procedures improved. Licensure and mandatory testing became commonplace by the end of the nineteenth century.

Advancements in professional competence, coupled with improved technology, contributed to an increased demand for hospital and physician services in the twentieth century. Access to care often depended on availability and affordability. A major study of health care economics done in 1927 resulted in several recommendations for organizing health care delivery. Although no immediate results were realized from the study, many innovative components were later integrated into aspects of health care administration (Dobson & Bialek, 1985).

Eventually, attempts to address the issues of access and affordable health care resulted in several innovative strategies. Financing mechanisms for addressing the issue of health care costs were implemented by the government through several programs between 1920 and 1950. The two major financing vehicles for health care services were the Social Security Act and the development of privately funded insurance programs. A hospital construction bill (The Hospital Survey and Construction Act) passed in 1946 was intended to increase health care facilities, thereby increasing access to care (Stoline & Weiner, 1993).

Hallmarks of the health care system between 1947 and 1965 were further technological advances, adequate hospital facilities, an increased demand for services, physician shortages, and increasing health care costs. Although the financial mechanisms were in place for addressing the needs of the majority of the population, low-income families were experiencing greater difficulty accessing adequate health care. In 1965, amendments to the Social Security Act created Medicare and Medicaid, resulting in health care funding for aged, disabled, and low-income families. Although these programs extended health services to a significant group of people, a health care gap still existed for ineligible Americans. The working poor remained a neglected population.

The Medicare and Medicaid programs resulted in increased demands for health services, incentives for growth within the health care delivery system, and increased health care expenditures (Smith, 1992). By 1980, competition within the health care industry and the demand for cost control measures had significantly altered health care practices, policies, personnel, and facilities. Downsizing of the health care industry has significantly revolutionized the delivery of health care services. Hospitals have become acute care facilities, managed in part by multinational corporations. Cost control efforts have emphasized less expensive outpatient and home care services. All facets of the current health care system are being held accountable for the effectiveness, efficiency, and quality of health care delivered to individuals (Wohl, 1989).

MAJOR COMPONENTS OF THE CURRENT U.S. SYSTEM

The health care system in the United States is a network of several interactive components that have contributed to the state of health care today. In the future they will provide some measure of solution to current problems. Simply stated, the system includes the payers, users, providers, facilities, and organizations involved in the health care delivery process.

Payers

Historically business, labor, and government have been involved in purchasing health services for employees. Health insurance was first offered by corporations following World War II as a part of employee benefits packages. In recent years, however, corporate America has been waging a battle against inflationary health care costs. Large corporations argue that they absorb the costs of the uninsured and underinsured populations in both the private and public sectors. The inadequate funding of government programs in the public sector, for instance, caps on Medicare and Medicaid spending, force health care services to devise creative measures of recouping their financial losses. One such practice is commonly referred to as cost-shifting. For example, if a hospital is not reimbursed adequately for a diagnostic procedure for a Medicaid patient, the loss is shifted to patients covered under private insurance plans through increased costs for the same procedure. In addition, large corporations often provide insurance coverage for spouses who do not have insurance benefits through their own employers. The spouse may be employed by a small corporation that cannot afford insurance coverage or does not provide adequate insurance coverage. Methods that have been utilized to reduce corporate costs include requiring workers to share in insurance or treatment expenses, group medical plans, preapproval for many medical or surgical procedures, and encouraging the use of more outpatient facilities (Altman, 1991).

Users

Most Americans will require some form of health care during their lives. According to Pol and Thomas, the U.S. system is effective in meeting the needs of the majority of the population, but demographic shifts will result in profound changes in the types of health services required by the various populations. Two major demographic shifts include an aging population and increasing cultural diversity (Pol & Thomas, 1992).

In 1900, the average life expectancy was 45 years of age. Today the average life expectancy is 75 years of age as a result of an improved standard of living and advances in the prevention and treatment of infectious disease. The 65-year-old age group, which comprises 12 percent of the population, is expected to increase to 21 percent of the population by the year 2030, and the number of people 85 years and older is growing at a rate three to four times any other age group. It is estimated that the health care needs of the 65-year-old age group consume 30 percent of the health care budget, even though they comprise 12 percent of the population (Stromborg, 1991, p. 1773). A study by Arnett shows that the average hospital days used by persons 75 years old are twice as high as for 65 year olds and three times the average of 55 year olds (Arnett et al., 1986). The advancing age of the baby boom generation will add to the burden of an already inadequate health care system. It is estimated that the middle-age population will increase from 14 million in 1991 to over 19 million in the year 2000 (U.S. Bureau of the Census, 1990). A decline in the birthrate during the 1960s will diminish the economic base available to fund health care. Health care costs are expected to continue rising with the "graying of America," and many experts feel the available resources will be exhausted unless other, less expensive methods of supporting the health care needs of this population are developed.

The structure of the current system does not accommodate the needs of the elderly, but is geared to meeting the requirements of the younger population and acute health care conditions. This is reflected in the statistics for practicing physicians at the end of the 1980s. It is estimated that only 1,000 of the 520,000 physicians had specialized training in the area of geriatric medicine. Researchers (Callahan & Wallack, 1982; Gilford, 1988; Pol & Thomas, 1992; Vogel & Palmer, 1985) who have studied long-term care needs of the elderly express concern that the U.S. system is organized primarily to cure disease, and does not adequately address the changes of an aging population that will require treatment for chronic diseases.

Many researchers (Avorn, 1984; Callahan, 1984; Callahan, 1987; Rundall, 1992; Schneider, 1989) express concern about the cost versus the benefit of delivering health care to an aged population, the ethics of rationing health care, the effective delivery of treatment, and a more aggressive use of the preventative model to ensure quality of life. There is fear that the allocation of limited health care resources will result in health policy decision making that discriminates against the aged and their needs. The American Geriatrics Society articulated this concern in a position paper (American Geriatrics Society, 1989).

A second major change in population characteristics is increasing cultural diversity. Because minorities are forced into adhering to mainstream treatment modalities, there has been little or no attempt to address specific sociocultural needs as they relate to health and medical care for these populations (Blendon et al., 1989). Demographic projections indicate that multiculturalism is the future of the United States. While 80 percent of the total population is white, whites will represent 72 percent of the total by the year 2000. The black population, which currently accounts for 12 percent of the population, increased 13 percent from 1980. The Hispanic population represents 9 percent of the population;

it increased 53 percent since 1980. Hispanics are expected to represent one out of every five Americans by the year 2050. The Asian/Pacific Island-born immigrant population now represents 7 percent of the American population, a 150 percent increase since 1980. Projections estimate they will represent 9 percent of the population by 1998 (Hagland, 1993). Pol extrapolates from census data that the black and Spanish-origin (Hispanic) populations are increasing at a faster pace than the white population. He notes that in 1950, "Blacks and Spanish-origin persons made up 12.7 percent of the U.S. population," and that "by the year 2000 this figure is expected to increase to 22.1 percent" (Pol & Thomas, 1992, p. 142). The price of not meeting the health care needs of these growing populations is one that American society cannot afford to pay. One physician stated that the combined pressure from these two underserved populations will eventually result in public consensus to finance a health care system that extends adequate health care to these populations (Munoz, 1988).

Providers

Approximately 8 million people are employed in the health care industry. It is becoming increasingly evident that many health professions share common concerns. Methods for predicting supply and demand factors within the health care economy need to be improved. Measures to recruit, educate, and retain health professionals also need to be addressed. Roles of the providers are changing as rapidly as the system itself. Two of the key providers in the delivery of health care services are physicians and nurses. They both seem to be facing the professional consequences of the same problems plaguing the overall health care delivery system. The practical reality of providing affordable, accessible quality care is the measure of their daily labors.

Physicians are frequently criticized for charging exorbitant fees for their services. Physicians argue that their fees are justified because of the cost and length of their educational process and the high cost of malpractice insurance. The current oversupply of physicians in the marketplace is contributing to a change in reimbursement practices. The private practice that was based on the fee-for-service model is rapidly being replaced by group practices that employ salaried physicians. However, physician roles are becoming increasingly complex and demanding as they attempt to strike a balance between their loyalty to patient care and the need to exercise cost-containment measures (Eisenberg, 1986). Access to advanced technology and the threat of malpractice litigation add to the burden of their decision-making process when treating patients (Roper et al., 1988).

Nursing is also undergoing a radical restructuring of its role within the health care delivery system. In contrast to the oversupply of physicians in the marketplace, there has been a nursing shortage since the early 1980s, which has contributed to a decline in the quality of patient care. One researcher summarizes the major concerns of the nursing profession as "status and power; economics; and numbers" (Cohen, 1992).

The introduction to the "Final Report of the 1988 Commission on Nursing" states that "a full and ongoing dialogue between nursing and its public is crucially important to the renegotiation of the contract between nursing and society. This is the essential task facing nursing and society over the next decade" (Secretary's Commission on Nursing, 1988, vol. 1, p. iii). In addition, goals for the 1990s will focus on advancing the scientific validity of the nursing profession and defining common issues of concern for a diverse practicing population.

INSTITUTIONS AND ORGANIZATIONAL STRUCTURES

The facilities and organizational structures that have historically provided health care services are also experiencing dramatic change in response to a multiplicity of factors associated with the health care crisis. Hospitals are a primary example of how the socioeconomic and political influences of American society have joined forces to completely revolutionize the mission of an institution and threaten its very existence. Eli Ginzberg has carefully studied and documented the downsizing and reorganization of hospitals since the 1980s. One study focuses on the problems with delivery of emergency medical services that exist in large urban areas where hospitals are closing at an alarming rate. Many large urban areas are inhabited by the poor and minorities, which means access to adequate health services is diminished further by such closures (Ginzberg, 1991).

The factors involved in the decline of hospitals are summarized by Ropes. A major change in funding resulting from Medicare and Medicaid programs altered economic and community ties to local hospitals. With the influx of federal dollars, the institutional mission changed from a service-oriented model to an industrial-driven model. The strategy of the Reagan administration to address the issue of alarming growth depended on the competitive market. This market approach allowed growth to proliferate in areas other than hospitals, such as Health Maintenance Organizations (HMOs) (Ropes, 1991).

During the early 1980s efforts to control rising costs for Medicare patients resulted in diagnosis-related groups (DRGs), a system of assigning categories to aspects of patient care for hospital reimbursement under Medicare. As the funding base declined and competition increased, hospitals could not afford to cover the costs of caring for the underinsured or uninsured. Recent developments have superimposed financial pressures by reducing the services hospitals provide. Cost-containment measures such as DRGs limited hospital admissions and length of stay. Technological advancements have revolutionized many procedures that previously required hospitalization and consequently can now be performed on a more cost-efficient outpatient basis. Technology has also added to the burden of financing expensive equipment to ensure quality patient care and avoid malpractice litigation. The demand for health care services is shifting to home care as the needs of an increasingly aging population shift to long-term care. This cameo provides one sterling example of the dynamic restructuring and reorganization process taking place at a rapid pace within the institutional and organizational settings of the health care system.

FINANCING MECHANISMS

An inequitable and inadequate funding base exists under the current financing system of the American health care system. Some experts argue that the Medicare and Medicaid programs, implemented in 1965, are the basis of the problem. These programs, in combination with sociopolitical forces, resulted in a major shift in the organization, financing, and delivery of medical care in the United States (Relman, 1980; Starr, 1983; Bergthold, 1990). One extensive work by notable researchers refers to this process as the "Corporatization of Medicine" (Salmon, 1990). Other researchers blame the third-party payment system because it shifts the responsibility for cost-effective care away from the consumer. Consumers tend to seek medical care more often because they are not directly paying for the service. Numerous proposals have been made to expand the funding base for health care. Expanding the economic base will most likely involve some form of additional tax. The alternative seems to be requiring all employers to provide some form of health insurance and providing tax incentives for corporations to do so. Americans will have to decide if initiatives will be taken to provide adequate health insurance coverage to everyone. Some hard questions remain. Is access to health care a basic human right and do American citizens have a moral obligation to provide for this need? Will American taxpayers bridge the gap?

The other major issue is controlling health care expenditures through cost-containment measures (Davis et al., 1990; Altman, 1991; Rice, 1992; Newhouse, 1993). Many experts feel this can be done through the existing competitive market-based system. The debate will continue to be about who controls managed care efforts. Physicians have always been involved in the process of managing patient care, but the term *managed care* has evolved since the 1960s to include third-party payment systems focused on efforts to promote cost containment. Major managed care systems include HMOs (Health Maintenance Organizations) and PPOs (Preferred Provider Organizations), but there are several variations of both major models and additional systems that interact in a complex networking environment to promote quality health care at a reasonable cost. Prepayment plans such as these differ from the traditional fee-for-service payment plans by contracting for health care services on a fixed monthly premium basis or contracting with medical care groups at reduced rates. In addition, a reviewer, such as a Peer Review Organization (PRO), is often relied upon to manage patient care in an effort to promote cost-containment measures. Detailed descriptions of prepayment plans are available in two separate works by Kongstvedt (1993) and Shouldice (1991). Managed care is expected to play a major role in any health care reform proposals considered by Congress and the Clinton administration. If managed care systems become an intricate part of the Clinton proposal for health care reform, the question will still remain as to whether regulation of these systems will take place at the local, state, or federal level.

REFORM PROPOSALS

Goals of Health Care Reform

The health care system is in the midst of major reform, but most experts hope that reform measures will be instituted in a series of carefully planned steps. The fear is that policy makers will view reform only in terms of financing the current system without addressing other important issues. Relief from out-of-control costs imposed on national, corporate, and individual budgets is viewed as a priority. Cooperative measures to reduce the economic burden of funding health care services are being sought by consumers, corporations, and government. Providing some mechanism for central control in the decision-making process will be the key to effective, comprehensive, and coordinated planning for the future.

The federal government has assumed a leadership role in the process of consensus building among the various constituencies involved in health care delivery. President Bill Clinton appointed a Task Force on National Health Care Reform, charged with cooperatively working with all levels of government to develop viable proposals for reform. Under the leadership of First Lady Hillary Rodham Clinton, working groups within the task force identified and analyzed policy options to form the basis of a comprehensive legislative proposal. Within nine months the task force effectively gathered data and focused national efforts to deal with the issues of health care reform (Toner, 1993).

Foremost in any legislative proposal will be an economic model that provides for relief from out-of-control costs. Managed competition is the major contender for inclusion in the president's economic reform package. Alain Enthoven is "responsible for the creation of the construct, and defines it as a blending of the competitive and regulatory strategies that have coexisted uneasily for years in the U.S. health care system" (Enthoven, 1993 p. 26). Managed competition divides providers into competing economic units within defined geographic regions (Cave, 1993). This arrangement is expected to encourage providers to compete for consumer business on the basis of cost and quality. Theoretically it places the burden of responsibility on health care consumers by making them more aware of the costs for individual services and giving them the power to choose between plans on the basis of qualitative data. The competition is expected to keep premium prices low as consumers shop for the highest quality at the lowest price.

Health Care Reform Proposals

On September 22, 1993, President Bill Clinton presented his health proposal to a joint session of Congress and the American people. The proposed National Health Security Act of 1993 is considered one of the most detailed, far-reaching pieces of social legislation in the history of the country. Although the Democratic and Republican parties agreed to hold off on the introduction of other reform proposals until President Clinton had the opportunity to present his ideas to Congress, there are several competing health reform bills that were introduced into Congress prior to the current administration. It is expected that five major plans will rival President Clinton's proposal and attempt to influence various elements of any final bill (Clymer, 1993). If the National Health Act is passed by Congress, the process will involve many concessions to the states, big businesses, insurers, health-care providers, and lawmakers. Any final version of reform legislation is expected to have little resemblance to the original document presented by the president. The proposed plan for health care reform is based on the economic model of managed competition and on several principles documented in the "Health Security Report" (1993).

Security. A comprehensive guaranteed benefits package for all Americans that cannot be taken away. The inclusion of preventative care and prescription drugs as a part of the package.

Simplicity. The reduction of paperwork for processing insurance claims through the use of one standard form.

Savings. The development of regional purchasing cooperatives or health alliances that will provide massive purchasing pools for health insurance plans. Individual health plans will compete for consumer enrollment on the basis of the price and quality they can provide.

Quality. An increased emphasis on a primary care system with incentives for physicians to become primary care providers. Required annual report cards from provider plans indicating accurate health outcome measures.

Choice. Consumers will have complete choice of three types of plans: Health Maintenance Organizations; Fee for Service; and Preferred Provider Organizations.

Responsibility. Consumers will be provided with detailed data about the cost efficiency and quality provided by the various plans. This will be available to consumers on an annual basis so they can make informed decisions about which plan they will elect for the next year. Choices will be made on a yearly basis.

An overview of the health reform plan is available in *The Clinton Blueprint: The President's Health Security Plan* (The White House Domestic

Policy Council, 1993). Operationally, the National Security Act includes the development of a seven-member National Health Board appointed by the president that will act as a steering committee responsible for setting policy and standards and monitoring state compliance with national requirements. Responsibilities also include establishment of a performance-based system of quality management and the formation of a committee to alert consumers to unreasonable drug pricing.

Individual states will assume the primary responsibility for developing a comprehensive health benefits package for all eligible citizens that complies with the national standard. Each state submits a health reform plan for approval by the National Health Board. Each plan will include a designated state agency responsible for coordinating state responsibilities under federal law. States establish the geographic boundaries for regional health alliances and determine incentives to enroll disadvantaged groups. States have the freedom to establish a single-payer system that meets with federal requirements or expand benefits beyond the comprehensive health benefits package.

Regional health alliances or HIPCs (health insurance purchasing cooperatives) will be developed at the state level to contract with health plans, educate consumers, and collect premiums. Their primary responsibility is to consumers and purchasers of health care services. The boards of each alliance will include an equal distribution of employer and consumer representatives. Health alliances will have to be large enough to provide a choice of three plans to consumers. (Large companies may create their own health alliances and small companies may be provided with subsidies.) Each plan must survey members and generate a report card that will be available to consumers and address the issues of quality, service, and health outcome measures.

Under certain conditions, corporations will have an option to form their own health alliances or join regional health alliances. Generally, this option applies to employers with more than 5,000 employees, and health plans must provide a similar comprehensive health care benefits package as guaranteed under federal law.

Health plans will be state-certified to provide a comprehensive health care benefits package to health alliances. Health plan providers are not allowed to cancel coverage until the individual enrolls in another health plan and may not discriminate by restricting enrollment on the basis of pre-existing medical conditions.

The National Health Board will include an advisory council responsible for the development and implementation of a quality assurance program focused on developing performance measures that will be reported to health consumers on a regular basis. In addition, the council will develop a core set of performance measures that will be applicable to all health plans, institutions, and practitioners. The measures are intended as a basis for evaluating and improving performance in all areas of health care delivery.

In an effort to simplify the processing of health care claims a reliable information infrastructure will have to be developed. The development of such a processing system will take fullest advantage of the information technology already available and require the development of a new paradigm for information and communication systems and rapid, efficient data sharing.

Malpractice reform measures will be inherent in each health plan through the provision of alternative dispute resolution (ADR) options for consumers. Consumers will be able to submit a claim and go through the process of arbitration, mediation, and possible settlement without going to court. However, the option of a court settlement is still viable if the consumer is dissatisfied with the outcome of the ADR.

The Clinton proposal is expected to cost $331 billion over a five-year period and provide universal coverage. Funding projections include savings of $189 billion from the reduction of Medicare and Medicaid spending, employer mandates to pay 80 percent of health premiums, a 75-cent tax increase on cigarettes, and a 1 percent payroll tax for self-insured big businesses that do not join the system. Big business levies are expected to raise $89 billion in revenues. Premium caps and subsidies to small businesses will be integral to effecting adequate funding. The Clinton administration projects that this will result in a deficit reduction from $91 billion to $58 billion over a five-year period (Hasson & Wolf, 1993).

The debate is beginning in earnest over health care reform and the Health Security Act. The Clinton plan itself is viewed by some as conservative because it builds on the current structure, relies on market incentives, and is financed through the reallocation of funds (Rivlin, 1993). Economic analysts propose that medical quality assurance will eventually reshape the health care market so that perverse incentives no longer remain the driving force, but warn that they may be replaced with a new variety of perverse incentives (Wallich & Holloway, 1993). Other advocates of managed competition project that the combined efforts of health alliances and consumers will result in improved health care at a reduced cost. Advocates also point to the ethical principles that serve as the basis of the plan. Certainly Americans would like to feel secure in the knowledge that they have health care coverage regardless of their job situation or pre-existing medical conditions. Most would also agree that a simplified method of processing health insurance claims is desirable and universal access to health care a right they are willing to fund.

Critics contend that managed competition is an untested theory and best serves the interests of those already in positions of power such as private business, publishing, and the health care industry. Pete Stark (D-Calif.), chairman of the House Ways and Means Subcommittee on Health, believes creation of new agencies to administer the plan will add to the bureaucracy, paperwork, and exorbitant costs (Inglehart, 1993). Imposed global budget caps may result in the rationing of health care services and the elderly may be discriminated against as a result (Pear, 1993a). Rural health care plans with limited resources may not be able to create enough of a competitive market between the various health plans (Kronick et al., 1993; Relman, 1993). Efforts to provide equitable access to all segments of the American population by mandating that all employers provide health care benefits may meet with resistance. Wester-field, an economist, predicts that mandated health care initiatives may result in employers reducing the workforce or trading benefits for income (Westerfield, 1991). Although universal coverage is viewed by most as desirable, funding may remain a major problem. As mentioned pre-viously, adequate measures of health outcomes do not exist and therefore are not available for consumers to make informed decisions regarding health plan options. In addition, the information infrastructure required to maintain the communication process for such a national health care plan will require extensive development and funding.

Other Reform Proposals

Congress has been evaluating five alternative health care reform plans besides the Clinton proposal. Four plans have already been intro-duced as bills in the Congress. In the Senate, the Gramm Bill (R-Texas), co-sponsored by Senators John McCain (R-Arizona) and Hank Brown (R-Colorado), opposes any form of health entitlement program for the middle class, such as the basic benefits package advocated in the Clinton proposal. The House Republican Bill already has extensive support in both bodies of Congress, but is viewed as only a first step in the process of reform. Sponsors are U.S. Representatives Newt Gingrich (Georgia) and Bob Michel (Illinois). The Chafee Bill (R-Rhode Island) is the result of a senate task force on health care reform. Chafee's plan includes features of managed competition but disagrees with the Clinton proposal on several major issues. The Cooper Bill (D-Tennessee) appears to be the most effective, comprehensive bipartisan effort for health reform in the 103rd Congress, but has been criticized by Hillary Rodham Clinton for not addressing the need for universal coverage. The last alternative under consideration is The McDermott Plan, sponsored by Representative Jim McDermott (D-Washington), which advocates a single-payer, Canadian-style system. Although this plan has approximately 90 cosponsors in the Congress, it is generally viewed as politically unviable. All of the health care reform proposals attempt to address several key issues including the restructuring process, financing, the provision of benefits, cost controls and quality (Health care reform . . . , 1993). Because none of the reform proposals were passed in the 103rd Congress, the next Congress will be left to tackle this thorny issue.

WHAT THE FUTURE MAY BRING

General predictions can be made from current observations. Any legislation under consideration will address the issues of affordability, accessibility, and accountability. Equitable access and universal coverage will be included in any final legislation. Demands for accountability for the quality of health care will continue to escalate. Increasingly, methods of researching and measuring quality related to the delivery of health services will be required by consumers, corporations, and government. Health care consumers will rapidly become more educated, sophisticated users of the system and assume more control over the treatment and financing of personal health care issues. The user population of the past deferred to physician knowledge and skill in treatment decisions, but many future users will want to be an integral part of the decision-making process. Users will also be concerned with the options and alternatives available to them for treatment modalities. Public health research and education will continue to make major contributions to providing information for health consumers. Major studies in the morbidity and mortality of major diseases and correlation with high-risk behaviors will continue to provide a basis for advocating preventative health practices. Consumers and payers will continue to demand cost-effective use of the health care dollar. The health care industry will be held accountable for measuring the output of what it produces.

The dynamic political process of negotiation and compromise regarding health care reform has just begun. In 1994 the nation will engage in a fierce debate over which health care reform measures will be adopted. The work of the Clinton task force has focused the major issues that need to be a part of any health care reform legislation. President Clinton has asked Congress to pass a bill for health care reform by the end of 1994 (Pear, 1993b). It is expected that Congress will meet the timetable and that following a year of intense debate, there will be a "Moment of Decision for Health Care" (Eckholm, 1993). For now, only tentative speculations can be made about what those final decisions will be and how health care reform legislation will reshape the future of health care delivery in the United States.

Once the legislation is passed, a timetable for implementation must be designated to aid in the transition process. President Clinton's plan includes a timetable for implementation of the various phases of his proposal, which would occur over several years. Many states and agencies are already involved in the business of reform as they try to anticipate the components of the final legislation and adopt state plans that will comply with national requirements. States such as California, Hawaii, and Florida have already enacted major health care reform efforts. This means that some states are already positioned to effectively meet the requirements of any mandated federal efforts for health care reform. Even before any federal legislation is passed many elements of health care reform will already have taken place nationwide.

While society is grappling with the problems of our complex health care system and all its ramifications, technology may prove to be the decisive force in restructuring and revolutionizing health care delivery. If the predictions of researchers and scientists become realities, technological advances will make it possible to predict and prevent disease at a cellular level, deliver home medical care through computerized systems, produce interchangeable, replaceable organs, and predict the health of an individual prior to birth (Fisher, 1992). Access to such crucial information about individuals will bring with it additional ethical dilemmas that will need to be addressed by society (Menzel, 1990). In this context, the eerie reverberations of Jonas's words, "Medicine and health must be defined socially, because as society changes, its state of health and view of what constitutes health changes as well" (Jonas, 1986, p. 12), echo down the halls of the future.

REFERENCES

Altman, S. H. 1991. Why healthcare executives should support a national cost-containment plan. *Healthcare Executive* (July-August): 21-24.

American Geriatrics Society. 1989. Equitable distribution of limited medical resources. *JAGS (Journal of the American Geriatrics Society)* 37: 1063-1064.

Arnett, R. H.; McKusick, D. R.; Sonnefield, S. T.; & Cowell, C. S. 1986. Projections of health care spending to 1990. *Health Care Financing Review* 7(3): 1-36.

Avorn, J. 1984. Benefit and cost analysis in geriatric care: Turning age discrimination into health policy. *New England Journal of Medicine* 310(20): 1294-1301.

Bergthold, L. 1990. *Purchasing power in health: Business, the state, and health care politics.* Brunswick, NJ: Rutgers University Press.

Blendon, R. J.; Aiken, L. H.; Freeman, H. E.; & Corey, R. C. 1989. Access to medical care for black and white Americans: A matter of continuing concern. *JAMA* 261(2): 278-281.

Blendon, R. J., & Edwards, J. N., eds. 1991 *System in crisis: The case for health care reform.* New York: Faulkner and Gray.

Buchanan, A. E. 1984. The right to a decent minimum of health care. *Philosophy and Public Affairs* 13: 55-78.

Callahan, D. 1984. Old age and new policy. *JAMA* 261: 905-06.

———. 1987. *Setting limits: Medical goals in an aging society.* New York: Simon & Schuster.

Callahan, J. J., & Wallack, S. S. 1982. *Reforming the long-term-care system.* Lexington, MA: D. C. Heath.

Cave, D. G. 1993. Making health reform work: Managed competition can succeed even in rural areas. *Business Insurance,* 24 May, 19-21.

Cleverly, W. O., & Harvey, R. K. 1992. Is there a link between hospital profit and quality? *Healthcare Financial Management*, September, 40-45.

Clymer, A. 1993. Many health plans, one political goal. *New York Times,* 17 October.

Coddington, D. C.; Keen, D. J.; Moore, K. D.; & Clarke, R. L. 1990. *The crisis in health care.* San Francisco: Jossey-Bass.

Cohen, L. B. 1992. Power and change in health care: Challenge for nursing. *Journal of Nursing Education* 31(3): 113-116.

Coile, R. C. 1990. Technology and ethics: Three scenarios for the 1990's. *QRB* 16(6): 202-08.

Davis, K.; Anderson, G. F.; Rowland, D.; & Steinberg, E. P. 1990. *Health care cost containment.* Baltimore: Johns Hopkins University Press.

Dobson, A., & Bialek, R. 1985. Shaping public policy from the perspective of a data builder. *Health Care Financing Review* 6(4): 120.

Donabedian, A. 1988. The quality of care: How can it be assessed? *JAMA* 260(12): 1743-1748.

Duhl, J. L. 1986. *Health planning and social change*. New York: Human Sciences Press.

Eckholm, E. 1993. The health debate: Moment of decision for health care. *New York Times,* 14 November.

Eisenberg, J. M. 1986. *Doctors' decisions and the cost of medical care*. Ann Arbor, MI: Health Administration Press.

Enthoven, A. 1993. The history and principles of managed competition. *Health Affairs* 12 (Suppl.): 24-48.

Fisher, J. A. 1992. *RX 2000*. New York: Simon & Schuster.

Flexner, A. 1910. *Medical education in the United States and Canada*. Bulletin 4. New York: Carnegie Foundation for the Advancement of Teaching.

Gilford, D. M., ed. 1988. *The aging population in the twenty-first century*. Washington, DC: National Academy Press.

Ginzberg, E. 1991. Can inner-city hospitals survive? *Healthcare Executive* (May/June): 24-26.

Glanze, W. D.; Anderson, K. N.; & Anderson, L. E. 1990. *Mosby's medical, nursing & allied health dictionary*. 3rd ed. St. Louis, MO: C. V. Mosby.

Hagland, M. M. 1993. New waves: Hospitals struggle to meet the challenge of multiculturalism now and in the next generation. *Hospitals* (20 May): 22-31.

Hasson, J. & Wolf, R. 1993. Health plan; First checkup comes today. *USA Today,* 27 October.

Havard, D. W. 1990. *Black's medical dictionary*. 36th ed. Savage, MD: Barnes & Noble.

Health care reform-focus on the hill. 1993. *Health Systems Review* 26(6): 22-30.

"Health Security Report Table of Contents." 1993. (On-line database). Referenced: 12/13/11:31 a.m. EST. Available on: *VMS Internet Gopher Information Clients* v2.0-10. Available from: cyfer.esusda.gov (FTP site).

Inglehart, J. K. 1993. Health Policy Report: Managed competition. *The New England Journal of Medicine* 328(2): 1208-1212.

Jacobs, P. 1991. *The economics of health and medical care*. 3rd ed. Gaithersburg, MD: Aspen Publishers.

Jonas, S. 1986. *Health care delivery in the United States*. 3rd ed. New York: Springer.

Kaplan, R. M. 1992. *The Hippocratic predicament*. San Diego: Academic Press.

Kongstvedt, P. R. 1993. *The managed care handbook*. 2nd ed. Gaithersburg, MD: Aspen Publishers.

Kronick, R.; Goodman D. C.; Wennberg, J.; & Wagner, E. 1993. The marketplace in health care reform: The demographic limitations of managed competition. *New England Journal of Medicine* 328: 148-52.

Lewin, T. 1992. Doctors consider a specialty focusing on women's health. *Wall Street Journal,* 7 November.

Menzel, P. T. 1990. *Strong medicine: The ethical rationing of health care*. New York: Oxford University Press.

Morey, R. C.; Fine, D. J.; Loree, B. S.; Roberts, D. L.; & Tsubakitani, S. 1992. The trade-off between hospital cost and quality of care. *Medical Care* 30(9): 677-695.

Munoz, E. 1988. Care for the Hispanic poor: A growing segment of American society. (Commentary) *JAMA* 260(18): 2711-2712.

Nelson, C. T., & Short, K. 1990. *Health insurance coverage, 1986-88*. Washington, DC: Government Printing Office.

Newhouse, J. P. 1993. An iconoclastic view of health cost containment. *Health Affairs* (Suppl.) 153-169.

O'Keeffe, J. E. 1992. Health care financing: How much reform is needed? *Issues in Science & Technology* VIII(3): 42-47.

Pear, R. 1993a. Influential group says health plan slights the aged. *New York Times*, 24 October.

———. 1993b. Congress is given Clinton proposal for health care: A bill of vast complexity. *New York Times,* 28 October.

Pol, L. G., & Thomas, R. K. 1992. *The demography of health and health care*. The Plenum Series on Demographic Methods and Population Analysis. New York: Plenum Press.

Raffel W. 1984. *The US health system: Origins and functions*. New York: John Wiley & Sons.

Reinhardt, U. E. 1989. Health care spending and American competitiveness. *Health Affairs* 8(4): 5-21.

Relman, A. 1989. Confronting the crisis in health care. *Technology Review* July, 31-40.

Relman, A. S. 1980. The new medical-industrial complex. *The New England Journal of Medicine* 303(17): 963-970.

———. 1993. Controlling costs by managed competition: Would it work? *New England Journal of Medicine* 328: 133-135.

Rice, T. 1992. Containing health care costs in the United States. *Medical Care Review* 49(1): 19-65.

Rivlin, A. 1993. Clinton's Conservative Health Plan. *The Wall Street Journal* 20 October.

The Robert Wood Johnson Foundation. 1991. *Challenges in health care: A chartbook perspective*. Princeton, NJ: The Robert Wood Johnson Foundation.

Roper, W. L.; Windenwerder, W.; Hackbarth, J. D.; & Krakauer, H. 1988. Effectiveness in health care: An initiative to evaluate and improve medical practice. *New England Journal of Medicine* 319(18): 1197-1202.

Ropes, L. B. 1991. *Health care crisis in America: A reference handbook*. Santa Barbara, CA: ABC-CLIO.

Rosner, R. 1993. Health care. In Cayton, M. K.; Gorn, E. J.; & Williams, R. W., eds., *Encyclopedia of American social history*. New York: Charles Scribner's Sons: 2399-2409.

Rundall, T. G. 1992. Health services for an aging society. (Editorial) *Medical Care Review* 49(1): 3-18.

Russell, L. B. 1987. *Evaluating preventive care: Report on a workshop.* Washington, DC: Brookings Institute.

Salmon, J. W., ed. 1990. *The corporate transformation of health care: Issues and directions.* Policy, Politics, Health and Medicine Series. New York: Baywood.

Schneider, E. L. 1989. Options to control the rising health care costs of older Americans. *JAMA* 261(6): 907-908.

Secretary's Commission on Nursing. 1988. *National centers for health care research and technology.* Washington, DC: Department of Health and Human Services.

Shouldice, R. G. 1991. *Introduction to managed care: Health maintenance organizations, preferred provider organizations, & competitive medical plans.* Arlington, VA: Information Resources Press.

Smith, D. G. 1992. *Paying for Medicare.* New York: Aldine De Gruyter.

Starr, P. 1983. *The social transformation of American medicine.* New York: Basic Books.

Stoline, A. M., & Weiner, J. P., eds. 1993. *The new medical marketplace: A physician's guide to the health care system in the 1990s.* Baltimore, MD: Johns Hopkins University Press.

Stromborg, M. F. 1991. Changing demographics in the United States. *Cancer* 67(6): 1772-1778.

Sulmasy, D. P. 1992. Physicians, cost control, and ethics. *Annals of Internal Medicine* 116(11): 920-926.

Toner R. 1993. Hillary Clinton's potent brain trust on health reform. *New York Times,* 28 February.

U.S. Bureau of the Census. 1990. *Population estimates and projections.* Current Population Reports, Series P-25. Washington, DC: U.S. Bureau of the Census, 1045.

U.S. Department of Health and Human Services. 1992. *Health United States, 1991.* Hyattsville, MD: U.S. Department of Health and Human Services, Public Health Service.

Vogel, R. J., & Palmer, H. C., eds. 1985. *Long term care: Perspectives from research and demonstrations.* Rockville, MD: Aspen Publication.

Wallich, P., & Holloway, M. 1993. The analytical economist: Health care without perverse incentives. *Scientific American,* July, 109.

Westerfield, D. L. 1991. *Mandated health care: Issues and strategies.* New York: Praeger Publishers.

The White House Domestic Policy Council. 1993. *The president's Health Security Plan: The Clinton blueprint.* New York: Times Books.

Wohl, S. 1989. The medical-industrial complex: Another view of the influence of business on medical care. In McCue, J. D., ed., *Medical cost containment crisis.* Ann Arbor, MI: Health Administration Press, 168-181.

SOURCES OF ADDITIONAL INFORMATION

The complexities and interdisciplinary nature of the health care system in the United States translate into an equally complex task when seeking relevant information on a particular topic. Materials in this section are grouped by format (i.e., Indexes/Databases) and broad subject categories (i.e., Health Professions) to provide a basic organizational structure for accessing the information more efficiently. All categories are representative of a small portion of information resources available and should not be interpreted as comprehensive.

Books

Aday, L. A. 1993. *Evaluating the medical care system: Effectiveness, efficiency, and equity.* Ann Arbor, MI: Health Administration Press.

Arnould, R. J.; Rich, R. F.; & White, W. D. 1993. *Competitive approaches to health care reform.* Washington, DC: Urban Institute/University Press of America.

Bailey, E. J. 1991. *Urban African American health care.* Lanham, MD: University Press of America.

Blank, R. H., & Bonnicksen, A. L. *Emerging issues in biomedical policy.* 1992. New York: Columbia University Press.

Boulder, A. F., ed. 1992. *Health policy and the Hispanic.* Boulder, CO: Westview Press.

Braithwaite, R. L., & Taylor, S. E., eds. 1992. *Health issues in the black community.* San Francisco: Jossey-Bass.

Cockerham, W. C. 1992. *Medical sociology.* Englewood Cliffs, NJ: Prentice-Hall.

Fincham, J. E., & Wertheimer, A. I., eds. 1991. *Pharmacy and the U.S. health care system.* Binghamton, NY: Haworth Press.

Geoffrey, R. 1992. *The strategy of preventive medicine.* New York: Oxford University Press.

Gitnic, G.; Rothenberg, F.; & Weiner, J. L., eds. 1991. *The business of medicine.* New York: Elsevier.

Goodman, J. C., & Musgrave, G. L. 1992. *Patient power: Solving America's health care crisis.* Washington, DC: Cato Institute.

Hawkins, J. W., & Higgin, L. P. 1989. *Nursing and the American health care system.* New York: Tiresias Press.

Hendricks, R. 1993. *A model for national health care: The history of Kaiser Permanente.* New Brunswick, NJ: Rutgers University Press.

Kos-Munson, B. 1993. *Who gets health care?: An arena for nursing action.* New York: Springer Publishing.

Lohr, K. N. 1991. *Quality of health care: An introduction to critical definitions, concepts, principles, and practices.* Ann Arbor, MI: Health Administration Press.

Mooney, G., & Hempstead, H. 1992. *Economics, medicine and health care.* Savage, MD: Barnes & Noble.

Newhouse, J. P. 1993. *Free for all?: Lessons from the Rand Health Insurance Experiment*. Cambridge, MA: Harvard University Press.

Pope, A. M., & Tarlov, A. R., eds. 1991. *Disability in America: Toward a national agenda for prevention*. Washington, DC: National Academy Press.

Rodwin, M. A. 1993. *Medicine, money and morals: Physicians' conflicts of interest*. New York: Oxford University Press.

Schechter, M. 1993. *Beyond Medicare: Achieving long-term care security*. San Francisco: Urban Institute Press.

Shortell, M. S. & Reinhardt, U. E., eds. *Improving health policy and management: Nine critical research issues for the 1990s*. Ann Arbor, MI: AHSR/HAP.

U.S. Senate. 1993. *National Health Care Senate Document 103-2*. Y1.1/3:103-2. Washington, DC: Government Printing Office. 31 March.

Winsow, G. R., & Walters, J. M. 1993. *Facing limits: Ethics and health care for the elderly*. Boulder, CO: Westview Press.

Bibliographies

Bibliography of Bioethics
Kennedy Institute of Ethics
Georgetown University
Washington, DC 20057
Print format

Bibliography of the History of Medicine
National Library of Medicine
8600 Rockville Pike
Bethesda, MD 20894
301-496-6308
Print format

Indexes/Databases

ABI / INFORM
UMI/Data Courier
620 S. Third St.
Louisville, KY 40202-2475
800-626-2823
Online and CD-ROM formats

AgeLine
American Association of Retired Persons
601 E. St., NW
Washington, DC 20049
Online format

American Statistics Index
Congressional Information Service
4520 East-West Hwy.
Bethesda, MD 20814-3389
Print, online, and CD-ROM formats

Biobusiness
BIOSIS Previews
BioSciences Information Service
2100 Arch St.
Philadelphia, PA 19103
800-345-4277
215-587-4847
Online format

Business Periodicals Index
H. W. Wilson Company
950 University Ave.
Bronx, NY 10452
212-588-8400
Print, online, and CD-ROM formats

CIS / Index
Congressional Information Service
4520 East-West Hwy., Ste. 800
Bethesda, MD 20814-3387
301-654-1550
Print, online, and CD-ROM formats

Cumulative Index to Nursing & Allied Health Literature
P.O. Box 871
Glendale, CA 91209-0871
818-409-8005
Print, online, and CD-ROM formats

Current Index to Journals in Education (CIJE)
Oryx Press
4041 N. Central Ave. at Indian School Rd.
Phoenix, AZ 85012-3397
602-265-2651
Print, online, and CD-ROM formats

ERIC
U.S. Department of Education
2440 Research Blvd., 5th Fl.
Rockville, MD 20950
301-656-9723
Print, online, and CD-ROM formats

Federal Register Index
National Archives and Records Administration
Superintendent of Documents
P.O. Box 371954
Pittsburgh, PA 15250-7954
Print and online formats

Government Reports Announcements and Index
U.S. Department of Commerce
National Technical Information Service
5285 Port Royal Rd.
Springfield, VA 22161
Print, online, and CD-ROM formats

Hospital Literature Index
American Hospital Association
840 N. Lake Shore Dr.
Chicago, IL 60611
312-280-6263
Print, online, and CD-ROM formats

Index Medicus
U.S. National Library of Medicine
8600 Rockville Pike
Bethesda, MD 20894-0001
301-496-6308
Print, online, and CD-ROM formats

International Nursing Index
American Journal of Nursing Company
555 West 57th St.
New York, NY 10019-2961
212-582-8820
Print, online, and CD-ROM formats

Monthly Catalog of United States Government Publications
U.S. Government Printing Office
Superintendent of Documents
Washington, DC 20402-0001
Print, online, and CD-ROM formats

PAIS INTERNATIONAL
Public Affairs Information Service, Inc.
521 W. 43rd St.
New York, NY 10036
202-336-5500
Print, online, and CD-ROM formats

Psychological Abstracts
American Psychological Association
750 First St. NE
Washington, DC 20002-4242
202-336-5500
Print, online, and CD-ROM formats

Sociological Abstracts
Sociological Abstracts, Inc.
P.O. Box 2206
San Diego, CA 92122
619-695-8803
Print, online, and CD-ROM formats

Women Studies Abstracts
Transaction Periodicals Consortium
Rutgers University
New Brunswick, NJ 08903
908-932-2280
Print format

Statistical Sources

Locating statistical data related to the health care system can be a time-consuming process, because it is such a large body of knowledge. There are volumes of health-related statistics. Here are a few guidelines to keep in mind to aid you in this process:

1. No centralized government agency or private organization exists to collect health statistics.

2. Is your question related to an area in which statistics might be collected on a regular basis?

3. What agency would most likely collect the information?

4. It is possible that no absolute statistics exist in answer to your question, or in the exact format you require.

5. Often, accurate interpretation of the data depends on knowledge of currency, definitions of the terms utilized, and careful review of the units of measurement.

6. The functions and responsibilities of the various government agencies often change with new administrations, which means the data collected may not be comparable from year to year.

7. When examining data, determine whether the figures presented are comprehensive, based on a limited survey, or general projections.

O'Brien, J. W., & Wasserman, S. R. 1988. *Statistics sources.* 12th ed. Detroit: Gale Research.

The universal healthcare almanac Phoenix, AZ: R-C Publications, irregular.

Demographics

U.S. Bureau of Census. *County and city data book.* Washington, DC: U.S. Government Printing Office, annual.

———. *Statistical abstract of the United States.* Washington, DC: U.S. Government Printing Office, annual.

Delivery and Financing

AHA guide to the health care field. Chicago: American Hospital Association, annual.

Hospital statistics. Chicago: American Hospital Association, annual.

Length of stay by diagnosis and operation. Ann Arbor, MI: Commission on Professional and Hospital Activities, annual.

Health Professions

Facts about nursing. Kansas City, MO: American Nurses' Association, irregular.

Handbook of labor statistics. Bureau of Labor Statistics. Washington, DC: U.S. Government Printing Office, irregular.

Physician characteristics and distribution in the U.S. Chicago: American Medical Association, annual.

Socioeconomic Characteristics of medical practice. Chicago: American Medical Association, annual.

Vital and Health

Accident facts. Chicago: National Safety Council, annual.

Centers for Disease Control. *MMWR: Morbidity and mortality weekly report*. Waltham, MA: Massachusetts Medical Society, weekly with an annual summary and supplements.

National Center for Health Statistics. *Advance data from vital and health statistics*. Hyattsville, MD: Public Health Service, irregular.

————. *Vital and health statistics*. Washington, DC: U.S. Government Printing Office, irregular.

Socio-economic factbook for surgery. Chicago: American College of Surgeons, annual.

Source book of health insurance data. Washington, DC: Health Insurance Association of America, biennial.

Economics and Financing

Health care financing review. Baltimore, MD: Health Care Financing Administration, quarterly.

Healthcare financial management. Oak Brook, IL: Healthcare Financial Management Association, monthly.

Source book of health insurance data. Washington, DC: Health Insurance Association of America, biennial.

Legal and Regulatory

Health care labor manual. Germantown, MD: Health Law Center, looseleaf.

Hospital law manual. Rockville, MD: Aspen Publishers, Inc., looseleaf.

Medicare and Medicaid guide. Chicago: Commerce Clearinghouse, looseleaf.

Directories

Health Facilities

AHA guide to the health care field. Chicago: American Hospital Association, annual.

Directory of nursing homes. Phoenix: Oryx Press, irregular.

Organizations, Associations, and Agencies

Encyclopedia of associations. Detroit, MI: Gale, annual.

Encyclopedia of health information sources. Detroit, MI: Gale , irregular.

Medical and health information directory. Detroit, MI: Gale, biennial.

Education and Training

AAMC directory of american medical education. Washington, DC: Association of American Medical Colleges, irregular.

Allied health education directory. Chicago: Committee on Allied Health Education and Accreditation, annual.

Associate degree education for nursing. New York: National League for Nursing, annual.

Baccalaureate education in nursing: Key to a professioanl nursing career. New York: National League for Nursing, annual.

Directory of graduate medical education programs. Chicago: American Medical Association, annual.

Doctoral programs in nursing. New York: National League for Nursing, annual.

Health services administration education. Arlington, VA: Association of University Programs in Health Administration, biennial.

Master's education in nursing: Route to opportunities in contemporary nursing. New York: National League for Nursing, annual.

State approved schools of nursing R.N. New York: National League for Nursing, annual.

Health Care Companies

The medical and healthcare marketplace guide. Philadelphia: International Bio-Medical Information Service, annual.

Health Maintenance Organizations (HMOs) and Preferred Provider Organizations (PPOs)

Directory of Health Maintenance Organizations. Bethesda, MD: American Medical Care and Review Association, annual.

GHAA's national directory of HMOs. Washington, DC: Group Health Association of America, annual.

HMO / PPO directory. Deerfield, IL: Whole World Publishing, annual.

Periodicals

Advance Data from Vital and Health Statistics
U.S. National Center for Health Statistics
6525 Belcrest Rd.
Hyattsville, MD 20782
Irregular

AHA News
American Hospital Publishing, Inc.
737 N. Michigan Ave.
Chicago, IL 60611
Weekly

American Health: Fitness of Body and Mind
Reader's Digest Association, Inc.
28 W. 23rd St.
New York, NY 10010
10 issues per year

American Health Systems Review
FAHS Review, Inc.
1405 N. Pierce St., Ste. 308
Little Rock, AR 72207
Bimonthly

American Journal of Health Promotion
American Journal of Health Promotion, Inc.
1812 S. Rochester Rd., Ste. 200
Rochester Hills, MI 48307-3532
Bimonthly

American Journal of Public Health
American Public Health Association, Inc.
1015 Fifteenth St. NW
Washington, DC 20005
Monthly

Business and Health
Medical Economics Company, Inc.
Five Paragon Dr.
Montvale, NJ 07645
Monthly

Caring
National Association for Home Care
519 C St. NE
Washington, DC 20002-5809
Monthly

Frontiers of Health Services Management
Health Administration Press
1021 E. Huron St.
Ann Arbor, MI 48104-9990
Quarterly

Hastings Center Report
Hastings Center
255 Elm Rd.
Briarcliff Manor, NY 10510
Bimonthly

Health Affairs
People-to-People Health Foundation, Inc.
Chevy Chase, MD 20815
Quarterly

Health Care Financing Review
Health Care Financing Administration
Oak Meadows Bldg., Rm. 1A9
6325 Security Blvd.
Baltimore, MD 21207
Quarterly

Health Care Management Review
Aspen Publishers, Inc.
7201 McKinney Cir.
Gaithersburg, MD 20878
Quarterly

Health Care Supervisor
Aspen Systems
200 Orchard Ridge Dr.
Gaithersburg, MD 20878
Quarterly

Health Facilities Management
American Hospital Publishing, Inc.
737 N. Michigan Ave.
Chicago, IL 60611
Monthly

Health/PAC Bulletin
Health Policy Advisory Center
47 W. 14th St., 3rd Fl.
New York, NY 10011
Bimonthly

Healthcare Executive
American College of Healthcare
Executives
840 N. Lake Shore Dr.
Chicago, IL 60611
Bimonthly

Healthcare Financial Management
Healthcare Financial Mangement
Association
Two Westbrook Corporate Center,
Ste. 700
Westchester, IL 60154
Monthly

Home Health Care Services Quarterly
Haworth Press, Inc.
10 Alice St.
Binghamton, NY 13904
Quarterly

Hospice Journal
Haworth Press
10 Alice St.
Binghamton, NY 13904
Quarterly

*Hospital and Health Services
Administration*
Health Administration Press
1021 E. Huron St.
Ann Arbor, MI 48104-9990
Bimonthly

Hospital Topics
Heldref Publications
1319 Eighteenth St.
Washington, DC 20036-1802
Bimonthly

Hospitals
American Hospital Publishing, Inc.
737 N. Michigan Ave.
Chicago, IL 60611
Semimonthly

Inquiry
Blue Cross and Blue Shield Association
676 N. St. Clair St.
Chicago, IL 60611
Quarterly

JAMA
American Medical Association
515 N. State St.
Chicago, IL 60610
Weekly

Journal of Health and Hospital
American Academy of Hospital Attor-
neys of the American Hospital
Association
840 N. Lake Shore Dr.
Chicago, IL 60611
Monthly

Journal of Health and Social Behavior
American Sociological Association
1722 N. St. NW
Washington, DC 20036
Quarterly

Journal of Health and Social Policy
Haworth Press, Inc.
10 Alice St.
Binghamton, NY 13904
Quarterly

*Journal of Health Care for the Poor
and Underserved*
Institute on Health Care for the Poor
and Underserved
Meharry Medical College
1005 D B Todd Blvd.
Nashville, TN 37208
Quarterly

Journal of Health Care Marketing
American Marketing Association
250 S. Wacker Dr., Ste. 200
Chicago, IL 60606
Quarterly

*Journal of Health Politics, Policy and
Law*
Duke University Press
6697 College Station
Durham, NC 27708
Quarterly

*Journal of Long-Term Care
Administration*
American College of Health Care
Administrators
325 S. Patrick St.
Alexandria, VA 22314
Quarterly

Journal of Public Health Policy
Journal of Public Health Policy, Inc.
208 Meadowood Dr.
South Burlington, VT 05403
Quarterly

Law, Medicine & Health Care
American Society of Law &
Medicine, Inc.
765 Commonwealth Ave., Ste. 1634
Boston, MA 02215
Quarterly

Medical Care Review
Health Administration Press
1021 E. Huron St.
Ann Arbor, MI 48104-9990
Quarterly

Milbank Quarterly
Cambridge University Press
40 W. 20th St.
New York, NY 10011
Quarterly

MMWR: Morbidity and Mortality
Weekly Report
Centers for Disease Control, Massa-
chusetts Medical Society
Superintendent of Documents
U.S. Government Printing Office
Washington, DC 20402
Weekly with annual summary
supplements

Modern Healthcare
Crain Communications, Inc.
740 N. Rush St.
Chicago, IL 60611-2590
Weekly

Nursing Administration Quarterly
Aspen Publishers, Inc.
200 Orchard Ridge Dr.
Gaithersburg, MD 20878
Quarterly

Provider
American Health Care Association
1201 L St. NW
Washington, DC 20005-4014
Monthly

QRB Quality Review Bulletin
Joint Commission on Accreditation of
Healthcare Organizations
1 Renaissance Blvd.
Oakbrook Terrace, IL 60181
Monthly

Trustee
American Hospital Publishing, Inc.
737 N. Michigan Ave.
Chicago, IL 60611
Monthly

Organizations

Nongovernmental Organizations

American Association of Blood Banks
1117 N. 19th St.
Arlington, VA 22209
703-528-8200

American College of Health Care
Administrators
8120 Woodmont Ave., Ste. 200
Bethesda, MD 20814
301-652-8384

American College of Healthcare
Executives
840 N. Lake Shore Dr.
Chicago, IL 60611
312-943-0544

American Health Care Association
1201 L St. NW
Washington, DC 20005
202-842-4444

American Hospital Association
840 N. Lake Shore Dr.
Chicago, IL 60611
312-280-6000

American Managed Care and Review
Association
1227 25th St. NW, No. 610
Washington, DC 20037
202-728-0506

American Medical Association
515 N. State St.
Chicago, IL 60610
312-464-4818

American Medical Record Association
875 N. Michigan Ave.
Chicago, IL 60611
312-787-2672

American Nurses' Association
2420 Pershing Rd.
Kansas City, MO 64108
816-474-5720

American Public Health Association
1015 15th St. NW
Washington, DC 20005
202-789-5600

Association for the Advancement of
Medical Instrumentation
1901 N. Fort Myer Dr., Ste. 602
Arlington, VA 22209
703-525-4890

Association of American Medical
Colleges
One DuPont Cir. NW
Washington, DC 20036
202-828-0400

Association of University Programs in
Health Administration
1911 N. Fort Myer Dr., Ste. 503
Arlington, VA 22209
703-524-5500

Blue Cross and Blue Shield Association
676 N. St. Clair St.
Chicago, IL 60611
312-440-6000

Group Health Association of American
1129 20th St. NW
Washington, DC 20036
202-778-3200

Hastings Center
25 Elm Rd.
Briar Cliff Manor, NY 10510
914-762-8500

Health Policy Advisory Center
17 Murray St.
New York, NY 10007
212-267-8890

Healthcare Financial Management
Association
1900 Spring Rd.
Oak Brook, IL 60521
312-571-4700

Joint Commission on Accreditation of
Healthcare Organizations
1 Renaissance Blvd.
Oakbrook, IL 60181
708-916-2138

Medical Group Management
Association
1355 S. Colorado Blvd., Ste. 900
Denver, CO 80222
303-753-1111

Medical Library Association
Six N. Michigan Ave., Ste. 300
Chicago, IL 60202-4805
312-419-9094

Milbank Memorial Fund
One E. 75th St.
New York, NY 10021
212-570-4805

National Association for Ambulatory
Care
21 Michigan St.
Grand Rapids, MI 49503
616-949-2138

National Association for Home Care
519 C St. NE, Stanton Park
Washington, DC 20002
202-547-7424

National Association for Hospital
Development
112-B E. Broad St.
Falls Church, VA 22046
703-532-6243

National Council on Patient Information and Education
666 11th St. NW, Ste. 810
Washington, DC 2001
202-347-6711

National Hospice Organization
1901 N. Moore St., Ste. 901
Arlington, VA 22209
703-243-5900

National League for Nursing
10 Columbus Cir.
New York, NY 10019
212-582-1022

National Rehabilitation Information
Center
8455 Colesville Rd., Ste. 935
Silver Spring, MD 20910-3319
800-346-2742

Government Organizations and Agencies

Bureau of Health Professions
5600 Fishers Ln.
Rockville, MD 20857
301-443-2060

Bureau of Labor Statistics
200 Constitution Ave. NW
Washington, DC 20210
202-523-1327

Centers for Disease Control
1600 Clifton Rd. NE
Atlanta, GA 30333
404-329-3286

Health Care Financing Administration
200 Independence Ave. SW
Washington, DC 20201
202-245-6726

National Center for Health Statistics
3700 East-West Hwy.
Hyattsville, MD 20782
301-436-8500

National Institute of Mental Health
5600 Fishers Ln.
Rockville, MD 20857
301-443-3877

National Institutes of Health
9000 Rockville Pike
Bethesda, MD 20892
301-496-4000

National Library of Medicine
8600 Rockville Pike
Bethesda, MD 20892
301-496-6308

National Technical Information Service
5285 Port Royal Rd.
Springfield, VA 22161
703-487-4600

Public Health Service
200 Independence Ave. SW
Washington, DC 20201
202-245 6296

Useful Library of Congress
Subject Headings

Allied Health Personnel
Health
Health and Race
Health Attitudes
Health Boards
Health Education
Health Facilities
Health Maintenance Organization
Health Occupations Licensing Boards
Health Occupations Schools
Health Planning
Health Promotion
Health Services Administration
Health Surveys
Health Systems Agencies
Home Care Services
Hospice Care
Hospital Administrators
Hospital Care
Hospital Consultants
Hospital Management Companies
Hospital Mergers
Hospitals—Proprietary
Hospitals—Rural
Hospitals—United States
Hospitals—United States—Accounting
Hospitals—United States—
    Accreditation
Hospitals—United States—
Administration

Insurance, Health—United States
Long-Term Care Facilities
Managed Care Plans
Medicaid
Medical Care—United States
Medical Ethics
Medical Personnel
Medically Underserved Areas
Medically Uninsured Persons
Medicare
Medicine
Medicine, Preventative
Medicine, Rural
Medicine—State
Medigap
Nursing
Nursing Home Care
Nursing Homes
Patient Advocacy
Patient Compliance
Patient Education
Patient Satisfaction
Patients
Physician and Patient
Physician Services Utilization
Preferred Provider Organizations
Preventative Health Services

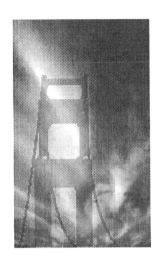

The family is changing, not disappearing. We have to broaden our understanding of it, look for the new metaphors.
Mary Catherine Bateson, 1989

12

Changing Family Structures

Diane Zabel

In the April 1993 issue of *The Atlantic Monthly*, Barbara Dafoe Whitehead declared that "Dan Quayle was right" (Whitehead, 1993a, p. 47). Whitehead, a researcher affiliated with the nonpartisan Institute for American Values, is a Democrat. According to Whitehead, a growing body of scholarship indicates that children raised in single parent or stepparent families fare worse on several indicators of well-being than children growing up in intact families. Her pronouncement referred to "Restoring Basic Values: Strengthening the Family," the infamous speech that former Vice President Quayle delivered at the Commonwealth Club of California on May 19, 1992. In his address, Quayle claimed that the breakdown of family values was represented by the decision of prime-time television character Murphy Brown to have a baby out of wedlock. Quayle's comment created an uproar, and family values subsequently became an issue in the 1992 presidential campaign. Although the ensuing flap over family values polarized voters in the 1992 election, the debate over whether the family is disintegrating is not new.

Diane Zabel has been the Social Science Reference Librarian at The Pennsylvania State University, University Park, since 1986. She has written several book chapters, including "Sociology" and "Psychology" in *The Social Sciences: A Cross-Disciplinary Guide to Selected Sources* (Libraries Unlimited, 1989); "Psychology and Psychiatry" in *Topical Reference Books* (Bowker, 1991); and "The Travel and Tourism Literature" in *The Leisure Literature: A Guide to Sources in Leisure Studies, Fitness, Sports, and Travel* (Libraries Unlimited, 1992). Her current research interests include flexible work arrangements and total quality management. She co-authored *Flexible Work Arrangements in ARL Libraries* (Association for Research Libraries, 1992) and "Total Quality Management: A Primer" (*RQ*, Winter 1992). She also reviews reference books for *RQ* frequently. Diane Zabel holds a Master of Urban Planning degree and a Master of Science in Library and Information Science from the University of Illinois.

There is an abundance of scholarly literature on the family. More than 800 English-language articles focusing on the family (excluding ethnologies and anthropological or historical works) were published between 1900 and 1938 (Broderick, 1988). The first issue of *Living* (the predecessor to the prestigious *Journal of Marriage and the Family*) was published in the beginning of 1939, coinciding with the founding of the National Conference on Family Relations (now the National Council on Family Relations), the leading professional organization in the field of family studies (Broderick, 1988). Within the next fifty years, several journals emerged in the area of family studies and articles on the family have appeared in a wide range of social science periodicals (Nye, 1988).

The family has also been the topic of many popular and scholarly books. Several excellent overviews of the evolution of American family life have been published (Gordon, 1978; Degler, 1980; Coontz, 1988; Mintz & Kellogg, 1988). Changes in family life are also traced in several demographic histories of the United States (Seward, 1978; Wells, 1982, 1985; Sweet & Bumpass, 1987). Although some books, such as Mary Jo Bane's *Here to Stay* (1976), have been optimistic about the future of the family, many have reflected the view that the family is troubled and on the verge of collapse. The decline of the family has been a persistent theme in both the scholarly literature and the popular media. Arlene Skolnick has chronicled the pessimism over the family in *Embattled Paradise*, her insightful analysis of trends that have affected the American family (Skolnick, 1991). Like Arlene Skolnick, social historian Stephanie Coontz believes that the family has been idealized. In her compelling book *The Way We Never Were*, Coontz argues that nostalgia about perfect families of the past (such as those represented in 1950s situation comedies like *Ozzie and Harriet* and *Leave It to Beaver*) burdens contemporary families who are trying to live up to unrealistic stereotypes of family life (1992a).

Is the family eroding or will it be stronger in the 1990s? Or is there some middle ground on this emotionally charged issue? Although the controversy may never be resolved, it is clear that the typical American family has not resembled June and Ward Cleaver's household for some time. The structure of the family has changed dramatically in the past three decades, reflecting several significant demographic and societal changes.

MAJOR TRENDS AND
SOCIAL FORCES IMPACTING
FAMILY LIFE

Delayed Marriage and Childbearing

In 1890, the median age at first marriage was 26.1 for men and 22.0 for women (Ambry & Russell, 1992). In 1950, when men and women married at an earlier age than in any other period in this century, the median age at first marriage dropped to 22.8 for men and 20.3 for women (Ambry & Russell, 1992). Since 1960, that trend has reversed. In 1990, the median age at first marriage was 26.1 for men (the same level as in 1890) and 23.9 for women (Ambry & Russell, 1992). Women are now marrying at a later age than ever before. Extensive data on first marriage rates and changing patterns of first marriage can be found in a study published by Rodgers and Thornton (1985). Coinciding with this trend of increasingly later marriages, there has been a rise in cohabitation (unmarried couples living together). Four times as many couples lived together outside of marriage in 1990 as compared to 1970 (Kellogg & Mintz, 1993). Census Bureau data indicate that whereas one-half million couples cohabitated in 1970, more than two million couples lived together in 1986 (Thornton, 1988). A detailed analysis of cohabitation trends has been published by Bumpass and Sweet (1989). In addition, women are delaying motherhood and bearing children until later in life (Riche, 1991; Crispell, 1992; Hatch, 1992). Census data indicate that 33 percent of babies were born to women in their thirties in 1988, compared to 19 percent in 1976 (*The new American family*, 1992).

Decreased Fertility

In the mid-1950s, at the height of the baby boom, American families averaged about three children per couple (*American households*, 1992; Haub, 1992). The fertility rate began to decline in the 1960s (Santi, 1987). Data from the 1990 census indicate that families now average about two children per couple (Popenoe, 1991; *American households*, 1992; Haub, 1992; Kalish, 1992). In addition to having fewer children, couples in the 1990s are also spacing their births further apart as compared to couples in the 1950s (Crispell, 1992; Hatch, 1992).

Increased Levels of Divorce

The divorce rate in the United States increased threefold from 1950 to 1990 (Kellogg & Mintz, 1993). If current trends continue, half of all marriages will end in divorce (London & Wilson, 1988; Hatch, 1992;

Kalish, 1992). University of Wisconsin demographers Teresa Martin and Larry Bumpass believe that this is an underestimation and predict that two-thirds of all first marriages will end in separation or divorce (Martin & Bumpass, 1989). When compared to other Western industrialized countries, the American divorce rate is double (Kellogg & Mintz, 1993). Although David Popenoe has referred to this propensity to divorce as "a divorce revolution" (Popenoe, 1991, p. 19), revisionist scholar Stephanie Coontz argued that divorce has replaced the function of death in the case of marital disruption (1992a). Coontz estimates that colonial American couples, on average, were likely to be married for less than twelve years because of high mortality rates. Consequently, in the past, many unhappy marriages were probably terminated by the death of one of the marriage partners. Now an unhappy marriage is more likely to be terminated by divorce. Andrew Cherlin has studied the historical development, causes, and consequences of divorce. His 1981 monograph, *Marriage, Divorce, Remarriage*, is regarded by family scholars as one of the most significant books on the topic of divorce (Adams, 1988). A revision of this classic work was published in 1992 (Cherlin). Cherlin found an association between economic conditions and divorce. Divorce rates have declined during periods of economic distress (such as the Great Depression of the 1930s) and have risen after depressions and wars, periods that have generally been marked by economic prosperity (Cherlin, 1981). Cherlin also noted that the divorce rate increased as more women entered the workforce. Women who are able to provide for themselves financially are more likely to divorce (1981).

Increasing Remarriage

The United States also has one of the highest remarriage rates in the world (Kellogg & Mintz, 1993). In 1988, only 55 percent of all marriages were between single (never previously married) men and single women (Ambry & Russell, 1992). Both bride and groom were previously divorced in 19 percent of marriages, and 25 percent of marriages were remarriages for one partner (Ambry & Russell, 1992). This means that 44 percent of marriages were remarriages for one or both partners in 1988. The interval between divorce and remarriage is relatively short. The average for both men and women is less than four years (London & Wilson, 1988). Increasing rates of remarriage have made stepfamilies common; an estimated 25 percent of children growing up in the 1990s will eventually live in a stepparent family (Whitehead, 1993a).

Increase in One-Parent Families

During the past three decades, there has been a dramatic increase in the number of one-parent families. This trend has been a result of two demographic factors: high divorce rates and an increase in out-of-wedlock births (Kalish, 1992). In 1960, 5 percent of all children born in the United

States were born out of wedlock (Hatch, 1992). Out-of-wedlock births now constitute 25 percent of all births, a fivefold increase over a 30-year period (*American households*, 1992; *The crisis of the absent father*, 1993). Census data from 1990 indicates that single-parent families are the fastest growing family type (*American households*, 1992). In 1960,9 percent of children under age 18 lived with one parent (Popenoe, 1991; Benokraitis, 1993). This figure rose to nearly 25 percent in 1990 (Popenoe, 1991; Benokraitis, 1993). If this trend continues, projections about the number of children living with only one parent in the future are alarming. Demographers estimate that between 42 and 70 percent of white children and 86 to 94 percent of black children born around 1980 will live with only one parent sometime during their childhood (Hofferth, 1987).

The percentage of children living with only their mother nearly doubled for both white and black children between 1970 and 1984 (Hofferth, 1987). This absence of fathers is particularly disturbing. The National Survey of Children found that in families disrupted by divorce, almost half of the children had no contact with their father over the course of a year, and, as time went on, more than two-thirds of these children did not see their father for a year (Whitehead, 1993a). According to David Blankenhorn, founder of the Institute for American Values, a research organization focusing on issues impacting the American family, "This trend of fatherlessness is the most socially consequential family trend of our generation" (Gibbs, 1993).

Increase of Women in the Workforce

A common misperception is that women, especially mothers, did not work outside the home in the 1950s. Diane Crispell has dispelled many of the myths surrounding families in the 1950s. In 1950, the labor force participation rate for married women was 25 percent, and 28 percent of married women with children aged six to seventeen had paying jobs (Crispell, 1992). Approximately 12 percent of married women with pre-schoolers worked outside the home in 1950 (Googins, 1991; Crispell, 1992). Women entered the workforce in record numbers over the next four decades. Two incomes have become an economic necessity for most American families. One of the findings of the 1990 Virginia Slims Opinion Poll was that 54 percent of women work to support themselves and their families (Townsend & O'Neil, 1990). In 1991, the labor force participation rate for married women was 59 percent (Crispell, 1992). Labor force participation rates have increased the most for married women with children aged one or under. Fifty-two percent of these women were in the workforce in 1988, compared to 31 percent in 1975 (Ambry & Russell, 1992). As a result, child care has become a critical issue for families in the 1990s (see chapter 5 for an analysis of the child care crisis).

Men and women have been reexamining and redefining their roles as more women enter the workforce. In *The Second Shift*, a groundbreaking study of dual-income couples, Arlie Hochschild demonstrated that women are responsible for a disproportionate share of housework and child care

(Hochschild, 1989). Hochschild concluded that "most women work one shift at the office or factory and a 'second shift' at home" (Hochschild, 1989, p. 4). In fact, Hochschild estimated that over the course of a year, women work an extra month of 24-hour days (Hochschild, 1989). Although men are doing less than women, they have gradually increased their share of cooking, cleaning, and other household chores. Men's share of housework increased from five to ten hours a week from 1965 to 1985 (Robinson, 1988). However, in a 1990 poll, 64 percent of women indicated that they wanted men to help more with housework and child care (Townsend & O'Neil, 1990).

AMERICAN FAMILIES IN THE 1990s

As a result of these demographic and social changes, a variety of family structures or forms is becoming increasingly common. The traditional family with a breadwinner dad, homemaker mom, and one or more children has become the exception. A significant number of children are now living in one-parent families, stepfamilies, gay families, or in households headed by unmarried cohabiting couples. What are the social and economic consequences of what has been described as the "flight from the nuclear family"? (Popenoe, 1991, p. 19).

Several social scientists have argued that many of these recent family trends affect children negatively. Rutgers University sociologist David Popenoe has warned that these trends suggest "that American society has been moving in an ominous direction—toward the devaluation of children" (1991, p. 20). Nicholas Davidson has referred to the 15 million children growing up without fathers as "casualties" and concludes that "life without father" is "America's greatest social catastrophe" (1990, p. 4). After a review of social science research on the changing family, Barbara Dafoe Whitehead recently determined that "the dissolution of two-parent families, though it may benefit the adults involved, is harmful to many children, and dramatically undermines our society" (1993a).

In particular, many experts are concerned that such serious problems as poverty, crime, and declining school achievement are related to changing family structures. Consider the following statistics:

- Children in one-parent families are six times as likely as children in two-parent families to be poor (Whitehead, 1993a).

- More than one-fifth (22 percent) of children in one-parent families will be poor for seven or more years. In comparison, only 2 percent of children in two-income families will experience poverty during childhood for seven or more years (Whitehead, 1993a).

- In 1990, the median income of a female-headed family was $17,000. In comparison, the median income of a two-parent, dual-income family was $47,000. If the wife did not work, the median income of a married-couple family was $30,000 (Kalish, 1992).

- If family structures had not changed since 1960, child poverty rates would have been one-third lower in 1988 (Eggebeen & Lichter, 1991).

- A growing number of minority children are at risk of poverty because of the greater likelihood that black families will be female-headed. Black children are three times more likely to be poor than white children (Eggebeen & Lichter, 1991).

- Children in families disrupted by divorce or out-of-wedlock birth are almost twice as likely as children in intact biological families to drop out of high school (Whitehead, 1993a).

- More than 70 percent of all juveniles in state correctional facilities come from homes where there is no father present (Whitehead, 1993a; Gibbs, 1993).

Statistically, children in two-parent families are better off financially than children in one-parent families. Eggebeen and Lichter have suggested that children have become "economically polarized" into two groups: "relatively advantaged children living in two-earner married couple households" and poor children living in "increasingly impoverished female-headed families" (1991, p. 814). This situation has been termed the "feminization of poverty" (Zopf, 1989, p. 1). The long-term consequences of poverty are profound: Poverty has been linked to hunger, poor health, drug and alcohol abuse, crime, and educational failure (Benokraitis, 1993).

THE FUTURE OF THE AMERICAN FAMILY

Demographers Ahlburg and De Vita have written that the American family is studied extensively because "the economic well-being of the family often serves as a barometer for measuring the well-being of the nation" (Ahlburg & De Vita, 1992, p. 4). If current trends continue, what does the future hold for the American family? Arizona State University professor Paul Glick calculates that one out of three Americans is now a member of a stepfamily and that this will increase to one out of two by the year 2000 (Ahlburg & De Vita, 1992; Larson, 1992). Sociologist Andrew Cherlin has noted that an increasingly common pattern will be "Cohabitation, Marriage, Divorce, More Cohabitation, and Probably Remarriage" (Whitehead, 1993a). Since Glick projects that 50 percent of stepfamilies will break up, the cycle is more likely to be marriage, divorce, remarriage, and divorce (Larson, 1992).

Although the statistics are gloomy, many typical Americans are far more optimistic about the future of marriage and family life. Since 1973, the National Opinion Research Center has polled a nationally representative sample of married adults and has asked them questions relating to marital and family satisfaction. The results have been surprising. Reported levels of marital happiness have remained relatively constant from 1973 to 1989. Sixty to 65 percent of married adults have described their marriage as "very happy" and 30 to 35 percent have rated their marriage as "pretty happy" (Chadwick & Heaton, 1992). Less than 5 percent of the respondents have described their marriages as "not too happy" (Chadwick & Heaton, 1992). Respondents were also asked questions relating to their satisfaction with family life. Again, the level of satisfaction has varied little over time. In 1986, 45 percent of respondents replied that they were "very satisfied" with family life, compared with 47 percent in 1980 (Chadwick & Heaton, 1992). Only 2 percent were "very dissatisfied" with family life in the 1980 and 1986 polls (Chadwick & Heaton, 1992).

Some family historians and sociologists have maintained that American families have always been diverse (Zinn & Eitzen, 1990; Hatch, 1992; Kellogg & Mintz, 1993). Susan Kellogg and Steven Mintz, two prominent family scholars, have concluded that American family structures have always been evolving and that "recent changes . . . represent simply the latest stage in an ongoing process of change and adaptation" (1993, p. 1941). Other family experts have reminded us that such problems as poverty, delinquency, drug abuse, and declining academic achievement have persisted for decades and are not necessarily a result of changing family structures (Skolnick, 1991; Coontz, 1992a). Carlfred Broderick's review of family scholarship in the 1920s and 1930s indicates that many of the articles and books published during this period focused on such family problems as poverty, delinquency, marital discord, divorce, and desertion (Broderick, 1988). Other experts, such as Arlene Skolnick, are optimistic because some negative societal trends such as infant and child mortality and teenage suicide appear to be declining or stabilizing (1991). Demographer Paul Glick has speculated that more couples will stay married in the next 10 to 20 years because of the fear of contracting AIDS (Glick, 1987). Another demographic expert has concluded that "the family is battered but not defeated" and that "the 1990s will be less disruptive to the family than were the 1970s and 1980s" (Ahlburg & De Vita, 1992, p. 2).

CONTEMPORARY
FAMILY PATTERNS

The following section examines four types of families that are prevalent today: nuclear families, stepfamilies, one-parent families, and gay families. Some of these contemporary family patterns, such as gay and lesbian couples with children, have created a dispute over the definition of a family. According to the Census Bureau, a family is "a group of two persons or more related by birth, marriage, or adoption, and residing together" (Benokraitis, 1993, p. 3). Some family scholars have argued for a more inclusive definition that does not include marriage (Benokraitis, 1993). Kris Franklin's thorough analysis of the legal definitions of what constitutes a family indicates that some legal scholars advocate expansion of definitions to include "previously unacknowledged family forms— such as unmarried partners, step-families, lesbian and gay families, communal households, group parents, extended families, and foster families" (1990, p. 1048). The current debate over the definition of a family is critical because any reformulation of the definition will affect decisions ranging from child custody to eligibility for federal programs (Franklin, 1990; Benokraitis, 1993).

Nuclear Families

In 1960, the majority of households were married couples with children (American households, 1992). However, recent Census Bureau data indicate that married couples with children have now lost ground to married couples without children (*American households*, 1992; Ahlburg & De Vita, 1992). In 1991, 37 percent of all families consisted of married couples with children, whereas 42 percent of all families consisted of married couples without children (Ahlburg & De Vita, 1992). Only 22 percent of these married-couple families are traditional "breadwinner/homemaker" families (Kalish, 1992, p. 2). In contrast, 61 percent of married-couple families included a male breadwinner and female homemaker in 1960 (Riche, 1991). Surprisingly, at the time of this writing, there are no current data on the number of children living with their biological parents. The most recent data are from 1985: That year, 77 percent of married couples with children were intact biological families (Ahlburg & De Vita, 1992).

However, additional evidence supports Barbara Dafoe Whitehead's conclusion about "the two-parent advantage" (1993a, p. 80). A Census Bureau analyst has found that "children living with two parents are more likely to be higher-income families, have parents that are educated, and to own their own home" (*American households*, 1992, p. 14). Moorman and Hernandez have found that intact biological families have higher family incomes than stepfamilies (1989).

Stepfamilies

High divorce and remarriage rates have resulted in a large number of stepfamilies. These families have sometimes been referred to as blended, combined, merged, remarried, mixed, reconstituted, reconstructed, or binuclear families (Ahrons & Wallisch, 1987, Wald, 1987; Di Canio, 1989; Mintz, 1991; Benokraitis, 1993). In 1987, an estimated 60 million adults and 20 million children (nearly one-third of the U.S. population) were members of a stepfamily (Larson, 1992). Because remarriage rates are higher for whites than blacks, stepfamilies are more likely to be white (Bumpass, Sweet, & Martin, 1990; Larson, 1992). Compared to biological families, stepfamilies have lower median incomes (Larson, 1992; Benokraitis, 1993). In 1987, 39 percent of stepfamilies had an annual income below $30,000, compared with 29 percent of intact families (Larson, 1992). This earnings differential is probably related to parental age and education. Stepparents are generally younger than biological or adoptive parents and are less likely to be college graduates (Larson, 1992; Benokraitis, 1993).

Because it is more common for a mother to retain custody of children following a divorce, the majority of children living in stepfamilies live with their biological mother and a stepfather (Ihinger-Tallman, 1988; Larson, 1992). However, stepfamilies vary greatly because there are many variant living and visitation arrangements for children involved in step-relationships (Jacobson, 1987; Visher & Visher, 1988). Experts generally agree that family relationships are more complex in stepfamilies than intact families because stepfamilies involve biological parents, stepparents, stepchildren, half-siblings, grandparents, stepgrandparents, and other family members (Ihinger-Tallman, 1988; Visher & Visher, 1988; Beer, 1989, 1992; Benokraitis, 1993). William Beer has referred to this as "the family maze" (1992, p. 8).

Although stepfamilies have always existed, research on stepfamilies is relatively new. Until the 1970s, few researchers studied remarriage and stepfamilies (Ihinger-Tallman, 1988). In her excellent literature review on stepfamilies, Marilyn Ihinger-Tallman (1988) noted that one of the earliest published books on remarriage was *The Old Love and the New* (Waller, 1930). During the 1950s and 1960s, scholars paid only slightly more attention to remarriage and stepparenting. Ihinger-Tallman (1988) reported that the few monographs published on this topic during this period included *Remarriage: A Study of Marriage* (Bernard, 1956), *After Divorce* (Goode, 1956), and *Stepchild in the Family* (Simon, 1964). This handful of books was supplemented by a few scholarly articles, notably those published by Bossard & Podolsky (1955), Bowerman & Irish (1962), Perry & Pfuhl (1963), and Burchinal (1964).

During the 1970s clinical psychologists and social workers became interested in the special problems encountered by stepfamilies (Ihinger-Tallman, 1988). Social scientists, however, did not increase their interest in the topic until the 1980s (Ihinger-Tallman; Coleman & Ganong, 1991). One seminal monograph published during this decade was *Remarriage and Parenting: Current Research and Theory,* a volume edited by Kay Pasley and Marilyn Ihinger-Tallman (1987). Several important books have been published since this edited volume. Emily and John Visher, founders of the Stepfamily Association of America, published a guide for therapists, counselors, and other professionals who work with stepfamilies (1988). The effects of remarriage and stepparenting on children is a topic that has generated much research. Hetherington and Arasteh have brought together papers that were presented at "The Impact of Divorce, Single Parenting and Stepparenting on Children," a 1985 conference sponsored by the National Institute of Child Health and Human Development (1988). Children's issues in stepfamilies have also been explored in a chapter written by Marilyn Ihinger-Tallman and Kay Pasley (1991), in a text authored by Australian sociologist Gay Ochiltree (1990), and in two books published by William R. Beer (1989; 1992). Beer's monograph, *Strangers in the House,* is particularly significant because it is the first extensive study of stepsibling relationships (Beer, 1992). Ihinger-Tallman's 1988 literature review has recently been updated by Coleman and Ganong in a chapter outlining the research that has been published on remarriage and stepfamilies in the 1980s (1991).

More than two hundred empirical studies have been published on remarriage and stepfamilies (Coleman & Ganong, 1991). What does this growing body of literature tell us about stepfamilies? Although negative perceptions about stepfamilies prevail, many stepfamilies successfully adapt to their new roles (Spanier & Furstenberg, 1987; Benokraitis, 1993). A longitudinal national study found that "most stepfamilies report high levels of parental satisfaction, low levels of intrafamily conflict, and relatively harmonious relations between stepparents and their children" (Spanier & Furstenberg, 1987, pp. 427-28). Stepfamilies are however subject to unique stresses. Common problems include loyalty conflicts, ambiguous roles, unrealistic expectations, and conflicts over such issues as finances and discipline (Cherlin, 1981; Macklin, 1987; Wald, 1987; Visher & Visher, 1988; Larson, 1992; Benokraitis, 1993). In addition, society has not changed to meet the special needs of stepfamilies. For example, many states only allow biological parents to authorize medical attention for a child (Wald, 1987; Larson, 1992). Even schools have not always accommodated this family form. When children are only allowed to invite two parents to a school function, children are forced to choose between their biological parents and stepparents (Di Canio, 1989).

Many findings relating to stepfamilies have conflicted. Lynn White and Alan Booth concluded that second marriages are more likely to end in divorce if there are stepchildren present (1985). However, Teresa Martin and Larry Bumpass (1989) determined that the presence of children is not a critical factor in the dissolution of second marriages. Most family scholars agree that there is a critical need for more extensive research on stepfamilies (Macklin, 1987; Coleman & Ganong, 1991). Because most studies have been based on white, middle class populations, it is imperative that future studies include minority and low-income families (Macklin, 1987). In particular, there is a need for more longitudinal studies, more precise demographic data, and research focusing on intervention and treatment strategies (Coleman & Ganong, 1991; Darden & Zimmerman, 1992).

One-Parent Families

An increase in divorce, out-of-wedlock births, and marital separation has contributed to the phenomenal growth of one-parent families. In 1990, 9 percent of all U.S. households were single-parent households, compared to 5 percent in 1970 (*American households*, 1992). There were 8.6 million one-parent families in 1990, and the majority (7 million) were headed by women (*American households*, 1992). One-third (33 percent) of these 7 million households were headed by black women (*American households*, 1992).

What are the consequences of this trend? Single mothers with children constitute the fastest growing segment of American poor (Garfinkle & McLanahan, 1986; Wattenberg, 1987; Gongla & Thompson, 1987). In 1990, single mothers and their children represented more than one-third of the poor (Benokraitis, 1993). Three monographs have made significant contributions to the scholarship on single mothers: *Single Mothers and Their Children* (Garfinkle & McLanahan, 1986); *Mothers Alone* (Kamerman & Kahn, 1988); and *Women as Single Parents* (Mulroy, 1988). These essential writings are supplemented by the literature on the economic consequences of divorce (Duncan & Hoffman, 1985; Weitzman, 1985, 1988; Hoffman & Duncan, 1988; Peterson, 1989; Zopf, 1989; Morgan, 1991; Weitzman & Maclean, 1992).

There is overwhelming evidence that female-headed households are likely to be poor and that divorce contributes to this poverty. Although most research indicates that a woman's income declines after divorce, there is disagreement over the magnitude of this economic loss (Chadwick & Heaton, 1992). In 1985, Lenore Weitzman, a leading authority on divorce, shocked researchers by reporting that the economic status of women declined by an average of 73 percent following divorce (Weitzman, 1985). Several scholars disputed Weitzman's findings. Saul Hoffman and Greg Duncan (1988) maintained that 30 percent was a more accurate estimation and other studies indicate that a woman's income declines by 20 percent the first year following divorce (Chadwick & Heaton, 1992).

One explanation for the economic distress of single mothers is the high probability that fathers will not meet their child support obligations. Fifty percent of divorced women are awarded child support (Chadwick & Heaton, 1992). However, only 75 percent of these women actually receive payments, and, then, only half of this group receive full payments (Chadwick & Heaton, 1992). Poor women are even less likely to receive payments (Chadwick & Heaton, 1992). The amount of awards has not increased appreciably between 1978 and 1987, with average awards ranging between $2,000 and $3,000 during this period (Chadwick & Heaton, 1992).

Douglas Besharov has written that "not all single mothers are created equal" (Besharov, 1992, p. 13). Never-married mothers are at greater risk of being poor than divorced mothers because only one in ten of these mothers receives child support, and awards are half as large as those received by divorced mothers (Wattenberg, 1987). In 1990, the median family income for never-married mothers was $8,337, compared to $15,762 for divorced mothers (Besharov, 1992). As a result, never-married mothers are more likely than divorced mothers to become long-term welfare recipients (Besharov, 1992).

Many researchers have studied the effects of divorce and father absence on children. In addition to the economic consequences, there are also behavioral and emotional consequences. For a summary of findings, consult Jenifer Kunz's review of the empirical literature published between 1930 and 1989 on the effects of divorce on children (Kunz, 1992). Her review builds upon an earlier review article published by David Demo and Alan Acock (1988). The psychosocial consequences of divorce are also the focus of a recently published monograph (Guttmann, 1993).

Many studies have concluded that divorce has negative consequences for children. More than one study found that children of divorce experienced greater anxiety (Hetherington, Cox, & Cox, 1979; Wyman et al., 1985). Some studies found that these children were more likely to be unhappy (Hetherington, Cox, & Cox, 1979; Guidubaldi & Perry, 1985). Other studies suggested that children in divorced families were more prone to delinquent behavior (Stolberg & Anker, 1983; Rickel & Langner, 1985; Kalter et al., 1985). Numerous studies have found that divorce has a negative effect on children's school behavior and achievement (Kinard & Reinherz, 1984; Kinard & Reinherz, 1986; Peterson & Zill, 1986).

Several studies have examined the long-term consequences of divorce. Verna Keith and Barbara Finlay found that divorce negatively impacts children's educational attainment (Keith & Finlay, 1988). One of the most important longitudinal studies is The California Children of Divorce Study, Judith Wallerstein's 15 study of 131 divorced children from 60 families. The results are reported in *Second Chances: Men, Women, and Children a Decade After Divorce*, a book Wallerstein wrote with the assistance of Sandra Blakeslee (1989). Some of the study's findings are disturbing. For example, the authors concluded that "almost half of the children entered adulthood as worried, underachieving, self-deprecating, and sometimes angry young men and women" (p. 299). Two recent studies on the long-term consequences of divorce have been more promising. Amato and Booth studied the impact of parental divorce on adult well-being and concluded that "a divorce causing minimal disruption to a child's life provides fewer long-term risks than does a marriage perceived by the offspring to be unhappy" (1991, p. 913). Based on longitudinal British and American studies of the effects of divorce on children, Andrew Cherlin and his colleagues determined that many behavioral and achievement problems were preexisting, especially in boys (1991).

Divorce research is still in its infancy. Jenifer Kunz (1992) noted that most results are based on small samples rather than nationally representative samples. In addition, adolescents and adults have not been widely studied because the focus has been on children. Kunz also identified a bias toward negative outcomes. Consequently, researchers in this area need to develop more objective measurement techniques.

Lesbian and Gay Parents

One out of five gay men and one out of three lesbian women have been previously married and have children from that marriage (Benokraitis, 1993). Many lesbian women have become mothers through adoption or artificial insemination (Pies, 1990). In addition, a growing number of homosexual men have become adoptive or foster parents (Harry, 1988). Researchers estimate that the number of gay and lesbian parents ranges from 6 to 14 million (Turner, Scadden, & Harris, 1990). As a result, increased attention has been given to gay and lesbian parents.

The literature on homosexual parenting is sparse when compared to the volume of literature on other contemporary family structures. More has been published on lesbian mothers than gay fathers. The revised edition of Delores Maggiore's guide to the literature on lesbianism can be used to locate books and articles published between 1976 and 1991 on lesbian families and lesbian mothers (Maggiore, 1992). The few existing studies on gay fathers have been summarized in a review article by Frederick Bozett, a leading authority on gay fathers (1989).

An earlier volume edited by Bozett provides an excellent introduction to the special problems experienced by homosexual parents (Bozett, 1987). Many lesbian and gay parents worry about losing their jobs, fear they will lose child custody or visitation rights, and are stigmatized by society. What do we know about the children of gay parents and the effects of homosexual parenting? Research indicates that most children of gay parents accept their parents' homosexuality (Benokraitis, 1993). There is no evidence that homosexual parenting impacts negatively on children (Falk, 1989; Gottman, 1990; Turner, Scadden, & Harris, 1990; Benokraitis, 1993). In fact, research has indicated that there are few differences between heterosexual and homosexual parents (Kirkpatrick, 1990; Turner, Scadden, & Harris, 1990; Benokraitis, 1993).

ISSUES FOR FAMILIES IN THE
1990s AND BEYOND

Family Values

In an interview, Barbara Dafoe Whitehead commented that she regretted the debate that Dan Quayle's Murphy Brown comment initiated because "The issue of family values was politicized and trivialized by politicians and the media" (*The crisis of the absent father*, 1993, p. 58). During the height of the controversy in 1992, Stephanie Coontz urged scholars to "bring realism to the debates on family values" (1993b, p. B1). What do researchers know about family values?

Surveys have consistently indicated that Americans value their families. Surveys taken from 1976 through 1986 found that a "good marriage and family life" was the top priority of high school seniors (Glenn, 1992). In a 1989 national survey of 200,000 incoming college freshmen, 69 percent of the students responded that raising a family was "an essential or very important" future goal (Benokraitis, 1993). Surveys have also indicated that family is important to adults. The 1989 Massachusetts Mutual American Family Value Study found that such objectives as "having a happy marriage" and "being able to provide emotional support to your family" ranked much higher than such objectives as "having nice things" and "being free from obligations so I can do whatever I want to" (Glenn, 1992). In a 1991 Gallup poll of 477 adults between the ages of 26 and 45, 93 percent reported that family life was "very important" to them and 81 percent indicated that it would be more important to them in the next five years (Benokraitis, 1993).

Why is there a gap between Americans' values and actions? Sociology professor Norval Glenn concluded that "some of it is probably due to economic, technological, and demographic trends that make it harder for families to stay together" (Glenn, 1992, p. 34). Glenn also believes that some of it is due to recent attitudinal changes. For example, surveys have indicated an increased acceptance of divorce. In order to close this gap between words and deeds, Americans will have to find a balance between individualistic goals and family responsibilities. Glenn asserts that "bridging the gap between family realities and personal expectations will be an important issue for families in the 1990s" (1992, p. 30). Kathleen Madigan has written that "no one is against family values," but because "they'll cost billions, . . . no one wants to pay for them" (1992, p. 88). Madigan's argument is that society needs to devote more money to social programs if it values the family. However, the reality is that neither the public nor the private sector has the resources to universally improve the schools, make neighborhoods safe, or increase wages to help families make ends meet. Barbara Dafoe Whitehead has been more optimistic, noting a recent shift away from individualism toward family commitment.

Whitehead and her colleagues have termed this "balance between '50s family values and '80s individualism," the "new familism" (1993b, p. 61-62).

Public Policy Responses to the Changing Family

In 1981, President Ronald Reagan signed a budget bill that included severe cuts in welfare, food stamps, Medicaid, and unemployment insurance (Waldrop & Exter, 1991). Urie Bronfenbrennner, one of the founders of Head Start, wrote that this massive reduction in funding for poverty assistance programs represented a political and social turning point in America (Bronfenbrenner, 1987). First, these cuts were made at a time when child poverty rates were rising. Second, these cuts signaled the public's disenchantment with the social welfare policies that were a legacy of the Johnson Administration's War on Poverty. Third, these cuts were part of a shifting of social responsibility from the federal government to state and local government (see chapter 2 for a detailed analysis of the development of public policies to assist families).

At the federal level, the government has introduced numerous bills to help families. Proposed legislation in recent years has covered child care, family leave, child support, and welfare reform. Although many pro-family bills have failed to pass Congress or have been vetoed by a president, there have been a few successes. The Family Support Act of 1988 requires states to record the Social Security numbers of both parents when issuing a birth certificate. This paternal identification is regarded as "the essential first step toward making a legally binding child-support award" (Whitehead, 1993a, p. 70). The Omnibus Reconciliation Act of 1990 will help states improve and expand the supply of day care, before- and after-school care, and early childhood education programs (Reeves, 1992). President Bill Clinton signed the Family and Medical Leave Act on February 5, 1993. This legislation took effect in August 1993 and guarantees workers at companies with more than 50 employees the right to take up to 12 weeks of unpaid leave in order to care for a child or ill family member.

Child support will continue to be a major public policy issue. Some states, such as Massachusetts, have taken dramatic measures, including "posters of 'deadbeat dads' on the six o'clock news" (Whitehead, 1993a, p. 71). Other policy experts have advocated a universal child support assurance program that would guarantee an established level of support for all single parents with dependent children (Whitehead, 1993a). Under this controversial scheme, the federal government would collect payments and send monthly checks to the parent with the child. If a parent failed to meet his or her child support obligation, the cost would be absorbed by taxpayers. There have also been proposals to reform the welfare system (Whitehead, 1993a). Many policy analysts argue that welfare reform is essential in order to eliminate the existing disincentives to marry. There is a strong likelihood that the Clinton administration will make changes to the welfare system because President Bill Clinton advocates the imposition of two-year limits for Aid to Families with Dependent Children (AFDC).

Corporate Responses to the Changing Family

Many corporations have implemented family-friendly policies and programs in order to help employees juggle work and family responsibilities. Some employers have established on-site or near-site child care, financial assistance for off-site child care, parental leave plans, and flexible work arrangements (Auerbach, 1988; Nollen, 1989; Solomon, 1991; Losey, 1992; Reeves, 1992; Tarrant, 1992). Flexible work arrangements include a range of options: flexible work schedules; compressed work weeks; job sharing; part-time work; and telecommuting. A survey of 521 of the largest American companies found that 93 percent of the companies surveyed had some form of alternative work arrangements in place, with part-time work and flexible scheduling being the most common options (Christensen, 1990). A recent study, however, indicates that not all working mothers have access to family-friendly work benefits (*Which moms fare best?*, 1993). The Employee Benefit Research Institute found that women who are highly educated, higher paid, and in professional occupations are more likely to be offered at least one family-friendly benefit, such as flexible scheduling or assistance with child care.

One issue that will receive increased attention in the 1990s is the revision of employee benefit packages to include nontraditional families. For example, survivors' benefits are generally only extended to survivors if there has been a legal marriage (Rubin, 1988). This affects unmarried cohabiting partners and homosexual couples. Such issues as health insurance can also be cumbersome for stepfamilies. One researcher concluded that "negotiating the health-care bureaucracy for an ex-spouse or stepchildren can be a nightmare" (Larson, 1992).

SUMMARY OF ISSUES AND TRENDS

In their revised edition of *What's Happening to the American Family?*, authors Sar Levitan, Richard Belous, and Frank Gallo (1988) outlined three trends that have polarized society into the "haves" and the "have nots": the growth in female-headed households, increased out-of-wedlock births, and rising child poverty rates. All three developments are linked to changes in family structure. Although a typical 1950s family consisted of a male breadwinner, female homemaker, and two or more children, contemporary families are diverse. Recent trends in American families include increasing numbers of stepfamilies and single-parent families.

It is neither realistic nor desirable for America to return to the lifestyle of the 1950s. Kathleen Madigan has calculated the economic costs of recreating families modeled after 1950s situation comedies. If one parent stayed at home to raise children, the economy would lose more than 14 million workers and a critical labor shortage would result (Madigan, 1992). Furthermore, a stay-at-home parent is a luxury that most families cannot afford. Additionally, such scholars as Arlene Skolnick and Stephanie Coontz have reminded us that that the 1950s were never a "golden age" (Skolnick, 1991; Coontz, 1993a). Even more conservative scholars, such as David Popenoe, have asked, "How can we uphold the virtues of the nuclear family without returning to the lifestyles of the 1950s . . . ?" (1992, p. 35).

The answer appears to be a cooperative effort by individuals, the private sector, and government (Cherlin, 1988; Popenoe, 1988; Blankenhorn, Bayme, & Elshtain, 1990). First, there is a growing public sentiment that individuals must take more responsibility for the families they create. Employers can help families by adopting family-friendly work policies, such as flexible scheduling, part-time work, job sharing, and parental leave. Corporations can acknowledge nontraditional families by extending benefits to stepchildren and unmarried partners. The government can strengthen families by enforcing child support awards, improving access to child care, and increasing job opportunities.

Steven Mintz has written that "the United States is a society deeply divided over the meaning of what constitutes a family and what role government should take in strengthening American families. Given this deep sense of division, it appears likely that the family will remain a major political battleground" (Mintz, 1991, p. 208). The reality is that American families will continue to be pluralistic in structure. In order to strengthen families and bridge the gap between the "haves" and the "have nots" in American society, America has to move beyond the polarized debate over family values.

REFERENCES

Adams, B. N. 1988. Fifty years of family research: What does it mean? *Journal of Marriage and the Family* 50: 5-17.

Ahlburg, D. A., & De Vita, C. J. 1992. New realities of the American family. *Population Bulletin* 47 (August): 1-44.

Ahrons, C. R., & Wallisch, L. 1987. Parenting in the binuclear family: Relationships between biological and stepparents. In Pasley, K., & Ihinger-Tallman, M., eds., *Remarriage and stepparenting: Current research and theory.* New York: Guilford Press, 257-72.

Amato, P. R., & Booth, A. 1991. Consequences of parental divorce and marital unhappiness for adult well-being. *Social Forces* 69: 895-914.

Ambry, M., & Russell, C. 1992. *The official guide to the American marketplace.* Ithaca, NY: New Strategist Publications & Consulting.

American households. 1992. *American Demographics Desk Reference Series* 3 (July): 1-24.

Auerbach, J. D. 1988. *In the business of child care: Employer initiatives and working women.* New York: Praeger.

Bane, M. J. 1976. *Here to stay: American families in the twentieth century.* New York: Basic Books.

Beer, W. R. 1989. *Strangers in the house: The world of stepsiblings and half-siblings.* New Brunswick, NJ: Transaction.

———. 1992. *American stepfamilies.* New Brunswick, NJ: Transaction Publishers.

Benokraitis, N. V. 1993. *Marriages and families: Changes, choices, and constraints.* Englewood Cliffs, NJ: Prentice-Hall.

Bernard, J. 1956. *Remarriage: A study of marriage.* New York: Russell & Russell.

Besharov, D. J. 1992. Not all single mothers are created equal. *The American Enterprise* 3 (September/October): 13-17.

Blankenhorn, D.; Bayme, S.; & Elshtain, J. B., eds. 1990. *Rebuilding the nest: A new commitment to the American family.* Milwaukee, WI: Family Service America.

Bossard, J. H. S., & Podolsky, E. 1955. The emotional problems of the stepchild. *Mental Hygiene* 39: 49-53.

Bowerman, C. E., & Irish, D. P. 1962. Some relationships of stepchildren to their parents. *Marriage and Family Living* 24: 113-21.

Bozett, F. W. 1989. Gay fathers: A review of the literature. *Journal of Homosexuality* 18: 137-62.

Bozett, F. W., ed. 1987. *Gay and lesbian parents.* New York: Praeger.

Broderick, C. B. 1988. To arrive where we started: The field of family studies in the 1930s. *Journal of Marriage and the Family* 50: 569-84.

Bronfenbrenner, U. 1987. Family support: The quiet revolution. In Kagan, S. L.; Powell, D. R.; Weissbourd, B.; & Zigler, E. F., eds., *America's family support programs: Perspectives and prospects.* New Haven, CT: Yale University Press, xi-xvii.

Bumpass, L. L., & Sweet, J. A. 1989. National estimates of cohabitation. *Demography* 26: 615-25.

Bumpass, L.; Sweet, J.; & Martin, T. C. 1990. Changing patterns of remarriage. *Journal of Marriage and the Family* 52: 747-56.

Burchinal, L. G. 1964. Characteristics of adolescents from unbroken, broken, and reconstituted families. *Journal of Marriage and the Family* 24: 44-51.

Chadwick, B. A., & Heaton, T. B., eds. 1992. *Statistical handbook on the American family.* Phoenix: Oryx Press.

Cherlin, A. J. 1981. *Marriage, divorce, remarriage.* Cambridge: Harvard University Press.

———. 1992. *Marriage, divorce, remarriage.* Rev. and enl. ed. Cambridge: Harvard University Press.

Cherlin, A. J., ed. 1988. *The changing American family and public policy.* Washington, DC: Urban Institute Press.

Cherlin, A. J., et al. 1991. Longitudinal studies of effects of divorce on children in Great Britain and the United States. *Science,* 7 June, 1386-89.

Christensen, K. 1990. Here we go into the "high-flex" era. *Across the Board* 27 (July/August): 22-23.

Coleman, M., & Ganong, L. H. 1991. Remarriage and stepfamily research in the 1980s: Increased interest in an old family form. In Booth, A., ed., *Contemporary families: Looking forward, looking back*. Minneapolis, MN: National Council on Family Relations, 192-207.

Coontz, S. 1988. *The social origins of private life: A history of American families 1600-1900*. New York: Verso.

———. 1992a. *The way we never were: American families and the nostalgia trap*. New York: Basic Books.

———. 1992b. Let scholars bring realism to the debate on family values. *Chronicle of Higher Education*, 21 October, B1-B2.

The crisis of the absent father. 1993. *Parents*, July, 54-56, 58.

Crispell, D. 1992. Myths of the 1950s. *American Demographics* 14 (August): 38-43.

Darden, E. C., & Zimmerman, T. S. 1992. Blended families: A decade review, 1979 to 1990. *Family Therapy* 19: 25-31.

Davidson, N. 1990. Life without father: America's greatest social catastrophe. *Policy Review* 51: 40-44.

Degler, C. N. 1980. *At odds: Women and family in America from the Revolution to the present*. New York: Oxford University Press.

Demo, D. H., & Acock, A. C. 1988. The impact of divorce on children. *Journal of Marriage and the Family* 50: 619-48.

Di Canio, M. 1989. Stepfamilies. In *Encyclopedia of marriage, divorce, and the family*. New York: Facts on File, 456-59.

Duncan, G. J., & Hoffman, S. D. 1985. A reconsideration of the economic consequences of marital dissolution. *Demography* 22: 485-97.

Eggebeen, D. J., & Lichter, D. T. 1991. Race, family structure, and changing poverty among American children. *American Sociological Review* 56: 801-17.

Falk, P. J. 1989. Lesbian mothers: Psychosocial assumptions in family law. *American Psychologist* 44: 941-47.

Franklin, K. 1990. "A family like any other family": Alternative methods of defining family in law. *New York University Review of Law & Social Change* 18: 1027-87.

Garfinkle, I., & McLanahan, S. S. 1986. *Single mothers and their children: A new American dilemma*. Washington, DC: Urban Institute Press.

Gibbs, N. R. 1993. Bringing up father. *Time*, 28 June, 52-61.

Glenn, N. D. 1992. What does family mean? *American Demographics* 14 (June): 30-37.

Glick, P. C. 1987. A demographer looks again at American families. *Journal of Family Issues* 8: 437-39.

Gongla, P. A., & Thompson, E. H. 1987. Single-parent families. In Sussman, M. B., & Steinmetz, S. K., eds., *Handbook of marriage and the family*. New York: Plenum Press, 397-418.

Goode, W. J. 1956. *After divorce*. Glencoe, IL: Free Press.

Googins, B. K. 1991. *Work/family conflicts: Private lives—public responses*. New York: Auburn House.

Gordon, M. 1978. *The American family: Past, present, and future.* New York: Random House.

Gottman, J. S. 1990. Children of gay and lesbian parents. In Bozett, F. W., & Sussman, M. B., eds., *Homosexuality and the family.* Binghamton, NY: Harrington Park Press, 177-96.

Guidubaldi, J., & Perry, J. D. 1985. Divorce and mental health sequelae for children: A two-year follow up of a nationwide sample. *Journal of the American Academy of Child Psychiatry* 24: 531-37.

Guttmann, J. 1993. *Divorce in psychosocial perspective: Theory and research.* Hillsdale, NJ: Lawrence Erlbaum.

Harry, J. 1988. Some problems of gay/lesbian families. In Chilman, C. S.; Nunnally, E. W.; & Cox, F. M., eds., *Variant family forms.* Newbury Park, CA: Sage, 96-113.

Hatch, L. R. 1992. American families. In *Encyclopedia of sociology,* vol. 1. New York: Maxwell-Macmillan, 65-74.

Haub, C. 1992. Storms over norms: Single life, empty nest, or married with children? *Population Today* 20: 6-7.

Hess, R. D., & Camara, K. A. 1979. Post-divorce family relationships as mediating factors in the consequences of divorce for children. *Journal of Social Issues* 35: 79-96.

Hetherington, E. M., & Arasteh, J. D., eds. 1988. *Impact of divorce, single parenting, and stepparenting on children.* Hillsdale, NJ: Lawrence Erlbaum.

Hetherington, E. M.; Cox. M.; & Cox, R. 1979. Play and social interaction in children following divorce. *Journal of Social Issues* 35: 26-49.

Hochschild, A. R. 1989. *The second shift: Working parents and the revolution at home.* New York: Viking.

Hofferth, S. L. 1987. Implications of family trends for children: A research perspective. *Educational Leadership* 44: 78-84.

Hoffman, S. D., & Duncan, G. J. 1988. What are the economic consequences of divorce? *Demography* 25: 641-45.

Ihinger-Tallman, M. 1988. Research on stepfamilies. *Annual Review of Sociology* 14: 25-48.

Ihinger-Tallman, M., & Pasley, L. 1991. Children in stepfamilies. In Edwards, J. N., & Demo, D. H., eds., *Marriage and family in transition.* Boston: Allyn & Bacon.

Jacobson, D. S. 1987. Family type, visiting patterns, and children's behavior in the stepfamily: A linked family system. In Pasley, K., & Ihinger-Tallman, M., eds., *Remarriage and stepparenting: Current research and theory.* New York: Guilford Press, 257-72.

Kalish, S. 1992. American families: Greater diversity but slower change ahead. *Population Today* 20 (November): 1-2.

Kalter, N.; Riemer, B.; Brickman, A.; & Chen, J. W. 1985. Implications of prenatal divorce for female development. *Journal of the American Academy of Child Psychiatry* 24: 538-44.

Kamerman, S. B., & Kahn, A. J. 1988. *Mothers alone: Strategies for a time of change.* Dover, MA: Auburn House.

Keith, V. M., & Finlay, B. 1988. The impact of parental divorce on children's educational attainment, marital timing, and likelihood of divorce. *Journal of Marriage and the Family* 50: 797-809.

Kellogg, S., & Mintz, S. 1993. Family structures. In Cayton, M. K.; Gorn, E. J.; & Williams, P. W., eds., *Encyclopedia of American social history*, vol. 3. New York: Charles Scribner's Sons, 1925-44.

Kinard, E. M., & Reinherz, H. 1984. Marital disruption: Effects of behavioral and emotional functioning in children. *Journal of Family Issues* 5: 90-115.

———. 1986. Effects of marital disruption on children's school attitude and achievement. *Journal of Marriage and the Family* 48: 285-93.

Kirkpatrick, M. J. 1990. Homosexuality and parenting. In Spurlock, J., & Robinowitz, C. B., eds., *Women's progress: Promises and problems*. New York: Plenum Press, 205-22.

Kunz, J. 1992. The effects of divorce on children. In Bahr, S. J., ed., *Family research: A sixty-year review, 1930-1990*, vol. 2. New York: Lexington Books, 325-76.

Larson, J. 1992. Understanding stepfamilies. *American Demographics* 14 (July): 36-40.

Levitan, S. A.; Belous, R. S.; & Gallo, F. 1988. *What's happening to the American family?: Tensions, hopes, realities*. Rev. ed. Baltimore: Johns Hopkins University Press.

London, K. A., & Wilson, B. F. 1988. D-I-V-O-R-C-E. *American Demographics* 10 (October): 22-26.

Losey, M. R. 1992. Workplace policies should be family-friendly. *Modern Office Technology*, May, 84-85.

Macklin, E. D. 1987. Nontraditional family forms. In Sussman, M. B., & Steinmetz, S. K., eds., *Handbook of marriage and the family*. New York: Plenum Press, 317-53.

Madigan, K. 1992. You want "family values"?: They'll cost billions. *Business Week*, 28 September, 88.

Maggiore, D. J. 1992. *Lesbianism: An annotated bibliography and guide to the literature, 1976-1991*. 2nd ed. Metuchen, NJ: Scarecrow Press.

Martin, T. C., & Bumpass, L. L. 1989. Recent trends in marital disruption. *Demography* 26: 37-51.

Mintz, S. 1991. New rules: Postwar families (1955-present). In Hawes, J. M., & Nybakken, E. I., eds., *American families: A research guide and historical handbook*. New York: Greenwood, 183-220.

Mintz, S., & Kellogg, S. 1988. *Domestic revolutions: A social history of American family life*. New York: Free Press.

Moorman, J. E., & Hernandez, D. J. 1989. Married-couple families with step, adopted, and biological children. *Demography* 26 (May): 267-77.

Morgan, L. A. 1991. *After marriage ends: Economic consequences for midlife women*. Newbury Park, CA: Sage.

Mulroy, E. A., ed. 1988. *Women as single parents: Confronting institutional barriers in the courts, the workplace, and the housing market*. Dover, MA: Auburn House.

The new American family: Significant and diversified lifestyles. 1992. New York: Simmons Market Research Bureau.

Nollen, S. D. 1989. The work-family dilemma: How HR managers can help. *Personnel Journal* 66 (May): 25-30.

Nye, F. I. 1988. Fifty years of family research, 1937-1987. *Journal of Marriage and the Family* 50: 305-16.

Ochiltree, G. 1990. *Children in stepfamilies.* New York: Prentice-Hall.

Pasley, K., & Ihinger-Tallman, M., eds. 1987. *Remarriage and stepparenting: Current research and theory.* New York: Guilford Press.

Perry, J. B., & Pfuhl, E. H. 1963. Adjustment of children in "solo" and "remarriage homes." *Journal of Marriage and the Family* 25: 221-223.

Peterson, J. L., & Zill, N. 1986. Marital disruption, parent-child relationships, and behavior problems in children. *Journal of Marriage and the Family* 48: 295-307.

Peterson, R. R. 1989. *Women, work, and divorce.* Albany, NY: University of New York Press.

Pies, C. A. 1990. Lesbians and the choice to parent. In Bozett, F. W., & Sussman, M. B., eds., *Homosexuality and family relations.* Binghamton, NY: Harrington Park Press, 137-54.

Popenoe, D. 1988. *Disturbing the nest: Family change and decline in modern societies.* New York: A. de Gruyter.

———. 1991. Flight from the nuclear family: Trends of the past three decades. *The Public Perspective: A Roper Center Review of Public Opinion and Polling* 2: 19-20.

———. 1992. Fostering the new familism: A goal for America. *The Responsive Community: Rights and Responsibilities* 2: 31-39.

Quayle, D. 1992. Restoring basic values: Strengthening the family. *Vital Speeches of the Day,* 1 June, 517-20.

Reeves, D. L. 1992. *Child care crisis: A reference handbook.* Santa Barbara: ABC-CLIO.

Riche, M. F. 1991. The future of the family. *American Demographics* 13 (March): 44-46.

Rickel, A. U., & Langner, T. S. 1985. Short-term and long-term effects of marital disruption on children. *American Journal of Community Psychology* 13: 599-611.

Robinson, J. P. 1988. Who's doing the housework? *American Demographics* 10 (December): 24-28, 63.

Rodgers, W. L., & Thornton, A. 1985. Changing patterns of first marriage in the United States. *Demography* 22: 265-79.

Rubin, R. H. 1988. Public policies and variant family forms. In Chilman, C. S.; Nunally, E. W.; & Cox, F. M., eds., *Variant family forms.* Newbury Park, CA: Sage, 254-89.

Santi, L. L. 1987. Change in the structure and size of American households: 1970 to 1985. *Journal of Marriage and the Family* 49: 833-37.

Seward, R. R. 1978. *The American family: A demographic history.* Beverly Hills, CA: Sage.

Simon, A. W. 1964. *Stepchild in the family*. New York: Odyssey Press.

Skolnick, A. 1991. *Embattled paradise: The American family in an age of uncertainty*. New York: Basic Books.

Solomon, C. M. 1991. 24-hour employees. *Personnel Journal* 70 (August): 56-63.

Spanier, G. B., & Furstenberg, F. F. 1987. Remarriage and reconstituted families. In Sussman, M. B., & Steinmetz, S. K., eds., *Handbook of marriage and the family*. New York: Plenum Press, 419-36.

Stolberg, A. L., & Anker, J. M. 1983. Cognitive and behavioral changes in children resulting from parental divorce and consequent environmental changes. *Journal of Divorce* 7: 23-41.

Sweet, J. A., & Bumpass, L. L. 1987. *American families and households*. New York: Russell Sage Foundation.

Tarrant, S. M. 1992. How companies can become more family friendly. *Journal of Compensation and Benefits* 7 (January/February): 18-21.

Teachman, J. D.; Polonko, K. A.; & Scanzoni, J. 1987. Demography of the family. in Sussman, M. B., & Steinmetz, S. K., eds., *Handbook of marriage and the family*. New York: Plenum Press, 3-35.

Thornton, A. 1988. Cohabitation and marriage in the 1980s. *Demography* 25: 497-508.

Townsend, B., & O'Neil, K. 1990. American women get mad. *American Demographics* 12 (August): 26-32.

Turner, P. H.; Scadden, L.; & Harris, M. B. 1990. Parenting in gay and lesbian families. *Journal of Gay & Lesbian Psychotherapy* 1: 55-66.

Visher, E. B., & Visher, J. S. 1988. *Old loyalties, new ties: Therapeutic strategies with stepfamilies*. New York: Brunner/Mazel.

Wald, E. 1987. Family: Stepfamilies. In *Encyclopedia of social work*, vol. 1. 18th ed. Silver Spring, MD: National Association of Social Workers, 548-55.

Waldrop, J., & Exter, T. 1991. The legacy of the 1980s. *American Demographics* 13 (March): 32-38.

Waller, W. 1930. *The old love and the new*. Carbondale: Southern Illinois University Press.

Wallerstein, J. S., & Blakeslee, S. 1989. *Second chances: Men, women, and children a second decade after divorce*. New York: Ticknor & Fields.

Wattenberg, E. 1987. Family: One parent. In *Encyclopedia of social work*, vol. 1. 18th ed. Silver Spring, MD: National Association of Social Workers, 548-55.

Weitzman, L. J. 1985. *The divorce revolution: The unexpected social and economic consequences for women and children in America*. New York: Free Press.

———. 1988. Women and children last: The social and economic consequences of divorce law reforms. In Dornbusch, S. M., & Strober, M. H., eds., *Feminism, children, and the new families*. New York: Guilford Press, 212-48.

Weitzman, L. J., & Maclean, M. 1992. *Economic consequences of divorce: The international perspective*. New York: Oxford University Press.

Wells, R. V. 1982. *Revolutions in Americans' lives: A demographic perspective on the history of Americans, their families, and their society*. Westport, CT: Greenwood Press.

————. 1985. *Uncle Sam's family: Issues in and perspectives on American demographic history*. Albany: State University of New York Press.

Which moms fare best? 1993. *Working Mother*, April, 6.

White, L. K., & Booth, A. 1985. The quality and stability of remarriage: The role of stepchildren. *American Sociological Review* 50: 689-98.

Whitehead, B. D. 1993a. Dan Quayle was right. *The Atlantic Monthly*, April, 47-84.

————. 1993b. The new family values: Striking a balance between '50s family values and '80s individualism. *Utne Reader*, May/June, 61-66.

Wyman, P. A.; Cowen, E. L.; Hightower, A. D.; & Pedro-Carroll, J. L. 1985. Perceived competence, self-esteem, and anxiety in latency-aged children of divorce. *Journal of Clinical Child Psychology* 14: 20-26.

Zinn, M. B., & Eitzen, D. S. 1990. *Diversity in families*. 2nd ed. New York: HarperCollins.

Zopf, P. E. 1989. *American women in poverty*. New York: Greenwood Press.

SOURCES OF
ADDITIONAL INFORMATION

Bibliographies

Gouke, M. N., & Rollins, A. M. 1990. *One-parent children, the growing minority: A research guide*. New York: Garland.

Sadler, J. D. 1988. *Families in transition: An annotated bibliography*. Hamden, CT: Archon Books.

Juvenile Literature

Berman, C. 1982. *What am I doing in a stepfamily?* Secaucus, NJ: Lyle Stuart.

Blume, J. 1972. *It's not the end of the world*. New York: Bradbury Press.

Bradley, B. 1985. *Where do I belong?: A kids' guide to stepfamilies*. New York: J. B. Lippincott.

Brown, L. K., & Brown, M. 1988. *Dinosaurs divorce: A guide for changing families*. New York: Little, Brown.

Cohen, S., & Cohen, D. 1989. *When someone you know is gay*. New York: M. Evans.

Gardner, R. A. 1983. *The boys and girls book about one-parent families*. Cresskill, NJ: Creative Therapeutics.

———. 1985. *The boys and girls book about stepfamilies*. Cresskill, NJ: Creative Therapeutics.

———. 1992. *The boys and girls book about divorce*. New York: J. Aronson.

Hazen, B. S. 1977. *Two homes to live in: A child's-eye view of divorce*. New York: Human Sciences Press.

Johnson, L. C. 1992. *Everything you need to know about your parents' divorce*. New York: Rosen.

Lehrman, R. 1990. *Separations*. New York: Viking.

Mayle, P. 1988. *Why are we getting a divorce?* New York: Harmony Books.

Newman, L. 1989. *Heather has two mommies*. Boston: Alyson Wonderland.

Nickman, S. L. 1986. *When mom and dad divorce*. New York: Messner.

Prokop, M. 1986. *Divorce happens to the nicest kids: A self help guide for kids (3-15) and adults*. Warren, OH: Alegra House.

Steel, D. 1989. *Martha's new daddy*. New York: Delacorte.

Watson, J. W. 1988. *Sometimes a family has to split up*. New York: Crown.

Willhoite, M. 1990. *Daddy's roommate*. Boston: Alyson Wonderland.

Nonprint Materials

For richer, for poorer. 1988. Montreal: National Film Board of Canada. 30-minute videotape or film.

Haley's home movie. Van Nuys, CA: AIMS Media. 23-minute videotape.

A kid's guide to divorce. Westport, CT: Words, Inc. 36-minute videotape.

A kid's guide to families. Westport, CT: Words, Inc. 35-minute film.

Playing for keeps. 1990. Montreal: National Film Board of Canada. 44-minute videotape or film.

Shattered dishes: Packing up the pieces of our parents' divorce. Rockville, MD: Deborah Ellmen. 28-minute videotape.

Teenage mothers: A global crisis. 1990. Washington, DC: Better World Society. 55-minute film.

Teens in changing families: Making it work. 1989. Pleasantville, NY: Sunburst Communications. 25-minute videotape.

Resources for Families

Artlip, M. A., et al. 1993. *The new American family.* Lancaster, PA: Starburst.

Bloomfield, H. H., & Kory, R. B. 1993. *Making peace in your stepfamily: Surviving and thriving as parents and stepparents.* New York: Hyperion.

Corley, R. 1990. *The final closet: The gay parents' guide for coming out to their children.* Miami: Editech.

Crosby, F. 1991. *Juggling: The unexpected advantages of balancing career and home for women and their families.* New York: Free Press.

Edelman, M. W. 1992. *The measure of our success: A letter to my children and yours.* Boston: Beacon Press.

Fassel, D. 1991. *Growing up divorced: A road to healing for adult children of divorce.* New York: Pocket Books.

Lansky, V. 1989. *Vicki Lansky's divorce book for parents.* New York: New American Library.

Martin, A. 1993. *The lesbian and gay parenting handbook: Creating and raising our families.* New York: HarperCollins.

Pollack, S., & Vaughn, J., eds. 1987. *Politics of the heart: A lesbian parenting anthology.* Ithaca, NY: Firebrand Books.

Rafkin, L. 1990. *Different mothers: Sons and daughters of lesbians talk about their lives.* Pittsburgh: Cleis Press.

Schulenburg, J. 1985. *Gay parenting: A complete guide for gay men and lesbians with children.* Garden City, NY: Doubleday.

Visher, E. B., & Visher, J. S. 1991. *How to win as a stepfamily.* 2nd ed. New York: Brunner/Mazel.

Indexes/Databases

ABI/INFORM
UMI/Data Courier
620 S. Third St.
Louisville, KY 40202-2475
1-800-626-2853
Online and CD-ROM formats

Business Periodicals Index
H. W. Wilson Company
950 University Ave.
Bronx, NY 10452
212-588-8400
Print, online, and CD-ROM formats

Current Index to Journals in Education (CIJE)
Oryx Press
4041 N. Central Ave. at Indian School Rd.
Phoenix, AZ 85012-3397
602-265-2651
Print, online, and CD-ROM formats

Family Resources
Database Information
National Council on Family Relations
3989 Central Ave. NE, Ste. 550
Minneapolis, MN 55421
612-781-9331
Online format

Inventory of Marriage & Family Literature
Corwin Press, Inc.
2455 Teller Rd.
Newbury Park, CA 91320
805-499-0721
Print format

PAIS INTERNATIONAL
Public Affairs Information Service, Inc.
521 W. 43rd St.
New York, NY 10036
212-736-6629
Print, online, and CD-ROM formats

Population Index
Princeton University
Office of Population Research
21 Prospect Ave.
Princeton, NJ 08544
609-258-4948
Print, online, and CD-ROM formats

Psychological Abstracts
American Psychological Association
750 First St. NE
Washington, DC 20002-4242
202-336-5500
Print, online, and CD-ROM formats

Sage Family Studies Abstracts
Sage Publications
2455 Teller Rd.
Newbury Park, CA 91320
805-499-0721
Print format

Social Sciences Index
H. W. Wilson Company
950 University Ave.
Bronx, NY 10452
215-588-8400
Print, online, and CD-ROM formats

Social Work Abstracts
National Association of Social Workers
7981 Eastern Ave.
Silver Spring, MD 20910
301-565-0333
Print, online, and CD-ROM formats

Sociological Abstracts, Inc.
P.O. Box 22206
San Diego, CA 92122
619-695-8803
Print, online, and CD-ROM formats

Periodicals

American Demographics
Box 168
Ithaca, NY 14851-0068
Monthly

American Journal of Sociology
University of Chicago Press, Journals
Division
5720 S. Woodlawn Ave.
Chicago, IL 60637
Bimonthly

American Sociological Review
American Sociological Association
1722 North St. NW
Washington, DC 20036
Bimonthly

Demography
Population Association of America
1722 North St. NW
Washington, DC 20036-2983
Quarterly

Family Process
29 Walter Hammond Pl., Ste. A
Waldwick, NJ 07463
Quarterly

*Family Relations: Journal of Applied
Family and Child Studies*
National Council on Family Relations
3938 Central Ave. NE, Ste. 550
Minneapolis, MN 55421
Quarterly

Journal of Family History
JAI Press, Inc.
55 Old Post Rd., No. 2, Box 1678
Greenwich, CT 06836-1678
Quarterly

Journal of Family Issues
Sage Publications, Inc.
2455 Teller Rd.
Newbury Park, CA 91320
Quarterly

Journal of Family Psychology
American Psychological Association
750 First St. NE
Washington, DC 20002-4242
Quarterly

Journal of Homosexuality
Haworth Press
10 Alice St.
Binghamton, NY 13904
Quarterly

Journal of Marriage and the Family
National Council on Family Relations
3938 Central Ave. NE, Ste. 550
Minneapolis, MN 55421
Quarterly

Personnel
American Management Association
135 W. 50th St.
New York, NY 10020
Monthly

Population Bulletin
Population Reference Bureau, Inc.
1875 Connecticut Ave. NW, Ste. 520
Washington, DC 20009
Quarterly

Population Today
Population Reference Bureau, Inc.
1875 Connecticut Ave. NW, Ste. 520
Washington, DC 20009
Monthly

Social Forces
University of North Carolina Press
Box 2288
Chapel Hill, NC 27515-2288
Quarterly

Organizations

Families and Work Institute
330 Seventh Ave.
New York, NY 10001
212-465-2044

Family Research Council
700 13th St. NW, Ste. 500
Washington, DC 20005
202-393-2100

Gay and Lesbian Parents Coalition
International
Box 50360
Washington, DC 20091
202-583-8029

Institute for American Values
1841 Broadway, Ste. 211
New York, NY 10023
212-246-3942

National Council on Family Relations
3989 Central Ave. NE, Ste. 550
Minneapolis, MN 55421
612-781-9331

New Ways to Work
149 9th St., Second Fl.
San Francisco, CA 94103
415-552-1000

Stepfamily Association of America
215 Centenniel Mall S, Ste. 212
Lincoln, NE 68598
402-477-7837

Useful Library of Congress
Subject Headings

Children of Divorced Parents—United
    States
Children of Gay Parents—United
    States
Divorce
Divorce—Economic Aspects—United
    States
Divorce—Law and Legislation—
    Economic Aspects
Divorce—Law and Legislation—
    History
Divorce—United States
Divorce—United States—History
Dual-Career Families—United States
Family—Research—United States
Family—United States

Family—United States—History
Family Policy—United States
Gay Fathers—United States
Gay Parents—United States
Lesbian Mothers—United States
Marriage—United States
Remarriage—United States
Single-Parent Family—United States
Single Parents—Government Policy—
    United States
Stepchildren
Stepchildren—United States
Stepfamilies
Stepfamilies—United States
Work and Family—United States

Index